Windows® 8
SECRETS

Windows® 8
SECRETS

DO WHAT YOU NEVER THOUGHT POSSIBLE WITH WINDOWS 8 AND RT

Paul Thurrott

Rafael Rivera

John Wiley & Sons, Inc.

EXECUTIVE EDITOR: Carol Long

SENIOR PROJECT EDITOR: Kevin Kent

TECHNICAL EDITOR: Todd Meister

PRODUCTION EDITOR: Christine Mugnolo

COPY EDITOR: Mildred Sanchez

EDITORIAL MANAGER: Mary Beth Wakefield

FREELANCER EDITORIAL MANAGER: Rosemarie Graham

ASSOCIATE DIRECTOR OF MARKETING: David Mayhew

MARKETING MANAGER: Ashley Zurcher

BUSINESS MANAGER: Amy Knies

PRODUCTION MANAGER: Tim Tate

VICE PRESIDENT AND EXECUTIVE GROUP PUBLISHER: Richard Swadley

VICE PRESIDENT AND EXECUTIVE PUBLISHER: Neil Edde

ASSOCIATE PUBLISHER: Jim Minatel

PROJECT COORDINATOR, COVER: Katie Crocker

COMPOSITOR: Craig Woods, Happenstance Type-O-Rama

PROOFREADERS: Sarah Kaikini and Scott Klemp, Word One New York

INDEXER: Johnna VanHoose Dinse

COVER IMAGE: © Chad Baker/Lifesize/Getty Images

COVER DESIGNER: Ryan Sneed

Windows ® 8 Secrets

Published by
John Wiley & Sons, Inc.
10475 Crosspoint Boulevard
Indianapolis, IN 46256
www.wiley.com

Copyright © 2012 by John Wiley & Sons, Inc., Indianapolis, Indiana

Published simultaneously in Canada

ISBN: 978-1-118-20413-9
ISBN: 978-1-118-22829-6 (ebk)
ISBN: 978-1-118-23769-4 (ebk)
ISBN: 978-1-118-26555-0 (ebk)

Manufactured in the United States of America

10 9 8 7 6 5 4 3 2 1

For general information on our other products and services please contact our Customer Care Department within the United States at (877) 762-2974, outside the United States at (317) 572-3993 or fax (317) 572-4002.

Wiley publishes in a variety of print and electronic formats and by print-on-demand. Some material included with standard print versions of this book may not be included in e-books or in print-on-demand. If this book refers to media such as a CD or DVD that is not included in the version you purchased, you may download this material at http://booksupport.wiley.com. For more information about Wiley products, visit www.wiley.com.

Library of Congress Control Number: 2012942054

To Stephanie, Mark, and Kelly

—Paul

To Janet, Rafael, Claudia, and Jenny

—Rafael

About the Authors

Paul Thurrott, the author of over 20 books, is a technology analyst at Windows IT Pro and the editor of the SuperSite for Windows (winsupersite.com). In addition to his daily contributions to the SuperSite, he writes a daily Windows news and information newsletter called *WinInfo*, a weekly editorial for *Windows IT Pro* UPDATE, and a monthly column for *Windows IT Pro* Magazine. He also co-hosts two highly-rated technology podcasts: *Windows Weekly* with Leo Laporte and Mary Jo Foley and *What The Tech* with Andrew Zarian. You can follow Paul's exploits on Twitter at @thurrott.

Rafael Rivera is a software developer for a VAR 500 company, Telos Corporation, where he works on mission critical systems. He is also a certified reverse engineering analyst and takes Windows apart for fun on his blog Within Windows (withinwindows .com). He has a growing interest in culinary arts and photography, and frequently shares his thoughts on Twitter at @WithinRafael. Secret: Rafael was born on the same day as Windows 1.0—November 20, 1985—which many believe is no coincidence.

About the Technical Editor

Todd Meister has been working in the IT industry for over 15 years. He's been a Technical Editor on over 75 titles ranging from SQL Server to the .NET Framework. Besides technical editing titles, he is the Senior IT Architect at Ball State University in Muncie, Indiana. He lives in central Indiana with his wife, Kimberly, and their five wily children.

Acknowledgments

Thanks to the anonymous souls from Microsoft who provided us with dozens of interim builds and important tidbits of internal information, both of which contributed to making this the best Windows 8 book on the market. We literally could not have completed this book in time without you and we hope that we lived up to the trust you placed in us.

—*Paul and Rafael*

This book was a truly collaborative venture that included daily check-ins on Skype, document sharing on Windows Live Mesh and SkyDrive, and even some in-person meet-ups at all-too-infrequent industry events. Thanks again to Rafael for accompanying me down the rabbit hole.

Thanks as always to Stephanie, Mark, and Kelly for giving me the time to make this book happen and for understanding why things got grouchy sometimes.

Thanks to Jill Lovato and Greg Chiemingo at Waggener Edstrom for being islands of calm in a sea of insanity. You guys are the best and were always ready to help. Much appreciated.

Thanks to Kevin and Carol at Wiley for the help, support, and understanding. Books are always stressful to make, with less time than I wish for and more work than I expect, regardless of how many times I've done it. But you get that.

Finally, thanks to my readers and listeners from around the world. I've enjoyed the conversations and hope they continue well into the future. It's always been fun, but what makes this worthwhile isn't the products and technologies, it's the relationships you make along the way.

—*Paul*

Thanks to my parents and sister for supporting my interests 100 percent. I love you all.

Thanks to Paul, for giving me another opportunity to do what I love doing—digging into and documenting Windows.

Thanks to Jennifer Ortiz for understanding my crazy late-night hours and a huge congratulations on being accepted to the PhD program at University of Washington.

A special thanks to David Golden, Patrick Laughner, and Paul Paliath whom I spend hours with on Skype daily playing Minecraft and other games.

Big thanks to Cliff Simpkins and Brandon Watson for helping me convince Microsoft there were merits in my hacking work on Windows Phone. And also Chris Walsh and Long Zheng for helping make a product of that hacking work, ChevronWP7 Labs, a huge success.

Last but not least, thanks to all my blog readers and Twitter followers. It's those conversations with real people that drive me every day.

—*Rafael*

Contents at a Glance

Read This First ▶ **xv**

Chapter 1 ▶ Choosing Windows 8 Versions, PCs and Devices, and Hardware   **1**

Chapter 2 ▶ Installing and Upgrading to Windows 8   **25**

Chapter 3 ▶ Metro: The New User Experience   **63**

Chapter 4 ▶ (Still) Alive and Kicking: The Windows Desktop   **103**

Chapter 5 ▶ Make It Yours: Personalizing Windows 8   **145**

Chapter 6 ▶ Windows Store: Finding, Acquiring, and Managing Your Apps   **183**

Chapter 7 ▶ Browsing the Web with Internet Explorer 10   **215**

Chapter 8 ▶ Get It Done with Windows 8's Productivity Apps   **247**

Chapter 9 ▶ Relaxing with Windows 8's Photo and Entertainment Apps   **305**

Chapter 10 ▶ Xbox Games with Windows 8   **349**

Chapter 11 ▶ Storage, Backup, and Recovery   **377**

Chapter 12 ▶ Accounts and Security   **413**

Chapter 13 ▶ Networking and Connectivity   **441**

Chapter 14 ▶ Windows 8 for Business   **463**

Appendix ▶ Windows Key Keyboard Shortcuts   **491**

Index ▶ **495**

Contents

Read This First   xv

Chapter 1 ▶ **Choosing Windows 8 Versions, PCs and Devices, and Hardware**... **1**

    Picking a Windows 8 Product Edition   2

    Picking a Windows 8 PC or Tablet   10

    Summary   24

Chapter 2 ▶ **Installing and Upgrading to Windows 8**...................... **25**

    That Was Then, This Is Now: How Setup Has Changed   26

    Using the Windows 8 Web Installer   28

    Advanced Setup: Using the Old-School Installer   45

    Post-Setup: Now What?   48

    Advanced Windows 8 Setup Configurations   51

    Summary   61

Chapter 3 ▶ **Metro: The New User Experience**........................... **63**

    Times They Are A-Changin': The New Windows Shell   65

    Lock Screen: A New Way to Sign In   67

    Start Screen: A New User Experience for Modern Apps   69

    Using the System-Wide Metro User Experiences   76

    Summary   101

Chapter 4 ▶ **(Still) Alive and Kicking: The Windows Desktop**.............. **103**

    What's New on the Windows Desktop?   104

    Where New Meets Old: Metro Features You Get in the Desktop, Too   109

    Managing Files and Folders   123

    Managing Classic Windows Applications   136

To the Cloud: Using the SkyDrive Desktop App   143

Summary   144

Chapter 5 ▶ Make It Yours: Personalizing Windows 8 .... **145**

Customizing Metro   146

Customizing Settings and Settings Sync   163

Customizing the Desktop   166

Power User Customization Tips and Tricks   178

Summary   181

Chapter 6 ▶ Windows Store: Finding, Acquiring, and Managing Your Apps **183**

What Is an App Store . . . and Why Does Windows 8 Need One?   184

First Rule of Windows Store: There Are Rules to Windows Store   186

Launching Windows Store   189

Using Windows Store   189

Configuring Accounts and Preferences   212

Summary   214

Chapter 7 ▶ Browsing the Web with Internet Explorer 10 .... **215**

Two Browsers, One Brain: Understanding Internet Explorer 10   216

Internet Explorer 10 for Metro   218

Using the Desktop Version of Internet Explorer 10   239

Configuring IE 10 Desktop   241

Where IE Metro and Desktop Meet . . . and Don't   242

IE 10 and Default Browser Selection   243

Summary   245

Chapter 8 ▶ Get It Done with Windows 8's Productivity Apps **247**

A Note About the Windows Productivity Apps and Your Microsoft Account   248

People   250

Mail   262

Calendar   272

Messaging   281

SkyDrive   287

Windows Reader   292

The Bing Apps   293

Microsoft Office Comes to Windows . . . Sort Of   300

Summary   303

Chapter 9 ▶ Relaxing with Windows 8's Photo and Entertainment Apps 305

A Note About the Windows 8 Entertainment
Apps and Your Microsoft Account   307

Enjoying Photos   308

Buying, Managing, and Playing Music   324

Buying, Managing, and Playing Movies and TV Shows   339

Summary   348

Chapter 10 ▶ Xbox Games with Windows 8. 349

Games and the Metro Environment   350

Finding and Acquiring Games for Windows 8   355

Finding and Acquiring Desktop Games   358

Xbox LIVE and Windows 8   359

Summary   375

Chapter 11 ▶ Storage, Backup, and Recovery 377

Storage Basics: NTFS Today, ReFS Tomorrow   378

Storage Spaces   379

File History   394

Using the Windows 8 Recovery Tools   400

Accessing System Image Backup and Recovery
Functionality with Windows Backup   407

What's Missing: Cloud Backup   409

Summary   411

Chapter 12 ▶ Accounts and Security **413**

User Accounts 414

Security and Windows 8: Keeping Your PC Safe 431

Summary 440

Chapter 13 ▶ Networking and Connectivity **441**

What Was Old Is New Again 442

Connecting to and Managing Wired and
Wireless Networks 443

Connecting to Cellular Data Networks 448

Sharing Files, Media, and Printers at Home with
HomeGroup 456

Summary 460

Chapter 14 ▶ Windows 8 for Business **463**

Domain Join and Group Policy 464

Disk Encryption 470

Virtualization 475

Features Exclusive to Windows 8 Enterprise 486

Windows RT and Business: A Tablet for All Seasons 488

Summary 489

Appendix ▶ Windows Key Keyboard Shortcuts **491**

Index 495

Read This First

In October 2009, I participated in the Windows 7 launch at the World Forum in the Hague, Netherlands. It was easily the most beautiful theater I've ever spoken in, and while I have many memories of that all-too-short trip to Europe, one stands out.

After my talk, I was signing copies of *Windows 7 Secrets* for attendees and I received a wonderfully blunt question that forever altered the book you're now reading.

"If Windows 7 is so easy to use," a bespectacled Netherlander asked as I signed my name, "then why is your book over a thousand pages long?"

Time stood still for a moment while I pondered this question. And though I replied, "To be fair, it's padded with screenshots," to laughs, the question hung in my mind for some time to come.

In my defense—*our* defense, since Rafael is of course my willing partner in this crime against both trees and those who would safely read before going to sleep—I have always taken the position, both in my writing for the SuperSite for Windows and in the *Secrets* books, that Windows isn't a standalone "thing"; it's the center of a vast ecosystem of related and connected products and services. That is, nobody buys Windows for Windows, per se. They buy Windows because of its promise of compatibility with the hardware, software, and, increasingly, services that they use and trust.

With Windows 7, that meant applications like those in Windows Live Essentials—which weren't technically included "with" Windows 7 but were very much required to "complete," if you will, Windows—but also Zune, Windows Home Server, Windows Media Center, and a slew of Windows Live services.

But with Windows 8, suddenly, everything is different. Yes, Windows still stands at the center of a vast ecosystem. But Windows 8 itself is quite different from its predecessor, and the solutions that make up its supporting cast have changed quite a bit since Windows 7, thanks to changes in the market.

Microsoft says it is "reimagining" Windows with Windows 8, giving Rafael and I the chance to, in turn, reimagine our *Secrets* books. A year before Windows 8 launched, as we plotted this next version of the book, it occurred to us that it was time to make a break with the past, similar to what Microsoft was doing with the product we're writing about. And so we came to Wiley with a tentative plan, since we feared failure, to not update *Windows 7 Secrets*. Instead, this next book, *Windows 8*

Secrets, would be an all-new book, with virtually no information taken and updated from previous books. It would be a shorter book, too, one that wouldn't harm you if you dropped it on yourself.

Oddly, and humorously, Wiley not only agreed, but they had also separately come to the same conclusion, and were likewise worried that the daunting task of starting over from scratch would be uninteresting to us.

Problem solved.

The resulting book, the one you now hold, is the product of this reimagining. It is significantly shorter than the previous book—about a third shorter, I guess—and doesn't drift into surrounding ecosystem products and services unless they're central to the discussion. Part of the reason we're able to do this is that Microsoft has simply built so much into Windows 8, while extending its support to cloud services in more seamless ways. But part of it is us just saying no to peripheral topics as well.

Our goal, as always, is to make you more efficient and proficient in Windows. It's to take you from your current skill level to the next level by revealing information about this new Windows that is new—simply because Microsoft has added whatever new features and functionality—and, as important, because it is new to you. In the old days, before the pervasive online connectivity we all now enjoy, the notion of "secrets" was pretty straightforward, and you could safely assume that you'd pick up a copy of whatever *Secrets* book and discover unique information—often obviously called out in gratuitous "Secret" boxes—that was not available anywhere else.

Today, that's not possible.

Both Rafael and I have discussed virtually every topic in this book online in some form already. I often test content on my own website before writing about it in the book to gather feedback and questions from users, which I can often present to Microsoft for further internal insights. The value of this book, then, is manifold. It's not just some simple compendium of previously published online articles. It's a deeper, more thorough examination of what's truly new in Windows 8, backed by months and months of research and usage, and feedback from the people at Microsoft who actually made the product. And it's all gathered in one organized and convenient place: this book.

Things have changed for you, the reader, as well. We're now making more assumptions than ever before. And while the bar isn't particularly high, both Rafael and I wanted to make sure that you understood what you are getting into here.

That is, we assume you know how to use Windows. And by this, we don't just mean how to translate the physical actions of moving a mouse on a surface into on-screen mouse cursor movements. We expect you to know Windows 7 inside and out, and to be familiar with the way it works. This is important, and different, because we're carrying over virtually no secrets, tips, or information from *Windows 7 Secrets*. This book is all-new, and assumes you already understand the features that were previously available, often in unchanged form, in Windows 7.

But don't worry that this book will be daunting in some way. It's not. We used the same approachable and conversational style that we've always used because, well, that's the way we do things. It's just that adding the relevant content from *Windows 7 Secrets* to this book would have necessitated a 1,500-page tome. No one wanted that. So we took what is a bold step for us. We think the book is better for it. And we hope you agree.

But we want to hear from you either way. We view this book in the same way we do our own websites and other work, as a conversation about technology between people who are truly interested in learning more, always. And that includes us. If we did something right or screwed up something terribly, please, do let us know.

These are our personal e-mail addresses and Twitter accounts. We're interested in continuing the conversation.

Paul Thurrott

thurrott@hotmail.com

@thurrott

Rafael Rivera

rafael@withinwindows.com

@withinrafael

Windows 8: Big Upgrade, or Biggest Upgrade Ever?

Some—including Microsoft—have described Windows 8 as the biggest change to Windows since the seminal release of Windows 95 in 1995. And while it's convenient to make such a claim—every Windows release in the years since has been compared to that milestone—the truth is far more dramatic.

Windows 8 isn't the biggest Windows release since Windows 95. It's the biggest release, *ever*.

To understand why this is so requires an understanding of the history of Windows and of the technologies that have driven each release. Early versions of Windows weren't even proper operating systems. Instead, they were graphical shells that ran on top of the real OS, called MS-DOS. MS-DOS was a product of its era—the early 1980s—which is to say it was an arcane command-line system that wasn't user friendly in the least. But since MS-DOS ran on the most popular computers of the day, many companies, including Microsoft, created user-friendly shells that hid the complexity of MS-DOS while retaining the system's most vital attribute, its compatibility with MS-DOS applications.

Some of these shells were essentially text-based, like MS-DOS itself, while some ran in special graphical modes. Microsoft's approach, called Windows, used the latter approach because the company had been deeply involved in the creation of the first consumer-oriented graphical OS, which shipped with the first Apple Macintosh. Sensing that graphical user interfaces, or GUIs, were the future, Microsoft cofounder Bill Gates drove his company to create a PC alternative that worked on top of DOS.

Thanks to its shaky MS-DOS underpinnings, early Windows versions weren't technically very elegant. They also weren't very pretty or usable, but by version 3.0 in the early 1990s, Microsoft suddenly had a hit on its hands and the industry began coalescing around this GUI, much as it had embraced plain old MS-DOS a decade earlier.

Without getting too deep into snooze-inducing technical arcana, there was a brief moment in the early 1990s when Microsoft was actually backing three desktop PC operating systems. First was MS-DOS and Windows, a homegrown solution with serious technical limitations. Second was OS/2, a joint project with IBM that would have replaced DOS/Windows on PCs had it been successful. And third was a more obscure project, first called NT, which was a stable and reliable UNIX alternative that had nothing in common with DOS/Windows at all.

But as NT evolved into Windows NT, Microsoft did two things to bring this system closer to its DOS-based cousin. First, it determined that NT would utilize the same GUI as DOS-based Windows, starting with the Windows 3.x Program Manager shell in 1993. And second, it created a 32-bit environment called Win32 that could run DOS-based Windows (and even some DOS) applications, creating a modicum of compatibility. Over time, the Win32 environment was ported to DOS-based Windows versions (starting with Windows 95), the driver models were combined, and Microsoft began its efforts to transition completely to the NT codebase, an event that was originally planned for Windows 2000 but had to be put off until Windows XP, in 2001.

Whew.

The point is that during all of this transition and evolution, Microsoft never changed the user experience, the Windows runtime, and the underlying technologies that developers use all at the same time. But with Windows 8, it has done just that.

Windows 8 includes a completely new user experience we call Metro that offers smartphone-like, full-screen experiences in lieu of (well, in addition to) the old-fashioned "windowed" interface provided by the desktop environment from previous Windows versions. And Metro runs on top of a completely new runtime engine, called Windows Runtime, or WinRT, which in turn offers developers a completely new set of native APIs, with new capabilities and a new way of doing things.

That's a whole lot of new.

NOTE Though we are calling this new environment Metro, Microsoft—for legal reasons—is not. One alternative style of naming we've seen used, in which Metro is called "the Windows 8 UI," and Metro-style apps are referred to as "Windows 8 apps," is, to us, inadequate. Windows 8 provides two user experiences, what we call Metro and the desktop. And both are "Windows 8 UIs" that contains "Windows 8 apps." So we're sticking with the Metro name, which has been in use for a couple of years now and which we feel perfectly encapsulates the new environment and the apps that run within it. Yep. We're rabble-rousers.

Compare this to Windows 7. In Windows 7, Microsoft provided a refined version of the Aero desktop experiences it previously offered in Windows Vista. And Windows 7 ran on top of the same Explorer runtime engine as all Windows versions dating back to Windows 2000, while offering developers the exact same Win32-based APIs, with of course a handful of new capabilities.

Put simply, there's no comparison.

What You Need to Know

We mentioned previously that we wrote this book for average users, and not technical experts. And that we assume you have used and understand modern Windows versions, especially Windows 7. And that your desire to learn more about Windows 8 has inspired this purchase. We won't disappoint you.

The book doesn't need to be read from cover to cover. That said, we do recommend reading through the first five chapters in sequence, if possible, since this is the foundation for understanding how the new operating system works and why things are the way they are. From that point on, feel free to cherry-pick as needed, as you discover and wonder about specific new features.

But before diving into Windows 8, it's important to understand a few basic concepts, especially if you'll be utilizing this system on a new tablet computer or similar multi-touch-based device. Throughout this book, we make no assumptions about *how* you'll interact with Windows 8, and we cover multi-touch, mouse, and keyboard throughout, so no one gets left out. But multi-touch-based Windows machines, while not technically new, are going to become a lot more popular with Windows 8. And more important, perhaps, Microsoft has seriously bolstered multi-touch support in Windows 8 so that it is now an incredible, integrated experience. And if you're using a multi-touch device of any kind, you'll want to know a few basics.

So let's start there.

USING WINDOWS 8 WITH MULTI-TOUCH

Those with multi-touch tablets and other touch-based Windows devices will soon discover that Windows 8 works quite naturally, and much like other familiar touch devices such as Windows Phone, iPhone, or Android smartphones or the iPad and other tablets. But Windows 8 is far more sophisticated than these other products, so while the basics are the same, understanding a few key multi-touch gestures and actions is key to getting off on the right foot, er, finger.

Here's what you need to know.

▶ **Tap:** To open an item, simply tap it with your finger, as shown in Figure 1. This works identically to clicking the item with the mouse.

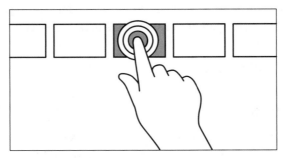

FIGURE 1: Tap an item to open it.

▶ **Tap and hold:** To get more information about an item, tap and hold on that item. (Microsoft calls this "press and hold" for some reason.) This works similarly to right-clicking an item with a mouse, and the result is often similar, with a menu appearing providing more information or options. Tap and hold can be seen in Figure 2.

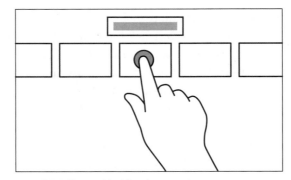

FIGURE 2: Tap and hold an item to view more information.

► **Slide to drag:** With some Windows 8 user experiences, you can tap and hold an item and then drag it to a new location on-screen by swiping your finger slowly in whatever direction you wish to go. This action, which is commonly used for rearranging tiles on the new Windows 8 Start screen, can be seen in Figure 3 and is similar to using a mouse to drag an item around.

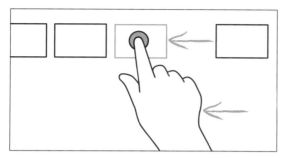

FIGURE 3: After tapping and holding, you can use a slide gesture to move an item.

► **Pinch to zoom out, stretch to zoom in:** Users of touch-based smartphones and tablets are probably familiar with the pinch and stretch methods of zooming out and zooming in a display, respectively. You touch the screen with two fingers simultaneously and then move them away from each other to zoom in, as seen in Figure 4. Or, if you move the two fingers toward each other, you can zoom out. These actions are typically used in apps like Photos or Maps where zooming is a common activity.

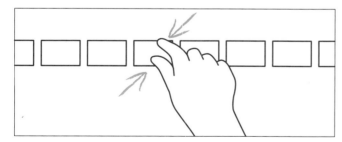

FIGURE 4: Pinch or stretch with two fingers to zoom.

► **Rotate:** With this fairly uncommon gesture, you can rotate the display either clockwise or counterclockwise. To do so, touch the screen with two fingers simultaneously and then turn your hand in either direction, as in Figure 5. Few apps support this gesture.

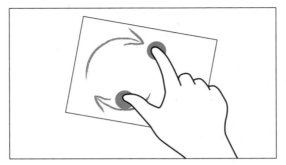

FIGURE 5: Rotate the display with two fingers.

▶ **Slide scrolling:** While smartphones often use a vertical form of scrolling, similar to document-based applications like Microsoft Word, Windows 8 was designed to be used in landscape mode by default, and its multiscreen experiences usually scroll from left-to-right, not up and down. To scroll quickly through these multiscreen experiences, you can swipe the display with your finger, as in Figure 6. A swipe to the left will cause the display to scroll to the right.

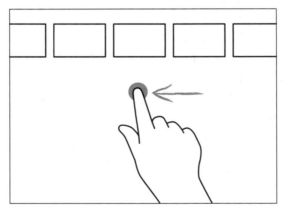

FIGURE 6: Scroll through a multiscreen display by swiping with your finger.

▶ **Swipe selecting:** To select an item in Windows 8, you can swipe on that item using a short downward gesture. When you do so, it will typically become visually highlighted in some way, indicating the selection, and additional options will appear, often in an app bar, which can be attached to the top or bottom edge of the screen. A swipe selection gesture can be seen in Figure 7.

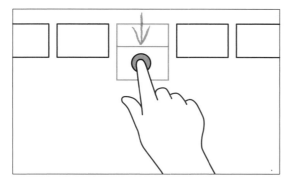

FIGURE 7: A short downward swipe can select an item.

▶ **Edge swiping:** Windows 8 provides app-specific and system-wide capabilities via so-called edge user interfaces, or edge UIs. To activate an edge UI, you swipe in toward the center of the screen from an edge. You swipe in from the top or bottom edge of the screen to display an app's edge UI. And you can trigger various system-level capabilities by swiping in from the left or right edge of the screen. (These actions are further discussed in Chapter 3.) You can see an example of edge swiping in Figure 8.

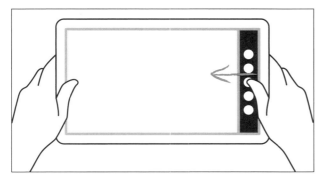

FIGURE 8: Activate edge UIs by swiping in from the edge of the screen.

▶ **Swipe app closing:** You can close any Metro-style app by swiping down from near the top edge of the screen to the bottom of the screen, as in Figure 9. As you do, the app display will appear in a large thumbnail and that thumbnail will visually disappear as it is dragged to the bottom of the screen, and the app is closed.

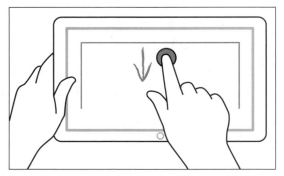

FIGURE 9: Closing an app by swiping from the top of the screen.

Note that swiping down from past the top edge of the screen will trigger the app's edge UI. To close the app, you must swipe down from near the top edge of the screen, but still on the app itself.

USING WINDOWS 8 WITH A MOUSE AND KEYBOARD

If you're using Windows 8 on a more traditional PC with a mouse and keyboard, things work largely as before and even when you're interacting with the Metro-style experiences and apps, you'll discover that all of your previous PC experiences are relevant. There are two things you should know about, however.

First, Windows 8 introduces a wide range of new keyboard shortcuts, many of which utilize the Windows key that is now common on all PC keyboards. We discuss these shortcuts throughout the book as the need arises, but you can reference the appendix for a complete rundown of Windows Key keyboard shortcuts.

Second, Windows 8 provides support for the edge UIs mentioned previously to mouse users via new "hot corners" on the screen. Since these interfaces are so central to using Windows 8 effectively, we discuss them fairly extensively in Chapter 3 and then again in Chapter 4. But a quick overview is provided here.

> ► **Start:** Microsoft has removed the Start button in Windows 8 so that it can provide a more consistent Start experience that works with both the Metro and desktop environments. To toggle Start, you can tap the Start key on your keyboard, press the Windows key button on your Windows device, or mouse the mouse cursor into the lower-left corner of the screen. (Yes, this is one of those

"hot corners" we just mentioned.) When you do so, the Start tip thumbnail, shown in Figure 10, appears. (Or, if you're already on the Start screen, a tip for the previous experience appears.) Click this to return to the Start screen (or previous experience.)

FIGURE 10: It's no button, but the Start tip works somewhat similarly to the old Start button.

▶ **Back and Switcher:** To access the previous experience, move the mouse cursor into the upper-left corner of the screen. A thumbnail of the previously used Metro app or other experience will appear, as in Figure 11. Click this to use that app. Or, move the mouse cursor down the left edge of the screen to display the new Switcher interface that lets you switch to any previously used app.

FIGURE 11: The Back tip

▶ **Charms:** If you move the mouse cursor into the upper-right or lower-right corner of the screen, you can display the new Charms bar, a set of system-level commands and capabilities. The Charms are shown in Figure 12.

▶ **App commands:** When you're using a new Metro-style app, you can display its app bar by right-clicking any empty spot on-screen. An app bar is shown in Figure 13.

OK, that's enough to get you started. Again, we cover these and other interactions you'll want to know throughout the book as needed.

FIGURE 12: The Charms bar can be accessed via hot corners on the right side of the screen.

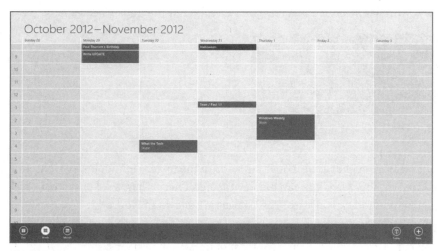

FIGURE 13: Metro-style apps offer more commands on hidden app bars.

What This Book Covers

Windows 8 is a strange new operating system that combines a completely new Metro environment with an evolved desktop environment. If you're familiar with Windows Phone, you will at least understand the basics of Metro, since that type of user experience debuted earlier on Microsoft's smartphone platform. But Windows 8 provides its own take on Metro, so even die-hard Windows Phone fans will find that there are some new skills to learn. For this reason, the book covers some background material related to the *whys* as well as the *hows* of Windows 8 before delving into specific apps and features.

This book covers everything you need to know to master Windows 8, from your pre-purchase considerations, to installing, upgrading, and understanding the new Metro user experience and the evolved desktop environment, and how the two sometimes intersect. From that point on, we dive deep into each of the new Metro apps that come with Windows 8 (or are at least core to the Windows 8 experience), as well as the new, more advanced interfaces for storage, backup and recovery, accounts and security, networking and connectivity, and, finally, those that are targeted specifically at businesses.

> **NOTE** One important point about Windows 8 is that the Metro-style apps Microsoft is providing with the system will all be updated on an ongoing basis through the new Windows Store. This means that the app descriptions we provide here are, of course, essentially slice-in-time overviews of their features and capabilities. We fully expect that these apps will only improve over time, sometimes in profound ways, and that could lead to discrepancies between the descriptions and figures in the book and what you're seeing on your own PC.

While it's impossible to see the future, we will be covering any changes to Windows 8 over time at our respective websites, the SuperSite for Windows (winsupersite.com) and Within Windows (withinwindows.com).

How This Book Is Structured

The structure of this book should help you easily find what you need to know. As noted before, we recommend starting with, and reading through, the first five chapters in sequence, if possible. This will give you a firm grounding in Windows 8.

From there, the book progresses through a series of chapters dedicated to the Metro-style apps and more advanced tools that make up the bulk of the Windows 8 upgrade. There's no reason to read these chapters in order. Instead, treat *Windows 8 Secrets* as a reference guide, referring to it as needed as you explore your own PC or device. Alternatively, you could use the book as an early exploration tool to find out about new features before you dive in yourself.

The point here is simple: For the most part, this book doesn't need to be read cover to cover. Instead, you can read it in the order that makes the most sense for you.

What You Need to Use This Book

To use a Windows 8 PC or device, and thus *Windows 8 Secrets*, effectively, you will of course need a Windows-based PC or device, preferably running Windows 7—if you're about to upgrade or migrate—or Windows 8. You will need a Microsoft account, formerly called a Windows Live ID, since Microsoft integrates with so many online services and utilizes a nice PC-to-PC sync functionality that relies on this account type.

Features and Icons Used in This Book

▶ Watch for margin notes like this one that highlight some key piece of information or discuss some poorly documented or hard to find technique or approach.

The following features and icons are used in this book to help draw your attention to some of the most important or useful information in the book, some of the most valuable tips, insights, and advice that can help you unlock the secrets of Windows 8.

SIDEBARS

Sidebars like this one feature additional information about topics related to the nearby text.

TIP The Tip icon indicates a helpful trick or technique.

NOTE The Note icon points out or expands on items of importance or interest.

CROSSREF The Cross-Reference icon points to chapters where additional information can be found.

WARNING The Warning icon warns you about possible negative side-effects or precautions you should take before making a change.

CHAPTER 1

Choosing Windows 8 Versions, PCs and Devices, and Hardware

IN THIS CHAPTER

▶ Understanding the different Windows 8 product editions

▶ Understanding the differences between each version of Windows 8

▶ Choosing the correct Windows 8 version

▶ Understanding the differences between Intel-compatible PCs and ARM-based devices

▶ Choosing a machine type

▶ New Windows 8 hardware capabilities to look for

With Windows 8, you suddenly have a lot of decisions to make. Fortunately, Microsoft has simplified the product lineup such that there are basically just two retail versions of Windows 8 that upgraders need to think about, plus a third version, called Windows RT, that will be sold only with new ARM-based PCs and devices.

But choosing a Windows version is only the start of the decision-making process. Beyond that, you have various machine types to choose from, including not just stalwart desktop PCs and laptops, but also new leading-edge all-in-ones, Ultrabooks, tablets, and hybrid PCs.

And within those different classes of machines are a variety of new hardware capabilities that work in tandem with Windows 8 to provide the best computing experience yet. Of course, getting there will require you to do a bit of homework first. And that's where this chapter comes in.

PICKING A WINDOWS 8 PRODUCT EDITION

Over the past decade, Microsoft has become involved in a controversy of its own making. And no, we're not talking about the antitrust issues that also dogged the software giant for much of the past decade. Instead, we're referring to its predilection for confusing users with too many product editions. That is, rather than make products called Windows and Office, Microsoft makes many product editions of each one, each of which comes with some almost arbitrary set of capabilities and features and, of course, individual price points.

The decision to diversify its product lineups wasn't made overnight, but it was made for all the wrong reasons. The thing is, Microsoft had research to fall back on that showed that users would generally spend more money on a supposedly premium version of a product. And the more versions they had, the studies suggested, the better.

To understand how the plan to diversify Windows quickly ran amok, consider what it was like when Windows XP debuted back in 2001. At first, it was the simplest product lineup of all time, with a Windows XP Home Edition aimed at, yes, the home market, and a Professional Edition that was aimed at businesses but also those who wanted every single possible capability.

And sure enough, the research paid off. Even consumers preferred the more expensive XP Professional edition and would pay extra while configuring a PC to get that version of the OS.

So then Microsoft went off the rails.

First, the company expanded the XP lineup with additional product editions that filled certain niches, including XP Tablet PC Edition (for Tablet PCs) and Media Center Edition (for so-called media center PCs), which were aimed at the living room. Then it added a 64-bit version, XP Professional x64, and a version for emerging markets called XP Starter Edition. There were "N" editions for the European market and "K" versions for the Korean market, both necessitated by antitrust action. And there was an Itanium version for Intel's then high-end (and now dead) 64-bit platform.

By the time Windows Vista shipped in 2006, it was hard to tell how many product editions were really available since most were also available in separate 32-bit and 64-bit (x64) versions. Counting them all, there were almost 20!

And Microsoft not only confused customers with packaging, but it also increased the ways in which users could purchase the product. There were the not-quite-retail versions of the software, called *OEM versions*, which were technically supposed to sell only to PC makers, but were widely available online. And there was a new option called Windows Anytime Upgrade, which let you upgrade in-place from one version of Vista to another.

Windows 7 arrived in 2009 with just a slightly simplified product lineup. This time around, the 32-bit and 64-bit (x64) versions of each edition were always bundled together, thankfully. And while there were just about as many mainstream versions of the product as with Vista, the choice was a lot simpler.

It boiled down to this: Most low-end netbook computers were bundled with a cut-rate version of Windows 7 called Starter Edition (which, in this version, graduated from emerging markets). Home PCs would typically come with Windows 7 Home Premium, and business PCs would typically come with Windows 7 Professional. If you wanted the version that had it all, you'd get Windows 7 Ultimate. But really, most people simply had to choose between Windows 7 Home Premium and Professional. It wasn't as hard as it looked.

With Windows 8, Microsoft has finally gone back to its roots. And while it is still delivering multiple product editions in this release, the choices are fewer and far more easily managed.

Introducing the Windows 8 Product Editions

With Windows 8, Microsoft is offering just three mainstream product editions, though choosing among them is easier than it's been since 2001. Two of the three versions, called Windows 8 and Windows 8 Pro, run on traditional PCs that utilize the same Intel/Intel-compatible x86/x64 processor architecture that has provided the backbone of our PCs for decades. The third, called Windows RT, is being made available only with new PCs and tablets that run on the ARM processor architecture.

▶ Internally, the entry level Windows 8 version is actually called Windows 8 Core. This name makes a lot of sense to us, and is how Microsoft should market it, we think.

Aside from the underlying architecture, Windows 8 and Windows RT are roughly comparable, with some key differences we'll note in a bit. That is, the feature sets are very similar. Windows 8 Pro is a superset of Windows 8, offering every single feature in Windows 8 plus several unique features.

And roughly speaking, Windows 8 is aimed at consumers—much like Windows XP Home was—and Windows 8 Pro is aimed at businesses and enthusiasts just like XP Professional was.

This makes picking a product somewhat easy, assuming you understand the differences between Intel-compatible PCs and ARM-based devices. (To more easily differentiate these platforms, we tend to refer to Intel-compatible machines as *PCs* and ARM-based machines as *devices*, though to be fair the differences are getting somewhat subtle. So your first choice is to pick a PC or a device.

If you're upgrading or clean installing Windows 8 on an existing PC, you will be choosing between Windows 8 and Windows 8 Pro. It's that simple.

If you're buying a new PC, that also means, generally, that you will choose between Windows 8 and Windows 8 Pro. But if you're buying a new tablet, you'll need to choose among all three: Windows 8, Windows 8 Pro, and Windows RT. And your choice will be limited by device type: Some models will only be available with an Intel-compatible chipset—where you can choose between Windows 8 and Windows 8 Pro—and some will come only with an ARM chipset, where your only choice is Windows RT.

We'll discuss some of these differences later in the chapter, but the big picture goes like this: Windows RT is a new, unproven product. It runs only on ARM-based platforms that could enable thinner and lighter iPad-like tablets that may get better battery life than Intel-compatible products. (That tale has yet to be told.) Windows RT is roughly comparable to the base version of Windows 8, but is lacking one very critical feature: It is not compatible with any existing Windows applications or utilities. And it's missing two interesting and potentially useful features, Windows Media Player and Storage Spaces. On the flip side, Windows RT offers a few unique features of its own: device encryption, and free, bundled versions of Microsoft Word, Excel, PowerPoint, and OneNote. These applications are based on Office 2013 and, like Windows RT, are branded with the RT name (for example, Word RT).

We mentioned that there were three *mainstream* Windows 8 editions. As it turns out, there are others. Microsoft is selling a version called, yep, Windows 8 Starter, in emerging markets only, so we can safely ignore that release. And a Windows 8 Enterprise edition is provided only to Microsoft's corporate customers that sign up for a volume licensing program called Software Assurance. This version of Windows 8 is in fact quite interesting as it offers some additional and useful features that are now available in Windows 8 or Windows 8 Pro. But since you can't actually acquire it normally, it's also something we won't be focusing on too much here.

To make the right choice, then, you'll need to understand the individual differences between each mainstream Windows 8 version. And you'll need to understand the pros and cons of the various hardware features you'll find in Intel-compatible PCs and ARM-based devices.

First, we'll discuss the software differences.

Understanding the Differences Between the Product Editions

There are various ways to present this kind of information, but we find that tables, logically divided by category, are easy on the eyes and mind. Tables 1-1 through 1-10 show how the mainstream product editions stack up.

TABLE 1-1: Hardware Capabilities

FEATURE	WINDOWS 8	WINDOWS 8 PRO	WINDOWS RT
Maximum number of processors	1	2	2
Maximum RAM	4 GB (x86), 16 GB (x64)	4 GB (x86), 64 GB (x64)	4 GB

TABLE 1-2: Upgrade Capabilities

FEATURE	WINDOWS 8	WINDOWS 8 PRO	WINDOWS RT
Upgrades from Windows 7 Starter, Home Basic, Home Premium	Yes	Yes	
Upgrades from Windows 7 Professional, Ultimate		Yes	

TABLE 1-3: Metro Features*

FEATURE	WINDOWS 8	WINDOWS 8 PRO	WINDOWS RT
Start screen, semantic zoom, live tiles	Yes	Yes	Yes
Windows Store	Yes	Yes	Yes
Mail	Yes	Yes	Yes
Calendar	Yes	Yes	Yes
People	Yes	Yes	Yes
Messaging	Yes	Yes	Yes
Photos	Yes	Yes	Yes
SkyDrive	Yes	Yes	Yes
Reader	Yes	Yes	Yes
Xbox Music	Yes	Yes	Yes
Xbox Video	Yes	Yes	Yes
Xbox Companion	Yes	Yes	Yes
Xbox Games	Yes	Yes	Yes
Camera	Yes	Yes	Yes
Bing	Yes	Yes	Yes

continues

TABLE 1-3:   *(continued)*

FEATURE	WINDOWS 8	WINDOWS 8 PRO	WINDOWS RT
Bing Maps	Yes	Yes	Yes
Bing News	Yes	Yes	Yes
Bing Sports	Yes	Yes	Yes
Bing Travel	Yes	Yes	Yes
Bing Weather	Yes	Yes	Yes
Internet Explorer 10 Metro	Yes	Yes	Yes
Snap	Yes	Yes	Yes
Touch and Thumb keyboard	Yes	Yes	Yes
Play To	Yes	Yes	Yes
Exchange ActiveSync (EAS) support	Yes	Yes	Yes
Mobile broadband features	Yes	Yes	Yes

* Note that some apps may not be preinstalled but can be downloaded from Windows Store

TABLE 1-4: Desktop Features

FEATURE	WINDOWS 8	WINDOWS 8 PRO	WINDOWS RT
Windows desktop with customization	Yes	Yes	Yes
Allows installation of desktop Windows software	Yes	Yes	
File Explorer	Yes	Yes	Yes
Windows Defender	Yes	Yes	Yes
Windows SmartScreen	Yes	Yes	Yes
Internet Explorer 10 Desktop	Yes	Yes	Yes
Task Manager	Yes	Yes	Yes
Microsoft Word, Excel, PowerPoint, OneNote			Yes
Windows Media Player	Yes	Yes	
Windows Media Center available as separate, paid add-on (includes MPEG-2 encoder and DVD playback)		Yes	
Shake	Yes	Yes	Yes

TABLE 1-5: Digital Media Features

FEATURE	WINDOWS 8	WINDOWS 8 PRO	WINDOWS RT
Dolby Digital encoder	Yes	Yes	Yes
AAC decoder	Yes	Yes	Yes
H.264 decoder	Yes	Yes	Yes

TABLE 1-6: File and Storage Features

FEATURE	WINDOWS 8	WINDOWS 8 PRO	WINDOWS RT
Storage Spaces	Yes	Yes	
File History	Yes	Yes	Yes
ISO and VHD mount	Yes	Yes	Yes
Dynamic volume support	Yes	Yes	Yes

TABLE 1-7: Account and Security Features

FEATURE	WINDOWS 8	WINDOWS 8 PRO	WINDOWS RT
Microsoft account	Yes	Yes	Yes
Picture password	Yes	Yes	Yes
PIN	Yes	Yes	Yes
Secure Boot	Yes	Yes	Yes
Device encryption			Yes
Family Safety	Yes	Yes	Yes

TABLE 1-8: Reliability Features

FEATURE	WINDOWS 8	WINDOWS 8 PRO	WINDOWS RT
Push Button Reset	Yes	Yes	Yes
Connected Standby	Yes	Yes	Yes

TABLE 1-9: Power User Features

FEATURE	WINDOWS 8	WINDOWS 8 PRO	WINDOWS RT
Language packs	Yes	Yes	Yes
Better multiple monitor support	Yes	Yes	Yes

TABLE 1-10: Business Features

FEATURE	WINDOWS 8	WINDOWS 8 PRO	WINDOWS RT
BitLocker and BitLocker To Go		Yes	
Boot from VHD		Yes	
Client Hyper-V		Yes	
Domain Join		Yes	
Encrypting File System (EFS)		Yes	
Group Policy		Yes	
Remote Desktop (host)		Yes	
Remote Desktop (client)	Yes	Yes	Yes
VPN client	Yes	Yes	Yes
Offline Files		Yes	

Choosing Between Windows 8 and Windows 8 Pro

Now that you are armed with the information in the previous tables, choosing between Windows 8 and Windows 8 Pro should be relatively straightforward. You just need to consider whether you need any of the following Pro-only features. If you do, then you should get Windows 8 Pro.

► **Upgrades from Windows 7 Professional, Ultimate:** If you intend to perform an in-place upgrade with an existing PC and are currently running Windows 7 Professional or Ultimate, you will need to purchase Windows 8 Pro.

► **BitLocker and BitLocker To Go:** These features provide full-disk encryption for fixed and removable disks, respectively, providing protection for your data even when the drive is removed and accessed from elsewhere.

- **Client Hyper-V:** Microsoft's server-based virtualization solution makes its way to the Windows client for the first time, providing a powerful, hypervisor-based platform for creating and managing virtual machines.

- **Boot from VHD:** This new capability allows you to create a virtual hard disk, or VHD, in Client Hyper-V and then boot your physical PC from this disk file rather than from a physical disk.

- **Domain join:** If you need to sign in to an Active Directory-based domain with Windows 8, you will need Windows 8 Pro (or Enterprise).

- **Encrypting File System:** EFS is somewhat de-emphasized in Windows 8 thanks to BitLocker and BitLocker To Go, but it provides a way to encrypt individual drives, folders, or even files, protecting them from being accessed externally should the drive be removed from your PC.

- **Group Policy:** Microsoft's policy-based management technology requires an Active Directory domain and thus Windows 8 Pro.

- **Remote Desktop (host):** While any Windows 8 PC or device can use a Remote Desktop client to remotely access other PCs or servers, only Windows 8 Pro can host such a session, allowing you or others to remotely access your own PC.

CROSSREF All of the aforementioned features are discussed in Chapter 14.

- **Windows Media Center:** For a small fee, Windows 8 Pro users can purchase Windows Media Center, a feature that used to be included in higher-end versions of Windows. This feature is not available to Windows 8 (or Windows RT for that matter). And it hasn't been upgraded since Windows 7 shipped.

And that's it. It really hasn't been this easy to choose between Windows product editions in over a decade.

What's Unique in Windows 8 Enterprise?

Windows 8 Enterprise is a superset of Windows 8 Pro. That is, it includes all of the features and capabilities in Windows 8 Pro plus provides some unique new features of its own. These include:

- **Windows To Go:** This very interesting feature lets you install Windows 8 on certain high-performance USB memory sticks, providing a highly portable Windows environment that can include all of your personal data, settings, and installed Metro-style apps and desktop applications.

▶ **Metro-style app deployment:** Corporations can bypass the normal requirement that all Metro-style apps must be stored, downloaded, and installed from the Windows Store. This capability, called side-loading, lets these businesses deploy Metro-style apps within their own environments securely.

▶ **DirectAccess:** A modern alternative to a VPN (virtual private network), DirectAccess lets remote users seamlessly access corporate network resources without dealing with the hassles common to VPN solutions.

▶ **BranchCache:** Aimed at distributed corporations, BranchCache lets servers and users' PCs in branch offices cache files, websites, and other content, so that it is not repeatedly and expensively downloaded across the WAN (wide area network) by different users in the same location.

▶ **AppLocker:** This feature provides white list and black list capabilities to control which files and applications that users or groups are allowed to run.

▶ **VDI improvements:** Windows 8 Enterprise also includes improvements to VDI (virtual desktop infrastructure), a way of virtualizing Windows client installs in a high-end data center and delivering them to thin client machines in a highly-managed environment.

PICKING A WINDOWS 8 PC OR TABLET

While the available selection of Windows 8-compatible PCs and devices is ever-changing, there are two primary issues to consider when it comes to hardware. First, you're going to need to choose between machines based on the new ARM platform and the more traditional, Intel-compatible platform. And second, since Windows 8 adds so many new hardware-based capabilities, you'll want to understand what those are and whether the availability of any in a given PC or device will color your decision-making process.

As with any purchasing decision, you may find yourself making trade-offs. For example, if you've determined that you simply must have the backward compatibility of an Intel-compatible PC, but then find that ARM-based devices deliver dramatically better battery life, you've got a decision to make. These features aren't point-by-point comparable, and no generalization we can make will help all readers. This means that, in the end, you'll need to decide which features or capabilities are more important to *you*. But we can at least start the discussion.

ARM vs. Intel Compatible

If you're one of the 1.3 billion active Windows users at the time of this writing, then you're using an Intel- or Intel-compatible PC running on what's arcanely described as an x86/x64 chipset.

Without getting too deep into the history of this nomenclature, it dates back to the original IBM PC, which featured an Intel processor, an early entry in the so-called x86 family of microprocessors. (More recent versions include the 80386, or 386, the 486, and the Pentium, which was originally called the 586.) Put simply, the x86 moniker describes two things: Intel compatibility (since both Intel and various copycats make the chips) and a 32-bit instruction set, which means, among other things, that these chips typically address up to 4 GB of RAM.

The x64 chipset, meanwhile, is a 64-bit variant of the x86 family of chipsets. Put simply, x64 is x86 on steroids: It is 100 percent compatible with x86 software, including Windows and its applications, but provides support for an astonishing amount of RAM: up to 256 TB (yes, terabytes).

Somewhat embarrassingly (to Intel), x64 was invented by Intel competitor AMD, but once it was embraced by Microsoft for use in Windows, Intel had to jump aboard, too. So when we refer to x86/x64 chipsets, we're referring to those that power all of the PCs made before late 2012: traditional, Intel-compatible, 32-bit or 64-bit microprocessors and supporting chips.

> **NOTE** If your PC came with Windows 7 preinstalled, then it's likely that it's utilizing a 64-bit, x64 chipset. Many such PCs come with 6 GB or even 8 GB of RAM, since one of the big advantages of these chips over older x86 chips is that additional memory support.

An Intel Core i7 processor, the latest in a long, long line of x86/x64 chips, is shown in Figure 1-1.

Most people vaguely understand that Intel-compatible chips sit at the heart of PCs. But things are really changing with Windows 8. Starting with this release, you can now also purchase PCs and tablets that are based on a competing and incompatible chipset called ARM (advanced RISC machine).

FIGURE 1-1: A modern Intel microprocessor carries a decades-old legacy inside it.

ARM is a different animal altogether. First, no one company makes ARM chips. Instead, the ARM platform is controlled by a company called ARM Holdings that licenses the technology for the chipsets to other companies; so unlike Intel and AMD, ARM Holdings doesn't manufacture its own chips.

The companies that do manufacture ARM chips—such as NVIDIA, Qualcomm, Texas Instruments, and others—are free to make their own changes to the design. So while ARM-based chipsets are broadly compatible with each other, they're not compatible in the way that x86/x64 designs from both Intel and AMD are compatible.

ARM chipsets are 32-bit designs, not 64-bit, but they run much more efficiently than x86/x64 chips. So they consume less power, with resulting devices normally providing fantastic battery life, especially when compared to traditional PCs. ARM designs are so efficient that they can be used in devices as small as phones. In fact, Windows Phone handsets are based on ARM chipsets. A typical ARM chipset is shown in Figure 1-2.

▶ As 32-bit designs, ARM systems can only utilize 4 GB of RAM. This isn't a huge issue for most users, but could be limiting for power users.

Microsoft's decision to port Windows to the ARM architecture was made for one reason, primarily: The company wanted its flagship product to run well on thin and light tablets and other devices. And while Intel-compatible chipsets provide amazing performance and good battery life on a wide range of device types, only ARM provides them with the ability to compete, point by point, with devices as thin and light and power efficient as the iPad. A representative ARM tablet is shown in Figure 1-3.

FIGURE 1-2: ARM designs are integrated into what is called system on a chip, or SoC.

Of course, the Windows 8 version for ARM, compromises. ARM chipsets are not compatible with Intel-compatible chipsets, so the amazing array of Windows-compatible application software that we all take for granted on the PC side will not run on ARM-based Windows devices.

▶ To be clear, we are referring to legacy desktop applications here. Most Metro-style apps will run identically on both ARM and Intel-based PCs and devices.

Likewise, you can't upgrade a traditional PC running Windows 7 to Windows RT. Instead, the system is made available only on new PCs and devices running a compatible ARM chipset.

FIGURE 1-3: ARM-based tablets will typically be thinner and lighter, and offer better battery life, than Intel-type designs.

Because of the differences in various ARM-based platforms, the Windows RT machines you see on the market are actually slightly different from each other under the hood, and Microsoft and its partners essentially have to custom-craft the OS and applications for each device. For this reason, Windows RT devices are sold almost like appliances, and there's a tight integration between the device and its software.

And as noted earlier in the chapter, some Windows 8 features simply aren't available on Windows RT. These include individual applications such as Windows

Media Player and Windows Media Center, as well as lower-level features such as Storage Spaces and BitLocker. (Windows RT overcomes the latter limitation with its own, unique full-device encryption functionality, however.)

So, which one do you choose?

In many ways, the decision comes down to need. A Windows RT device—like a tablet—will generally provide better battery life than an equivalent Intel-compatible device and come in a thinner and lighter form factor. Both can be turned into "full PCs" using a docking station and attached keyboard, mouse, screen, and other peripherals. Both can run virtually all Metro-style apps, but only the Intel-compatible machine will be capable of running legacy software designed for Windows.

Perhaps the best way to decide from a form factor/architecture perspective is to ask yourself a few simple questions, the first few of which will be aimed at seeing whether you can remove ARM/Windows RT from the equation.

Are you upgrading from Windows 7?

If yes, then you simply cannot choose Windows RT. You'll need to upgrade to either Windows 8 or Windows 8 Pro (depending on which version of Windows 7 you're currently using.)

Do you need compatibility with legacy, desktop-based third-party applications like Photoshop?

If yes, then you simply cannot choose Windows RT. You'll need to choose from the many Intel-compatible Windows 8 PCs and devices.

Do you need to sign in to an Active Directory–based domain for work purposes?

If yes, then you simply cannot choose Windows RT. You'll need to choose from the many Intel-compatible Windows 8 PCs.

Do you need Windows Media Center, perhaps for a living room–based DVR (digital video recorder) solution?

If yes, then you simply cannot choose Windows RT. You'll need to choose from the many Intel-compatible Windows 8 PCs. In fact, you'll need to use Windows 8 Pro.

Those are the four biggest Windows RT blockers. If you are still a candidate for a Windows RT-based device, your choice is now a heck of a lot less clear, unfortunately. And that's because it's just really hard to know whether to choose Intel (Windows 8) or ARM (Windows RT).

Consider this quandary. You've decided on a Windows RT tablet because it's super thin and light and it runs for days on a charge. (We're fantasizing here; stick with us.) So you make the purchase, discover a bunch of fun and useful Metro-style apps and go happily on your way. You are able to connect it to a docking station and take advantage of the large, widescreen display, external keyboard, and mouse you keep in your home office. All is well.

But then you receive an attachment for work that includes a file type that's not supported by any Metro-style app, perhaps an Adobe Photoshop file or WordPerfect document. If this were a traditional Windows 8 PC, you'd be able to install software to open this file. But on Windows RT, you're kind of stuck until a Metro-style alternative appears.

There are a hundred scenarios like this where the lack of real Windows compatibility can hurt: browser alternatives, browser add-ins, games, and more.

As a rule, the decision will often come down to the very general difference between the Metro-style environment that will be your primary interface on Windows RT devices and the Windows desktop, which will be far more powerful and usable on Intel-compatible PCs (and will certainly be the primary interface as well, especially on traditional desktop PCs and laptops). And that difference is this: Metro is (largely) for consuming content and the desktop is (largely) for productivity. When you want to browse the web, check Facebook, perform simple e-mail activities, enjoy music or a movie, and perform other consumption-style activities, Metro is the place to be. And if this is all you're doing with the PC or device, or almost all you're doing, an ARM-based Windows RT device should be ideal. You need a device, not a PC.

If you need to do anything creative or productive—regularly create word processing documents, edit spreadsheets, or make presentations, and so on—you need a Windows 8-based PC running on an Intel-compatible chipset. You need a PC, not a device.

What's confusing is that the lines are blurring between the two types of products. That is, there are Intel-compatible tablets, and there are ARM-based laptops. The adoption of the ARM platform gives Windows users a choice. But it also provides a new bit of confusion.

Speaking of which, let's talk device types.

Picking a PC or Device Type

With a few exceptions, the PC world has consisted of two major device types to date: the venerable desktop PC and the laptop. Sure, there were exceptions, like the poorly-selling Tablet PCs that barely made a blip in the marketplace in the early 2000s, the successful but short-lived and inexpensive netbooks, and so on. But for the past 20 years or more, we've pretty much had two choices: desktops and laptops.

With Windows 8, that's changing. On the desktop side, all-in-one computers modeled on Apple's successful iMac are becoming more and more popular, and out-selling traditional tower PCs with detached monitors.

But portable computers, overall, are far more successful than any desktops, and with Windows 8 (and RT), an estimated 80 percent of new computers sold will be portable PCs and devices. And in addition to traditional laptops and the thin and light Ultrabooks, we're seeing interesting new hybrid PCs—laptops where the screen can flip around to turn the device into a tablet—as well as slate-like tablet devices similar to Apple's iPad.

Here's a rundown of PC and device types to consider.

DESKTOP PC/WORKSTATION

For those who prefer or need the ultimate in expandability, PC makers still offer tradi-tional desktop computers, which typically come in some form of tower configuration in which the guts of the computer—or what some erroneously describe as the CPU—are separated from the display, keyboard, mouse, and other external peripherals, including speakers, microphone and web camera, external drives, and more.

The advantage of a desktop computer is manifold, but the primary advantage is expandability: You can install multiple internal hard drives inside the PC's case, as well as external expansion cards for USB, video capture, and the video card, among others. Desktop computers also tend to have more ports—especially of the USB variety—and can be easily expanded to accommodate more.

Desktop computers will remain the machine of choice for power users of all kinds, as well as those with high-end needs, including graphic designers, CAD designers, hard-core gamers, and others. Some desktop PCs are referred to as workstations, though that name is quickly losing favor. That said, PCs that utilize server-class CPUs can be considered workstations.

A typical desktop PC is shown in Figure 1-4.

The vast majority of traditional desktop PCs are Intel-compatible machines, not ARM-based PCs. One exception is ultra-small form factor PCs, which can be found in both configurations.

FIGURE 1-4: Traditional desktop PCs are less popular than they were 10 years ago, but they're not going anywhere.

ALL-IN-ONE

Thanks to Apple's iMac, there's been a resurgence in all-in-one computers, a special form of desktop PC in which almost all of the components—including the CPU and "guts," the screen, the speakers, the microphone and web camera, and all of the ports—are found in a single, generally slim and attractive form factor. All that's found separately from the box are the keyboard and mouse, and of course any additional external peripherals.

All-in-one computers, like the one shown in Figure 1-5, are typically very attractive, with a sleek and modern design.

While both Intel-compatible and ARM-based all-in-ones are available, most are Intel-compatible designs.

FIGURE 1-5: All-in-one PCs utilize laptop parts but offer much more on-screen real estate.

LAPTOP AND PORTABLE WORKSTATION

The venerable laptop computer survived a temporary wave of competition from low-end netbooks. But with those toy-like computers disappearing from the market, there's a new more ideal option arriving in the form of Ultrabooks, thin and light laptop computers that generally cost under $1,000—often well under $1,000—and things don't look good for traditional laptops (see Figure 1-6). Suffice to say that laptops will of course continue in the market, and some high-end models might be considered portable workstations. But the Ultrabook, described in the next section, will almost certainly take over this segment of the market during Windows 8's lifetime.

Most laptops and all portable workstations are Intel-type designs, but you can find ARM-based Windows RT laptops as well.

FIGURE 1-6: Traditional laptops are on the way out, but will still be common in businesses.

NETBOOK

Although netbooks (Figure 1-7) were all the rage when Windows 7 first shipped in 2009, this low-cost alternative to the laptop has since fallen out of favor. And while Windows 8 is certainly capable of running rather well on the low-end hardware that's found in such machines—a 1 GHz Atom-class processor and 2 GB of RAM—this version of Windows is not suited to netbooks very much at all.

The issue is the screen. Most netbooks ship with 1024 x 600 resolution screens, which is fine for the Windows desktop but below the 1024 x 768 minimum—and the recommended 1366 x 768—resolution needed for the Metro environment. This means that if you do install Windows 8 on a netbook class computer and try to run any

▶ There is a fix, as it turns out. We discuss this in Chapter 5, which deals with personalization.

Metro-style app, even Windows Store, you're going to get a full-screen error message. It just won't work.

You won't see Windows RT-based netbooks. These machines have come and gone.

FIGURE 1-7: Netbooks can't run Metro-style apps.

ULTRABOOKS

Most people understand the basic concept behind a laptop: It's a portable computer with a clamshell case design in which the laptop lid can be closed over the keyboard for easy portability. An Ultrabook is simply a modern take on the laptop, but with some rules. First, Ultrabooks are much thinner and lighter than traditional laptops and are thus much easier to carry around. Second, Ultrabooks feature the latest Intel CPUs and chipsets, which are designed to perform well and offer excellent battery life. Third, Ultrabooks must obtain at least five hours of battery life, which is decent, though most offer more. And they must offer USB 3.0-based connectivity (which we discuss later in the chapter).

A typical Ultrabook is shown in Figure 1-8.

There's a final, unofficial requirement of Ultrabooks, and it's perhaps the best of them all. Ultrabooks generally cost less than $1,000, and many cost closer to $650. (On the flip side, some high-end Ultrabooks cost almost as much as low-end Mac laptops. Almost.)

Speaking of Macs, the Ultrabook design was clearly based on Apple's trendsetting MacBook Air line. And not surprisingly, many of the first

FIGURE 1-8: Beauty and brains: Ultrabooks have it all.

generation Ultrabooks—which appeared in the year before Windows 8's release— looked an awful lot like the Apple entry, albeit it while costing hundreds of dollars less. You can expect more innovative and unique designs to appear in the coming years as PC makers become more familiar with this type of device.

Ultrabooks are available in both Intel-compatible and ARM-based designs, but the Intel underpinnings are far more common.

TABLET/SLATE

We assume most people have seen an iPad, and given that device's popularity, it should come as no surprise that Microsoft and its PC maker partners have raced to create both an operating system, Windows 8/RT, and a wide variety of multi-touch-based tablet devices that can blow the iPad's doors off.

The nice thing about Windows 8/RT-based tablets is the variety. You have numerous machines to choose from, on both the Intel-compatible and ARM sides of the fence, and they come in a variety of sizes, with screens that range from 7 inches on up. A standard slate-style tablet can be seen in Figure 1-9.

Tablets are also not limited by their form factor. Many can be docked and easily expanded with an external screen, keyboard, mouse, and other peripherals, becoming, in effect, a full-fledged PC in the process. In this usage scenario, a tablet can work much like an iPad while you're out and about, accessed solely through its multi-touch capabilities. But when you get home—or to work—and dock the device, you have a real PC (Figure 1-10).

FIGURE 1-9: The looks of an iPad but the power of a PC

FIGURE 1-10: A docked tablet can function as a desktop computer by adding a keyboard and mouse.

The tablet market is pretty evenly split between ARM- and Intel-compatible designs, and many of both types are available. This is the one type of PC where ARM-based products may eventually outsell the entrenched Intel juggernaut. In fact, Microsoft is betting pretty heavily on this market and is releasing its own Windows RT-based tablet device, called Surface, and a Windows 8-based tablet PC, called Surface Pro. Both look almost identical, and resemble the device shown in Figure 1-11. But the Intel-based PC version is more powerful and a bit thicker and heavier.

FIGURE 1-11: Microsoft Surface RT

HYBRID PC

Ultrabooks are obviously a huge improvement over traditional laptops but they suffer a bit when compared to tablets in certain situations. For example, Ultrabooks aren't as personal as tablets and aren't as easily used in casual situations, such as when you are sitting in bed. Fortunately, PC makers have created a range of hybrid devices that bridge this gap, offering the best of both product lines.

The most basic of such hybrid PCs dates back to Microsoft's first foray into Tablet PC computing in the early 2000s. This type of machine, called a convertible laptop, is essentially a laptop or Ultrabook computer in which the screen is permanently attached on a swivel. So you can use a convertible laptop like a regular laptop or Ultrabook, or you can flip the screen around and lock it over the keyboard, creating a somewhat thick tablet device in the process.

A convertible laptop like the one shown in Figure 1-12 is ideal for those who usually need a full-fledged laptop but would occasionally like to use the device in tablet mode.

Slate hybrids are essentially tablets that can accommodate a clip-on keyboard base, sometimes with an extra battery under the keyboard to provide better off-power run time. This design essentially reverses the convertible laptop usage pattern and is best used by those who will use the PC in tablet mode primarily but sometimes need to type as well.

You will find both Intel-compatible and ARM-based hybrid PCs of all kinds.

FIGURE 1-12: A hybrid laptop lets you use the machine as a laptop or a tablet.

Hardware Capabilities to Look For

Once you've determined whether to stick with an Intel-compatible machine or switch to an ARM-based device, chosen the Windows version you need, and picked out the type of PC or device that suits your fancy, there's one more area of concern. And it concerns new hardware capabilities, some of which won't be available on certain PCs or devices.

With each new Windows release, Microsoft supports a wider range of hardware devices and peripherals, of course. But with Windows 8 and the new portable scenarios that are opened up by tablets, Ultrabooks, and hybrids, the possibilities have expanded dramatically. And many of these possibilities are tied directly to new hardware capabilities that you should be aware of.

Here are some of the more relevant new hardware capabilities you should consider.

MULTI-TOUCH

While Windows has offered pervasive multi-touch support since Windows Vista, the release of Windows 8 has changed things pretty dramatically. Instead of simply tacking multi-touch support on top of Windows as was done in previous releases, Windows 8 has been re-architected so that multi-touch is a full-fledged input type, alongside the mouse and keyboard. And in the new Metro environment, multi-touch is arguably even better supported than is mouse and keyboard. It is, as Microsoft puts it, a touch-first environment.

We discuss multi-touch throughout this book, but it's important to know that multi-touch isn't just relegated to tablets. In fact, once you start using Windows 8 via multi-touch, you're going to expect this capability on all of your PCs. And not surprisingly, multi-touch devices of all kinds have come to market alongside Windows 8, including touch-capable displays that can attach to desktop computers, and touch-based Ultrabooks, hybrid PCs, and even all-in-ones.

You may not believe it until you try it. But once you've experienced multi-touch, you'll find yourself touching all of your screens, whether they're touch-capable or not.

NOTE Still not convinced? Know this: Microsoft requires that all Windows 8 devices support at least five touch points. That translates to a hand of fingers— or foot of toes—that are able to interact with Windows and apps all at once. And many devices will of course support even more touch points.

CROSSREF Check out Chapter 3 for more information about Metro and its multi-touch interactions.

CONNECTED STANDBY

While Windows's support for power management has evolved over the years, the new emphasis on highly portable computing in Windows 8 has triggered the development of an excellent new power management mode called Connected Standby. This mode isn't generally available on PCs created before 2012 and is designed for new, highly portable devices that will only rarely be turned off. In other words, it works much like power management on a modern smartphone.

Instead of using a standard sleep state, Connected Standby allows your PC or device to enter a nearly powerless state in which battery life is only minimally impacted but Metro-style apps can run in the background, performing tasks like updating e-mail and triggering notifications. Of course, traditional desktop applications are unaware of this new power mode, so Windows 8 utilizes a new Desktop Activity Monitor to reduce the resource utilization of desktop applications while in this mode.

Connected Standby is available in all Windows 8 versions, including Windows RT, but will work best on new hardware designed specifically for this mode. But even if your PC or device doesn't support Connected Standby, Windows 8 includes numerous power management improvements that should improve battery life and performance when compared to performing similar tasks in Windows 7.

SENSORS

Many of Windows 8's new capabilities are inspired by smartphones and other highly mobile devices and the new wireless scenarios these devices enable. Key among these capabilities is a support for a variety of sensors, small hardware devices that provide interaction between the outside world and Windows itself. Some of the new scenarios supported by Windows 8 and sensors include:

- ▶ **Adaptive screen brightness control:** In the past, controlling screen brightness was at best semi-automatic. You could manually configure a brightness setting in Power Options. Or those with portable computers could use power modes to automatically change the screen brightness to one of two settings, depending on whether the machine was attached to power. In Windows 8, the situation is much more sophisticated, and if you have a PC or device with an ambient light sensor (ALS), Windows 8 will automatically change the brightness of the screen on the fly. This capability is better for your eyes and for readability, but it can also improve battery life when you use the PC or device in a dimly lit area.

- ▶ **Automatic screen rotation:** Tablets and hybrid devices and other screens can utilize an accelerometer to determine the orientation of the screen and rotate the on-screen display appropriately as it's changed. This type of activity is common on smartphones and, with Windows 8, it's come to PCs as well.

- ▶ **Tilt and motion:** Using a gyroscope sensor, a Windows 8-based PC or tablet can register its movements in 3-D space, providing feedback to games and apps. In this way, you might tilt a tablet forward to accelerate during a driving game, or tilt the device to the left and right to steer. This isn't limited to just games, however, and the types of motions gyroscope sensors can detect—including shakes, twists, and rotations in multiple dimensions—are quite sophisticated.

- ▶ **Location and directions:** Using a standard GPS sensor, a Windows 8 PC or device can accurately report its geographic location and then plot routes and distances to other destinations. Mapping and driving apps are obvious applications for this capability.

- ▶ **Compass:** Using a 3-D accelerometer and a 3-D magnetometer, or a gyroscope, a Windows 8 PC or device can emulate a compass. In fact, they can be used to create a multi-axis, tilt-sensitive compass.

TAP TO SEND (NFC)

Utilizing new Near Field Communication (NFC) chipsets, Windows 8-based PCs and devices can send content to another compatible device (Windows 8 PC or device, Windows Phone 8, or other NFC-compatible device) using a new method called Tap to

Send. This method additionally requires a unique tap zone on the device's exterior, which is used to initiate a send or receive action, but even without this part, NFC can still be used via Bluetooth to send information wirelessly.

So what's the big deal with NFC? As an emerging standard, NFC is being used to perform contactless (that is, wireless) payments at retail locations, data exchanges, and other duties. And while these activities may seem better suited to a smartphone, the inclusion of NFC in Windows 8 means that these PCs and devices will be able to participate with coming NFC-based systems as well.

UEFI FIRMWARE

New Windows 8-based PCs and devices will utilize a new type of firmware called Unified Extensible Firmware Interface, or UEFI, instead of the old-fashioned BIOS firmware we've been using for decades. UEFI provides many advantages over BIOS, but key among them is performance: UEFI-based PCs and devices will boot much more quickly than those based on BIOS.

UEFI offers other advantages over BIOS, of course. The user interface for this firmware type can be graphical instead of text-based like BIOS. And it enables a new security feature called Secure Boot that protects system components from tampering during boot.

CROSSREF UEFI and Secure Boot are discussed a bit more in Chapter 12.

USB 3.0

Don't buy a Windows 8 PC that includes only USB 2.0 ports. Rated at throughput speeds of up to 5 Gbps, USB 3.0 is up to 10 times faster than USB 2.0 (480 Mbps), which can have a significant impact on the performance of certain peripherals, especially hard disks.

USB 3.0 has other advantages over USB 2.0, though. You can mix and match USB 2.0 and 3.0 devices on a single controller without impacting the speed of the faster USB 3.0 devices. (This was an issue with USB 2.0 controllers, which would ratchet the speed of all devices down to 12 Mbps if a USB 1.0 device was attached.) USB 3.0 also provides more power to devices, removing the need for USB 2.0-type double connectors and speeding the charge time of battery-powered devices. And while the plugs look a bit different, they're 100 percent compatible with previous generation devices.

SUMMARY

With every Windows release, customers face challenges when it comes to picking the correct Windows version. And while Windows 8 is no different in this regard, it does at least offer the simplest product lineup we've seen in over a decade, with just two mainstream retail versions—Windows 8 and Windows 8 Pro—being offered alongside a version for ARM-based devices that's called Windows RT.

The addition of an ARM-based variant of Windows 8, sold only with new Windows-based devices, is perhaps where things get trickiest. Picking between such a device and a PC based on more traditional Intel-compatible chipsets can be difficult, but not insurmountable if you understand the differences and issues.

Also, for the first time in many years, you're going to want to pay close attention to the hardware peripherals and sensors that come with your PC or devices. Windows 8 and Windows RT are far more useful when used on a machine with the latest hardware capabilities, so be sure to shop carefully, regardless of which Windows 8 version or processor architecture you choose.

CHAPTER 2

Installing and Upgrading to Windows 8

IN THIS CHAPTER

- ► Understanding the different options for installing and upgrading to Windows 8
- ► Understanding how the web-based installer works
- ► Using new Windows Setup features
- ► Choosing a sign-in type
- ► Employing post-setup tasks for a complete install
- ► Looking at advanced Windows 8 configurations
- ► Using a dual-boot configuration
- ► Installing Windows 8 on a Mac

With previous Windows versions, Microsoft offered a fairly static set of capabilities by which one could install the OS onto a new or existing computer. These capabilities were based on the same underlying functionality but were designed to serve three basic audiences: end users, businesses, and PC makers, and not necessarily in that order. As such, the process was pretty technical for the typical user, which wasn't much of a problem because very few users actually installed Windows this way anyway. Most acquired Windows with a new PC purchase or, perhaps, through a work-based PC.

With Windows 7, however, those usage patterns changed somewhat. For the first time, a significant percentage of Windows users upgraded existing PCs running a previous version of Windows to Windows 7, and to do so they typically purchased a retailed, boxed copy of the new OS, in Upgrade form, and then performed the upgrade manually.

The reason for this sudden change is obvious: With Windows 7, for the first time, a new version of Windows actually had system requirements that matched, not exceeded, those of the previous version. So while many users did of course buy new, Windows 7-based PCs—several hundreds of millions of them, in fact—many also chose to continue using their existing computers as well.

With Windows 8, Microsoft expects a mix of both traditional PC sales and retail upgrades, again because Windows 8 does not exceed the system requirements of its own predecessor. And many users will simply purchase a Windows 8-based device, such as a tablet, and then upgrade their existing PC as well so that they can take advantage of this Windows version's excellent PC-to-PC sync and integration capabilities. So, since many users would still be installing Windows 8 on their own going forward, Microsoft has evolved the Windows Setup process yet again. And this time, finally, we think they got it right.

As is the case throughout this book, we'll be focusing largely on new features and functionality, in this case with regards to Setup and installing Windows 8 on your own PCs. But don't worry, power users: If you have specific setup needs, we cover those as well.

> **NOTE**   What about Windows RT? This ARM-based version of Windows 8 comes only with new hardware and cannot be purchased in software-only form, either in retail packaging or electronically, as with Windows 8. So the only Windows Setup experience you'll have will involve the so-called out-of-box experience, or OOBE, that's discussed later in the chapter. But since that bit is so obvious, Windows RT users can feel free to skip much of the information in this chapter.

THAT WAS THEN, THIS IS NOW: HOW SETUP HAS CHANGED

With Windows 7 and previous Windows versions, Microsoft provided a monolithic installation application called Windows Setup that was custom-tailored for managed businesses and PC makers but could also be used, in manual form, by end users. This same Setup application came with both the Full and Upgrade versions of Windows and provided a consistent interface between the two.

Those who purchase Windows 8 today in retail, boxed form will find that Setup—shown in Figure 2-1—hasn't changed much since Windows 7. The color scheme is a bit different, the out-of-box experience (OOBE) steps / those that appear after Setup is complete and you have to enter some information about yourself and the PC) are now touch-enabled and evolved, and the whole process is a bit shorter. But overall, things haven't changed much.

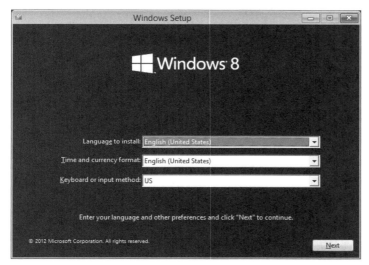

FIGURE 2-1: Windows Setup

This is both good and bad.

For businesses and PC makers, it means that the tools and methods they use to blast Windows 8 images onto PCs will be familiar and efficient, and not require training. This, after all, is what Windows Setup was really made for anyway.

But for end users, this old-fashioned setup routine is incomplete and inefficient. It doesn't include vital and important tools such as the Upgrade Advisor, which provides you with a compatibility report for your hardware and software *before* you install Windows, or Windows Easy Transfer, which makes upgrades and migrations of data possible. Furthermore, Setup won't work well electronically, so those who hope to install or upgrade to Windows 8 over the Internet would need to first download the massive Windows installer file set—roughly 3.5 to 5 GB, depending on the version, then burn it to disc or copy to a specially made, bootable USB hard drive or flash drive. And then they would need to boot the computer with that device and go through the manual setup process.

Yes, you can do this if you really want to. But there's a better way.

> **NOTE** Those who wish to install Windows 8 the old-fashioned way should consult Paul's website, **winsupersite.com**, where the clean install and upgrade/migration scenarios are fully documented. But we provide some related information later in the chapter for those who are forced to continue using these methods.

USING THE WINDOWS 8 WEB INSTALLER

With Windows 8, Microsoft has combined three of its Windows installation tools into a single web-based version of Setup that overcomes virtually all of the problems with the traditional, monolithic Setup application. Available at windows.com, this new installer can perform a clean install, upgrade, or migration to Windows 8 more quickly and more reliably than ever before.

Understanding Why the Web-Based Setup Is Superior

To understand why this new web-based Setup is superior, consider how you used to install Windows (and how, optionally, you still can with the retail-type Setup application in Windows 8) and why you would be performing this task in the first place.

The most common reason you'd find yourself wasting an afternoon—or more commonly, an entire day—futzing around with Windows Setup and the attendant activities you must undergo is that you've got an existing PC running the previous Windows version and you'd like to upgrade. This Setup type was fraught with the possibility of disaster, and since you may want to bring your settings and data along with you—called a *migration*—or even your currently-installed applications—called an *in-place upgrade*—the times and places in which something could go wrong—resulting, perhaps, in data loss—could multiply as well.

The second most common reason to run the traditional Windows Setup routine is that you've been using Windows for a while and your PC is starting to slow down. And what you'd like to do is back up all your settings and data, run Setup, wipe out Windows, and just reinstall it from scratch. This is called a *clean install* of Windows, though Microsoft for some reason refers to it as a custom install.

Clean installs are a tricky business. Assuming you get through Setup without any issues—which, to be fair, doesn't require a lot of skill—that doesn't mean you're done. The trouble is that Setup might not have found all the drivers for your PC. Even though Windows Update can often find more drivers, that won't help if your network adapter driver is among the missing and you can't get online. Regardless, it's very common to visit Device Manager and discover that some hardware devices were not properly configured with drivers. And the name of a device in Device Manager sometimes doesn't even provide a hint about what the device really is, making the process of finding the correct driver next to impossible.

A related issue is that even the most fastidious advocate of backing up may miss something. As you recover your data and start reinstalling applications after a clean install, you may discover that you forgot to de-authorize an application like Apple iTunes or Adobe Photoshop, didn't back up a critical but hidden data file (like Outlook's notorious PST file), or missed some other palm-slap-to-the-forehead, obvious-after-the-fact thing that you really wish you had remembered. But once you've blown away your previous Windows install, it's too late.

Microsoft tried to alleviate these issues in the past with solutions that were separate from and ran outside of Setup. One, called Upgrade Advisor, evaluated the hardware, devices, and installed software on your PC and then presented you with a report containing, potentially, a list of issues you may need to address before installing Windows. A second utility, called Windows Easy Transfer, took the guesswork out of files (documents, pictures, movies, and so on), e-mail, and settings from the previous version of Windows to the new version. You would run Windows Easy Transfer twice: once against the previous version of Windows to acquire this data and then again under the new version to apply it all back.

Upgrade Advisor and Windows Easy Transfer are both excellent tools, but they suffer from the same basic problems: You need to know they exist, and obtain them, and do so before you install Windows. And there's nothing in Windows Setup to even suggest that such tools are available. As a result, many users simply don't know about them and run into problems these tools could have easily fixed.

> Windows Easy Transfer had other onerous requirements. You needed an external hard drive, network location, or even a crazy, specially designed USB cable to use this utility.

In Windows 8, the traditional Windows Setup routine doesn't solve these issues, and it works much like that of its predecessor. But the new web-based installer *does* solve these issues, and it does so in the most obvious way possible: It integrates both the Upgrade Advisor and Windows Easy Transfer directly into Setup, making these processes not just discoverable but obvious and unavoidable.

The web-based installer has other advantages as well.

For example, with traditional, media-based installs of Windows, you need to know whether you have a 32-bit (x86) or 64-bit (x64) version of Windows and then buy and use the appropriate Upgrade media when performing an in-place upgrade. With the Windows 8 web-based installer, this is handled for you behind the scenes.

Each Windows Setup disc or download also comes with an associated product key, a complex, 25-digit sequence of letters and numbers that you must manually enter accurately before Setup will continue and, later, activate Windows. With the web-based installer, this product key is tied to your Microsoft account and automatically applied to the install during setup. It's yet another thing you don't need to be worried about.

Also, the Windows 8 web-based installer uses a new form of compression that is specially tuned for the massive Windows Imaging (WIM) file that makes up the majority (size-wise) of the files that form Windows Setup. So it's far more efficient to stream this file from the web while running Setup than the old method of downloading a disc image file (in ISO format), burning that to disc (or installing to USB), rebooting the computer, and running Setup that way.

Put simply, the new web-based installer is faster and far more full-featured than the traditional, media-based Setup variant. Like we said earlier, we can't imagine why you wouldn't want to use it.

> **NOTE**   Well, there are always reasons, of course. Enthusiasts who purchase or build their own computer without a copy of Windows preinstalled may need to install Windows 8 the old-fashioned way. For such cases, Microsoft does allow you to download an ISO version of Windows Setup as before, and then create your own Setup disc or USB device. Remember, Windows is all about choice.

> **NOTE**   Okay, there's one other reason. If you've been running Windows 8 for a while and would like to reinstall the OS from scratch, there's a new, quicker way than with previous methods. It's called Push Button Reset, and it can work in one of two ways: A factory-fresh, literally new install of Windows or a new install of Windows in which your settings and Metro-style apps are retained as well. This new feature is so amazing and so useful that we devote a lot of time to it in Chapter 11.

Step-by-Step: Installing Windows 8

▶ You can access the web-based Windows 8 Setup from the Microsoft Store (store .microsoft.com) as well.

Before you can install Windows 8 with the web-based installer, you will need to visit Microsoft's Windows website (windows.com), sign in with your Microsoft account, and purchase the version of Windows you'd like to use. Microsoft will provide you with a product key, which you won't need if you're using these instructions, and then provide you with an opportunity to run Windows Setup from the web or download the operating system in ISO format so that you can burn it to disc or copy it to a bootable USB device later. Choose the former.

This initial download is tiny, about 5 MB, and it initiates Windows 8 Setup. You can run this file directly from your browser or choose to save it to the hard drive and then run.

In the first phase of the wizard-based Setup application that launches, an Upgrade Advisor-type tool runs and polls your software applications and hardware devices to see whether everything is compatible with Windows 8. When the compatibility check is complete, the wizard will indicate whether you have any items that need your attention. (See Figure 2-2.) If you're lucky, this will be a short list, but no worries yet. As you may discover, most of the items that require your attention are minor.

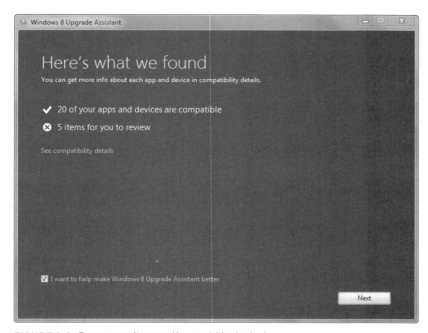

FIGURE 2-2: Cross your fingers. You could be lucky here.

To see what's wrong, click the link titled See compatibility details. This report, shown in Figure 2-3, can be printed or saved to disk, but oftentimes you can deal with the pertinent issues immediately.

FIGURE 2-3: The Compatibility details report

In our experience, some typical issues do arise here. These include:

▶ **Microsoft Security Essentials:** Microsoft's free antivirus solution is not compatible with Windows 8, so you will need to uninstall it before Setup will continue. (You will be prompted to do so.)

▶ **Apple iTunes:** The compatibility checker is nice enough to remind you to de-authorize your iTunes account from within the iTunes application before continuing. However, you should remember that some other applications will need to be de-authorized as well, including some from Adobe, such as Photoshop.

▶ **Other software issues:** The compatibility report lists any software applications that will not work in Windows 8, many of which will be accompanied by a link so you can get help on the application's website. If you see such a message, save the compatibility report to disk, back it up, and use it later to make the fix(es).

▶ **Other hardware issues:** Some hardware drivers may need to be updated after Windows 8 installs, and the compatibility report will call out some of them with a message to get updated drivers from Windows Update or the manufacturer's website. This necessity is discussed in the section about post-Setup tasks later in the chapter.

When you're ready, close the compatibility report and click Next.

Next, Setup says it's ready to download Windows and notes that a product key has been "pre-keyed," or pre-applied to the installation. This means you won't have to type a 25-digit alphanumeric product key as you do with a manual clean or upgrade install.

Click Next and the wizard will download the rest of Windows 8 Setup. This procedure should just take a few minutes on a high-speed connection, but it could take much longer, of course. As Setup notes, you can continue using the previous Windows version during this process.

Once the full set of installation files are downloaded, Setup will check the integrity of the downloaded files. This is important because large chunks of the Setup process occur when the PC is offline and once it begins, there's no way to elegantly recover should a corrupt file be encountered.

When that process completes, Setup reports that it is getting files ready. This is a plain English way of explaining that Setup is decompressing the compressed files it previously downloaded. So this process could take a few minutes as well.

When it completes, Setup then prompts you to select one of several choices, as shown in Figure 2-4. These can include Install now, Install by creating media, or Install later from your desktop.

▶ A fourth option, Install on another partition, can also appear if you're using a PC with multiple disk drives or partitions.

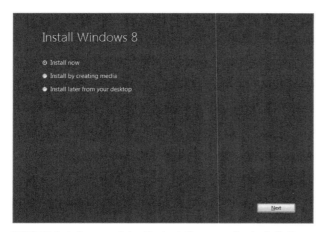

FIGURE 2-4: You can defer the install or copy the installation files to DVD or USB.

▶ This is similar to the process utilized by the Windows 7 USB/DVD Download Tool, yet another previously separate tool that is integrated into the web-based installer. We told you this thing was special.

These choices seem straightforward, but the second option is a cleverly disguised way to trigger a process whereby you can install the Setup files to a DVD or USB memory device. This allows you to perform a more traditional, if less seamless, installation later, or to another PC.

If you're ready to go for it, choose Install now and then click Next.

> **NOTE** Setup may prompt you to check for software updates here. We strongly recommend performing this check, since there are occasionally newer components available online. That said, this will be more of an issue if you previously deferred the install for some reason using the Install later option in the previous step of the wizard.

After a bit of churning, Setup will present the End User License Agreement (EULA). You must accept the license terms before you can click the Accept button to continue. It's like you're accepting it twice.

The next screen, shown in Figure 2-5, determines what type of install you will perform. Because this is so important, and can vary from PC to PC, we'll need to spend a bit of time on this. (This figure was obtained by running the Windows 8 Setup from Windows 7.)

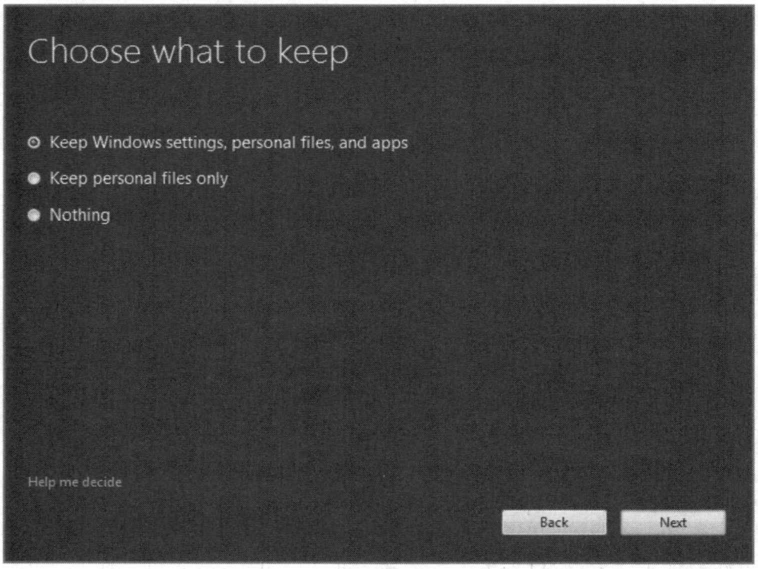

Choose what to keep

⦿ Keep Windows settings, personal files, and apps
● Keep personal files only
● Nothing

Help me decide

[Back]   [Next]

FIGURE 2-5: Think wisely here.

You are asked to choose what you want to keep, and there will be some mix of the following choices here, depending on which version of Windows you're currently running:

▶ **Keep Windows settings, personal files, and app[lication]s:** This install type equates to what used to be called an in-place upgrade. This means that virtually everything from your existing Windows installation, including applications—we're not sure why Microsoft uses the term *apps* here—will come forward as the OS is upgraded to Windows 8. This is the most complete install type because nothing will be lost. And it's available only to those who are currently running Windows 7.

▶ **Keep Windows settings and personal files only:** This hybrid option, which can be considered an advanced migration, saves your custom settings as well as everything in your personal folders (all of your documents, desktop files, and so on, as well as those for any other user accounts). This option is available only to those upgrading from Windows Vista with Service Pack 1 or 2.

▶ **Keep personal files only:** This will perform what we used to call a migration, meaning that Setup will save everything in your personal folders (all of your documents, desktop files, and so on, as well as those for any other user accounts), wipe out the current Windows version, perform a clean install, and then copy the personal files back. What you lose with this type of install are your custom settings and your installed applications. This option is available to all supported Windows versions, including Windows 7, Windows Vista (all versions), and Windows XP with Service Pack 3.

▶ **Nothing:** This is the clean install, or what Microsoft calls a custom install. In this install type, Setup will wipe out all of the files and data on the disk and then install a factory-fresh version of Windows. Everything that was there will be lost. This option is also available to all supported Windows versions, including Windows 7, Windows Vista (all versions), and Windows XP with Service Pack 3.

> **WARNING** We can't stress this enough: Trust technology to do the right thing, but have a backup plan, in this case literally. That is, yes, Setup will most likely not lose any data during a migration or in-place upgrade. But just in case, be sure to copy your important data to a removable drive and then remove that drive during Setup.

▶ And yes, these options are part of what used to be Windows Easy Transfer.

After making your selection, Setup will collect its wits and determine if there are any more steps to perform before it begins the actual process of applying Windows 8 to the PC.

You may recall that Setup could have previously informed you that one or more applications will need to be uninstalled before Windows 8 can be installed. If this is the case, you will see a prompt like the one in Figure 2-6. Here, Microsoft Security Essentials will need to be uninstalled before Setup continues. Click the Uninstall button next to any applications that need to be uninstalled.

FIGURE 2-6: Some applications will need to be uninstalled before Setup will complete.

After this process completes, Setup may need to restart the PC, depending on which types of tasks it asked you to complete. If so, Setup will resume immediately and automatically after the reboot, and it will prompt you to continue from where you left off or start over from the beginning. Choose the former and then click Next.

Setup will again check to make sure there are no more steps to take before it can install Windows 8. Finally, it will present the screen in Figure 2-7 that verifies the type of install you've chosen. You can make a last minute change to that install type if you're unsure.

Click Install to continue. Setup will switch into a full-screen mode install Windows 8. During this process, which will involve a few reboots, Setup will configure hardware and install device drivers. It will also reapply your Windows settings, personal files, and other files if you configured it to do so.

FIGURE 2-7: One last check and you're ready to install Windows 8.

When Windows 8 is finally ready, the computer will reboot for the last time and the out-of-box experience, or OOBE, will appear. In the first phase of the OOBE, Personalize, you have just a single choice to make: your Metro color scheme, a set of two colors that includes an accent (or foreground) color and a background color. This scheme is used on all Metro experiences, including the Windows 8 Start screen (but not to the desktop), and all Metro apps. This screen is shown in Figure 2-8. Pick a color scheme then click Next.

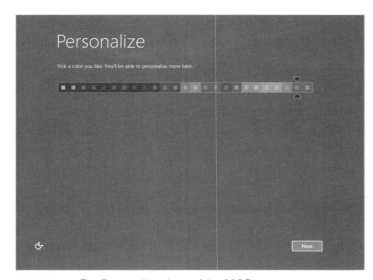

FIGURE 2-8: The Personalize phase of the OOBE.

If you are using a Windows PC or device with wireless networking hardware, you will next be asked to choose a wireless network and then, if required, enter a password. Do so and then click Next.

> **NOTE** What you're not asked is which type of network you're joining. In Windows Vista and 7, this was done via a network location, where you could choose between Home, Work, or Public. This occurs a bit later in Setup and is hidden if you choose a certain option, as you'll see.

▶ Speaking of cute, if you don't choose anything, Setup will assume you want a custom install and just start you down that path regardless. You can click the Back button, however, to choose Express Settings.

In the next part of OOBE, called Settings and shown in Figure 2-9, you can choose between Express Settings and Customize, which is a cute way to potentially cut the number of OOBE steps dramatically.

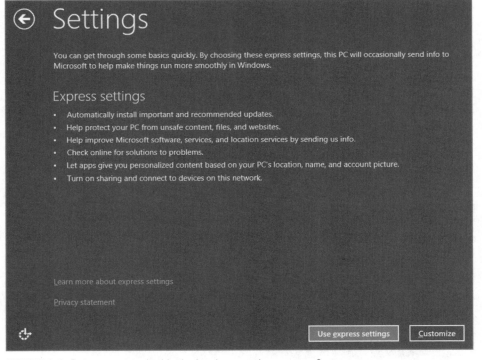

FIGURE 2-9: Do you want to do this the hard way or the easy way?

Long-time readers know that we have always preached the need to perform the more difficult and time-consuming configuration type in situations like this because Microsoft and other companies don't always choose the correct defaults in their express-type options. That said, we actually choose Express settings here. But for purposes of full disclosure, let's examine what options you'll configure if you choose the customized route, and what the defaults are if you choose Express.

These options include:

▶ **Sharing and Connect to Devices:** A simplification of the Select your computer's current location step from Windows 7 Setup, here you can choose Yes, turn on sharing and connect to devices (for home or work networks) or No, don't turn on sharing or connect to devices (for networks in public places). The Express default is Yes, turn on sharing and connect to devices. (See Figure 2-10.)

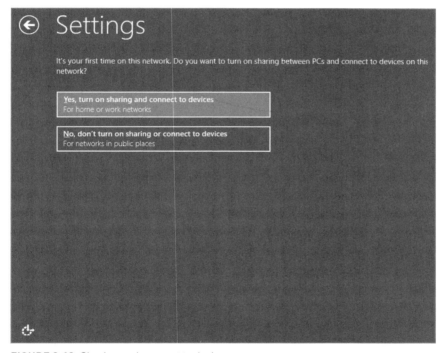

FIGURE 2-10: Sharing and connect to devices.

▶ **Help protect and update your PC:** Here, you configure Automatic Updates, including those for device driver updates, and the SmartScreen filter (separately for both Internet Explorer and the file system). The Express default is to enable all of these features. (See Figure 2-11.)

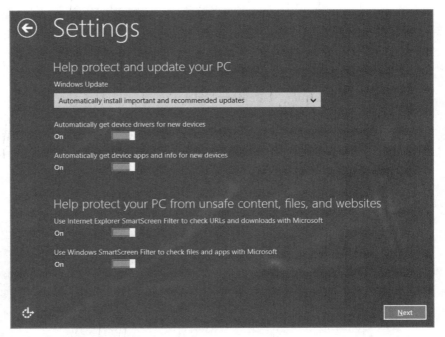

FIGURE 2-11: Protect and update settings

▶ **Send Microsoft info to help make Windows and apps better:** Here you
choose whether to send diagnostic information to Microsoft to improve
Windows, Windows Store, Microsoft's anti-malware online service, Location
Services, the Customer Experience Improvement Program, and Windows Help,
as shown in Figure 2-12. The Express default is to enable all of these features
except for Location Services.

▶ **Check online for solutions to problems:** In this step, you can configure Windows
Error Reporting, Internet Explorer 10 Compatibility lists, user name and account
picture sharing with (Metro-style) apps, and the Windows Location Platform, as
shown in Figure 2-13. The Express default is to enable all of these features.

▶ **Password:** If you upgraded from a previous Windows version, you may be
asked to supply the password for the user account you previously used to sign
in. Do so and click Next.

NOTE Don't see an option to sign in to your Microsoft account? You won't see
this if your PC is offline. Granted, this isn't a huge issue for a web-based install of
Windows 8 since, by definition, you have to be online to get it started. But it happens. You can later convert a local account to a Microsoft account if you'd like.

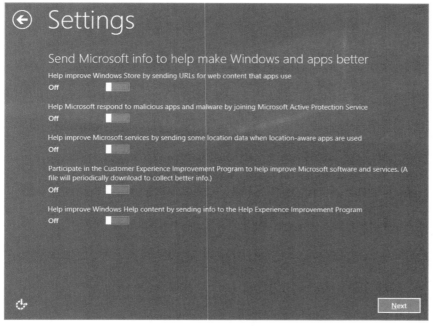

FIGURE 2-12: Windows and app settings

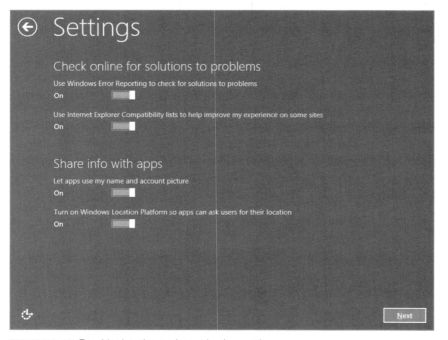

FIGURE 2-13: Troubleshooting and app sharing settings

Finally, you'll be asked to sign in to your PC, using a Microsoft account, as shown in Figure 2-14. You'll see this regardless of whether you performed a clean install, upgrade, or migration using the web-based installer.

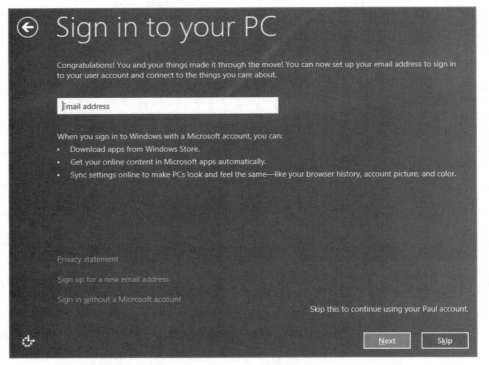

FIGURE 2-14: First Windows 8 sign-in

▶ You can click Skip to use your old local account.

Windows 8 supports a new type of user account that is based around your Microsoft account, or what used to be called a Windows Live ID. And while you could still use the old-fashioned local account that you previously configured, we recommend accepting Setup's offer to switch this account to one based on your Microsoft account. Doing so is highly recommended: You gain impressive PC-to-PC settings synchronization and integration functionality by enabling this account type. As a result, we will assume you do this.

Click Next.

In the next screen, you'll be prompted for your Microsoft account password. Enter the password for your existing Microsoft account or click Sign up for a Microsoft account to turn any e-mail address into a Microsoft account.

After clicking Next, you'll be prompted to enter (or at least verify) your security verification info. To help you recover your password and keep your Microsoft account safe from hacking, this screen, shown in Figure 2-15, lets you configure a mobile phone number and alternate e-mail address. You'll receive a confirmation e-mail at your primary e-mail, and if agreed to, you can make the current PC a trusted PC for authentication purposes.

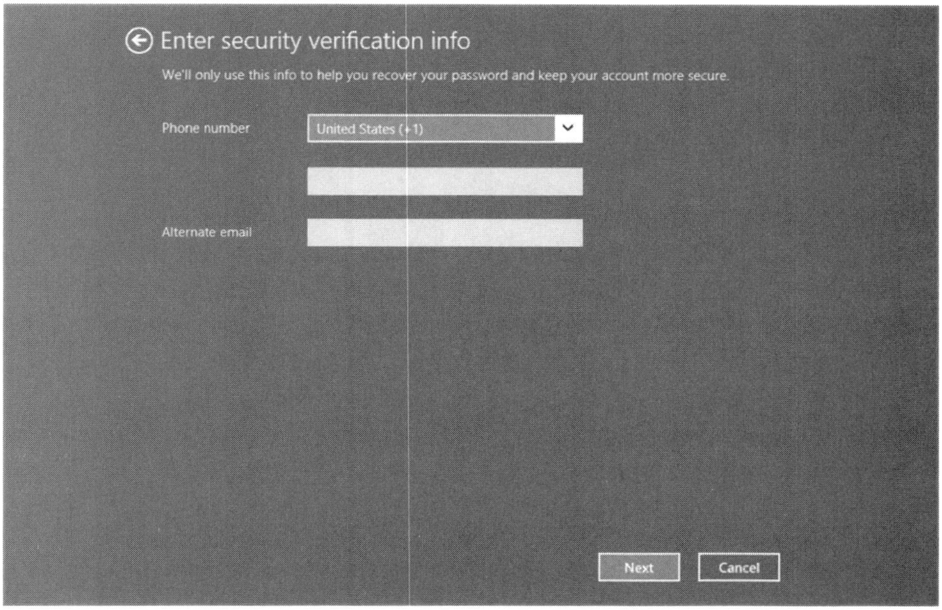

FIGURE 2-15: Security verification info

Click Next to continue.

Now, Setup creates your account on the PC and finalizes settings, and then further prepares the PC and logs on to the Start screen. When it's done, you should be presented with a Start screen similar to the one shown in Figure 2-16.

If you performed an in-place upgrade or a migration, now is the time to see which customizations made it across—check by clicking the Desktop tile—and to ensure that your documents and other files are where they belong. We examine post-Setup tasks later in the chapter, but this is a good place to begin.

FIGURE 2-16: Welcome to Windows 8!

WINDOWS SETUP: A DYING BREED

In some ways, this is all academic, even given the improvements Microsoft has made to Setup, especially with the web-based installer. That's because perform-ing a clean install will typically be a one-time affair with Windows 8, even for those that really need it: This version of Windows includes new Push Button Reset functionality that allows you to wipe out and quickly reinstall Windows 8 without needing to step through Setup again, as is the case with Windows 7 and previous Windows versions. So once you've got Windows 8 on a PC, it's unlikely you'll ever need to do this again. And since most people acquire Windows with a new PC, or upgrade from a previous release to the new version, most will never run through Setup this way at all. We examine Push Button Reset, and other ways to back up and restore, in Chapter 11.

ADVANCED SETUP: USING THE OLD-SCHOOL INSTALLER

If you purchased a boxed, retail version of Windows 8 or would simply prefer to install Windows 8 the old-fashioned way, even with an electronic purchase, you can of course still do so. We don't recommend it. But it's important to realize that this option is still available.

If you purchased Windows 8 electronically from Microsoft, the web installer is the default install type. But you are also given the option to download the installer files as a disc image, or ISO, which you can then use to create a bootable Setup disc (or USB flash drive) so you can install Windows 8 at a later time or perhaps on another PC.

Getting Started

A couple of notes about this process:

- ▶ **Product key:** Microsoft will provide you with a 25-digit product key that you must have handy during the Windows Setup process. We recommend printing this out if possible or having a second PC or device available nearby so that you can read this key from that second device and input it on the PC to which you are installing Windows 8.

- ▶ **Upgrade or Full:** With previous Windows versions, Microsoft offered Upgrade and Full versions of each product edition. This time around there are only Upgrade versions, which can be used for both clean and upgrade installs.

- ▶ **32-bit or 64-bit:** Like Windows 7, Windows 8 is available in both 32-bit (x86) and 64-bit (x64) variants. Generally speaking, you will want the 64-bit version for a clean install or migration. But if you plan to perform an in-place upgrade, you will need to use the same version, 32- or 64-bit, as your current Windows version. You can find this information in the System control panel.

- ▶ **Product version:** Windows 8 is available in multiple product versions, or SKUs (Stock Keeping Units). For a clean install, ensure that you're buying the Windows 8 product version you want. For an upgrade or migration, ensure that you're buying a product version that meets or exceeds the product version of your current version of Windows.

▶ **Drivers:** If you are performing a migration or in-place upgrade, it's highly likely that Windows 8 will not recognize every hardware device and peripheral attached to your PC. So you will need to be ready with the drivers you may potentially need. At the least, make sure you have a Windows 7- or 8-class driver for your PC's network adapter so you can get online. Then, you can navigate to your PC vendor's support website to download any remaining missing drivers. We discuss this process in more detail later in the chapter.

Creating a Bootable Windows Setup Disc or USB Key

If you downloaded an ISO file from Microsoft, you can use this file to create a bootable Windows 8 Setup DVD disc or USB memory key. How you do this will depend on which version of Windows you're currently running. In this section, we'll look at some common scenarios.

CREATING A WINDOWS SETUP DISC WITH WINDOWS 7

▶ You will need a blank recordable DVD with a capacity of 4.7 GB or higher for this purpose.

To create a bootable Windows Setup disc with Windows 7, simply double-click on the Windows 8 ISO file. The Windows Disc Image utility, shown in Figure 2-17, will launch and help you create this disc.

FIGURE 2-17: The Windows Disc Image utility can help you create a bootable Windows Setup disc.

CREATING A WINDOWS SETUP DISC OR BOOTABLE USB KEY WITH WINDOWS 7 OR WINDOWS VISTA

If you would rather use a bootable USB key to install Windows, or are using an older Windows version, you can use Microsoft's excellent USB/DVD Download Tool, available from the Microsoft Store. This utility, shown in Figure 2-18, will guide you through the process of creating a bootable Windows 8 Setup disc or USB memory key.

FIGURE 2-18: The USB/DVD Download Tool

You can find this tool at `tinyurl.com/4qfdm4x` online.

Installing Windows 8 with Bootable Media

You can use the following basic steps to install Windows 8 using the boot media (Setup disc or USB flash drive) you just created. Note that since this process is advanced, we assume you know what you're doing and will only be providing basic instructions.

▶ **Back up:** You're pretty much on your own with this one, but you will want to back up all of the important data and other files on your PC if you are installing Windows 8 onto an existing machine. This is true regardless of whether you plan to perform a clean install, in-place upgrade, or migration. Remember: better safe than sorry.

▶ **Boot the PC with your Windows Setup media:** You will most likely need to interrupt your PC's boot process in order to boot from a USB memory key, especially. But this could be true for a bootable DVD as well. Consult your PC documentation—or pay attention when the BIOS screen appears—to discover how this works on your particular machine.

▶ If you're upgrading or migrating, you will run Windows Setup from within your existing version of Windows and not boot the PC with the media you created.

▶ **Run Windows Setup:** The Windows 8 boot disc (or disk) will prompt you to Install Windows or access its recovery tools. Choose Install Windows, of course, and step through the wizard-based application. The initial steps are very similar to those described in the previous section about the web-based installer, though you will not be provided with an opportunity to generate a compatibility report.

▶ **Use the OOBE:** After a few reboots, Windows Setup will load the out-of-box experience (OOBE), stepping you through the final configuration of your PC and user account. This process is identical to that described in the previous section about the web-based installer.

▶ **Post-install tasks:** After you've signed in to Windows and have accessed the Windows 8 Start screen for the first time, the real fun begins. You'll need to copy back any data, documents, and other files, reapply your personal settings, install Windows-based applications and new Metro-style apps, and, of course, ensure that Windows is up to date, both with software and driver updates.

We discuss this latter activity in the next section.

POST-SETUP: NOW WHAT?

However you choose to install Windows 8, at some point you will be confronted with the blank slate of the new Start screen and may be wondering what happens next. Windows 8 may look quite a bit different than its predecessors, but this is one case where the general strategy remains the same. It's time to engage in some post-Setup activities to ensure that your PC is up and running as efficiently as possible. More to the point, you need to ensure that you're really done configuring Windows 8 so you can begin actually using it.

First, Complete the Driver Installs

The first step is to check your hardware drivers: Ideally, all of the hardware connected to your PC has been correctly detected and assigned an up-to-date driver. But that's often not the case. There are two ways in which to trigger driver updates after Setup is complete: one automatic (and thus preferable) and one manual and considerably more difficult.

Let's try the automatic route first: Visit Windows Update to trigger a check of the Microsoft Update service, which will be polled for three things, by default: software updates, security patches, and, yes, driver updates. There are many ways to run Windows Update, and Windows 8 confusingly offers two interfaces to this functionality, the old control panel interface and a new, Metro-style version. Let's use the latter.

To find the new Windows Update, tap Winkey+I from anywhere in Windows 8 to bring up the Settings pane. Then, choose the Change PC Settings link at the bottom of the screen. This will launch the new, full-screen PC Settings interface, a Metro-style control panel experience. In the left pane, choose Windows Update from the bottom of the list and you'll see a display similar to that shown in Figure 2-19.

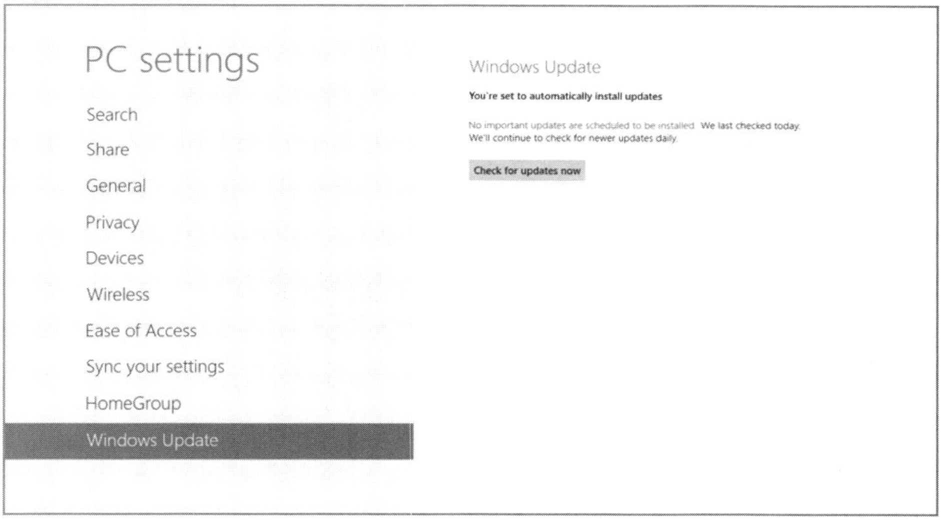

FIGURE 2-19: The new Windows Update

Now, click Check for updates now to manually check for new updates. Download and install any updates and reboot as required. Repeat this process until Windows 8 is completely up to date.

Once that's done, you use a legacy Windows desktop tool called Device Manager, which is the easiest and most detailed way to ensure that all of your hardware is properly configured with drivers. As always, there are a number of ways to access the Device Manager, but the quickest (as is so often the case) is to use Start Search: Type Winkey+Q to bring up Search and then type *device man.* In the right pane, select Settings, and then select Device Manager from the results list on the left.

This time, something interesting happens: The classic Windows desktop—that familiar environment from Windows 7 and previous Windows versions—appears and the old-school Device Manager window opens (see Figure 2-20).

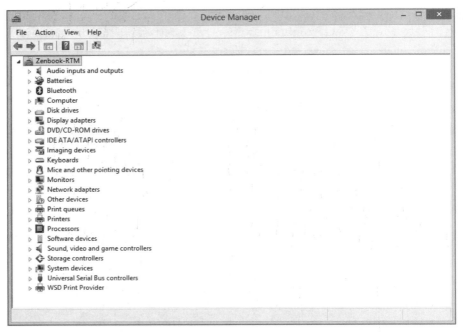

FIGURE 2-20: Device Manager tells you at a glance which hardware devices are connected and properly configured for your PC.

If any of the entries, or nodes, in the Device Manager tree view are open, displaying a device with a small yellow exclamation point, or *bang*, then you're going to need to install some drivers. If not, you're in luck—truly, truly in luck—and you can jump ahead to the next section: Your PC is magically completely up to date.

For the rest of us poor slobs, there are a few options for rectifying this situation.

▶ **Automatically:** Right-click the unsupported device and choose Update Driver Software. Windows will search the Internet (that is, Microsoft Update, the cloud-hosted service behind Windows Update) and the local system, including any setup disks, to find the appropriate driver. In our experience this method almost never works, but it's worth trying.

▶ **Manually, with an executable setup disk or download:** Many drivers come in self-contained executables whereby you run a setup routine just as you would for an application program. If possible, be sure to use a Windows 8- or 7–compatible setup application or, if really pressed, one designed for Windows Vista.

In the latter case, you will want to visit your PC maker's support website and search for the drivers that are specific for your system. Most of them will be fairly obvious, but in some cases you'll run into devices in Device Manager that are listed with dummy or unhelpful names like "unsupported device," "SM Bus," or similar. Our advice is to start with chipset drivers, because these low-level, multi-device drivers often clear up any missing, or banged, devices.

Note, too, that Windows 8 will sometimes assign a default graphics driver and not use an up-to-date, optimized driver. You will know this is the case if Windows isn't using the full resolution of your display. Right-click the Windows desktop and choose Screen resolution to check. If you can't select the appropriate resolution, you'll need to update the graphics driver too, even if it's not banged out in Device Manager.

Next, Install Core Applications

With Windows 8 and older Windows versions, it was generally important to install a security solution, such as Microsoft Security Essentials, before continuing on to other applications. But Windows 8 includes the functionality from Security Essentials as part of the Windows Defender solution, so this is no longer necessary. If you prefer a third-party security solution for some reason, however, you should install that first.

Next, install your core applications one at a time and reboot if necessary after each install as requested. This process can often take a long time and is mind-numbingly boring, but you should have to do it only once.

Recover Your Data

After your key applications are installed, it's time to restore any data that you might have backed up from your previous Windows install. How you do this will vary depending on how you backed up that data, but we use the Microsoft SkyDrive application to sync key documents, photos, and other folders between the web and our Windows PCs. So installing SkyDrive (available from skydrive.com) copies the documents, photos, and other critical files over automatically.

ADVANCED WINDOWS 8 SETUP CONFIGURATIONS

While the preceding parts of this chapter document the most common Setup scenarios, sometimes you need a bit more advanced or unusual configuration. Here, we'll examine some of the more common ways in which you can install Windows 8 in such configurations.

Since the actual process of installing Windows 8 in each case resembles the procedure detailed previously, here we'll just focus on the specific differences of which you need to be aware.

Dual Boot

While most users will want just a single version of Windows installed on their PC, some power users or others will require two (or more) installs of Windows, which sit side by side on the PC's hard disk in separate partitions. When you boot the PC in such a configuration, you're presented with a menu listing the various OS choices, and you pick one and boot into the appropriate OS version.

Such a configuration is often called a *dual-boot* configuration, though of course it's possible to install three or more OSes, assuming you have the disk space. (Maybe *multi-boot* is a better term.) But however many versions of Windows you wish to install, the basic advice is simple: Install them in order of age, from oldest to newest. If you want to dual-boot between Windows 7 and Windows 8, for example, install Windows 7 first and then Windows 8.

Why is this, you ask? Each Windows version comes with an updated version of the Windows boot loader, which includes both the menu that users will see and the underlying code that selects which OS to boot. The Windows 7 boot loader is not familiar with Windows 8. But the version for Windows 8 is very much familiar with Windows 7, and with older Windows versions. So install that last.

Assuming you have a Windows 7 install up and running already, you must use a media-based Setup to install Windows 8 after booting the PC from that disc or USB flash drive. That is, you cannot use the web-based installer.

GETTING THE PC READY FOR THE SECOND OS

Before you do that, however, there is one absolutely critical task you must perform: You must make room for the new Windows 8 install. This can occur on its own disk, so if you have one sitting in the PC waiting to go, you're all set. But if you have just one hard disk, as in a typical laptop, you'll need to segregate it into separate partitions, segments of the disk that work and act like individual hard disks. And to do this, you must use a fairly complex and well-hidden tool called Disk Management.

To find this tool from Windows 7, use Start Menu Search: Open the Start Menu, type **disk part**, and hit Enter. The Disk Management utility, shown in Figure 2-21, will open.

On a single disk PC, you must select the partition on which Windows 7 is installed—it's almost always the C: drive—right-click it, and choose Shrink Volume. In the Shrink window, shown in Figure 2-22, enter the amount of space to shrink the partition in MB. This space will be used for the Windows 8 partition, which you'll create next.

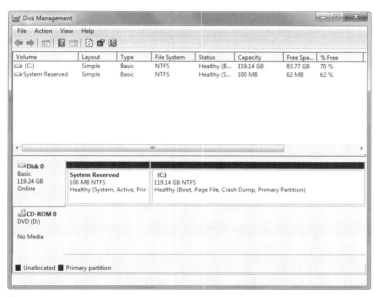

FIGURE 2-21: Disk Management

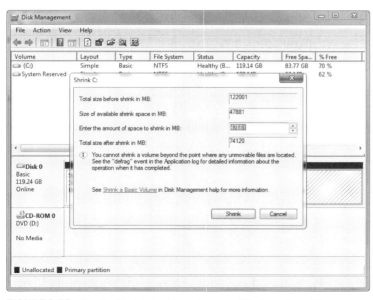

FIGURE 2-22: Use the Shrink tool to resize your Windows 7 partition and make room for Windows 8.

Then, click the Shrink button.

Back in Disk Management, you'll see the new empty disk space you just created. Right-click this and choose New Simple Volume. Step through the wizard, give it all the available space, assign it a drive letter, and be sure to assign it an obvious name, like *Windows 8*.

INSTALLING WINDOWS 8 ALONGSIDE WINDOWS 7

Now you're ready to install Windows 8 in a dual-boot configuration. Reboot the computer, and boot it using the Setup media you previously acquired or created.

In Windows Setup, there are two critical points where you must choose correctly:

▶ **Install type:** You will be prompted to choose between Upgrade and Custom install types. You must choose Custom here, since you are not upgrading Windows 7 and are instead clean installing Windows 8 alongside Windows 7.

▶ **Where do you want to install Windows?** In the next Setup step, you will be asked to pick a partition or hard drive on which to install Windows 8. *You cannot install Windows 8 to the same partition or hard drive to which Windows 7 is installed*. Instead, you must choose a different partition or hard drive. So choose the partition you created earlier.

Windows 8 will install normally and eventually boot into the new OS.

CHOOSING BETWEEN WINDOWS 7 AND WINDOWS 8 AT BOOT

By default, your PC will boot into the most recently-installed OS, which in this case is Windows 8. But it will briefly stop at a new boot menu, which gives you the opportunity to choose the OS at boot time. This menu will resemble Figure 2-23 and will contain entries for both Windows 8 and Windows 7.

This menu only displays for several seconds, so you need to think quick if you want to change from the default boot choice. (Or simply tap an arrow key on the keyboard to stop the countdown.)

You can configure this boot menu by clicking Change defaults or choose other options. When you do so, you'll be presented with the screen shown in Figure 2-24.

The following options are available:

▶ **Change the timer:** By default, the boot menu only appears for 30 seconds (which, frankly, is reasonable). Here, you can change this to other time limits, including 5 minutes or 5 seconds.

- ▶ **Choose a default operating system:** By default, your PC will boot into the most recently installed OS if the menu timer expires. With this option, you can choose a different Windows version as the default.

- ▶ **Choose other options:** This option triggers the Windows 8 recovery tools menu, which we discuss in Chapter 11.

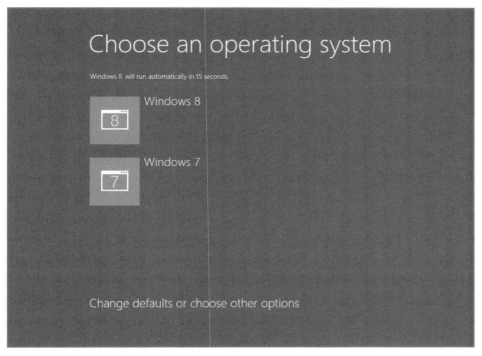

FIGURE 2-23: The Windows 8 boot menu

You can also modify this boot menu a bit from within Windows 8 (but not from within Windows 7). Of course, you may be wondering: Why bother? Well, this other interface provides a bit more fine-grained control over the boot options, especially for the boot menu timer.

To access these capabilities, you have to find a very well-hidden Startup and Recovery interface that's available via the classic System control panel from previous Windows versions. There are numerous ways to find it, but the easiest, as always, is Start Search: Look for **system**, select Settings, and then choose System from the results list. In the System window, click Advanced system settings on the left, then select the Advanced tab of System Properties. And then click the Settings button in the Startup and Recovery section. (Whew!)

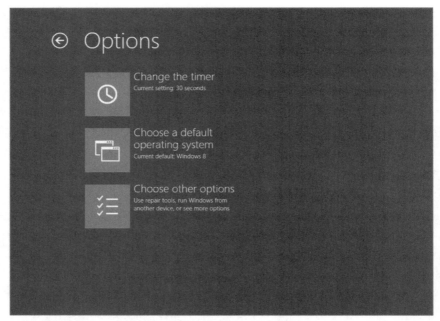

FIGURE 2-24: The Options screen for the Windows 8 boot menu

You'll be presented with the window shown in Figure 2-25.

FIGURE 2-25: You can configure Windows 8 boot options from this well-hidden interface.

From this window, you can configure the following boot menu options:

▶ **The default operating system:** It will be Windows 8 initially, but if you prefer it to default to Windows 7, this is the place.

▶ **The time to display the list of operating systems:** By default, the Windows 8 boot menu will display for 3 seconds. Here, you can change the value to any number of seconds you like.

Installing Windows 8 on a Mac

For a few years there, Mac "switchers" made inroads in the PC world, starting with the poorly received Windows Vista and Apple's antagonistic "I'm a Mac, I'm a PC" advertisements. But then something interesting happened. Microsoft got its mojo back with Windows 7, releasing an OS that was both competent and efficient. And then it released Windows 8 and triggered renewed excitement in Windows in a way we hadn't seen in, well, a couple of decades.

Of course, with thousands of Mac users out there wondering what went wrong, it's no surprise that many are suddenly regretting their expensive side-trip to the Apple side of the computing fence. But have no fear, unhappy Mac users. Windows 8 will work on your computer too. After all, Macs are nothing more than expensive and beautiful PCs.

As with previous versions of Windows, you can install the Windows 8 Consumer Preview on your Mac in three basic ways: virtualized, using a solution like Parallels Desktop or VMWare Fusion, in a dual-boot configuration using Apple's Boot Camp utility, or as the sole OS, replacing Mac OS X once and for all.

Nothing would make us happier than recommending the latter approach because, after all, every time someone uses Mac OS X a unicorn dies. But we can't recommend it for a simple and pragmatic reason: There are some things you can only do on a Mac using Mac OS X, including updating the device's firmware. So you really should keep at least a small OS X partition available, if only for that reason.

The Mac's various virtualization solutions are straightforward and have their own unique advantages, but since the goal here is to replace Mac OS X to the extent possible, we'll focus on the Boot Camp approach. Besides, it's free and comes with every Mac. Wasn't Apple nice to do that?

Before getting started, make sure that OS X is up to date with all the latest software updates and that you have a bootable Windows 8 Setup DVD; a USB flash drive-based Setup type doesn't work with Boot Camp. And depending on which kind of Mac

▶ You can also use this interface to enable the recovery options at boot time if you'd like. Generally speaking, this isn't advisable, but if you're having issues with the computer, it's not a bad idea to have this capability at the ready.

you have, you may need a 32-bit version of Windows. But modern Macs generally can work with the preferred 64-bit versions of Windows 8.

INSTALLING WINDOWS 8 WITH BOOT CAMP

You will find the Boot Camp Assistant utility in Applications, Utilities on any modern Mac. (Or, just use the handy keyboard shortcut Command + Space to bring up OS X's version of Start Menu Search and type **boot c** and then press Enter.)

Boot Camp Assistant is a very simple, wizard-based application that walks you through the process of getting the drivers you need and partitioning your Mac to accommodate both OSes and then installs Windows. It's a pretty straightforward process, but be sure to download Apple's Windows Setup drivers when prompted since you'll need them later. Burn them to disc (or copy them to a USB flash drive).

Boot Camp Assistant will also prompt you to choose how much disk space to allot to both Mac OS X and Windows, as shown in Figure 2-26. We recommend giving as much space to Windows as possible since, of course, you'll be using this superior platform almost exclusively going forward. But choose accordingly, understanding that you will not be able to easily change this configuration later.

Once that's done, click Install and Boot Camp will trigger the Windows 8 Setup routine, or prompt you to insert the Setup disc so it can do so.

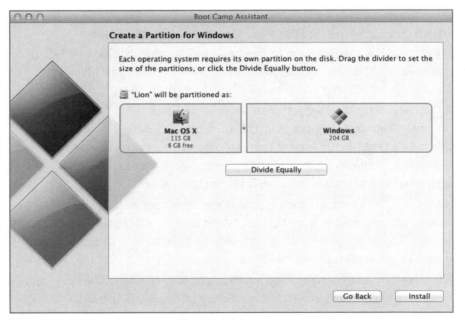

FIGURE 2-26: Apple actually lets you install another OS on a Mac. They're so cute.

Setup will run normally, as described previously. There are two crucial choices to make during this process, however. First, choose the Custom install type at the appropriate screen. And then choose the right partition, of course, and not the one on which OS X is installed. This screen will be a bit messy, given the way Boot Camp laid out the disk. But the correct partition is named Bootcamp and will be roughly the size you previously configured. You will have to format it using the Advanced options before Setup can proceed.

After a few reboots, you'll step through the out-of-box experience as is usual, and then sign in to Windows 8 for the first time.

POST-INSTALL TASKS

Once Windows 8 is installed, you will need to install Apple's Boot Camp drivers in order to complete the installation. So you should insert the driver disc you created as part of the Boot Camp Assistant and let it do its thing, rebooting as required. From there, follow the general post-install advice provided earlier in this chapter.

OF MAC KEYBOARDS AND WINDOWS

One of the weirdest things about using a Mac is that Apple's computers use non-standard keyboards. It will take a little getting used to, but this handy guide (Table 2-1) to common key conversions should get you started.

TABLE 2-1: Mac Keyboard Conversion for Windows 8

WINDOWS KEY	MAC KEYBOARD EQUIVALENT
Ctrl	Control
Alt	Alt/Option
Winkey	Command
Prtscn	fn + Shift + F11
Ctrl + Alt + Del	Control + Option + Delete
Backspace	Delete
Delete	fn + Delete
Insert	fn + Enter

CHOOSING BETWEEN WINDOWS AND OS X

Apple is nice enough to configure Boot Camp such that the machine will boot automatically into Windows 8 every time you restart the PC. This is almost always what you'll want, but you may occasionally need to boot into OS X for some reason. You can do so on the fly, when the Mac boots, or configure the Mac to boot into OS X just once, the next time you restart. (Okay, you could also make OS X the default boot OS. But we're not documenting that particular option since you will never, ever, ever want to do that. Got it?)

BOOTING INTO OS X ONCE

To boot into OS X just once, you need to access the Boot Camp control panel that was installed when you installed Apple's various Boot Camp drivers. This control panel, shown in Figure 2-27, will be accessible from an icon in the system tray. (It's the tiny gray diamond.)

FIGURE 2-27: The Boot Camp control panel

To restart in OS X just once, right-click the Boot Camp system tray icon and choose Restart in Mac OS X. You'll be prompted about whether you're sure you want to do this, as even Apple can't believe it. Click OK to reboot into OS X.

CHOOSING BETWEEN OS X AND WINDOWS 8 AT BOOT TIME

You can also choose between Mac OS X and Windows 8 when the Mac boots up. To do so, wait for the Mac's *bong* sound at restart and then hold down the Alt/Option key.

You'll see a graphical boot menu appear with choices for Mac OS X, Windows, Recovery HD, and, if available, a bootable optical disc. Select the partition you want and enjoy.

Virtual Machine Installs

Like previous versions of Windows, it's possible to install Windows 8 in virtual machine environments such as Microsoft Hyper-V, Oracle VirtualBox, VMware Workstation, and so on. Generally speaking, there's no real magic to making Windows 8 work with such products, though you lose out on some graphical niceties and, usually, the touch-based goodness that makes Windows 8 special.

From an installation perspective, you will want to download a Windows 8 disc image in ISO format and use that to install Windows 8. You cannot use the web-based installer. Since these environments are well understood and utilize generic virtualized hardware components, you will usually not need to hunt around for drivers after Setup concludes.

Windows to Go: Windows 8 on a USB Flash Drive

With Windows 8, Microsoft has finally answered a long-time request from power users, businesses, and educational institutions and has provided a unique new way to install the OS to a USB flash drive, providing users with a complete operating environment they can carry in their pocket. To use this special version of Windows 8, called Windows to Go, all you need to do is insert it in any PC, reboot, and boot from the USB drive. After about 20 seconds, you'll be presented with your familiar, customized Windows 8 environment, complete with all your apps and data. And if you lose the USB flash drive, no problem: The entire disk can be encrypted with BitLocker and protected against data theft.

▶ Windows 8 is the first client version of Windows to include its own hypervisor-based virtualization solution. This is called Hyper-V, and because this solution is generally aimed at businesses, we discuss it in Chapter 14.

SUMMARY

With its latest operating system, Microsoft has significantly improved the process by which you take a new or used PC and install, upgrade, or migrate to Windows 8. This procedure, called Windows Setup, now comes in a streamlined new web-based installer that bundles useful but previously separate tools for a more complete and error-free experience. But you can still install Windows 8 using the old-fashioned, media-based installer from a bootable DVD disc or USB flash drive.

Windows 8 can also be installed in various advanced configurations, including dual- and multi-boot, where multiple versions of Windows sit side by side on a single PC. It can be installed on a Mac in a variety of ways. It can be installed in virtual machines, and it can be installed to a bootable, self-contained USB flash drive in a new configuration called Windows to Go.

However you choose to install Windows 8, you can be sure that at the end of this process, you'll have a fully functioning install, complete with all of the drivers you need to power your PC. And this chapter showed you how to make that happen.

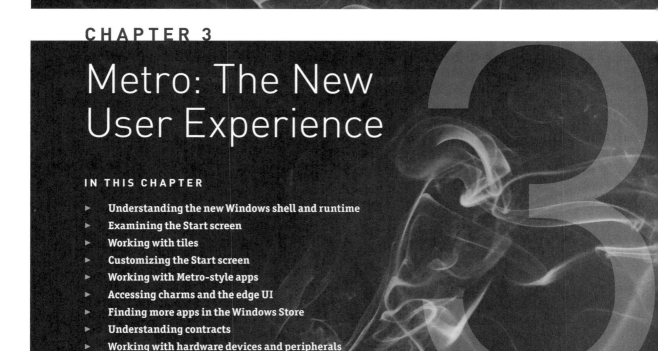

CHAPTER 3

Metro: The New User Experience

IN THIS CHAPTER

▶ Understanding the new Windows shell and runtime
▶ Examining the Start screen
▶ Working with tiles
▶ Customizing the Start screen
▶ Working with Metro-style apps
▶ Accessing charms and the edge UI
▶ Finding more apps in the Windows Store
▶ Understanding contracts
▶ Working with hardware devices and peripherals

You don't have to spend too much time with Windows 8 before it hits you: This Windows version is like nothing that's come before. The biggest and most visual change, of course, is the new Metro environment, which includes the Start screen, various full-screen Metro-style apps, and several Metro user experiences that all sit on a brand-new runtime engine called WinRT. Not only does Windows 8 look different from its predecessors, it really is a brand-new operating system, built from scratch to meet the needs of today's quickly evolving technology landscape. Yes, all your old desktop applications and hardware devices still work. But the underpinnings of Windows—its soul, really—has completely changed.

This chapter dives deep into the new Metro environment and explains how it works and why it works the way it does. You'll look at how to use this new UI on PCs of all kinds—including desktop, laptop, tablet, and hybrid devices—and how you can get the most out of it regardless of the hardware you're using. You'll also look at the hidden new features available to the Start screen and the new Metro-style apps that run on top of this environment. In Windows 8, it may seem like everything has changed, and in many ways it has. There are only two ways to face change as dramatic as this: fear or excitement. We choose the latter. And if you get through this chapter with us, you will, too.

SO, IT'S CALLED METRO, RIGHT?

One of the tough decisions we had with this book concerned naming conventions. See, we think names are important. They provide a simple and obvious way to refer to the things we're describing throughout the book. It's nice to be able to point out a new on-screen gadget and tell you, hey, look, that's the new *thingamawhatsis* or whatever.

Unfortunately, there's a new trend at Microsoft where the (we assume) well-intentioned designers behind all the fun new interfaces in Windows 8 not only don't want to name things, but seem actively engaged in rewriting history by retroactively simplifying the names of objects that appeared in previous Windows versions. So the Start Menu is now simply called *Start*. That way, when we move forward to Windows 8, Microsoft can claim that Start—or, more pretentiously, the *Start experience*—works like before but is now a full-screen experience and not a menu. Even though in reality, they're completely different.

So it is with the Metro environment. Microsoft does not refer to the *Metro* environment as anything in particular; they just claim that it's *Windows*, generically, as if wanting or needing to call out these completely new and different user experiences was a ludicrous notion. Indeed, right after it completed Windows 8, Microsoft decreed that it would not use the term Metro to describe these new experiences, ostensibly for legal reasons.

We're not buying into this. In the interests of clarity, we're naming things. And in those places where Microsoft refuses to name names, we're giving them names. And sometimes we're deviating from the way Microsoft does things. But to be clear, we're doing this for you, to make things obvious and simpler, and to prevent clever or lengthy turns of word that would annoy all of us.

For example, Microsoft has gotten the app bug. Everything to them is an app these days. And that includes new Metro-style apps—those apps that run in the new environment described in this chapter—as well as old-school, Windows desktop-based applications. Folks, desktop applications are not apps. They're applications. And we differentiate them from Metro-style apps—because they are very different—by giving them a different name. So when we use the term *app*, we're referring only to Metro-style apps. When we use the term *application*, we're referring only to desktop-based applications.

Ditto for *Metro*. Microsoft refuses to name this environment, or even use the term Metro, but we're not so shy. There are two main user experiences in Windows 8, and while one is the desktop environment we all know and love from previous Windows versions, the other is. . .Metro. At least that's what we're calling it.

Sometimes, of course, Microsoft does get it right. In Windows 7, for example, there was a feature called Start Menu Search, which we liked quite a bit. In Windows 8, this has been replaced by something we'd be inclined to call *Start Screen Search*, which will make a lot more sense once you see it in action. But Microsoft's name for this feature, which it has retroactively applied to the Windows 7 feature as well, is *Start Search*. And you know what? That works just fine, since it's clear and obvious, and simpler. Ultimately, we're just trying to be pragmatic here.

TIMES THEY ARE A-CHANGIN': THE NEW WINDOWS SHELL

In previous versions of Windows, you would boot the PC (or wake it from Sleep mode), provide your login credentials when prompted (after bypassing the lock screen if using a corporate-connected domain account), and then be presented with the Windows desktop. The desktop was only part of a wider series of applications and services known as the Windows shell. And in all of the versions of Windows released over the past 15 years or more, this shell was called Windows Explorer, or simply Explorer.

In Windows 8, this entire sequence of events is generally unchanged. But the specifics are all new, creating what is in effect an entirely new experience.

Now, your PC's boot process is measured in just a handful of seconds—under 20, certainly, and well under 10 for most SSD-based systems—and waking from sleep is near simultaneous. The lock screen is always present by default, whether you're using your own PC or one from work. When you sign in—Microsoft no longer uses the terms *log in* or *log out*—you're presented with the new Metro-style Start screen, not the desktop. And the Metro environment in which the Start screen and new Metro-style apps run is the new shell. In Figure 3-1, you can see a selection of full-screen Metro experiences, including the new Start screen, PC Settings, and a representative Metro-style app.

FIGURE 3-1: It's not your father's Windows.

▶ In Windows 3.X, Program Manager was the shell. And in Windows 95, you could still run Program Manager as an application if you wanted to. So Microsoft making the new and old available simultaneously is not unprecedented.

Oddly enough, however, the familiar desktop and Explorer interfaces are still present in Windows 8, though in keeping with the "everything is new again" approach in this release, even Windows Explorer has been renamed, to File Explorer. This lets you switch back and forth between the new shell, along with its apps and experiences, and the old shell, with its own applications. You can even run both environments, Metro and the desktop, side by side in very limited ways, as you'll see later in this chapter.

Regardless of which version of Windows you're talking about, the shell is both the look and feel of this OS—the user interface or experience—and the part of Windows that controls how things look and work. It is responsible for the controls—buttons, windows, tabs, and so on—that make up the environment as well as their behaviors.

Replacing the Windows shell is a big step, and this fact alone should signal that Windows 8 is a major release of the operating system since, after all, the last time Microsoft swapped out the shell was in 1995. But we're making the case that Windows 8 represents the biggest change to Windows in the history of the product line. And that's because Microsoft is not only swapping out the shell, but it's also swapping out the underpinnings of Windows, or the runtime engine, as well as the APIs that developers use to write Windows apps. And this is the first time in history that the company has ever done all of that in a single release.

The new runtime engine is called, logically enough, Windows Runtime, or WinRT. This engine provides the system's platform for applications (or, in this case, "apps"), and it mostly replaces Win32, which was (and still is) the basis for desktop-based applications. (Under the hood, WinRT does access some Win32 functionality that's still missing in WinRT.) Win32 debuted in Windows NT in 1993. (And even that was just a 32-bit conversion of the then-current Windows runtime, which was retroactively renamed to Win16.)

But you don't need a history lesson to know that Windows 8 is different. It hits you right in the face the first time you use it, and as you can see in its new lock screen, the Start screen and its apps, and the pervasive Metro-style user experiences, there's a lot that's new here. And that's what this chapter is all about.

LOCK SCREEN: A NEW WAY TO SIGN IN

When you boot the computer or wake it up from Sleep, you'll be presented with the new lock screen, a full-screen Metro-style experience that is basically new to Windows 8 and visually sits on top of the sign-in screen where you select a user account and optionally provide a password.

As you can see in Figure 3-2, the lock screen looks and works much as it does on a smartphone OS like Windows Phone. It provides a nice photographic background image, the time and date, and a number of status notifications, most of which are icons.

FIGURE 3-2: The Windows 8 lock screen

Virtually every aspect of this lock screen can be customized, and it provides what Microsoft calls a "glance and go" interface where you can glance at the screen even when the system is locked—indicated by the presence of the lock screen—and see information that is useful, such as the date and time and your next upcoming appointment.

> **CROSSREF**   We describe customizing the lock screen in Chapter 5.

To bypass the lock screen, tap any key (such as Enter), or click the mouse. Or, on a touch-based system, swipe up from the bottom of the screen as you do with Windows Phone. When you do, you'll be presented with the sign-in screen similar to the one shown in Figure 3-3.

FIGURE 3-3: The Windows 8 sign-in screen

This screen will vary somewhat based on how many user accounts you've config-ured on the PC, but the first time you use Windows 8, you'll just see the one account you configured during Setup.

To sign in to Windows, enter your password and tap Enter. If you're using a touch-based system, you can do so using the on-screen keyboard, as shown in Figure 3-4.

You can also choose accessibility options from the Ease of Access button in the lower-left of the screen, or Sleep, Shut down, or Restart the PC using the button in the lower right of the screen. If you don't do anything, the lock screen will reappear after a short period of time.

FIGURE 3-4: The on-screen keyboard

WARNING If you have not configured your user account with a password, and have only the one account configured on the PC, you will bypass the sign-in screen and proceed directly to the Start screen, as described in the next section. Don't do this. We strongly recommend configuring all user accounts with passwords for what we assume are obvious security reasons.

You can lock the PC at any time by typing Winkey + L. Note that this keyboard shortcut will lock the screen without any confirmation request. It's immediate.

START SCREEN: A NEW USER EXPERIENCE FOR MODERN APPS

In Windows 7 and previous Windows versions, applications were said to run "on" or "within" the Windows desktop since that is how they visually appeared, and because the desktop provided different user interfaces for managing and launching applications and performing other system-level tasks.

In Windows 8, these activities are performed from the new Start screen. As you can see in Figure 3-5, this screen is decidedly different from the old Windows desktop.

FIGURE 3-5: The Start screen

Understanding the Design of Metro

The Start screen is what's called a Metro-style user experience. That is, it employs the techniques of a new "design language" at Microsoft that is guiding the look and feel of many of the software giant's core platforms, including Windows, Windows Server, Windows Phone, Xbox, and Office. And while we don't want to get too bogged down in designer talk, it's worth noting a few general tenets of these interfaces, since they're so pervasive in Windows 8.

> ► **Typography and white space:** Metro-based user experiences feature beautiful typography, often surrounded by lots of white space. This is a very different approach than with typical technology interfaces, which tend to overwhelm users with obscure rows or grids of icons, buttons, and other on-screen elements.
>
> Consider the Start screen as a typical example. The Start logo and user tile (in the upper-right corner) are offset deliberately from the live tiles below by a wide swath of white space. Those tiles don't butt up to the left edge of the screen, but rather sit to the right. But the tiles also appear to disappear off the right edge of the screen, suggesting that you can scroll in that direction to see more. There's no awful looking chevron graphic or whatever to spell it out for you. Instead, the design is confident and beautiful, and something that would be fun to touch.

▶ **Animation and motion:** Interfaces come to life with animation and other motion, and in Metro these motions aren't just fun to look at, they're useful. Animation can also give the appearance of performance, though to be fair, Windows 8 performs so well it's almost redundant.

It's not possible to show you how animations and motion improve the Windows 8 user experience, but suffice to say these elements are everywhere, from the live tiles that animate between various status updates, to the animation that occurs each time you launch a Metro-style app, and to the floating notification "toasts" that slide on-screen rather than jar you by appearing suddenly and without warning.

▶ **Minimal user interface chrome:** Until recently, most computer software was designed by the engineers who wrote the code. And let's face it, these guys don't get good design. They were responsible for such UI extremes as the dialog with multiple rows of tabs and the Office applications so loaded up with toolbars you couldn't even see the document you were supposed to be editing.

With Metro, it's the content that's emphasized, not the surrounding application user interface, or *chrome*. In fact, with most Metro-style designs, there is little to no chrome at all. Instead, Metro provides full-screen experiences that use every available pixel to display the app or experience. Accessory interfaces that used to be on-screen all the time, like an app bar—Metro's all-in-one replacement for the toolbar and menu—are now hidden by default and displayed only when needed.

For example, in Figure 3-6, you can see the Start screen's app bar, which is not normally shown since its few options are rarely needed.

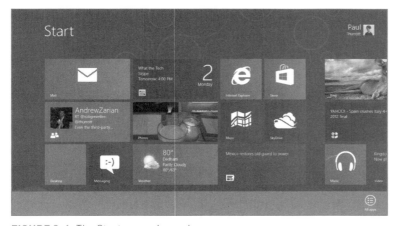

FIGURE 3-6: The Start screen's app bar

▶ **Honesty of design:** While some systems treat their users like idiots, Metro design specifies that user interfaces should be "authentically digital" and true to the system on which they run. That is, your $1,000 Ultrabook isn't a paper-based calendar. Why should a calendar app be designed to resemble one? After all, most users today have never even used such a calendar, so that design is at best nostalgic and at worst inefficient. Instead, Metro designs are designed explicitly for the device form factor: a high-resolution, high-performance screen that could employ multi-touch interactions. On such a device, a calendar could look very different from that old-fashioned paper calendar that some companies seem to like so much.

You can see this type of design throughout Metro, but the best example, perhaps, is in the various opaque icons that appear throughout, in such places as the live tiles on the Start screen and the buttons on various app bars. Instead of being photorealistic representations of a store (Windows Store), a pair of headphones (the Xbox Music app), or a video game controller (Xbox LIVE Games app), these icons are authentic to the digital nature of the device itself. In fact, they're designed to be as obvious as possible, and are modeled on the signage one sees in public transportation hubs throughout the world.

▶ And yes, this is where Metro gets its name. It's based on the simple graphics found in the transportation hubs that people use every day.

Using the Start Screen

The Start screen provides just a few basic functions: It's a place to organize live tiles that represent the apps you care about the most, so you can launch those apps and, while viewing the Start screen, see live updates that are rendered on their surfaces.

This functionality alone makes the Start screen far more useful than the Windows desktop. With that interface, applications had very limited ways in which to provide you with any kind of status information. An e-mail application, for example, might provide a small number badge on its icon, indicating how many unread e-mails it contained. But this badge could be seen only when you pinned the application to the taskbar, as in Figure 3-7.

Application developers tried to overcome this lack of capability through several means. Many wrote customized notification schemes that could alert users when something important happened, but the sheer number of variety of these notifications was often more annoying and distracting than useful. And Microsoft even briefly pushed a new type of utility, called the Windows Gadget, which would sit on the desktop and update the user from time to time. Gadgets failed for all kinds of reasons: Full-screen applications would cover them up, they were disconnected from full-fledged Windows applications, and they were written with completely different technologies.

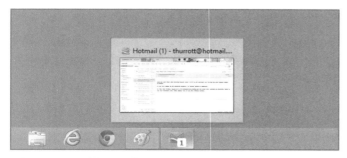

FIGURE 3-7: In Windows 7, an e-mail application could provide you with an unread e-mail count through its taskbar button's icon.

In Windows 8, each app (and many desktop-based interfaces) can expose a single live tile on the Start screen. This live tile is more expressive and useful than any icon and can provide all kinds of information in real time. By arranging the tiles for apps you use most often, you can create a live dashboard of sorts where your e-mail, calendar, social networking, weather, and other apps are all providing you with ongoing live updates over time. And you can see these updates without ever entering the app in question. Glance and go, as Microsoft says.

To use the previous e-mail example again, Windows 8 includes an app called Mail. And unlike its desktop-based predecessor, it not only tells you how many unread e-mails you have, but it also cycles through previews of each of those e-mails. In Figure 3-8, you can see two of the different types of displays it animates between.

Not all live tiles are expressive. Some don't have to be, like the tile for a game or web browser. You can configure tiles to be one of two sizes—Bigger and Smaller, with the former being rectangles and the latter being smaller squares.

Consider Figure 3-9, where you can see a grid of live tiles, some big and some small. Here, the Internet Explorer, Windows Store, Bing Maps, and SkyDrive Explorer tiles are all configured to be smaller and don't provide any rich, animated information. But the Calendar, Photos, Weather, and Bing Finance live tiles are larger and provide dynamic information about their contents.

▶ In the smaller size, a normally expressive live tile is effectively rendered mute.

FIGURE 3-8: The Mail app cycles through previews of your most recent e-mails; here are two examples from the same tile.

FIGURE 3-9: A mix of small and large live tile sizes

The Start screen can be configured in various ways so you can tailor the system as you prefer. For example, you can organize the tiles visually into various groups, and can add and remove tiles for the apps (and Windows desktop applications and websites) you use most frequently.

CROSSREF We explain how to customize the Start screen in Chapter 5.

Launching Apps

To launch an app, you simply tap its live tile from the Windows 8 Start screen. (Mouse users can of course click the tile.) When you do so, you'll see a quick-loading animation as the app runs and fills the screen. This is typical for Metro-style apps, which typically run full screen all the time.

▶ Typically, but not always. As you'll see later in the chapter, it's possible to "snap" two Metro-style apps, or one Metro-style app and the desktop side by side, using a new form of multitasking that's really just screen sharing.

To return to the desktop, you can tap the Windows key on your keyboard or tap the Windows key button on your Windows device. (There's also a software-based approach related to the so-called edge UIs, which we'll discuss in just a moment.)

Note that the Windows key (or Windows key button) works like a toggle in Windows 8, another big change from previous versions. In Windows 7, for example, if you tapped the Windows key repeatedly, the Start menu would simply open and close repeatedly. But in Windows 8, tapping this key repeatedly will toggle between the current Metro-style app and the Start screen.

Windows 8 ships with a large number of apps and you can find even more in Windows Store, Microsoft's new app store.

CROSSREF We discuss the various built-in Windows 8 Metro-style apps throughout this book, of course, but you can find out more about Windows Store in Chapter 6.

Accessing the Windows Desktop

In Windows 8, the desktop environment is treated like an app, and you should find a Desktop tile somewhere on the Start screen. (If you don't, you can use Start Search, described in the next section, to find it.) When you tap the Desktop tile, the familiar desktop interface appears, as shown in Figure 3-10.

FIGURE 3-10: The Windows desktop lives.

The Windows desktop looks and works much like the desktop in Windows 7, but with a few differences. The biggest is that the Start button and Start menu are missing: Windows 8 has replaced the old Start menu with the new, full-screen Start screen, so the Start button is gone. You will typically use the Windows key, Windows key button, or the other methods described later in this chapter, to access the Start screen.

▶ With just a few exceptions, all of the built-in Windows 7 applications and utilities—Paint, WordPad, Windows Media Player, and the like— are included in Windows 8 as well.

Other than that, things work as before. You can run traditional Windows applications, in windowed or full-screen mode, install new applications, and so on. Chances are if it worked in Windows 7, it will work fine in Windows 8 as well.

Also, the Start toggle mentioned earlier works with the Windows desktop as well: Tapping the Windows key (or Windows key button) repeatedly will toggle the display between the desktop and the Start screen.

CROSSREF The desktop is important enough that it gets its own chapter. Check out Chapter 4 for more information.

USING THE SYSTEM-WIDE METRO USER EXPERIENCES

While the Start screen, Metro-style apps, and the Windows desktop are all full-screen experiences that you generally access in isolation, Windows 8 also offers a variety of other Metro user experiences that you can access from elsewhere. In many cases, these experiences are new system-level interfaces, and most are available from the Windows desktop as well as from the Start screen or Metro-style apps.

Before digging into individual interfaces, it's helpful to know that Windows 8 exposes many of these user interfaces in different ways depending on whether you're using the keyboard, mouse, or your fingers on a multi-touch screen. And yes, in most cases, all three input types are available.

- **Keyboard shortcuts:** For keyboard users, Microsoft has delivered a startling number of keyboard shortcuts in Windows 8, many of which utilize the now-common Windows key (or Winkey). For example, Winkey + D will display the Windows desktop, while Winkey + E will open a new Windows Explorer window. Keyboard shortcuts are such a big deal in this release, in fact, that we supply an amazing list of such shortcuts in the appendix. But we also discuss each applicable shortcut as needed throughout the book.

- **Hot corners:** For mouse users, Microsoft utilizes the corners of the screen, providing what it calls hot corners that activate different features. These features include Back, Switcher, Start, and Charms, and they're discussed individually in just a moment.

- **Edge UIs:** Touch users can utilize various edge UIs to achieve the same actions for which mouse users use hot corners. For example, if you swipe down from the upper edge of the screen (or up from the bottom edge), you will activate the current app's (or other Metro experience's) app bar. You can perform simple task switching via the left edge of the screen and access the Charms bar from the right edge; these interfaces are all described later in this chapter as well.

Okay, let's look at the various system-level Metro experiences in Windows 8.

Charms: The Uber-Metro UI

If you learn just one Metro-based user experience, it should be how to access the Charms bar, a menu of useful system-level options that is perhaps the key to mastering Windows 8. This is shown in Figure 3-11.

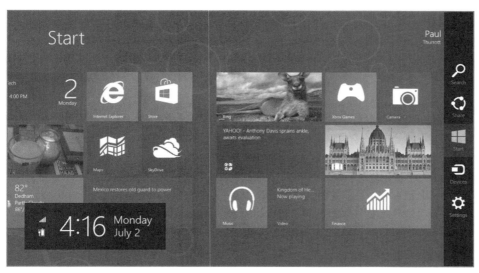

FIGURE 3-11: Charms

Before explaining Charms further, however, let's discuss how to invoke them. Each of these access types works from anywhere in Windows 8, including the Start screen, any Metro-style app or game, or from the Windows desktop.

- ▶ **Keyboard:** Type Winkey + C.
- ▶ **Mouse:** Move the mouse cursor into the top-right corner of the screen. As you do, the Charms bar will appear in a translucent mode. Then, move the cursor down toward the middle of the right edge of the screen to fully engage the bar. (Conversely, you can mouse into the lower-right corner of the screen and then move the mouse cursor up toward the middle of the right edge of the screen.)

▶ Accessing the Charms bar on a multiscreen configuration can be tricky, depending on the location and orientation of your secondary screens. Though some workarounds exist, the simplest is to use the Winkey + C keyboard shortcut instead of the mouse.

> **NOTE**   Why the translucency? Microsoft is accounting for other user interface elements that might be bumped up against the right edge of the screen, including a desktop application's scroll bar or the Peek button in the taskbar. If you don't immediately move the mouse cursor toward the middle, the Charm bar will disappear, allowing you to access whatever else is on-screen in that area.

- **Touch:** To display the Charms on a multi-touch screen, swipe in to the left from the right edge of the screen.

As you can see, there are five items, or "charms", in the Charms bar. They are as follows:

- **Search:** This charm provides easy access to the system-wide search functionality in Windows 8. It's context-sensitive, so if you tap it from the Start screen or Windows desktop, it will trigger the new Start Search experience, which lets you find apps (and applications), settings, and files on your PC. But if you access this charm from within an app, you will instead search that app. For example, you can use this to search for e-mail from within the Mail app.

  We discuss Search in the next section of this chapter.

- **Share:** Via this unique charm, you can share what's on-screen with others using another Metro-style app. Like many of the other charms, including Search, this functionality is tied to a new, low-level capability in Windows 8 called contracts, in this case the Share contract. And any Metro-style app can implement this contract to send and/or receive share requests.

  Share doesn't work at all from the Start screen (or the desktop) since these interfaces have nothing to share. To use Share, you need to be using a Metro-style app first.

  We discuss Share in more detail a bit later in the chapter.

- **Start:** This charm, which is color-coded to the accent color in the Metro theme you chose, simply emulates the Windows key or Windows key button. That is, it will navigate to the Start screen from any other Metro-based experience or the desktop. But if you're already on the Start screen, you'll return to the previous experience you were using.

- **Devices:** Like most charms, Devices is also context-sensitive, so what you see here will be determined by two things: which compatible devices are attached to (or included in) your PC or device and what you're doing at the time. The Device charm is most often used to access a printer or, for those with two or more screens, to determine how the secondary screens are used.

We discuss the Devices charm, and Windows 8's support for hardware peripherals, later in the chapter.

▶ **Settings:** Another context-sensitive charm, Settings provides an interesting array of features. At the top of the Settings pane that appears, shown in Figure 3-12, you'll see links to settings that pertain to the current view, which could be the Start screen, a Metro-style app, or the desktop environment. But at the bottom, you will find links to settings that are always available, from any of those experiences.

▶ Keyboard users can more quickly open the Settings pane by tapping Winkey + I.

FIGURE 3-12: Settings pane

From the Start screen, you'll see a Tile settings link that provides a short list of settings for the Start screen. These include whether to show administrative tools on the Start screen and a button for clearing personal information from the tiles.

From within an app, you'll see different settings depending on the app. For this reason, we examine app settings in the respective chapters throughout this book.

The grid of settings icons you see at the bottom of the Settings pane is perhaps the most interesting bit here.

The Network icon provides access to your PC's networking connections, discussed in Chapter 13.

The Volume icon provides a way to change the system volume using a slider that appears when the icon is clicked, as in Figure 3-13.

▶ You can also change the volume using hardware keys, either on your device (volume buttons are common on modern tablets, for example) or via your keyboard, where some PC makers are reassigning function keys to control the volume.

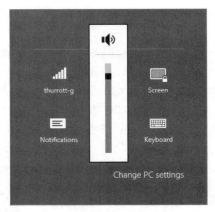

FIGURE 3-13: Adjusting the volume

The screen brightness icon similarly provides a way to control the brightness of the screen on compatible devices. (Generally, it will be available on portable machines but not on desktop computers.)

Notifications lets you determine whether notifications, described a bit later in the chapter, are globally on or disabled ("hidden") for some period of time so you can get work completed without interruption.

Power toggles between the power states Sleep, Shutdown, and Restart, meaning that it's a fairly important control (see Figure 3-14). You may recall that you would perform these operations in Windows 7 from the Start menu. But with the Start button and menu missing in Windows 8, Microsoft opted to put this functionality in a location that would be accessible from anywhere in the system, whether you were using the Start screen, a Metro-style app, or the desktop. So here it is.

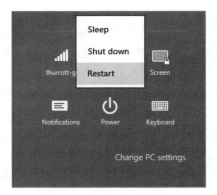

FIGURE 3-14: Power options

The keyboard icon lets you switch between the different keyboard language layouts your PC or device supports. For most, this will be just one, such as US English, but Windows 8 is the first version of Microsoft's flagship OS in which every single product edition—Windows 8, Windows 8 Pro, Windows 8 Enterprise, and Windows RT—supports switching languages on the fly using Language Packs. So now everyone can get their multilingual game on.

Finally, take note of the More PC Settings link at the bottom of the Settings pane. PC Settings is the Metro-style replacement for the Control Panel—though to be fair, you'll still be accessing various control panels, too, as you'll see throughout this book—and as such, it's pretty darned important. We look at PC Settings in depth in Chapter 5.

Finding What You Need with Start Search

Start Menu Search was one of the best features in Windows 7, and its successor, simply called Start Search, is even better in Windows 8, or at least it will be once you get used to the new full-screen interface. If you weren't familiar with Start Menu Search, it worked like this: You would tap the Start button (or hit Winkey on your keyboard) and just start typing the name of the application, document, or control panel you needed to find. As you typed, the search results would appear, inline within the Start Menu. This can be seen in Figure 3-15.

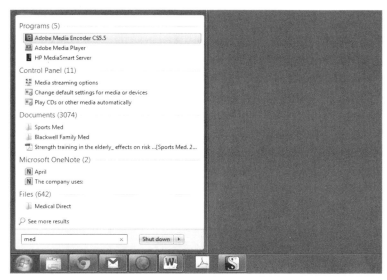

FIGURE 3-15: Windows 7's Start Menu Search

Of course, Windows 8 doesn't have a Start menu. But it does still offer searching capabilities. And it works exactly the same way: From any Metro-style app or the Windows desktop, just tap Start (or Winkey) and start typing. If you're already viewing the Start screen, it's even easier: Just start typing.

When you do, the new full-screen Search experience appears as shown in Figure 3-16. And while it may look a bit balky at first, it's actually really powerful: It can help you find new Metro-style apps, Windows desktop applications, various PC Settings or desktop-type control panels, and files. And as you'll see, it can even search within (Metro-style) apps! It really puts Windows 7 Start Menu Search to shame.

FIGURE 3-16: Windows 8's new Start Search

By default, Start Search will provide search results for Apps, which is really a combination of new, Metro-style apps and old-school, desktop-type applications. As you can see in Figure 3-17, telling the difference between the two is a bit subtle, but Metro-style apps typically have solid-colored, square, tile-like icons while older, desktop-type applications have the more familiar, old-school icons.

You can perform a variety of actions on the icons in the search results. For example, to launch the application or app, simply click or tap it. But you can perform many more actions if you right-click one of the items in the search results list: When you do, a new app bar will appear providing the additional options, as in Figure 3-18.

▶ To perform a right-click with a touch-based screen, tap the item and drag down a bit.

What you see here will vary according to the type of item you select. But some of the more common options include the following:

▶ **Pin/Unpin from Start:** This option lets you pin a tile for the application or app to the Start screen. If it's already pinned, you can unpin it.

FIGURE 3-17: Applications and Metro-style apps mixed in the search results

▶ **Pin/Unpin from taskbar:** This option lets you pin a desktop-type application to the taskbar on the desktop (or reverse that effect for an item that is already pinned there).

▶ **Open new window:** This option is applicable to Windows Explorer and it lets you open a new Explorer window. (The same as typing Winkey + E.)

▶ **Open file location:** This option is available only to desktop-type applications and it opens a new Explorer window in the location in which the application can be found.

▶ **Run as administrator:** This option, which is also only available to desktop-type applications, lets you run the application within an elevated security context. (You'll be prompted with a User Account Control dialog to authenticate or confirm this option.)

▶ **Uninstall:** This option lets you uninstall the app. Note that it works only for Metro-style apps; you uninstall classic Windows desktop applications as you did before (using the Programs and Features control panel).

▶ Why is this called "Run as administrator" when most Windows 8 users will most certainly be using an administrator account anyway? It's just an unfortunate artifact from the past. What it really means is, "Run under an elevated security context."

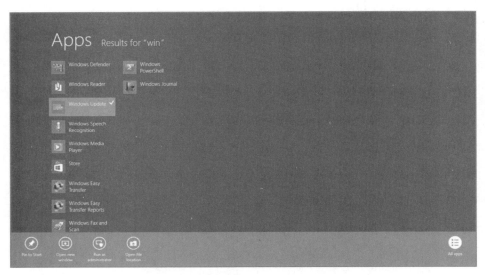

FIGURE 3-18: The Search results app bar provides more options.

Of course, Start Search isn't just for applications. You can also filter the view for settings (a combination of PC Settings and control panels), files, and individual apps.

To filter the search results for settings, type your search and then tap the Settings item in the search pane on the right. As you can see in Figure 3-19, the search results will filter to show only the relevant PC Settings and control panels.

FIGURE 3-19: Search results showing settings

This interface is a bit different from the search results list for apps: The PC Settings choices appear first and are segregated from the control panels. And there are no right-click options to be had. You can only tap the item you wish to access. PC Settings items will launch the appropriate screen in Windows 8's new PC Settings interface (which is described in a moment), while control panels will open in a window over the Windows desktop as in previous Windows versions.

To filter the search results for files, type your search and then tap the Files item in the search pane. As Figure 3-20 shows, this reveals yet another take on the search results view, where the files on your PC that match the search term can be further filtered by documents, pictures, music, videos, or others.

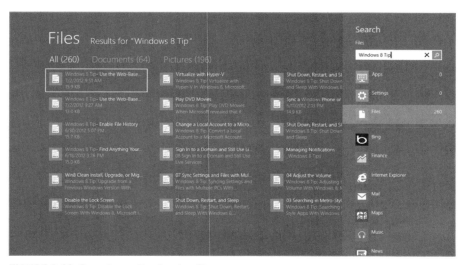

FIGURE 3-20: Search results showing files

You can also redirect this search type across your homegroup, meaning that the files on other PCs on your home network will be included in the search results, too. To do so, tap the Files header and select Homegroup from the short menu that appears.

As with settings search results, there are no additional (right-click) options for files search results.

The ability to search within Metro-style apps is of course app-specific, and thus something we'll discuss as appropriate throughout this book. But it's worth noting that this feature is a key advantage of the new underlying software platform in Windows 8: As with many other key Metro features, apps can utilize this useful capability fairly easy and thus extend the way that Windows 8 works.

Sharing Between Apps

Windows 8 supports a new low-level feature called Contracts that works much like Copy and Paste does in that the applications (or, in this case, apps) on either end of the sequence—those that are participating in the contract—don't need to know anything about the other. That is, they only need to support the appropriate contract. One of the most common is the Share contract, which lets one app share information with another.

A contract, of course, is a two-way street, with one app initiating the operation, or "sending" the share request, and the other completing the operation by "accepting" it. So while you are able to share information between many Metro-style apps using the Share contract, most will only support one end of the contract. That is, they will send, or they will receive.

The canonical example of such a transaction is the web: You're browsing around your favorite website one morning and come across an article that you simply *must* share with someone else. In the days before Windows 8 and Metro, this kind of sharing would have occurred in two fairly limited ways. Either the browser would have been specifically designed (or "hard-coded") to facilitate the sharing of web pages (perhaps via e-mail or a social networking service like Facebook) or a third-party developer would have written a browser add-on, or extension, to add that capability to the browser.

Either would work. But both solutions are specific to that one browser. If you decide to use a different web browser, you're out of luck. And if you want to share via a service or other mechanism that's not supported by the browser you use—perhaps one that's not been invented yet—you're equally out of luck.

In Windows 8, Metro-style apps simply need to support the Share charm. They can support initiating a share action, and they can separately (or only) support receiving a share action. The Metro-style version of Internet Explorer 10, Microsoft's web browser, supports initiating a share action, so you can share web pages with others. But it doesn't need to know which app you're using to share that page. And that's because any number of apps support receiving the share. One that's included in Windows 8 is the Mail app: You can use this app to share a page from IE 10 via e-mail, as shown in Figure 3-21. But as time goes on, many other apps will appear that will let you share web pages via other means, such as with different social networks.

This capability means that Windows 8 will get better over time without Microsoft needing to update the OS itself. Third-party developers will extend the system's abilities by implementing the Share contract, and by doing so will make Windows 8, and many other apps that run within it, better than they were before.

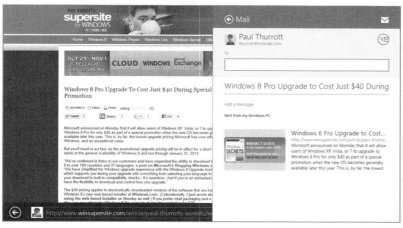

FIGURE 3-21: Sharing a web page from Internet Explorer, with Mail.

Managing Running Apps

Anyone who's used Windows knows about the Alt + Tab keyboard shortcut that lets you quickly switch between running applications. It's still there in Windows 8, and it's still called Windows Flip, though we suspect few knew *that*.

What's different is that Windows Flip now includes Metro-style apps as well as desktop applications and the Windows desktop, as you can see in Figure 3-22. And Windows Flip is no longer the primary way to switch between running applications and apps.

▶ Oddly, you can't access the Start screen itself with Windows Flip.

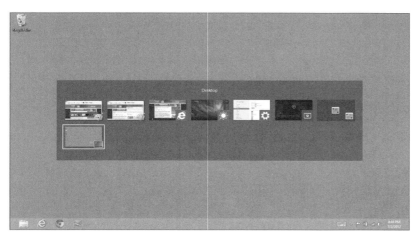

FIGURE 3-22: Windows Flip is still in Windows 8 and works with both apps and applications.

Instead, Windows 8 employs new Metro-style UIs for switching between running apps, applications, the desktop and the Start screen. These include a new touch-based interface for quickly swiping between views, plus the new features Back, Switcher, and the Start notification tip. And as you should expect, they're each available from anywhere in the system, including the Start screen, any Metro-style app, and the desktop. So let's look at each in turn.

SWITCHING APPS BY SWIPING

You can very easily switch between running apps, and the Windows desktop, using a new swipe gesture for multi-touch-based devices. To do so, swipe in from the left-most edge of the screen. As you do, a large thumbnail of the next app in the "app stack"—the list of running apps—will appear, as in Figure 3-23.

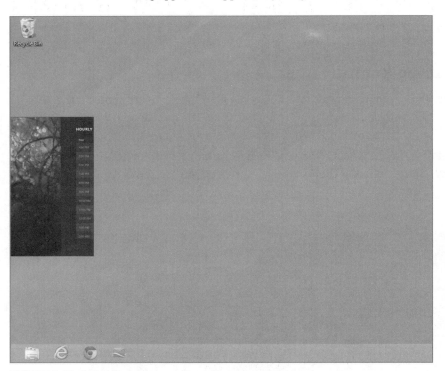

FIGURE 3-23: Switching to the next app with a touch-based swipe gesture.

There are a number of things you can do with this gesture:

▶ **Switch to the next app:** A single swipe will cause the next app to appear, replacing the app you were using as the only app on-screen.

▶ **Switch repeatedly through available apps:** If you perform the aforementioned gesture repeatedly, you will quickly switch from app to app, navigating through each app in the app stack in turn. You will typically do this when the next app isn't the app you're looking for.

▶ **Snap the next app:** Windows 8 supports a unique side-by-side screen-sharing mode called Snap. It can be engaged using this swipe gesture, but is important enough that we describe it separately later in the chapter.

▶ **Enable Switcher:** Windows 8 also includes a new app-switching interface called Switcher. This, too, can be enabled via this swipe gesture, and we describe it in just a bit.

BACK

The new Back experience is a toggle and it works much like quickly tapping Alt + Tab once: When you use it, you will return to the previous Metro-style app or to the Windows desktop. To access the Back experience, move the mouse cursor into the top-left corner of the screen. As you hit the corner, you'll see a Back tip appear, as in Figure 3-24, representing the previous app (or desktop) you used. To access that app, just click the tip.

▶ For those readers lucky enough to own a multi-touch-based device, you can use the swipe-based app switching gesture described a bit later instead. There's no way to display the Back tip via touch.

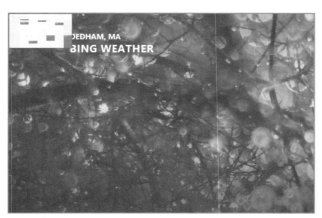

DEDHAM, MA
BING WEATHER

FIGURE 3-24: The new Back experience lets you switch to the previously used app easily.

SWITCHER

Back works well if you're using a small number of apps. But if you're a heavy multi-tasker, you're going to want and expect a way to more easily access a particular app.

So Windows 8 has a new interface called Switcher that provides Windows Flip-like functionality in a Metro-style interface. Shown in Figure 3-25, Switcher can be enabled by typing Winkey + Tab.

FIGURE 3-25: Switcher provides a Metro-style list of your running apps.

▶ The Windows Flip 3D application-switching feature from Windows Vista and 7 has been replaced by Switcher in Windows 8. Sorry, Flip 3D fans.

Mouse and touch users can also utilize Switcher, though with a bit more difficulty.

With a mouse, the simplest way is to first trigger the Back tip by moving the mouse into the top-left corner of the screen. When you do, you may notice that there are in fact a number of ghost-like tile previews that run down the left edge of the screen, indicating that there are more running apps. To display Switcher, then, move the mouse down the left edge of the screen. As you do, the full Switcher interface will appear.

(If you're familiar with Charms, you may understand that this behavior mimics how that interface is activated with a mouse. Likewise, you can alternatively mouse into the lower-left corner of the screen and then move the mouse cursor *up* the left edge of the screen if that's more natural.)

While most touch interactions are by definition simple, enabling Switcher with touch is actually pretty difficult. It goes like this: You swipe in from the left edge of the screen, but a bit more slowly than normal. When the large thumbnail for the next app appears, you stop swiping to the right and move your finger instead backward a bit, to the left. If you do it just right, Switcher will appear.

START NOTIFICATION TIP

While many will mourn the loss of the Start button from Windows 8, Microsoft removed it for a good reason: As a desktop-based interface, it was only available in that environment and not in any Metro-style apps. So the company came up with a decent replacement, called the Start notification tip, that works from anywhere in the system—the Start screen, the desktop, or any Metro-style app—and works exactly like the Windows key (or Windows key button on devices); that is, it's a toggle.

To see the Start notification tip, move the mouse into the lower-left corner of the screen. As you do, a thumbnail will appear, representing either the Start screen or the previous screen (a Metro-style app or the desktop). This is shown in Figure 3-26.

To navigate to the Start screen (or to the previous experience), just click it.

The Start notification tip isn't available with a keyboard or touch because it's not necessary. Keyboard users can use the Winkey as a toggle, as noted earlier, and touch users can use the Windows key button on their device or access the Start thumbnail that's in Switcher.

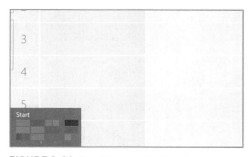

FIGURE 3-26: The Start notification tip

Snap

After the wonder of Metro's full-screen experiences wears off, you may start to feel a bit constrained by this environment. After all, Windows is named Windows for a reason: It has historically provided access to multiple on-screen windows—each representing applications and various system interfaces—simultaneously. And as our experience with Windows grew, many have come to expect this type of behavior. And yes, it's still available with the desktops. But all of the Metro-style apps are full-screen only.

Well, not quite.

No, you're not going to be running multiple Metro-style apps on-screen, as you can do with desktop-based applications. There are security, performance, and battery life reasons for that, but no matter. What Microsoft is providing is a simple screen-sharing feature called Snap, which lets you use two Metro-style apps—or one Metro-style app and the desktop—side by side, albeit in limited ways. In this configuration, one app—the so-called snapped app—will occupy a small channel on the left or right side of the screen. And the other app, the so-called main app, will occupy the rest.

Not all apps support snapping fully, because they're either useless or next to useless in a snapped configuration. But some apps provide specifically tailored snap interfaces—like Calendar and Mail—and can be quite useful in this way.

Since a picture really is worth about a thousand words in this case, examine Figure 3-27 to see what Snap looks like. Note that the app in the main area, on the right in this figure, can be the desktop or any Metro-style app.

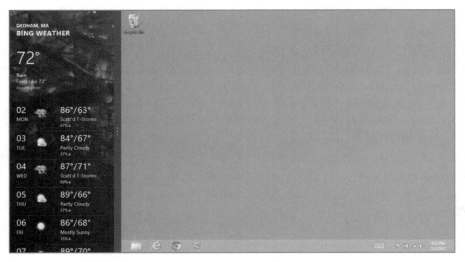

FIGURE 3-27: Snap: Simple screen sharing

While there are a number of ways to snap an app, the most reliable—and consistent across mouse and touch—is to use Switcher. Here's how you do so using either the mouse or touch.

After ensuring that the app (or desktop) you wish to have in the main view is on-screen, enable Switcher. Then, grab the app you wish to snap from the Switcher list of app thumbnails, and then pull it out of Switcher. As you do, the Snap border bar, shown in Figure 3-28, will appear. When it does, release the mouse button (or lift your finger from the screen) to snap the app.

Note that you can perform these same basic steps to snap the app on the right side of the screen. But instead of releasing the thumbnail when you pull it out of Switcher, drag it all the way over to the right edge of the screen until the Snap border bar appears there. Then release the mouse button (or lift your finger).

FIGURE 3-28: Snapping an app

There are a few other things you can do with Snap. For example, you can reverse the snapped and main apps so that the previously snapped app now takes up most of the on-screen real estate. To do so, just double-click the Snap border bar. Or, with a touch screen, just drag the bar toward the middle of the screen and then lift your finger.

If you're a keyboard shortcut junkie, Snap supports some cool shortcuts. For example, from any Metro-style app, you can tap Winkey + . (period) to engage the Snap border bar and then tap that repeatedly to keep moving it to the right. (Winkey + Shift + . moves to the left.) We provide a complete list of Winkey keyboard shortcuts in the appendix.

> **TIP** If this is still too limiting, consider a multi-monitor configuration. In this case, you can have the Start screen and all Metro-style apps on one screen and the desktop and its applications spread across one or more other screens. We discuss this configuration in Chapter 5.

Getting Alerted with Notifications

Back in the "Longhorn" days, when Microsoft was prepping the version of Windows that was eventually released in diminished form as Windows Vista, the software giant revealed that it was working on a new centralized notifications system that would be used by the OS as well as any third-party applications that needed this functionality. The idea was a good one since most Windows applications simply do their own thing when it comes to notifications. But because of delays in getting Vista to market, that notifications system—like many other good ideas from the Longhorn project—never made it to into Windows.

Flash forward a decade and Microsoft has finally realized its vision for a central notifications system in Windows. That said, Windows 8 bears little resemblance to Longhorn, and it's not likely that many from the Longhorn era of Microsoft could have foreseen the rise in touch-based devices that necessitated the full-screen Metro experiences in this release.

No matter. It's here now. And while only Windows itself and new Metro-style apps can take advantage of this new notifications platform, they work on the desktop as well. So if you get a new e-mail or have an upcoming appointment, you will still get alerted.

Windows 8 supports two types of notifications: full-screen, modal notifications that must be dealt with before continuing, and small, floating notification *toasts* that appear and then disappear on their own. The former are the province of Windows and system-level features only and are generally very important. Notification toasts, meanwhile, can vary in importance, but since they're app-based, they're never going to involve a decision that could render your PC inoperable.

Figure 3-29 shows a full-screen notification. As you can see, it's a fairly jarring and attention-getting interface, and something you won't miss.

FIGURE 3-29: A full-screen notification really gets in your face.

An app-based notification toast, like the one in Figure 3-30, meanwhile, can be subtle, unless of course you are getting repeated toasts appearing back to back as you might with an instant messaging app. These notifications appear in the top-right corner of the screen and disappear if you do nothing.

Notifications are configured via PC Settings: From anywhere in Windows 8, press Winkey + I (or access the Charms bar and then choose Settings) to access the Settings pane. Then, select the link titled More PC Settings. In PC Settings, select Notifications on the left. The screen will resemble Figure 3-31.

FIGURE 3-30: A notification toast

FIGURE 3-31: Notifications settings

There are two basic areas to this interface. On the top are three options related to notifications generally. And on the bottom is a toggle for each Metro-style app that can provide notifications.

Each of these should be relatively straightforward. In the case of the apps list, each toggle provides you with an opportunity to determine whether individual apps can provide notifications. So if you feel that Messaging notifications are annoying, just toggle those off.

CROSSREF We discuss PC Settings further in Chapter 5.

There are actually two other places where you can configure notifications somewhat.

If you navigate to Personalize and then Lock Screen in PC Settings, for example, you'll see that there's a Lock screen apps section where you can determine which, if any, apps can provide notifications on your PC's or device's lock screen. As you can see in Figure 3-32, this interface includes seven slots of normal notifications and one for an app—like Calendar—that can provide detailed status information.

FIGURE 3-32: Notifications can be configured separately for the lock screen, too.

▶ Note that this toggle applies only to app-based notifications.

Also, earlier in the chapter we mentioned the Notification icon in the Settings pane (Winkey + I). This interface is useful because it lets you temporarily toggle all notifications off for set periods of time. That way, if you're busy, you can disable notifications using one of the three time periods shown in Figure 3-33 and then be sure they'll automatically come back later; if you turn them off from the main Notifications interface in PC Settings, you may simply forget to turn notifications back on again later.

FIGURE 3-33: The Notification icon lets you temporarily disable all app-based notifications.

Working with Devices

While new apps and other software-based capabilities can extend the functionality of Windows 8 and make it better than it was before, adding new hardware devices is another approach. Add a printer, for example, and many of your apps will suddenly be able to print. Plug in an external USB-based hard drive, and your PC has more storage, which can also be used by the OS and by many apps.

OK, we know you understand why adding a few hardware peripherals can make for a better computing experience. But we mention this here because the way in which Windows 8 interacts with these devices has changed, thanks to the switch to Metro. So while some legacy interfaces for dealing with hardware devices remain for backward compatibility reasons, much of your interactions with the devices in Windows 8 will now occur through Metro-style experiences. And more often than not, that means the Devices charm.

Let's look at some common examples.

PRINTING

The ability to print is obviously a core capability. And while installing printer drivers works as it did in earlier versions of Windows—through the desktop interface using familiar methods—as does printing from desktop-based Windows applications, Metro-style apps interact with printers through the Devices charm.

Consider the Metro-style version of Internet Explorer 10. You've found a web page you want to print for posterity, but there's no printer button in the app bar and no menu system at all. How do you print?

In Metro, printing—like other device access—is now consistent, and it happens through the Devices charm. So you display this charm (perhaps through the Charms bar, but Winkey + K is quicker), and you'll see something resembling Figure 3-34. And in that list of devices will be one or more printers, depending on how your PC is configured.

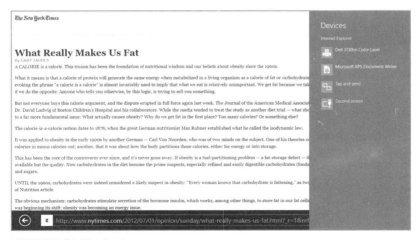

FIGURE 3-34: The Devices pane

▶ Too ponderous? Depending on the app, Ctrl + P still works for printing, too.

When you select the printer, the Devices pane will expand to reveal options related to that specific printer, as in Figure 3-35. This interface will let you make last-minute configurations before actually printing, with many of the options available via a More settings link.

To print, just tap Print.

USING PORTABLE STORAGE

You may recall from previous Windows versions that an Auto Play window would appear when you plugged in an external storage device like a USB-based hard drive. In Windows 8, Auto Play is now a Metro-based experience. So when you plug in an external drive, you'll see the interface in Figure 3-36.

And if you click this notification, you'll be confronted by the user interface in Figure 3-37, though the options you see here will vary from device to device.

FIGURE 3-35: Printer settings

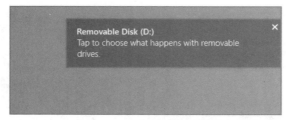

FIGURE 3-36: Auto Play for portable storage

FIGURE 3-37: Deciding what to do when this type of device is plugged into the PC

As is the case with desktop applications, this storage is now available to any Metro-style app as well. You can see this for yourself in apps that support the Metro-style File Picker, a new full-screen experience for selecting files on disk. As you can see in Figure 3-38, a USB-based hard drive is automatically available to the File Picker just as it is to Windows Explorer on the desktop.

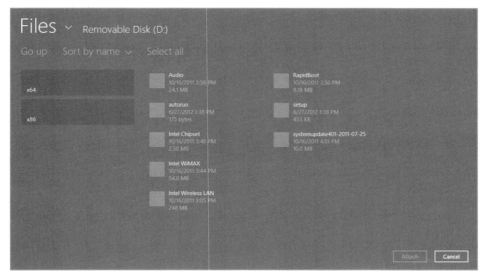

FIGURE 3-38: External storage is available to Metro-style apps too, via the File Picker, a sort of Metro "Open File" interface.

USING A SECOND SCREEN

When you plug a second display into your PC, you can choose between a variety of display modes, including duplicating the display on both screens, extending the display across the screens, or using only one of the two screens. In earlier Windows versions, finding and then configuring this feature was fairly ponderous. But Windows 8 provides a handy new Metro-style experience that makes this easier than ever.

To see it, make sure you have a second display attached to your PC. Then, access the Devices charm (Winkey + K) and select Second screen. You'll see the Second screen pane appear as in Figure 3-39.

▶ You can press Winkey + P to jump directly to the Second screen pane.

CROSSREF This was only a short example. We thoroughly discuss multiple display usage in Chapter 5.

FIGURE 3-39: This pane lets you configure how a secondary screen works.

SUMMARY

Windows 8 provides an exciting and new full-screen user experience we call Metro that brings the best of mobile devices to your PC and positions Windows for the 21st century. Yes, Metro is a touch-first interface that will be most at home on touch-based, iPad-like devices. But Metro works just fine on all kinds of PCs, including those with a keyboard and mouse, and it provides an amazing new platform upon which a new generation of full-screen, Metro-style apps run.

As important, the Metro experience pervades other Windows 8 experiences, including the Windows desktop, providing charms, search, sharing, app switching, app snapping, notifications, and device interactions that work everywhere in Windows. In this way, we can see that Metro isn't a "thing on a thing" or even a "thing next to a thing." It's the heart and soul of Windows 8. It is, ultimately, what makes Windows 8 so special.

CHAPTER 4

(Still) Alive and Kicking: The Windows Desktop

IN THIS CHAPTER

▶ Understanding what's changed with the Windows desktop

▶ How Metro experiences are exposed on the desktop

▶ Using the new File Explorer

▶ Managing files and folders

▶ Managing classic desktop applications

▶ Managing running tasks

▶ Using SkyDrive with the Windows desktop

While the touch-friendly Metro-style user experience is clearly the big story in Windows 8, most Windows users have a rich history with the Windows desktop and the many, many applications and utilities that have run in this environment for years. Fortunately, all of these things are still available in Windows 8, since this OS includes an updated and enhanced version of the traditional Windows desktop environment, its File Explorer file manager, and the other related capabilities Windows users know and love. And this is true whether you're using a traditional desktop PC or laptop, or a newfangled tablet computer or hybrid PC, and whether you're using Windows 8 or Windows RT.

> **NOTE** There is one major exception to this rule. While Windows 8-based PCs and devices of course provide all of the desktop features you've come to know and love, those based on Windows RT—the ARM-based variant of Windows 8—are somewhat limited in that they cannot run any third-party Windows desktop software. That said, all of the features described in this chapter work equally well and identically in Windows RT as they do with their Intel-type Windows 8 brethren.

How the Metro-style environment and Windows desktop interact with each other is an important consideration for anyone moving to this new operating system. After all, in previous Windows versions, the Windows desktop was the entire user interface, the face that Windows presented to the world. But in Windows 8, the desktop behaves, conceptually at least, as an app that works within the new Windows Runtime (WinRT) and the Metro-style user experience. As such, even users who stick strictly to the desktop environment will still need to deal with, and understand, various Metro-style user interfaces, including the new Back and Start experiences, Switcher, and the Charms bar. And indignities of indignities, you'll even need to use Metro to shut down your PC!

This chapter examines each of these issues as well as all of the new Windows desktop features that Microsoft added to this version of the OS. If you were expecting very little in the way of desktop enhancements thanks to a focus on the Metro environment, prepare to be surprised. There are some very nice updates to the desktop in Windows 8.

WHAT'S NEW ON THE WINDOWS DESKTOP?

To best understand what's new with the Windows 8 desktop, let's take a quick look back at the Windows 7 desktop, shown in Figure 4-1. This was the default (and only) user experience in the previous version of Windows, and aside from a few minor bits that differed between various product versions, this was essentially what all Windows 7 users saw when they booted into the operating system.

The Windows 7 desktop comprises a few key items, most of which hadn't changed at all since Windows 95. These include one or more desktop icons (with Recycle Bin being the only icon pretty much guaranteed to appear every time), an optional selection of desktop gadgets (graphical utilities that would "float" over the desktop but under any open windows; these first appeared in Windows Vista), a Start button (or Start orb, as it was officially called), a taskbar, a system tray (with white notification icons and a clock), and the Aero Peek button, which temporarily hid the on-screen windows so you could peek at the underlying desktop.

FIGURE 4-1: The Windows 7 desktop

The Windows 8 desktop, perhaps not surprisingly, doesn't look all that different. As you can see in Figure 4-2, it looks almost identical to the Windows 7 desktop, though the Aero "glass" look and feel has been replaced with a flatter, more opaque, and somewhat Metro-like user experience that is battery-life friendly and a bit more consistent with the new Metro user experiences in Windows 8.

FIGURE 4-2: The Windows 8 desktop looks and works like its predecessor, but with some minor differences.

Look a bit closer, however, and you will notice some other differences. For the most part, these differences involve user interface elements that were present in Windows 7 but are now missing in Windows 8. What's interesting is that the two biggest—the Start and Aero Peek—are in fact still functionally available in Windows 8, even though they're no longer visually there.

The Start Button Is Dead. . .Long Live the Start Button

▶ As discussed in Chapter 3, many capabilities of the old Start menu can now be found in other Metro interfaces, such as the Charms bar.

Microsoft's decision to remove the Start button is, perhaps, one of the more controversial decisions in Windows 8, because this on-screen button has been a ubiquitous mainstay of the Windows user interface since 1995. But before you get too upset over the change, it's helpful to understand why it happened and how Windows 8 makes an onscreen button on the desktop superfluous anyway.

The *why* part is straightforward. With the addition of the Metro environment as the default user interface in Windows 8, Microsoft has replaced the application launching capabilities of the desktop-based Start menu (and, in Windows 7, the taskbar) with a new Metro-style interface called the Start screen. Microsoft calls this the new Start experience. (They do love the word *experience*.) And they wanted it to work equally well—and consistently—from both of Windows 8's user interfaces, Metro and the desktop.

What this means is that every time you tap the Windows key button on your Windows device, or press the Windows key on your keyboard—while the desktop is displayed, that is—the desktop will disappear and be replaced by the new Start screen. This happens instead of the old behavior where the Start menu would display.

▶ If you're using an older or nonstandard keyboard that doesn't have a Windows key, try Ctrl + Esc instead.

But what about mouse or touch users? Your muscle memory is telling you to tap the Start button. But the Start button is gone.

Or is it?

As it turns out, Windows 8 includes methods for triggering this new Start experience for both the mouse and touch. As with other system-wide actions, these new triggers are part of a collective series of *edge UIs*, and while we cover this topic pretty heavily in Chapter 3, this one is worth discussing here as well since they work with the desktop, too, and many users coming to Windows 8 on a traditional PC will interact with it mostly from the desktop.

To trigger the Start experience with the mouse, move the mouse cursor down into the lower-left corner of the screen, into the area where the Start button used to be.

> **NOTE** You can simply push that cursor right into the corner, since Windows will stop it from moving beyond the edges of the physical display, even on multi-monitor setups.

As you hit the lower-left corner of the screen with the mouse cursor, something new happens: A Start tip appears, providing a visual thumbnail of the Start screen as an indication of what will happen if you click it. This can be seen in Figure 4-3.

FIGURE 4-3: The new Start tip appears when you mouse into the lower-left corner of the screen.

To navigate to the Start screen, simply click the Start tip. (To get back, you'll need to do one of the following: Click the Desktop tile on the Start screen, press the Windows key on your keyboard, or tap the Windows key button on your Windows device.)

▶ Power users will want to right-click the tip. When they do, they'll see the magical power user menu shown in Figure 4-4. Winkey + X will also trigger this menu.

Programs and Features
Mobility Center
Power Options
Event Viewer
System
Device Manager
Disk Management
Computer Management
Command Prompt
Command Prompt (Admin)

Task Manager
Control Panel
File Explorer
Search
Run

Desktop

FIGURE 4-4: A hidden power user menu can be found by right-clicking the Start tip.

To trigger this edge UI with a multi-touch-based device, you can choose between two different edge UIs: the Switcher or the Charms bar. Both are discussed in Chapter 3, and then again later in this chapter, but since the Switcher method more closely mimics the mouse-based description above, let's look at that quickly here.

To activate the Switcher edge UI from the desktop, swipe in from the left edge of the screen, and when the previous app thumbnail appears, swipe back to the left. If you do it just right, the Switcher appears, as in Figure 4-5. Just tap the Start tip at the bottom to return to the Start screen.

FIGURE 4-5: Switcher can appear over the desktop, too.

In case it's not obvious, all of these methods for accessing the new Start experience from the desktop work like a toggle. So when you're on the desktop and engage it, using any available method, you will navigate to the Start screen. But if you immediately repeat that step, without launching any other apps, you'll navigate *back* to the desktop.

Peek Lives On, Too

Where the Start button disappearing act will no doubt cause much wailing and pontificating, few will cry for Aero Peek, which is also missing, seemingly, in Windows 8. But as with the Start button, rumors of Aero Peek's death are exaggerated. Although the small UI button that used to trigger this effect is gone, the Peek lives on.

To trigger Peek, you can employ one of the following methods:

▶ **Keyboard:** Press Winkey + , (comma)

▶ **Mouse:** Move the mouse cursor into the very lower-right corner of the screen.

▶ There's no way to trigger Peek via touch.

Either way, the effect is the same, and you will visually peek through to the desktop, so that any floating windows that were on-screen will disappear temporarily, replaced by the outlines shown in Figure 4-6.

Beyond the Start button and Peek, much of what you'll see initially on the Windows desktop is identical, or nearly so, to the Windows 7 desktop. But with this being a new OS, there are indeed numerous other changes to discover. To find them, all you need to do is move the mouse around a bit or start clicking on things.

Or simply read on.

FIGURE 4-6: With Peek, you can peek under any windows and see the desktop and the icons it contains.

> ► If you press Winkey + D from the Start screen or from any Metro-style app, you will navigate to the desktop, sans the Peek effect.

NOTE You can also right-click on the Peek area to display a context menu that provides an additional choice, Show Desktop. This option minimizes all on-screen desktop windows so you can actually access the icons on the desktop if you'd like, and not just view them as you do with Peek.

WHERE NEW MEETS OLD: METRO FEATURES YOU GET IN THE DESKTOP, TOO

While many users of traditional PCs—desktops, laptops, and other devices without touch screens—are likely wondering what good the Metro user experiences are to them, especially if they're committed to using old-school Windows applications like Office or Photoshop, it's worth remembering that Metro is, in fact, the underlying operating system and that it pervades (some might say *invades*) the desktop environment as well. So Metro isn't an all-or-nothing proposition. Indeed, even those firmly committed to the desktop will find themselves dealing with Metro experiences throughout the day.

This isn't as bad as it may seem. These experiences work just as well with your keyboard and mouse as they do with touch screens, for example, and they provide a fairly gentle way for recalcitrant desktop holdouts to dip their toes into the Metro waters, so to speak. As a result, these users become acclimated to the new way of doing things, and then perhaps make a future Windows tablet or other touch-based device purchase not just doable but even preferable.

▶ Remember, these Metro features are discussed further in Chapter 3.

OK, no promises. But you need to know how this stuff works, and at the very least, becoming proficient—and thus more efficient—with Metro is a key step toward mastering Windows 8.

Back

▶ The Back stack does not replace existing multitasking actions, such as using the Windows Flip (Alt + Tab) keyboard shortcut or the new Switcher interface, which is described shortly.

As part of the simplified multitasking model in Windows 8, users can access a smartphone-like Back experience (or Back stack) that provides a quick way to return to the most recently used app. And yes, this is part of the reason we describe the desktop as if it were an app (even though, technically, it's a bit more nuanced than that: The entire desktop is placed in the Back stack, not any of its individual Windows applications.

You can access the most recently used Metro app in the Back stack in the following manner:

> ▶ **Mouse:** Move the cursor to the top-left corner of the screen. A Back tip, in thumbnail form, will appear as shown in Figure 4-7, indicating the most recently used app. Click it to navigate to that app.

FIGURE 4-7: The Back tip is a thumbnail that indicates the previously used app in the Back stack.

> **TIP** You can right-click the Back tip to see other options related to snapping applications in a side-by-side display, which is described shortly.

▶ **Touch:** Swipe in from the left edge of the screen to navigate immediately to the previous app.

▶ **Keyboard:** You can't directly access Back using the keyboard, but you can still use Windows Flip (Alt + Tab) or the new Switcher interface (Winkey + Tab), described shortly, to access recently used apps.

▶ *You can swipe repeatedly to quickly navigate through every app in the Back stack.*

Start

In previous Windows versions dating back to Windows 95, the Start experience was centered completely on the Start menu. This menu was evolved over the years and expanded in functionality and usefulness fairly dramatically in subsequent Windows versions. So did the ways in which we accessed the Start experience: first via a software button called the Start button (later renamed Start orb) and then via a Windows key on PC keyboards.

In Windows 8, everything is changing yet again. The Start experience is now a full-screen Start screen, though if it helps you to think of it as a Start menu, there's some logic to that. And Start now acts as a toggle, which is another difference: Activate it from the desktop, or from a Metro-style app, and you'll navigate to the Start screen. But activate Start from the Start screen and you will return to the previously used app (including the desktop).

How you activate Start has changed, too. And while you can still use the Windows key on a keyboard to access the Start experience, the software Start button is gone. So there are some new ways of doing things.

Here's how you activate the Start experience from the Windows desktop:

▶ **Mouse:** As described earlier in the chapter, the Start button is gone, but you can still move the mouse cursor down to the same basic place on-screen— the lower-left corner—and the Start tip will appear. Click this thumbnail to activate Start and, in this case, navigate to the Start screen.

▶ **Keyboard:** Tap the Windows key (Winkey) on your keyboard or use the keyboard shortcut Ctrl + Esc.

▶ **Touch:** Touch users have two methods to activate Start. You can swipe in from the right side of the screen to display the Charms bar, and then tap the Start charm. Or, you can activate Switcher (described next) by swiping in from the left, and then quickly to the right; then tap the Start thumbnail.

▶ *You can mix and match, too. For example, type Winkey + C to display the Charms bar and then tap (or click) the Start charm. There are many other combinations, but you get the idea.*

> ► Remember: The desktop is conceptually just an app. So Switcher provides only a single entry for the entire desktop and its contained applications, not one for each Windows application.

> ► In Windows 7, Winkey + Tab triggered a unique task switcher called Windows Flip 3D. That action is no longer available in Windows 8.

Switcher

Windows 8 features a convenient and consistent new task-switching interface called Switcher that lets you switch between and manage running tasks, including Metro-style apps and the Windows desktop. While we introduced Switcher earlier in the chapter, there are a few additional details that may be of interest.

ACTIVATING SWITCHER

Here are the ways in which you can activate Switcher:

► **Keyboard:** This is, by far, the easiest way. Just tap Winkey + Tab to activate Switcher. You can hold down Winkey and repeatedly tap Tab to navigate through each of the various available apps. Just let go of Tab when you find the one to which you want to switch.

► **Mouse:** Move the mouse cursor to the upper-left corner of the screen to activate the Back experience as described previously. Then, move the mouse cursor down the left edge of the screen to activate Switcher and select the app to which you'd like switch.

Note that there is a subtle indication that the Switcher is waiting for you when you engage Back; as you can see in Figure 4-8, there are a few app thumbnail outlines barely visible down the left edge of the screen.

► **Touch:** This is the hardest one of all. You need to swipe in from the left side of the screen as if you are going to switch to the previously used app. When the previous app thumbnail appears under your finger, move back to the left until Switcher appears. If you do it just right, Switcher will actually dock on the screen and stay there until you do something.

FIGURE 4-8: Look closely, and you'll see a hint that Switcher is available.

ADVANCED SWITCHER USAGE

While Switcher is visible on the screen, either by being docked with touch or just by being made visible with the mouse, there are some additional capabilities you can use. These include the following:

▶ **Removing an app from the Back stack:** If you'd like to remove a Metro-style app from the Back stack—effectively closing or quitting it—you can do so by dragging its thumbnail out of Switcher and down to the bottom of the screen. You can do this with the mouse or touch input types.

▶ *This will not work with Start or the desktop, only Metro-style apps.*

> **NOTE** You can also remove apps from the Back stack by right-clicking and choosing Close.

▶ **Snapping an app for use in side-by-side mode:** As described next, Windows 8 supports a unique side-by-side screen sharing mode called Snap that lets you use two apps next to each other on-screen. There are a few different ways to enable this functionality, as you'll see, but if you'd like to snap a previous app that's visible in the Switcher to a side of the screen alongside the current app (or desktop), you can right-click it in the Switcher and choose either Snap left or Snap right, as shown in Figure 4-9.

FIGURE 4-9: A power user method for snapping secondary apps to a side of the screen

Don't worry if the notion of side-by-side apps is confusing. That's right: Side-by-side is our next topic.

SWITCHER VS. WINDOWS FLIP

With all this new task switching goodness, you may be thinking that good old Windows Flip—the familiar Alt + Tab task switcher that dates back decades—is on life support in Windows 8. Not so fast. As it turns out, Windows Flip has some important advantages over Switcher, particularly for those who will be spending a lot of time in the desktop. And since Microsoft sees Metro and the desktop coexisting for the foreseeable future, we think it's fair to say that Windows Flip has some life left in it indeed.

The key advantage of this interface is that it differentiates between multiple desktop applications as well as individual Metro-style apps. So if you have Microsoft Word and File Explorer windows open on the desktop, and Mail and Calendar open in the Metro runtime environment, and then engage Windows Flip, you'll see five items: Word, Explorer, Mail, Calendar, and Desktop. But in Switcher, you'll see just three: Mail, Calendar, and Start. (This assumes you activate Switcher from the desktop.) There are no desktop applications—or even the desktop itself—available in Switcher if you use it from the desktop.

This means that Switcher isn't of use to individual desktop applications at all, especially if you activate it while using the desktop. So Windows Flip will remain a frequently used tool for all desktop users in Windows 8.

That said, it is a bit curious that Start doesn't appear in the Windows Flip task list. But keyboard users simply need to use the Windows key instead.

Snap: Side-by-Side Apps

The new Metro environment in Windows 8 is designed for apps that run full screen, similar to how smartphone and tablet device apps work. But Windows 8 kicks things up a notch by offering a special side-by-side mode in which two apps can share the screen, albeit in limited ways. And one of those two apps can be the desktop, which is why we're discussing it here.

▶ Yes, we're sure this name is an allusion to the Aero Snap window docking feature that debuted in Windows 7 and is still available on the Windows 8 desktop.

Sadly, side-by-side display sharing is not particularly customizable. You can have just two apps, and the one that is considered the primary app takes up about two-thirds of the available on-screen real estate. Meanwhile, the secondary app is stuck with just one-third, roughly, of the available space. Apps that are side by side in this fashion are said to snap into place.

Confused? A picture will make things clearer. Consider Figure 4-10, in which Microsoft's Calendar (Metro-style) app is snapped next to the Windows desktop.

That configuration in the previous figure is one of two possible ways in which a snapped, or secondary, app can be snapped in place next to another app. The other, of course, has the snapped app placed on the right side of the screen, as shown in Figure 4-11. Which side you use is a matter of taste.

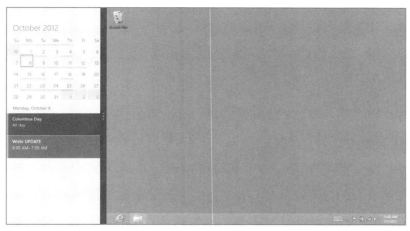

FIGURE 4-10: You can snap Metro-style apps next to the desktop.

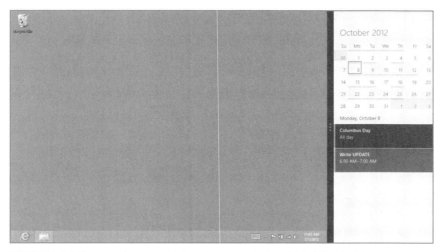

FIGURE 4-11: You can also snap Metro-style apps to the right of the desktop.

▶ So why would you ever want to snap the desktop? The best reason we've seen is to monitor a download that's occurring in a desktop-based web browser. But frankly, it's not very useful otherwise.

Conversely, it's also possible for the Windows desktop to be the snapped, or secondary, app. However, when you enable this view, as in Figure 4-12, you'll notice that the snapped desktop only displays thumbnails of the available open windows and isn't too useful.

FIGURE 4-12: You can even snap the desktop.

> **NOTE**   One interface you *can't* snap is the Start screen. And to be honest, such a capability would be truly useful, since it could provide a snapped list of tiles with live updates. Maybe in Windows 9.

USING SNAP TO PLACE APPS SIDE BY SIDE ON THE DESKTOP

The new side-by-side app mode can be enabled in various ways, but here are some instructions for the common input types. In each case, it's best to launch the app you intend to use in the secondary, or snapped, mode first and then launch the app you intend to use as the primary app. Then you can use one of the following techniques to enable the snap mode:

▶ **Mouse:** Move the mouse cursor to the upper-left corner of the screen to display the Back thumbnail. Then, while holding down the mouse button, drag the thumbnail downward. It will turn into a larger, floating thumbnail, as shown in Figure 4-13, and the side-by-side Snap bar will appear.

Release the mouse button to snap the app into the Snap area on the left.

▶ **Touch:** Swipe in from the left edge of the screen. As you do so, the previous app in the Back stack will appear as a thumbnail image under your finger. Stop moving your finger and the side-by-side Snap bar will appear. When it does, release your hold on the screen and the secondary app will snap in place.

FIGURE 4-13: You can drag a previous app off Back or Switcher and then snap it in place alongside the desktop or another primary app.

> While there is no keyboard-based shortcut for enabling side-by-side mode, as you'll discover next, there are keyboard shortcuts for modifying the presentation of side-by-side apps.

CUSTOMIZING SIDE-BY-SIDE MODE

Once you've got two apps snapped into position in side-by-side mode, you can further customize the display, albeit in fairly limited ways. Here are the options available at your disposal:

▶ **Snap to the right instead:** While many are happy to snap a secondary app to the left side of the screen, some will prefer the snapped app to appear on the right. While performing the snap operation, simply drag the app thumbnail to the right side of the screen instead of down and to the left.

If you've already snapped an app to the left side of the screen and would like it to appear on the right side instead, the easiest way to do so is via a mouse: Just move the mouse cursor to the top edge of the snapped app, and when the cursor changes into a small hand, grab the app and then drag it to the right side of the screen. With a keyboard, you may find it easier to simply close the snapped app, as described shortly, and just redo the snap action and place it on the right instead. But the convoluted way in which you can do this goes like so: Press Winkey + . (period) three times to snap the secondary app to the right. Then press Alt + Tab (or Winkey + D) to return the desktop to the primary display area.

▶ **Swap the snapped and primary apps:** Press Winkey + J to swap the snapped (secondary) and primary apps on-screen. Or via touch or mouse, simply drag the Snap bar toward the other side of the screen, letting go before you hit the screen edge.

▶ **Close the snapped app:** If a secondary app is snapped on the left, press Winkey + Shift + . (period) to close the snapped app. Otherwise, press Winkey + . (period). You can close the snapped app via touch or mouse by dragging the Snap bar to the closest screen edge.

> **NOTE** Side-by-side screen sharing is more interesting for those who wish to stick with Metro-style apps, and we cover this feature in Chapter 3 as well as a result. But it's worth mentioning here, because the desktop is considered an app, too, and can participate in this task management solution. Certainly, some apps will work well in this snapped mode, even when used in tandem with the desktop.

Charms

In Windows 8, Microsoft exposes many system-level services through a new user experience called Charms. These Charms are accessible via a bar that appears on the right edge of the screen in a manner that is consistent across every user experience in Windows 8, including the Start screen, all Metro-style apps, and the desktop. This can be seen in Figure 4-14.

> **CROSSREF** Charms are central to using and understanding Windows 8, so we cover them as needed throughout this book. The main discussion about this experience, however, can be found in Chapter 3.

OPENING THE CHARMS BAR

You can access the Charms bar in a variety of ways, and as a top-level interface in Windows 8, it has simple triggers for all the major input types:

▶ **Mouse:** Move the mouse cursor into the lower-right corner of the screen. As the cursor hits against the natural edge of the screen, a transparent preview of the Charms bar appears, as shown in Figure 4-15.

FIGURE 4-14: The Charms bar is a system-wide user experience that works in the Start screen, Metro-style apps, and the desktop. When the Charms bar displays, an overlay for the time and date also appears.

FIGURE 4-15: A preview of the Charms bar appears when you mouse into one of the screen's rightmost corners.

▶ Mouse-based Charms access also works from the top-right corner of the screen. But when the transparent preview of the Charms appears, you must move down the right edge of the screen to fully activate the Charms bar.

To fully enable the Charms, move up the right side of the screen. The Charms bar will appear normally and you can access the various options normally.

▶ **Keyboard:** To enable the Charms bar from the keyboard, type Winkey + C.

▶ **Touch:** With a multi-touch display, you can swipe in from the right edge of the screen to enable the Charms bar.

▶ This is perhaps the simplest way to enable the Charms, and if you remember just one Windows 8 keyboard shortcut, this should be it.

> **NOTE** Why is the Charms preview shown here? Microsoft realized that many users would move the mouse cursor near the right edge of the screen for a variety of reasons, such as to access the Peek functionality or to click an application's scroll bar. So the Charms bar appears in preview mode first. If the user doesn't move the mouse cursor along the right edge of the screen when this preview appears, the Charms will disappear and you can continue doing whatever it is you were doing.

ACCESSING CHARMS FEATURES

Once you've displayed the Charms bar, you can then access the various Charms and perform system-wide or context-sensitive actions. Some of the more common actions you may access from this interface include Settings, Search—by which you can find desktop applications (as well as Metro apps and PC Settings and Control Panels)—and Devices, which helps you interact with various hardware devices, including secondary displays, removable storage devices like hard drives and USB memory devices, and the like. These functions are all discussed later in this chapter.

Of the remaining two Charms, one, Share, does not work with the desktop or Windows applications at all. Instead, the Share charm is aimed solely at Metro-style apps, which use this system capability to share information with other apps. The other remaining Charm, the Start icon, can be used as a toggle for the Start screen.

How you access these Charms varies by input device. With the mouse, you simply navigate the mouse cursor to the appropriate Charm and click it once. Via touch, it's a simple tap. And if you access the Charms bar from the keyboard, you can use the arrow keys to navigate around and then press Enter (or Space) to activate a Charm.

Settings

While Windows 8 offers the same Screen Resolution and Personalize context menus from the desktop as did its predecessor, Windows 7, Windows 8 also expands on this notion of desktop settings by making some of these features available via a handy new Metro-based Settings interface as well. This feature is accessed via the Charms bar, as noted previously. But if you're a keyboard maven, you can also access Settings from the desktop (or from any Metro-style experience) more quickly by tapping Winkey + I.

However you choose to enable it, the Settings pane for the desktop should resemble Figure 4-16.

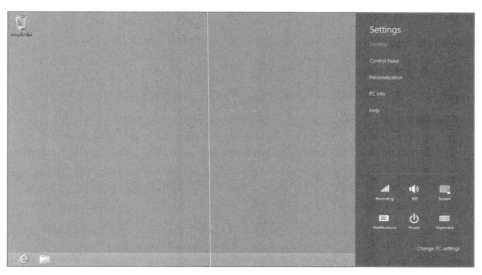

FIGURE 4-16: The Settings user experience

The following options are available:

- **Control Panel:** Opens the classic Control Panel interface, which is largely unchanged from Windows 7. Note that many—but not all—system configuration options can now be accessed from the new Metro-style PC Settings interface instead. This interface is described in Chapters 3 and 5, the latter of which concerns system customization.

- **Personalization:** Opens the Personalization control panel, which works much like the version from Windows 7, while offering a few new or different options, some as a result of the move away from Aero on the desktop. We discuss this interface in Chapter 5.

- **PC Info:** This opens the System control panel, which is also largely unchanged since Windows 7. From this interface, you can access your PC's Windows Experience Index score, Device Manager, Remote Settings, System Protection, Advanced System Settings, and other useful configurations.

- **Help:** This option launches Windows Help and Support, Microsoft's attempt at in-product documentation. They try.

While the top part of the Settings pane is context-sensitive and will change depending on what you're viewing on-screen, this interface is also a system-wide interface. So the Settings pane also provides various system settings, which always appear near the bottom of the pane. We discuss these settings in Chapter 3.

▶ You can also access Control Panel from the power user tasks menu that appears when you mouse into the lower-left corner of the screen to display the Start tip and right-click.

▶ You can also access Personalization by right-clicking on a blank area of the desktop and choosing Personalization from the context menu that appears.

▶ You can access Windows Help and Support more quickly by pressing F1 from anywhere in the desktop user interface.

Notifications

Windows 8 supports new kinds of system and app notifications, both of which work consistently in the Metro and desktop environments. And, as we're sure you must suspect by now, these notifications are of course Metro-based experiences. So they appear as an overlay of sorts over the screen, whether you're looking at the Start screen, a Metro-style app, or, yes, the desktop.

The new Windows 8 notifications are also discussed in Chapter 3—along with a ton of other Metro user experiences—but let's see how they interact with the desktop. There are two key notification types to consider: Full-screen, modal notifications and notification *toasts*, small floating windows that don't prevent you from getting other work done.

▶ Okay, they're not technically modal in that you can, in fact, interact with the underlying screen if you really want to. But the full-screen notifications do make it hard to do so.

An example of a full-screen notification is shown in Figure 4-17. These notifications are modal in the sense that they must be addressed before you can move on. You'll see this type of notification when something important happens, such as when the new SmartScreen security feature suspects you're downloading a malicious file and wants you to think twice before proceeding.

FIGURE 4-17: A full-screen notification

Notification toasts are far more subtle. They appear as small floating windows near the top right of the screen, as shown in Figure 4-18. If you don't address this kind of notification, it will simply disappear.

FIGURE 4-18: A notification toast

Notification toasts appear for all kinds of reasons, including when you install a new application that can change file associations, when you plug in a USB-based storage device, and so on. Also, many Metro-style apps, like Mail, Calendar, and Messaging, utilize these types of notifications. For example, Mail can be configured to notify you each time a new e-mail arrives.

MANAGING FILES AND FOLDERS

As with previous versions of Windows, you use the desktop interface to interact with the filesystem and manage files and folders. This occurs, as before, via the File Explorer interface, which has been nicely updated in Windows 8 with a new, ribbon-based design similar to that used by Microsoft Office and Windows applications, such as Paint and WordPad and a new Metro-like (but *not* Metro-based) window design. This section examines the new File Explorer and the improvements to the ways in which you interact with files and folders in Windows 8.

▶ File Explorer was called Windows Explorer in previous Windows versions.

Understanding the New File Explorer

File Explorer debuted (as Windows Explorer) in Windows 95, but Windows has of course always had a graphical interface for managing files and folders. In fact, even the first version of Windows, dating all the way back to 1985, included a basic file manager application called MS-DOS Executive.

While File Explorer was evolved over previous Windows versions, it's been thoroughly overhauled with a new, Metro-like and ribbon-based UI in Windows 8, and as a result, this version is the best yet. But don't take our word for it. Let's compare the Windows 8 version of Explorer to Windows Explorer from Windows 7 to better understand what's changed.

First, take a look at Windows 7. As you can see in Figure 4-19, this version of File Explorer is streamlined, with most advanced options hidden under the Organize command bar item.

In Windows 8, Explorer drops the Aero glass and adopts the new ribbon-based UI, replacing the previous version's command bar with a more powerful but denser interface that puts all the options you'll ever need—and then some—right up front. Fortunately, thanks to feedback during the Windows 8 prerelease cycle, Microsoft opted to hide the ribbon by default. So the Explorer UI you'll probably see the first time you use this application will likely resemble the one shown in Figure 4-20.

FIGURE 4-19: Explorer from Windows 7

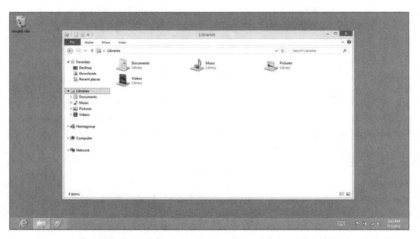

FIGURE 4-20: The Windows 8 Explorer has a ribbon UI, but it's hidden by default.

To expand the ribbon and see more commands, click the Expand the Ribbon control in the top-right corner of the window. (It resembles a downward-pointing arrow. You can also type Ctrl + F1.) When you expand the ribbon UI, File Explorer will resemble Figure 4-21.

Interestingly, what you see here only represents a subset of the commands that are available in the new File Explorer. And that's because the ribbon has several tabs, and only one of them—Home, in this case—is displayed at a time. You can click the other two tabs that are always available, Share and View, to see the commands they provide.

▶ Other tabs are possible. For example, if you select an image file, you'll see a Manage: Picture Tools tab appear. Select a disk and Drive: Disk Tools appears.

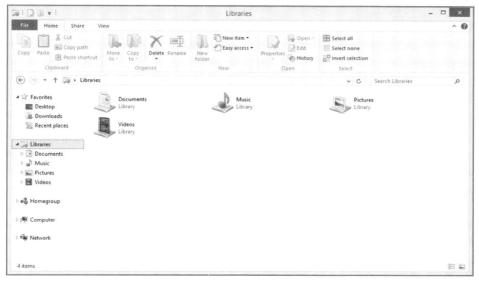

FIGURE 4-21: With the ribbon displayed, far more commands are readily available.

While it would be overly pedantic to step through every single command in this interface—we do have certain assumptions about your capabilities, after all—a short discussion of each of the new default tabs is perhaps in order.

First, there's a tab that's not a tab: The colored File tab is really a button that displays the new File menu. Shown in Figure 4-22, this menu provides several useful options, including the ability to open a new window, ideal for side-by-side file copying, open a command prompt or PowerShell window, delete the history in your recent places and address bar history lists, and access help.

▶ You can also access Explorer's Frequent Places list from this menu. This list is otherwise available via the File Explorer taskbar button.

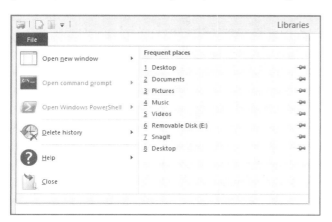

FIGURE 4-22: The new File Explorer File menu

▶ You can jump quickly to the Home tab from another Explorer tab by tapping Alt + H.

▶ Need to access Share quickly? Type Alt + S.

▶ The View tab can be displayed by typing Alt + V.

Next, the Home tab includes the most commonly needed commands related to files and folders, and for the most part, this is the obvious place to start if you're a heavy mouse user and like to click on icons to initiate actions, such as Move to, Copy to, and Rename.

The Share tab contains commands related to sharing, of course, and for this reason it's a location you most likely won't be using very often.

The View tab, conversely, contains a number of commands we wish were more easily accessible, including the various icon sizes—Extra Large Icons, Large Icons, Medium Icons, Small Icons, List, Tiles, Details, and Content—and the various grouping options. It's perhaps not coincidental that File Explorer has a miniature set of buttons in the status bar in the lower-right corner of the window that lets you toggle between two of the most common icon sizes, Details and Large Icons.

NOTE   If you enjoy creating your own libraries, Windows 8 does have a new feature where you can customize a library's icon to any icon in the system, offering a much more personalized look.

Put simply, the File Explorer ribbon is something that new users should leave displayed until they're comfortable with the new interface. But power users will likely want to keep it hidden and enjoy the simpler interface afforded by this configuration.

NOTE   Hidden in the upper-left corner of the File Explorer window is a new Quick Access Toolbar, which can be customized with the commands you need most often. That's ideal for power users who want to hide the ribbon but also want access to a handful of useful commands.

OK, it's time to see what you can really do with this thing. While most of the behaviors you'll see in File Explorer are the same as with previous Windows versions, there have been some key changes and improvements as well. In keeping with the focus of this book, we'll assume that you understand the basics, and how things used to work, and highlight only these new features.

Working with Files

While we await a future in which the data we work with is managed for us automatically via some cloud-based mechanism, the reality of today is that we work with files regularly. These include documents related to work, such as Word documents, Power-Point presentations, and Excel spreadsheets, as well as photo files, music files, video files, and many others. Windows 8, like all previous versions, includes all the basic file operations one might expect—copy, move, rename, delete, and so on—and many of these have been improved nicely in this release.

COPYING AND MOVING FILES

Microsoft has significantly updated the file copy and move experience in Windows 8, making it both faster and easier to manage. If you're familiar with how this works in Windows 7 and older Windows versions, you know that each file and/or move operation you begin creates its own file or move window, and that each subsequent operation slows everything down to an eventual crawl. The multi-window file copy/move experience in Windows 7 can be seen in Figure 4-23.

So how does one improve on a cluttered, slow experience? Simple: Make it streamlined and faster. And that's exactly what's happened in Windows 8. Now, file copies and moves all occur in a single window in which you can pause any copy or move processes if you'd like to give precedence to another operation. This can be seen in Figure 4-24

FIGURE 4-23: In older Windows versions, multiple file copies (and moves) resulted in slower performance and required multiple windows.

FIGURE 4-24: The new file copy/move experience in Windows 8

You can also click the More Details button to display a new detailed view of the file copy/move experience that shows the speed of the operation, how much data is left to transfer, and so on. This More Details view can be seen in Figure 4-25.

FIGURE 4-25: Detail view of the new file copy/move experience

Under the hood, things have improved dramatically, and file copies and moves occur much more quickly than before, even when you have multiple file operations going at once.

But what about when things go wrong? One of the most common things that can happen during a file copy or move operation is that one or more of the files involved in the operation already exists in the destination folder. So Windows has always offered up a dialog or window in these situations, asking the user what to do.

In Windows 7, Microsoft improved what it calls Explorer's "confliction resolution" logic to pretty good effect. But in Windows 8, it's done so again, offering its most obvious interface yet. This is actually quite important, because when you see the window shown in Figure 4-26 in Windows 7, it's not always clear which option you should choose.

Things are considerably clearer in Windows 8. Now, when a file conflict occurs, you see the window shown in Figure 4-27. The Replace or Skip Files window lets you choose which files have precedence globally or choose them on a file-by-file basis.

▶ You can find out more about each of the files in the conflict windows by mousing over them. A small tooltip will appear, displaying its path. Want to view the file? Just double-click it. Yes, really.

FIGURE 4-26: Windows 7 made it somewhat difficult to resolve file copy and move conflicts.

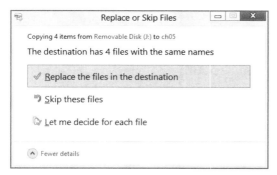

FIGURE 4-27: In Windows 8, file copy/move conflicts are more easily resolved.

RENAMING FILES

While the act of renaming a file is simple enough and hasn't changed markedly since Windows 7, there is one neat aspect to multi-file renaming that's worth mentioning, since so few are aware of it. And that's that Windows 8 supports a cool way of renaming multiple files in a folder.

To recap, you can rename an individual file by selecting it and pressing F2, by selecting it and then clicking it again with the mouse, or via touch by selecting it and then tapping it again. When a file is in rename mode, its name is highlighted as shown in Figure 4-28. If you start typing now, you will replace the current name with whatever you type.

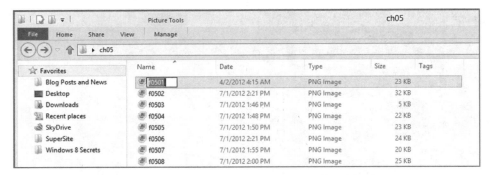

FIGURE 4-28: When a file is in rename mode, its name appears highlighted.

► This renaming trick works with folders, too, not just files.

Normally, you hit Enter when you're done renaming a file. But if you want to move to the next file and rename that, tap Tab instead. This will put the next file in rename mode, allowing you to instantly rename it next. You can keep tapping Tab, instead of Enter, to rename subsequent files in the current folder.

PIN TO START

In Windows 7, Microsoft allowed us to pin application shortcuts to the taskbar for the first time, providing a new way to launch applications. (Previously, you could only pin applications to the Start menu.) And starting with Internet Explorer 9, Microsoft provided this same capability to web apps, letting sites like Hotmail, SkyDrive, Amazon.com, *The New York Times*, and many others work like pseudo-applications, pinned to the taskbar or Start menu for quick access.

This is very useful because most Windows users don't spend all day using just Windows applications. They also use a lot of popular web apps and services. And by mixing and matching shortcuts for all of these things side by side on the taskbar, as shown in Figure 4-29, users can organize their workspace in a way that mimics what they're really doing all day long.

FIGURE 4-29: You can mix desktop application and web app shortcuts on the taskbar in Windows 7 and 8.

These capabilities carry forward in Windows 8, and you can pin applications and web apps (via Internet Explorer 10, now) to the taskbar just as you did before, using exactly the same methods. But as you know, Microsoft is also replacing the Start menu with the new Start screen in Windows 8, and that interface is the primary place for you to manage and launch the apps you use most frequently. As discussed in Chapter 3, you can easily pin new Metro-style apps to the Windows 8 Start screen. Can you do the same for classic, Windows desktop applications like Microsoft Word, Adobe Photoshop, and the like?

Yes, you can.

There are two basic interfaces for accomplishing this. You can use the new system-wide search functionality that is available in Windows 8, as described later in this chapter. Or you can do so directly from File Explorer.

Here's the best part. This functionality works for applications, as you'd expect. But it also works for libraries and folders. And you can pin favorite web apps and sites via Internet Explorer 10, though we cover that in Chapter 7.

To pin a folder or library to the Start screen, navigate to the location's container in File Explorer, right-click it, and choose Pin to Start as shown in Figure 4-30.

FIGURE 4-30: You can pin applications to the Metro-style Start screen from the desktop environment.

As with anything else that's pinned to the Start screen, the folder or library is placed at the end of the Start screen. From there, you can position it as needed. (This functionality is discussed in Chapter 3 and Chapter 5.)

Using External Storage

Windows 8 works with external storage devices, such as USB-based hard drives and memory sticks, in a manner that is very similar to Windows 7. That said, the user experience that appears the first time you plug such a device into your computer has

▶ You can also Pin to Start from the new Explorer ribbon. Just select the folder or library and then choose Easy Access and then Pin to Start from the Home tab of the ribbon.

changed in Windows 8, and is now a Metro-based notification rather than a dialog box or pop-up window as before.

The first time you plug in a USB storage device, you will see the Metro-style notification toast shown in Figure 4-31.

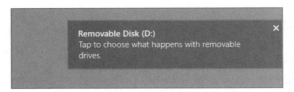

Removable Disk (D:)
Tap to choose what happens with removable drives.

FIGURE 4-31: A Metro-style notification toast appears the first time you plug in a USB storage device.

► Don't see an option for ReadyBoost? It's a technology that requires both the USB device and the PC's USB hardware to meet certain performance characteristics. So it won't always appear as a choice.

Tap the notification to choose what to do with these types of devices going forward. As you can see in Figure 4-32, the available choices can include using the device to speed up the PC with ReadyBoost, to back up File History (which is described in Chapter 11), to view the files with File Explorer, or to take no action. Choose wisely because this interface will never appear again, at least not automatically.

Removable Disk (D:)

Choose what to do with removable drives.

Configure this drive for backup
File History

Open folder to view files
File Explorer

Take no action

FIGURE 4-32: The choices you see here will vary according to the performance characteristics of your PC and the USB storage device.

► You can also configure AutoPlay options at any time, and reset them to their default values. To do so, use Start Search to query auto play, Settings.

Okay, you don't have to get it right the first time. If you want to change your choice later, you can. Just navigate to the Computer view in File Explorer, right-click the icon for an attached USB-based storage device and choose Open AutoPlay from the context menu that appears. You'll be provided with the same Metro-style experience shown earlier.

Using Disk Images

In Windows 8, Microsoft has added support for two very popular disc (and disk) image formats, ISO and VHD, allowing users to browse within these special files as if they were physical discs (or disks) connected to the PC.

If you're not familiar with these formats, a quick overview should get you up to speed. ISO is a disc image format in which the contents of an optical disc (CD, DVD, and the like) are packaged into a single archive file, generally with an .iso extension, which is similar to a ZIP file. You can then later burn this ISO file to disc, creating a copy of the original.

VHD, or virtual hard disk, files are created for Microsoft's virtualization solutions, including Hyper-V and Windows Virtual PC. These files represent a hard disk drive, and as you'll discover in Chapter 14, they are useful in a number of scenarios, such as testing operating systems and other software, for help desk support, and for software developers.

While Microsoft has used both ISO and VHD file formats to distribute evaluation and even final versions of Windows and other software in the past, it's never really formally supported these formats in Windows to any major degree. The one exception is ISO burning support: Starting with Windows 7, you can burn ISO files to disc natively with the integrated Windows Disc Image Burner utility. (This capability also exists in Windows 8, as you'd expect.) But you couldn't browse into them as you would with a physical disk.

Now you can.

Windows 8 automatically mounts both ISO and VHD files so that they become, in effect, part of the PC's filesystem, just as with any other attached storage device. For example, when you plug a USB hard drive into your PC, it may become the E: drive, or whatever. So it is with both ISO and VHD files: Simply by opening such a file—by double-clicking it with the mouse, say—it becomes part of the filesystem and immediately picks up the next available drive letter.

Let's see how this works.

USING AN ISO FILE WITH FILE EXPLORER

If you double-click on an ISO file in Windows 8, two things happen. First, a new Explorer window opens, letting you browse into the contents of the file as if it were a physical storage device. And second, a new virtual optical drive is mounted in the filesystem and given the next available drive letter. Both of these things can be seen in Figure 4-33.

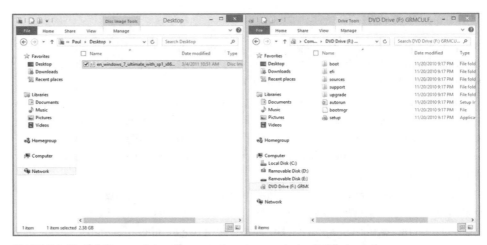

FIGURE 4-33: ISO files work just like any other storage device in Windows 8.

Because an ISO file works like physical storage, it can be used like any other storage device. You can navigate through its virtual directory structure using File Explorer, copy files out as needed, and even run applications contained within the file. This means, for example, that you no longer need to burn an ISO file to disc if you don't want to. Instead, you can just mount it in the filesystem and run whatever Setup or other applications it contains.

You may have noticed that an ISO file creates a new tab in Explorer when the file is mounted. This Disk Tools: Drive tab is of more use for other types of drives, but for an ISO file it's pretty much there to provide a way to eject—really, unmount—the ISO. This will remove the ISO from the filesystem, along with its drive letter.

USING A VHD FILE WITH FILE EXPLORER

VHD files work similarly to ISO files in Windows 8, and offer other unique virtualization-related capabilities. However, there is one subtle but important difference. Whereas an ISO file is treated as a removable disc when it is mounted, a VHD file is treated as a fixed hard disk.

When you double-click a VHD file in Windows 8, a new drive letter is added to Explorer, just as with an ISO file, but it appears as a fixed disk, not a removable disk. You can see this in Figure 4-34, where the VHD appears next to the PC's main storage device (which is typically a hard drive or SSD).

Okay, so you may be thinking: So what? The icon's different, but you can still navigate around in the VHD as you do with an ISO, and of course use all the standard file management actions you can with physical storage or ISO files. But there is an

▶ This is, in fact, the primary reason that Windows 8 offers this capability: It allows you to run the Setup application from an ISO file without first burning the file to disc.

▶ You can also mount an ISO file by right-clicking and choosing Mount from the context menu.

▶ Want to burn an ISO to disc? Right-click the file and choose Burn to disc.

important distinction to mounting a VHD vs. an ISO: With a VHD, you get the full
suite of Windows 8 disk utilities to work with.

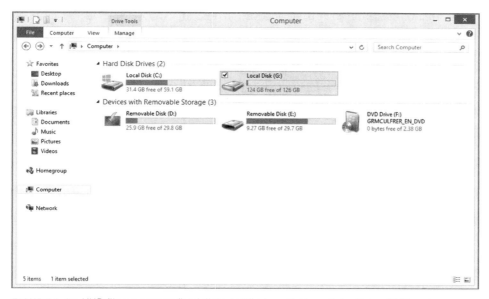

FIGURE 4-34: VHD files mount as fixed disks in Windows 8: Here, Drive G: is a VHD, not a
physical hard disk.

To see what this means, open File Explorer, navigate to the Computer view and
select the VHD. As you can see in Figure 4-35, the Disk Tools: Drive ribbon tab is now
fully enabled, providing access to advanced capabilities, such as BitLocker, disk
optimization and cleanup, format, and more.

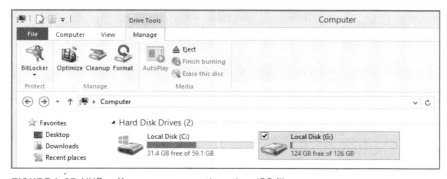

FIGURE 4-35: VHDs offer many more options than ISO files.

That said, you can still eject a mounted VHD just as you do with ISO: Right-click
and choose Eject, or select Eject from the Disk Tools: Drive tab in the Explorer ribbon.

MANAGING CLASSIC WINDOWS APPLICATIONS

While Windows does offer some basic applications and, in Windows 8, some new Metro-style apps as well, most Windows users will want to install a number of more full-featured Windows applications, such as Microsoft Office, as well. And while Microsoft is moving inexorably to a future of Metro-style apps, Windows 8 also works with traditional (one might say, "old-fashioned") Windows applications almost exactly like its predecessors. But there have been a handful of improvements in this area, so we'll discuss the changes in this section.

Configuring Desktop Applications

From a compatibility perspective, Windows 8 works just like Windows 7, though you can now use the built-in Application Compatibility tools to emulate Windows 7 if needed. But from our regular usage of Windows 8, it's pretty obvious that little in the way of compatibility work will be required, and if you have an application that works with Windows 7, it should work fine with Windows 8 as well.

Of course, with the move to a Metro-like user experience, Windows 8 users will need to deal with a few Metro-related nuances when it comes to working with classic desktop applications. And the big two, in our experience, involve file associations and the pinning of applications to the Metro-style Start screen.

DESKTOP APPLICATIONS AND FILE ASSOCIATIONS

Most Windows users are probably familiar with the notion of file associations, where various applications are known to be compatible with different file types and Windows provides an interface by which you can select which of those applications is used by default. Likewise, Windows has long supported an Open With functionality that lets you override the default file association on the fly and use a different application. This latter capability is usually accessed by a right-click context menu such as the one shown in Figure 4-36. Here, we're overriding the default file association for .jpg picture files and opening them with Windows Photo Viewer instead.

This functionality works as it did in Windows 7. But there is one major difference in this version of the OS: Windows 8 supports both new, Metro-style apps as well as classic Windows applications. So it's possible that the list of applications you could use to open a file will contain a mix of both Metro and desktop applications. And aside from Open With, which works as an Explorer extension as before, the interfaces you use to configure file associations are now Metro-based.

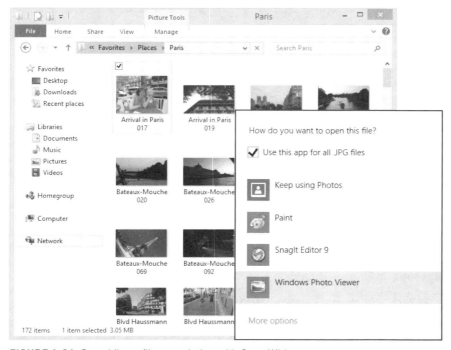

FIGURE 4-36: Overriding a file association with Open With

There are two key times you'll run into these new interfaces. When you install a new application that tries to associate itself with various file types, Windows 8 will display a notification toast, like the one in Figure 4-37, alerting you that there are new file association choices to make.

If you click the toast, you'll be presented with a window similar to the one shown in Figure 4-38. (It will, of course, vary according to the file type.) Here, you see a list of Metro-style apps and desktop applications that can open a certain file type. And if you always want to open that file type with a certain application, this is a great time to make sure that happens.

And be sure to click the See All link to expand the window, when available, to see more options.

But what if you're not quick enough and the toast disappears? Or perhaps you

FIGURE 4-37: The new file association notification toast

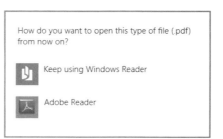

FIGURE 4-38: The new Metro-style file association interface

simply want to change the file association at a later time. In these situations, you can redisplay the new, Metro-style file association interface in a surprisingly old-fashioned way. Simply find a document or file type for which you want to change the associated application, right-click it, and choose Open With and then Choose Default Program. *Voila!*

HOW PIN TO START WORKS FOR NEW APPLICATION INSTALLS

We discussed how you can pin any application to the Metro-style Start screen earlier in the chapter. What you might not realize, however, is that Windows 8 automatically pins application shortcuts to the Start search for you. This happens when you install any classic desktop application, and depending on the application, it can get ugly.

Some applications are simple, standalone affairs, and thus won't pollute your Start screen with dozens of new icons. Install the desktop version of Google Chrome for example, and you'll find that a single new tile is added to the end of the Start screen as shown in Figure 4-39.

FIGURE 4-39: When you install a desktop application, one or more tiles are added to the Start screen.

When you install more complex applications like Microsoft Office or Visual Studio, you could be in for a surprise: Some will populate the Start screen with multiple tiles, many for applications you'll never (or perhaps rarely) need.

First, the bad news. You can't stop this from happening. And the reason is simple: Because the Start screen replaces the Start menu, it emulates the Start menu, and this is the same behavior from Windows 7 and previous Windows versions, just a bit more in your face.

We discuss the many ways in which you can personalize the Start screen (and other aspects of Windows 8) in Chapter 5, but it's wise to check this screen after each Windows application install to see which tiles were added. And then you can delete the ones you don't want and, if desired, reorganize those you do.

Remember that deleting tiles from the Start screen won't remove those applications. You can see this by opening the All Apps view by tapping Winkey (or Start) and then choosing All Apps from the Start screen app bar, which appears at the bottom of the screen. In this All Apps view, all of the installed applications are available and are even segregated in groups.

Switching Between Running Applications, Apps, and Open Windows

Even when Windows was just a simple graphical front end to MS-DOS, it supported means by which users could switch between various running applications, bringing one to the visual forefront and making it the current application. These task management capabilities have long worked with both keyboard and mouse, and even with touch, and include such well-understood tools as Windows Flip, the familiar Alt + Tab keyboard shortcut.

These capabilities largely come forward in Windows 8, which for the most part provides a superset of the multitasking and task-switching capabilities in Windows 7. But because Windows 8 includes the new Metro-style environment and full-screen Metro-style apps, there are a few differences.

First, it's now possible to task switch between Metro-style experiences (like the Start screen) and apps and the desktop. To do so, you can use Windows Flip as before, tapping Alt + Tab repeatedly until you find the application or app you want. In Windows 8, Windows Flip provides access to individual desktop applications, individual Metro-style apps, and the desktop, as shown in Figure 4-40.

You can also use the new Switcher user experience, which was discussed earlier in this chapter. Switcher is mouse- and touch-friendly, and provides a new way to switch between running tasks.

Finally, it's worth noting that the Windows Flip 3D task-switching interface that was available in both Windows Vista and 7 is no longer available in Windows 8. Now, the Windows Flip 3D keyboard shortcut—Winkey + Tab—activates Switcher instead. Sorry, Flip 3D fans.

▶ To display the toolbar-like control called the app bar at the bottom of the screen, right-click with the mouse, swipe up from the bottom of the screen with touch, or press Winkey + Z.

▶ What's missing from Windows Flip? The Start screen. If you wish to go there, use the new Start experience, the Windows key on your keyboard, or the Windows key button on your device.

▶ Switcher treats the desktop environment as a single app, and doesn't differentiate between individual desktop applications.

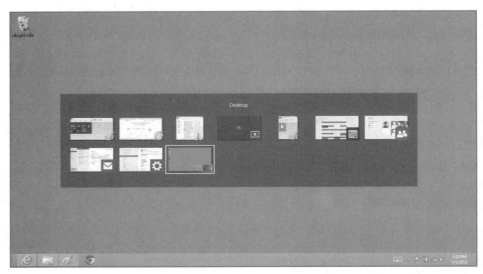

FIGURE 4-40: Windows Flip now works with both Metro-style app and desktop applications.

Using Task Manager

As with the task-switching functionality described earlier, Windows has also offered an interface called Task Manager that, among other things, provides a way for users to manually kill processes and applications. It's perhaps a sad statement that this interface is one of the most frequently used tools in Windows, but there you go. And in Windows 8, it's gotten its most impressive upgrade in years, with a simple new user interface that offers a superset of the functionality from previous versions.

Task Manager is accessible many ways, but the simplest is the tried-and-true method of right-clicking a blank area of the taskbar and choosing Task Manager from the context menu that appears. As you can see in Figure 4-41, the Windows 8 version of Task Manager offers a much simpler interface by default than its predecessors.

From this very simple interface, you can right-click an application and perform a number of actions, the most commonly used of which are End task (kill the application dead), Switch to (to bring that application to the forefront), and Open file location (which will display the application executable in File Explorer). But since End task is the single most common option, there's a button just for that: To kill any application immediately, select it in Task Manager and click End task.

While it's possible that the End task button and right-click menu will meet most users' needs, the power users in the audience are probably looking at the interface and thinking that there are many missing features. But that's only true because they're

▶ You can also access Task Manager from the power user tasks menu that appears when you activate the Start tip and right-click the Start tip thumbnail as described previously in this chapter.

hidden by default. Click More details and Task Manager will expand into a power user's dream come true. Not only are all the capabilities from the Windows 7 Task Manager present, but there are new capabilities here as well. The advanced Task Manager interface is shown in Figure 4-42.

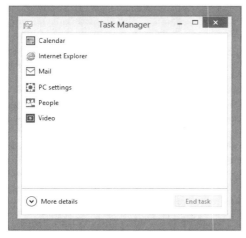

FIGURE 4-41: The simpler new Task Manager

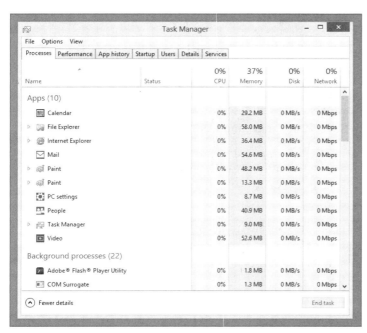

FIGURE 4-42: Task Manager's advanced UI

There's a lot going on here, but the highlights include:

▶ **Filtering for better application management:** Using the various columns available in the Processes tab—CPU, Memory, Disk, Network, and so on—you can filter and pivot the view of running processes using a visual heat map view and get a better idea of how individual applications are impacting system performance. By filtering on Memory, for example, you can see which applications are sucking up the most RAM.

▶ **Metro-style apps and desktop applications managed together:** As you may have noticed, Task Manager lets you manage both traditional desktop applications and new Metro-style apps. And you do so with the same interface and commands.

▶ **Manage startup applications:** Task Manager now provides an excellent new capability on its Startup tab that helps you manage which desktop applications—not Metro-style apps—auto-start when Windows boots.

▶ **Services:** Users who wished to manage system services previously needed to use the Services control panel. While this control panel is still available in Windows 8, Microsoft replicates it in the Task Manager as well. In retrospect, this is a fairly obvious place for this functionality.

Finding and Launching Applications with Search

Windows 7 includes a fantastic feature called Start Menu Search. To use it, you simply tap the Start button, type the term you're looking for, and the search results are returned right in the Start menu. It provides an amazingly handy way to quickly find an application you want without mousing around the labyrinthine Start menu submenus.

OK, fine. But with Windows 8 doing away with the Start menu, you may be wondering how you can accomplish the same feat in the new operating system version.

Surprise: It works exactly the same way.

That is, if you're using the desktop environment and would like to find and then run an application, just tap the Windows key on your keyboard (or otherwise return to the Start screen) and start typing. Instead of a Start menu–based search, you'll see the new full-screen Search experience, now called Start Search, as shown in Figure 4-43. And it's far more powerful than the old Start Menu Search.

This new Search experience now provides a filter capability where it returns both traditional Windows applications and Metro-style apps by default. But you can use

---

Marginal notes:

▶ Try not to micro-manage Metro-style apps. Unless one is hanging, there's little reason to kill it from Task Manager. Windows 8 will automatically close Metro-style apps when needed.

▶ Metro-style apps cannot auto-start at boot time.

▶ You can also trigger app search by pressing Winkey + Q.

the various items in the Search pane on the right to change the search to Settings (and control panels), Files (documents and other files), and, interestingly, within Metro-style apps that support this functionality.

Keep typing to refine the search. When you see the application (or app) you want, simply click (or tap, or select) it. If it's a desktop application, the view will switch back to the desktop and the selected application will launch immediately.

Knowing that Start Search now works for settings, files, and apps, you'll probably use it more than ever. But even if a desktop application search is all you need, you can rest easy knowing that one of Windows 7's best features has carried forward to Windows 8.

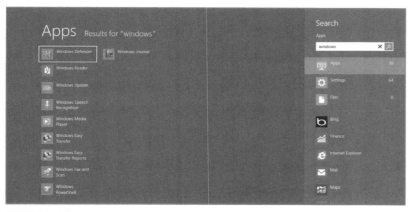

FIGURE 4-43: The new Windows 8 Search experience

▶ If you know the type of search you wish to perform, you can use different keyboard shortcuts. Winkey + F works for file searches. And Winkey + W will jump right to settings search. Check the appendix for a full list of Windows key keyboard shortcuts.

TO THE CLOUD: USING THE SKYDRIVE DESKTOP APP

While Microsoft built SkyDrive support into the Metro environment, providing File Picker-based access to the files on that cloud service, as well as integrated setting sync for those who want it, there is one crucial bit missing for desktop users: you can't natively navigate your SkyDrive storage using File Explorer.

Fortunately, you can overcome this issue by downloading a SkyDrive desktop application that integrates your SkyDrive storage with File Explorer, providing a libraries-like interface for exploring SkyDrive, copying and moving files to and from this cloud storage service, and syncing those files with your PC.

▶ The SkyDrive desktop application works in Windows Vista and 7 as well.

Shown in Figure 4-44, the SkyDrive application integrates with File Explorer and also lets you upload large files (up to 2 GB in size) to the service, which isn't possible through the normal web interface. And even more exciting, it provides a unique

Remote Fetch functionality that lets you access files on remote PCs through the SkyDrive web interface.

The SkyDrive application and Remote Fetch aren't really features of Windows 8, per se, so we won't waste too much space on them here. But you should know that this application is available, since this functionality will make your Windows 8 experiences even richer.

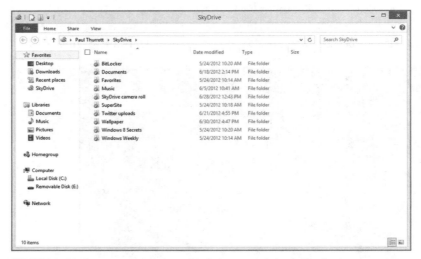

FIGURE 4-44: Access and sync your SkyDrive storage from File Explorer.

SUMMARY

While Microsoft is very clearly heading to a future in which increasingly sophisticated and full-featured versions of the Metro user experience will eventually squeeze out the classic Windows desktop, we're a long way from that future. And honestly, Metro and the desktop will coexist for the foreseeable future, thanks to the over one billion PCs out there still running classic Windows applications and the vast depth of experience that users have with this environment.

Fortunately, Microsoft hasn't left desktop users in the lurch with Windows 8. This version of Microsoft's client OS includes deep integration with new core Metro user experiences, and many desktop-related improvements like a new File Explorer, a new Task Manager, a new file copy and move experience, and more. So even if you spend most of your day in the desktop, Windows 8 will be a useful and desirable upgrade.

CHAPTER 5

Make It Yours: Personalizing Windows 8

IN THIS CHAPTER

▶ **Customizing the lock screen**

▶ **Customizing the Start screen**

▶ **Customizing app tiles and tile groups**

▶ **Customizing user account pictures and other settings**

▶ **Customizing settings and settings sync**

▶ **Customizing the desktop**

▶ **Using a multi-monitor setup more efficiently**

▶ **Using Libraries with SkyDrive**

▶ **Easing the transition between Metro and the desktop**

▶ **Booting (almost) directly to the desktop**

With its brand-new Metro interface, you won't be surprised to discover that there are new ways in which to customize Windows 8 to work the way you want it to. Aside from the app-specific tweaks we discuss throughout this book, Windows 8 provides an entirely new PC Settings interface for customizing many Metro- and system-level features; new personalization features for the lock screen, Start screen, and app tiles; and more.

And customizing Windows 8 is not just about Metro. As with previous versions of Windows, this OS also provides a number of ways in which you can customize the Windows desktop, including useful new multi-monitor capabilities that will be valuable in a number of usage scenarios, especially for those who pick up a new Windows 8 (or RT) tablet and decide to dock it to a larger display—and a keyboard and mouse—at home or at work.

Rounding out the Windows 8 customization capabilities are a handful of ways in which you can make the Metro and desktop environments interact a bit more seamlessly with each other. Ultimately, the goal here is to help you make Windows 8 work the way you want it to.

CUSTOMIZING METRO

When it comes to customizing the Metro user experience, you'll be spending much, but not all, of your time in the new PC Settings, a Metro-based interface that partially replaces—augments, really—the old Control Panel interface from older Windows versions.

The easiest way to access PC Settings will depend on the type of PC or device you're using and whether you prefer to use the keyboard, mouse, or touch screen.

▶ **Keyboard:** Those who prefer keyboard shortcuts should remember the Win-key + I shortcut, which displays the Settings pane from anywhere in Windows 8. This pane, shown in Figure 5-1, provides two areas: a top area that is context-sensitive to the experience—Start screen, desktop, or Metro-style app—you're currently viewing and a bottom area that is global, and thus the same everywhere. That is, the top area will look different depending on what you're doing at the time, whereas the bottom area will always look the same.

FIGURE 5-1: The Settings pane

Here, you're concerned with the bottom area. Below the grid of system icons, you'll see a link titled Change PC settings. Select that to access PC Settings.

▶ **Mouse and touch:** Those with a touch screen, or those who prefer to the use the mouse, will find that accessing the Charms bar, as shown in Figure 5-2, and then Settings, will be the easiest route. Then, from Settings, click the link Change PC settings.

FIGURE 5-2: You can get to Settings and then PC Settings from the Charms bar.

Accessing the Charms bar, of course, varies a bit between the two interfaces. For touch, simply swipe in from the right edge of the screen. With a mouse, you need to move the mouse cursor into the upper- or lower-right corner of the screen and then move the cursor along the right edge of the screen toward the center-right edge of the screen; as you do, the Charms bar will appear.

However you access it, the PC Settings interface should resemble Figure 5-3.

OK, got your bearings? Good; let's go customize the Metro interfaces in Windows 8!

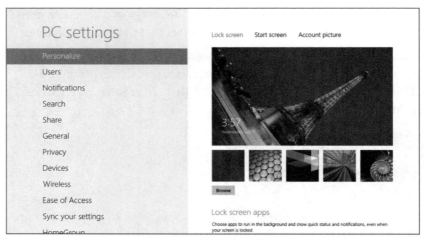

FIGURE 5-3: PC Settings

Customizing the Lock Screen

In Windows 8, the lock screen has taken on renewed importance and it now works much like the lock screen on Windows Phone handsets. This is by design: While users of traditional PCs will be a tad uninterested in the lock screen, the success of Windows 8 hinges in part on a new generation of iPad-like tablets and other nontraditional devices. And on these machines, the lock screen can behave as a nice "glance and go" front end to the time and date and your daily activities, with a favorite photo as the backdrop.

The lock screen is customized in PC Settings, Personalize, Lock screen. Since this is the default view in PC Settings, you won't have to do much navigating unless you've previously used PC Settings for some other purpose.

There are three basic lock screen features you can customize in PC Settings: the background picture, which apps can run in the background while the PC is locked and provide simple status updates via the lock screen, and which app can run in the background while the PC is locked and provide detailed status updates.

▶ **Background picture:** If you click or tap the Browse button, you can use a standard Metro-style File Picker interface to find a favorite photo and use that as the lock screen's background. If you're not familiar with this interface, shown in Figure 5-4, note that it can be used to find pictures not just on your local PC, but also via an online service for which you've installed a compatible app. For example, installing the SkyDrive app lets you navigate your SkyDrive-based storage as well.

FIGURE 5-4: With the File Picker, you can find the perfect lock screen background image.

▶ **Lock screen apps with basic status updates:** The lock screen can be configured with up to seven notification icons that provide simple status updates from your favorite apps. Not all Metro-style apps support this functionality, so you can tap an empty square (denoted by the "+" sign) to see which apps are available, as shown in Figure 5-5.

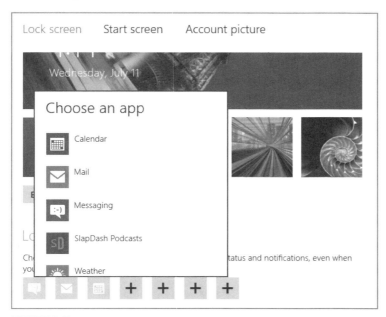

FIGURE 5-5: Choosing apps that can run in the background while your PC is locked and provide you with very simple status updates

Generally speaking, it makes sense to configure icons for apps like Mail, which will show you how many new e-mail messages you've received, and Messaging, which will likewise show you how many instant messages you've missed.

▶ **Lock screen app with detailed status updates:** While the seven notification icons noted previously are somewhat useful, Windows 8 also provides for a single app to provide you with more detailed status updates.

Of course, you may not be a fan of the lock screen, and this will be especially true of the many, many people using Windows 8 on a traditional desktop PC. If this is the case, you can simply disable the lock screen.

To disable the lock screen, you'll need to run the Local Group Policy Editor, an old-school management interface that's been in Windows for years but hidden so that normal users don't stumble across it by mistake. To find the Local Group Policy Editor, use Start Search, and search for *gpedit.msc*; it will pop up in the Apps list and resemble Figure 5-6 when running.

In the leftmost pane of this console, navigate to Computer Configuration, Administrative Templates, Control Panel, and then Personalization. When you do, the application will resemble Figure 5-7.

Double-click the entry titled "Do not display the lock screen" and then select Enabled in the window that appears. Click OK to close that window, and then close the Local Group Policy Editor. The change will take effect immediately.

▶ We typically choose Calendar for this purpose, as it will provide information about the next scheduled event right on the lock screen. But other apps can be useful this way, too, like Weather.

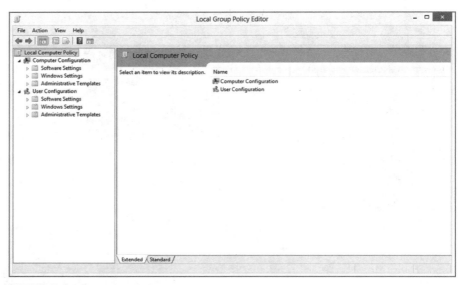

FIGURE 5-6: Local Group Policy Editor

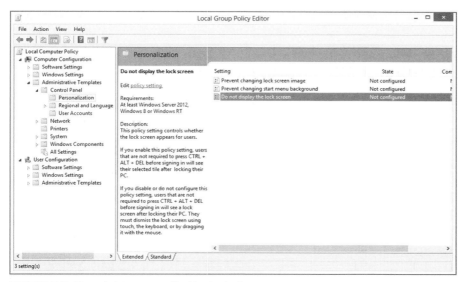

FIGURE 5-7: There it is: a way to disable the lock screen.

Now, when you restart the PC, you'll bypass the lock screen entirely and be presented with the sign-in screen instead. Likewise, when you lock the PC (Winkey + L), you'll go immediately to the sign-in screen, not the lock screen.

Customizing the Start Screen

The Start screen is unique for many reasons. As the new default user interface for Windows 8 and the place by which you will launch and, via their live tile updates, monitor your running apps, it's the central dashboard that many users will face, literally, each day. Not surprisingly, it offers a number of useful customizations. Oddly, however, these customizations can occur through two interfaces. That is, some of the customizations occur through PC Settings, as with other Metro features. But some occur directly from within the Start screen itself.

CHANGING THE START SCREEN THEME

If you navigate to PC Settings, Personalize, Start screen, you'll see the interface shown in Figure 5-8. From here, you can choose the theme that is applied to the Start screen, a combination of background pattern, accent color, and background color.

If you're not a fan of the background patterns, you can thankfully choose no pattern, which is the final square in the grid of pattern squares. What you can't do is choose an arbitrary combination of accent and background colors. Instead,

Microsoft has chosen combinations that it thinks work well together. For example, if you like a dark purple background color, your only accent color options are two shades of light purple. You'll find that the gray backgrounds tend to have the most accent color choices for whatever reason.

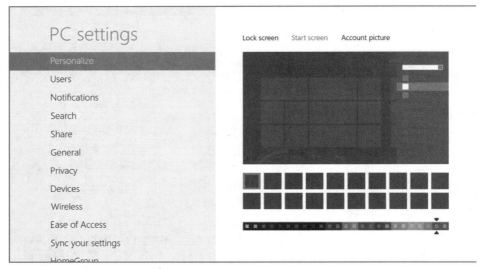

FIGURE 5-8: Start screen theme selection

DETERMINING WHICH TILES APPEAR ON THE START SCREEN

Windows 8 ships with a default selection of live tiles, and of course PC makers can add their own. And as you install Metro-style apps and traditional Windows applications, more tiles will be added to the Start screen so that, over time, it becomes a mess of useful and non-useful tiles alike. Fortunately, you can configure which tiles appear on the Start screen.

▶ **Remove a tile:** To remove a tile, you must first select it. This is most easily done with a mouse, where a simple right-click is all that's required. But it can be done via touch, of course, and far less easily via the keyboard, too. With touch, you must perform a short downward swipe on the tile to select it. With the keyboard, use the arrow keys to navigate to the tile in question—you'll see a selection rectangle as you go—and then press the spacebar on the appropriate tile.

However you do it, when you select a tile on the Start screen, you will see that an app bar like the one in Figure 5-9 appears. This bar includes an Unpin from Start button: Just select that option to remove the tile.

FIGURE 5-9: Selecting a tile on the Start screen

You can also select multiple tiles at once. To do so, simply select one tile and then perform the same selection action—based on whichever input type you prefer—on other tiles in sequence. You can arbitrarily select as many tiles as you'd like and then unpin them all at once.

▶ **Add a tile:** You can also add a tile to the Start screen. There are two methods for doing so.

From the Start screen, you can search for the item you wish to pin. To do so, just start typing and Start Search will appear. For example, if you wish to pin WordPad to the Start screen, type *wordpad* in Start Search. Then, as shown in Figure 5-10, right-click (or otherwise select) WordPad in the search results and choose Pin to Start.

▶ Various items can be pinned to the Start screen, such as Metro-style apps; Windows desktop applications; File Explorer and various Explorer-based locations, including folders, libraries, and the like; and websites.

FIGURE 5-10: Pinning a new application or app to the Start screen

You can also pin some items from the Windows desktop environment. Some desktop icons—like Recycle Bin, Computer, Network, and similar—can be pinned: Just right-click one on the desktop and choose Pin to Start. You can do the same for libraries, the homegroup, and various folders from within File Explorer as well. For example, in Figure 5-11, you can see that Pin to Start is an option when you right-click any location in the Explorer navigation bar.

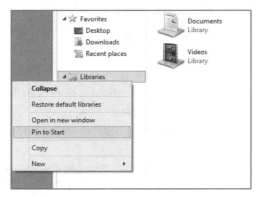

FIGURE 5-11: Pinning from the desktop

ARRANGING AND GROUPING TILES ON THE START SCREEN

Adding and removing tiles is nice, but of course most people will also want to arrange tiles on the Start screen so that they appear in the order they prefer. This is obviously possible, as is the ability to group icons into visually segregated groups.

To move a tile's location, simply select it with the mouse or, on a touch screen device, with your finger and drag it around on the screen. As you can see in Figure 5-12, as you do so, tiles will part and redistribute intelligently to accommodate the tile you're moving.

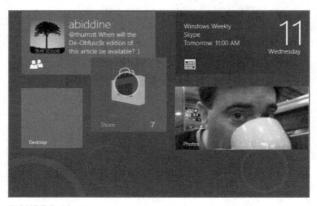

FIGURE 5-12: Rearranging the tiles layout on the Start screen

You can also group Start screen tiles. To create a new group, select a tile and move it to the far left or right of the current group until you see a new group bar appear as in Figure 5-13; this is your indication that dropping the tile there will create a new group.

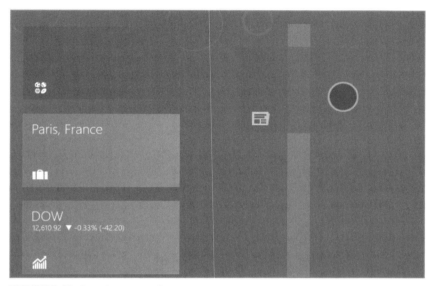

FIGURE 5-13: Creating a new tile group

And when you *do* release the tile, you can see that it's by itself in a new group (Figure 5-14). Now you can just move other tiles into that group as you would normally.

FIGURE 5-14: A lonely tile group of one

TIP How you arrange and group tiles is of course up to you, but many people like to group them logically, with media apps (Music, Video, and so on) together in one group, productivity apps in another, and so on.

You can also move and even name groups. To do so, you need to take advantage of a cool Metro feature called semantic zoom which lets you visually zoom the entire Start screen so you can see the whole layout at once in a kind of thumbnail view.

You can enable semantic view most easily via touch or mouse. With touch, simply pinch the Start screen. As you do, the tiles will visually shrink until they're a small group of thumbnails as in Figure 5-15.

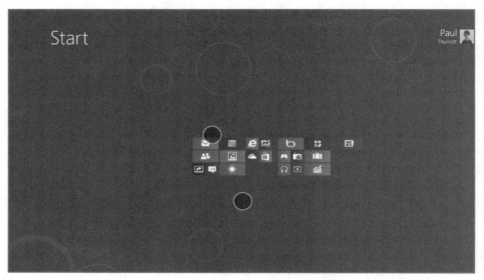

FIGURE 5-15: Semantic zoom

With a mouse, move the mouse cursor in the lower-right corner of the screen and click the tiny semantic zoom button, which can be seen in Figure 5-16. This tiny button will immediately place the screen into semantic zoom view as well.

FIGURE 5-16: It's easy to miss, but this button will display the Start screen with semantic zoom.

There are two basic actions you can perform in this view.

► First, you can arrange groups. To do so, simply select a group—using the same methods that are used to select an individual tile—and then drag it around the thumbnail view of the Start screen, positioning it where you want, as in Figure 5-17.

FIGURE 5-17: Rearranging the layout of tile groups

► Second, you can optionally name each tile group. To do this, select the group you wish to name while in semantic view—again, using the same selection technique you learned for tiles—and then tap the Name group app bar button that appears. It will provide a text box for you to type the name. And when you are done, the group name will appear over the top-left area of the group, as shown in Figure 5-18.

FIGURE 5-18: A named tile group

To exit semantic zoom, use the stretch gesture (a sort of "reverse pinch") on a touch-based screen. Or, with a more traditional PC, type Esc or click on any empty spot on the screen.

CUSTOMIZING INDIVIDUAL START SCREEN TILES

Looking at your Start screen, you've probably noticed that the tiles are two different sizes. There are large rectangular tiles and then smaller, square tiles. This raises a few questions, but key among them is whether it's possible to customize individual tiles so that they are one or the other size. It depends.

Tiles that represent Metro-style apps can support both tile sizes. And most do, though it's not a requirement. So you may occasionally run into a Metro-style app that offers only one tile size. But in either large or small variants, these tiles can optionally be live, offering app-related updates graphically or textually.

Tiles that represent websites, traditional Windows applications, or Explorer locations support only the smaller, square tile size. These types of tiles are not live: They provide the name of the app or experience only, and some icon. That's it.

You can customize a live tile in the following ways:

▶ **Make it bigger/smaller:** A large rectangular tile can be resized to be a smaller, square tile if you'd like. Likewise, a smaller, square tile can be resized as a larger, rectangular tile. Doing so will generally impact the amount of information displayed by a live tile, though the exact change will differ from app to app, depending on how it was created. In Figure 5-19, you can see different versions of the same live tile, one large and one small.

FIGURE 5-19: The same tile in its two supported size configurations

▶ **Turn live tile on/off:** While some will really appreciate the constantly updating live tiles on a typical Windows 8 Start screen, others will find it distracting or even annoying. There are two things you can try to cut down on the noise if you're in the latter group. First, you can experiment with resizing the tiles from large to small, since those smaller tiles—while still "live"—tend to be less dynamic than their larger versions. But if you just want it to stop, you can also turn off live updating on a tile-by-tile basis. And this works for large as well as small tiles. In Figure 5-20, you can see the effect this has on a typical app tile.

FIGURE 5-20: Same tile with live updates on (left) and off (right)

To perform either of the preceding customizations, select the tile in question and then choose the appropriate app bar button as shown in Figure 5-21.

FIGURE 5-21: Tile options in the app bar

▶ You can't customize the color of a tile, which is designated by the app's creator and cannot be modified. Still, some apps let you customize the tile face in some ways. For example, the Photos app lets you apply a favorite picture as the tile face.

Customizing User Accounts

While we dedicate a large chunk of Chapter 12 to user accounts, it's worth mentioning here that PC Settings is also the home for most user account customizations as well. There are two basic interfaces: one for your user account picture and then a more general Users settings area that lets you configure other aspects of your account and other user accounts. (And no, we don't know why these two things are separate.)

CHANGING YOUR ACCOUNT PICTURE

To change your user account picture, navigate to PC Settings, Personalize, Account picture. Or, select Change account picture from the Start screen-based user tile in the upper-right corner of that screen. Either way, you'll be presented with the screen in Figure 5-22.

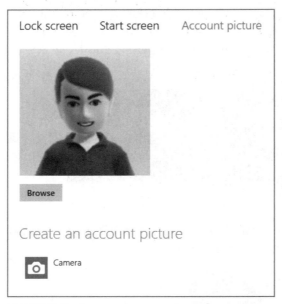

FIGURE 5-22: Account picture settings

Using this interface is pretty straightforward. The Browse button lets you find a picture on your PC or elsewhere using a standard Metro-style File Picker. The Camera tile lets you capture a still image using the Camera app. (And you can see other apps listed there as well, of course.)

If you sign in with a Microsoft account as we recommend, note that changing this account picture will also change the account picture associated with your online account. Likewise, if you change your Microsoft account picture elsewhere—such as on the web—it will change the image you see here in Windows 8 as well.

CHANGING OTHER ACCOUNT SETTINGS

Other settings related to your user account, and other accounts that are (or will be) configured on this PC can be found in PC Settings, Users (Figure 5-23).

Here, you can change your password, associate a PIN or picture password with your account, add other users, switch your account between a local and Microsoft account type and, if you're signing in with a domain account, connect that account to your Microsoft account. (And these are in addition to other options, depending on how things are configured when you view this screen.) This is all covered in Chapter 12.

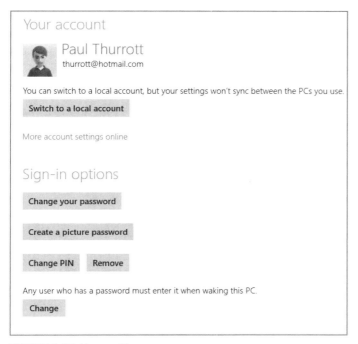

FIGURE 5-23: User settings

Other Customizations in PC Settings

The PC Settings interface provides an obvious and discoverable way to customize many aspects of Windows 8, so there's no need to step through every conceivable option. That said, there are a few you may want to pay special attention to. And these are as follows:

▶ **Notifications:** As with live tiles, new Metro-style apps—including the ones that come with Windows 8—can provide floating notification *toasts* to alert you when something happens, such as an e-mail arriving (Mail), a new instant message (Messaging), or a pending appointment (Calendar). But like live tiles, these notifications can get a bit chatty and depending on your needs and temperament, you may want to turn them off or determine whether individual apps can even use notifications. Notifications can be configured in PC Settings, Notifications.

▶ **Devices.** You can rename certain types of devices—Xbox 360 consoles and DLNA-compatible set top boxes, both of which you may want to use with the

▶ You should also consider turning off notification sounds. Now that gets annoying.

Xbox Music and Xbox Video apps in Windows 8—by selecting them in the Devices view and typing a new name. That way, when you select them from the Devices pane, they'll have names that make sense to you, and not names like WDTVLiveHub.

▶ **Ease of Access:** While Windows 7's excellent accessibility tools have been updated only somewhat in Windows 8, this new OS does of course have a new Metro environment to deal with as well. So you will find some interesting accessibility features in PC Settings under Ease of Access. Key among them are the high contrast mode, which works in both Metro and the desktop, and the Winkey + Volume Up shortcut, which can be used to toggle Magnifier, Narrator (the default), the onscreen keyboard, or nothing.

▶ **Sync your settings:** This is the most important set of settings, arguably, in PC Settings and is directly tied to why signing in with a Microsoft account is such a big deal. This one is important enough that we describe it in the next section of this chapter, "Customizing Settings and Settings Sync."

▶ **Windows Update:** While there is still a control panel-based Windows Update in Windows 8, it's a bit hard to find and not the primary interface for Microsoft's software updating service. Now, the new, Metro-style front end to Windows Update can be found in PC Settings, Windows Update. As you can see in Figure 5-24, this interface is simple and obvious.

▶ One item in Ease of Access might be of interest to any user of a large screen display: If you enable Make everything on your screen bigger, you might find the Start screen to be less unwieldy, with bigger tiles.

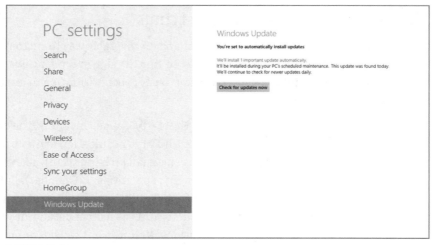

FIGURE 5-24: Windows Update

CUSTOMIZING SETTINGS AND SETTINGS SYNC

In PC Settings, Sync your settings, you will find a long but surprisingly incomplete list of the groups of features that you can sync from PC to PC if you sign in with a Microsoft account. You can see this interface in Figure 5-25.

▶ Indeed, this list of features—as well as those that are inexplicably not noted in this UI—is collectively the single best reason to sign in to Windows 8 with a Microsoft account.

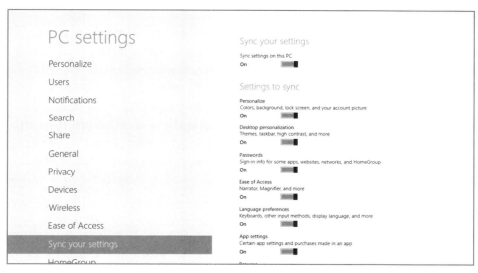

FIGURE 5-25: Sync your settings

While signing in with a Microsoft account is enough to trigger the synchronization of most settings between the current PC and your other machines, one settings group—for Passwords, as shown in Figure 5-26—won't be synced until you make the current PC a "trusted PC."

FIGURE 5-26: Passwords won't sync unless your current PC is a trusted PC.

You may have already made your PC a trusted PC, by the way: At the end of Setup, you're prompted to provide a mobile phone number as part of the security verification info. Doing so causes Microsoft to send that number a text message with an embedded hyperlink that, when tapped, verifies the Windows install and makes that PC a trusted PC. Likewise, you should have received an e-mail to this effect at the time you set up Windows as well. Like the text message, this e-mail contains a hyperlink that lets you mark the PC as a trusted PC.

If you didn't perform either of these actions earlier, you can enable password syncing by tapping the Trust this PC link provided in PC Settings. This will launch your default browser and navigate to account.live.com/p, where you can click a Confirm link to make the current PC a trusted PC.

With that out of the way, you can examine the entire list of settings groups, each of which can be enabled for syncing or not. Microsoft is nice enough to list some of the features that are synced with each group, but not all of them. That's where we come in: In the list that follows you'll find a much more complete list of the features that get synced with each group.

▶ **Sync settings on this PC:** This global switch determines whether PC to PC sync is enabled on this PC. If this switch is set to off, none of the other settings will be available for syncing.

▶ **Personalize:** This settings group concerns settings related to Start screen, lock screen, and user tile personalization. But it also syncs two other very useful settings. First, as described earlier in this chapter, it's possible to individually configure app tiles to provide live information or not; this settings group determines whether those customizations are synced. And second, it includes file type associations: If you configure, say, Windows Reader to open PDF files on one PC, it will be auto-selected as the default app for that file type across your PCs.

▶ **Desktop personalization:** As its name suggests, this settings group relates to some Windows desktop settings (but not all; see the related Other Windows settings group later in the list). Chief among these is the desktop theme (as configured in the Personalization control panel), which includes the desktop background, the Explorer window color, sounds, and screen saver. But it also includes taskbar customizations (including which edge of the screen to which the taskbar is connected) and desktop-based photo slideshow (triggered from the Explorer shell or Windows Photo Viewer) customizations.

- ▶ **Passwords:** This includes sign-in info for some apps, including Mail (for your e-mail accounts), Calendar, Messaging, and People, websites (through IE), networks, and HomeGroup.

- ▶ **Ease of Access:** As you may expect, this settings group includes all of the Windows accessibility features, including Narrator, Screen Magnifier, high contrast, and so on.

- ▶ **Language preferences:** Here, you'll find settings such as the display language, additional installed languages and input methods (IMEs), and settings related to the onscreen keyboard. But there's another important setting that's synced via this group: The new Windows spelling dictionary, which can work from any Metro-style app.

- ▶ **App settings:** This settings group curiously notes that it will sync "certain settings in your apps." That's a bit of a stretch as installed Metro-style apps can actually participate in Microsoft account-based PC-to-PC sync on their own. Instead, this settings group is really related to Windows Store-purchased app information.

- ▶ **Browser:** This settings group encompasses a wide range of Internet Explorer settings, including browser history, Favorites, homepage, Tracking Protection, domain suggestions, and more.

- ▶ **Other Windows settings:** This settings group, strangely separated from Desktop personalization, incudes settings related to two specific desktop features: File Explorer and mouse.

- ▶ **Sync settings over metered Internet connections:** This determines whether your settings are synced over metered Internet connections.

- ▶ **Sync settings over metered Internet connections when I'm roaming:** Like the previous settings, but on a more expensive roaming connection. This is disabled by default.

As noted previously, each Metro-style app you install can optionally use your Microsoft account to sync its own settings from PC to PC, and some apps will provide their own granular control over this and other features. Check the app's settings—through the Settings charm, or Winkey + I—from within the app itself to see whether this functionality is available.

CUSTOMIZING THE DESKTOP

If you're familiar with Windows 7 or previous Windows versions, many of the same customization options that were available before are also available in Windows 8. As is the case throughout this book, however, we'll be focusing only on those aspects of the system that are new or at least notably changed in this release. And believe it or not, there have been some interesting improvements to desktop customization in Windows 8 despite the obvious focus on the new Metro environment in this release.

Automatic Explorer Window Color

With Windows 8, Microsoft has removed the translucent glass effects of Windows Aero and replaced it with a more opaque and flat new Explorer desktop theme. But that doesn't mean you can't customize the look of the desktop to your heart's content.

For example, in Windows Vista and 7, you could configure the color of the transparent or "glass" parts of File Explorer windows (and, in Windows 7, the taskbar) to match the underlying desktop background. So if you set up your desktop to cycle through a favorite set of photos from a recent trip to Ireland, for example, you might change the window color to a pleasant green to match.

This capability was nice, and of course you could save background and window color combinations as desktop themes. But it was a bit tedious if you changed backgrounds regularly, or used a dynamic theme like those provided by Bing that changes background pictures on a schedule. So in Windows 8, there's a new option that will automatically change the File Explorer window and taskbar color to match the desktop background. You will see this option in the Color and Appearance control panel shown in Figure 5-27.

Of course, you have to find it first. You can find Windows Color and Appearance much as you did in Windows 7: Right-click the desktop, choose Personalize, and then click Color in the resulting window. Or, you can get there directly—and more quickly—from Start Search: Simply search for *window color* and look under Settings.

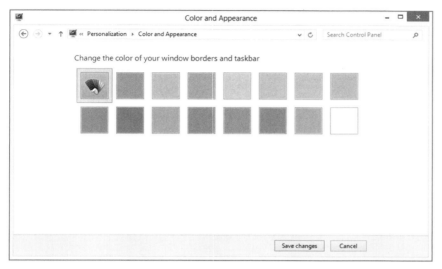

FIGURE 5-27: A new automatic window color option will keep your windows and taskbar in sync with the desktop background.

Make Items Bigger

While Windows 7 included a display scaling feature that made it a snap to enlarge the appearance of all desktop items using percentages like 125 percent and 150 percent, Windows 8 goes a step further by providing a new interface for just increasing the text size for specific items. It's also found in the Display control panel, which can be accessed in a variety of ways, though the easiest is Start Search: Search for *display* and then select Display from the search results.

In the Change only the text size section of the Display control panel, you can select individual desktop UI elements—Title bars, Menus, Message boxes, Palette titles, Icons, and Tooltips—and provide them with custom sizes, as seen in Figure 5-28.

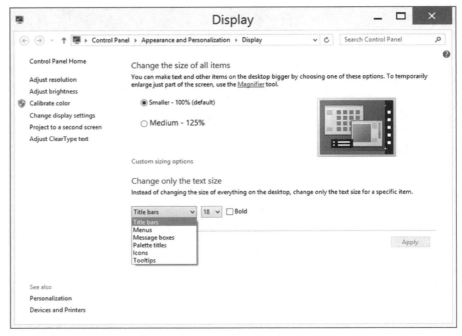

FIGURE 5-28: Just make certain items bigger, like window title bars

Metro-Style Apps on Netbooks: A Workaround

If you want to run Metro-style apps on your Netbook, there is a fix, as it turns out. But be warned that modifying a Windows 8 install to allow Metro-style apps to run will cause the desktop environment look a bit skewed, or squished. But if your goal is to enjoy Metro, this will do the trick.

Run the Registry Editor, Regedit (Start Search, *regedit*), and search for the term *display1_downscalingsupported* (using Ctrl + F). Find each instance of this entry and change its value from 0 to 1. (Use F3 to repeat the previous search.) Do this until you've found them all, close Regedit, and reboot.

You will now have additional resolution options, such as 1024 × 768 and 1152 × 864. If you do have multiple resolution choices, try each (that's above 1024 x 600) to see which looks best. But either way, Metro apps will now work.

More Efficient Multi-Monitor

While previous versions of Windows offered only basic multi-monitor capabilities, Windows 8 addresses past issues and adds some unique new features that let you customize how you can view the Metro and desktop environments side by side on multiple displays.

> **NOTE** First, a general rule: While it's possible to span your desktop across multiple displays, the Metro environment can only appear on a single screen. So if you have a four-monitor system for some reason—perhaps you're James Bond or are a little too excited about flight simulator games—you can have this setup configured in one of two basic ways: one screen showing Metro and three showing the desktop, or all four screens showing the desktop.
>
> Given this limitation, let's look at some of the ways in which you can configure your PC for multi-monitor use in Windows 8.

BASIC MULTI-MONITOR CONFIGURATION

There are two interfaces you will use to configure a multi-monitor setup. The most basic is the Metro-based Second Screen pane, which replaces the old "presentation" mode from previous Windows versions. You can access this screen, shown in Figure 5-29, in several ways.

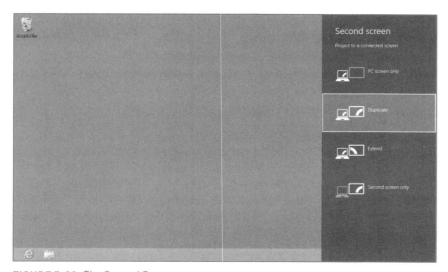

FIGURE 5-29: The Second Screen pane

The simplest, we think, is to use the Winkey + P (where P = "presentation") keyboard shortcut. However, you can also find this interface via touch or mouse by displaying the Charms bar and choosing Devices and then Second Screen.

While it is clearly aimed at those who need to project a presentation to a secondary screen or projector, the Second Screen pane will meet the needs of many users who have two screens attached to their PC, including laptop or tablet users who dock their device at home or work in order to use a larger screen.

This pane lets you configure the screens as follows:

- **PC screen only:** In this mode, the second screen is simply ignored and only the PC's primary display is used.

- **Duplicate:** In this mode, the second screen duplicates, or mirrors, the primary display. There are some limitations here based on the capabilities of the screen. For example, the mirrored screens will both utilize the resolution of the lowest resolution screen of the pair. This is a common choice for those giving presentations who wish to see the same display as the audience.

- **Extend:** In this mode, the PC display is extended across the two screens. This common configuration allows you to have a desktop that spans two screens or a configuration in which you use Metro on one screen and the desktop on the other. Unlike with Duplicate, each display will use its own native resolution. Presenters can also utilize this mode with the Presenter mode in recent versions of Microsoft PowerPoint.

- **Second screen only:** Here, the main PC display (on a laptop or tablet, the display that's built into the device) will be disabled and only the secondary screen is used. This is a common choice for those with portable computers who wish to use a docked display, keyboard, and mouse while not moving around.

MORE ADVANCED MULTI-MONITOR CONFIGURATION

The Second Screen interface is fine for basic usage, but if you have more than two screens or need to configure how the screens work, you'll need more control. And that comes via a legacy control panel called Screen Resolution. Shown in Figure 5-30, this control panel can be accessed by right-clicking the desktop and choosing Screen Resolution, or via Start Search (*screen resolution*).

A number of configuration options are available here, including the following:

▶ **Visual positioning and orientation of the displays:** You can move the graphical representations of the displays in the window to approximate how the physical displays they represent are in fact oriented in real life (Figure 5-31). Because you will need to move the mouse cursor from screen to screen, it makes sense to line up the displays so that they work onscreen as they do in real life.

You may recall that Windows 8 utilizes the corners of the primary screen as "hot corners," which are required by Metro interfaces such as Back, Start, and Charms. Fortunately, Microsoft has configured Windows 8 such that if a corner of the primary display is lined up exactly with a corner of a secondary display, that corner will become "sticky," and the mouse cursor will hard stop when it reaches such a corner. This feature prevents you from accidently overshooting the hot corner, moving the cursor to the next display, and missing out on the Metro feature you meant to trigger.

▶ Of course, anyone using a multi-monitor setup can probably remember a keyboard shortcut, too: Winkey + C. This shortcut opens the Charms bar so you don't have to use the mouse.

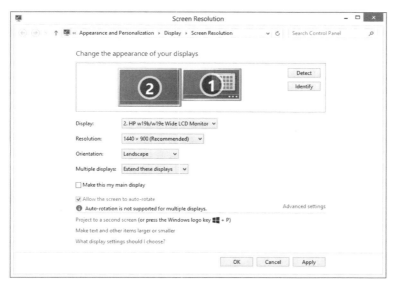

FIGURE 5-30: The Screen Resolution control panel provides more fine-grained control over multiple displays.

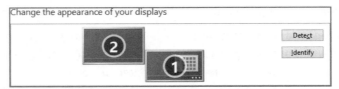

FIGURE 5-31: You should orient the onscreen displays to mirror how the displays line up in real life.

▶ **Set screen resolutions:** Using the Resolution drop-down, you can ensure that the resolution of each display is set correctly to the optimal resolution (generally the highest possible resolution, or the display's "native" resolution). Select a display in the graphical representation area first and then make sure the resolution is correct.

▶ **Orientation:** You can choose between landscape, portrait, landscape (flipped) and portrait (flipped) orientations, which can be handy for those displays that can be rotated.

▶ **Multiple displays:** This drop-down works much like the Second Screen pane described in the previous section. It lets you choose between the same four options, though they are annoyingly described somewhat differently: Duplicate these displays (Duplicate), Extend these displays (Extend), Show desktop only on 1 (PC screen only), and Show desktop only on 2 (Second screen only).

FINE-TUNING MULTI-MONITOR CONFIGURATION

OK, you've got your multiple displays configured and oriented the way you like. But what about the desktop wallpaper and taskbar? By default, Windows 8 will simply duplicate both the wallpaper and taskbar across two or more displays, even if you've chosen the Extend view, which extends the desktop across the multiple displays. Wouldn't it be nice if you could extend a panoramic wallpaper across the displays, or use a different picture for each display? And what about having the taskbar be unique to each display so that, say, the taskbar on the second display only shows buttons for the windows that are actually open on that display?

Yep, you guessed it. You can configure how each of these features works, too.

CONFIGURING THE DESKTOP BACKGROUND TO SPAN MULTIPLE DISPLAYS

To configure the desktop background for multiple displays, you will use the Desktop Background control panel, which is accessible through the Personalize control panel (right-click the desktop, Personalize, and then Desktop Background) or directly from Start Search (*desktop background*). In this interface, shown in Figure 5-32, you can click the Picture location drop-down to choose between a variety of background types.

The Span option lets you span a single image across multiple displays. This works best, of course, with panoramic images, and while you're free to make your own, Microsoft is stepping up by providing panoramic wallpapers (and even desktop themes, which also include other unique configurations) that are designed specifically for this use.

Some are included in Windows 8. To see what's available, select Windows Desktop Backgrounds from the Picture location drop-down near the top of this window. There, you'll find a few panoramic options that, when selected, span nicely across two displays as in Figure 5-33.

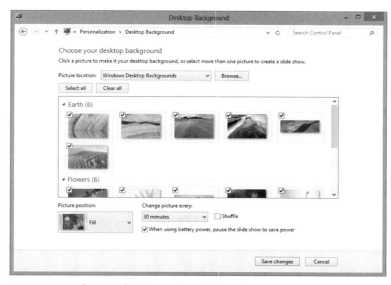

FIGURE 5-32: Desktop Background control panel

FIGURE 5-33: With a panoramic background picture, you can create a seamless display across multiple monitors.

Be sure to select Span from the Picture position drop-down as well to see the effect correctly. It also helps if the displays are lined up properly, since otherwise the picture will stagger from screen to screen.

Note that Microsoft is also making panoramic wallpapers and themes available from its Windows Personalization Gallery website at windows.microsoft.com/en-US/windows/downloads/personalize. This collection is updated regularly, so be sure to check it out from time to time.

▶ In case it's not obvious, all desktop themes designed for Windows 7 still work the same with Windows 8, too.

CONFIGURING A DIFFERENT BACKGROUND PICTURE FOR EACH DISPLAY

Another choice is to use a different background picture for each display. This is absolutely possible in Windows 8, though it's not particularly obvious.

To do so, navigate to the Desktop Background control panel. (Again, via Personalize and then Desktop Background or from Start Search, with *desktop background*). Select a (picture) location from the Picture location drop-down list and then select the picture you want for the first display. Then, right-click that picture and choose Set for monitor 1, as shown in Figure 5-34.

▶ It can't be a solid color for some reason.

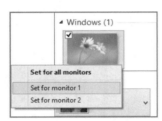

FIGURE 5-34: Specifying a background picture for the first display only

Then, find the picture you want for the second display, right-click it, and choose Set for monitor 2. Repeat as necessary for further displays.

CONFIGURING THE TASKBAR FOR MULTIPLE DISPLAYS

By default, the taskbar will duplicate on each display even if you've chosen the Extend option. But you can change this so that the taskbar on each screen is specific to that screen. To do so, right-click an empty area of the taskbar (any screen will do) and choose Properties. You'll see the Taskbar Properties window shown in Figure 5-35.

There are four possible configurations for the taskbar on a PC with multiple displays:

▶ **Duplicated across all displays:** By default, the same taskbar will appear on all displays and its collection of buttons will be duplicated on each. That is, the taskbar on each display will be identical.

▶ **Taskbar only on the primary display:** If you'd like to display the taskbar only on the primary display, uncheck the option titled Show taskbar on all displays in Taskbar Properties. This will eliminate the taskbar on all secondary displays, and display it only on the first, or primary, display.

FIGURE 5-35: New to Taskbar Properties: a way to control how the taskbar works with multiple displays

▶ **A unique taskbar on each display:** If you'd prefer to have a taskbar on each display but would like each to hold buttons (shortcuts for running and non-running programs) that are specific only to that display, choose "Taskbar where window is open" from the Show taskbar buttons on drop-down. In this configuration, the secondary displays will only display buttons for windows and applications that are open on that screen.

▶ **A unique taskbar on each display, but all open windows available on primary display, too:** This most confusing of options is basically identical to the previous configuration, but with a twist: Open windows and applications will display a button on the taskbar of both the display they're open on as well as the primary display.

CONFIGURING METRO FOR MULTIPLE DISPLAYS

You may recall that you can only use the Metro environment on one display. The question is: Which display?

As it turns out, there's no user interface for specifying which display is used for Metro, and of course it uses the primary display, or what's sometimes referred to as Monitor 1, by default. You can, however, change which display Metro uses. As is so often the case, you just need to know the trick.

To switch Metro from the primary display to a secondary display, you need to launch any Metro-style app. That is, you cannot do this from the Start screen. Once you have a Metro-style app running, "grab" the top of the app via touch or mouse—the cursor will change into a gloved hand cursor if you're using the mouse—and then drag the app to the display you prefer.

▶ The only issue with this tip is that it's not persistent across reboots. Metro will stay on the secondary display until you reboot, but once you do, you'll need to perform this drag-and-drop operation again.

To the Cloud! Do More with Libraries

When it comes to libraries, Windows 8 works much like Windows 7, with the only major difference being that the new ribbon-based File Explorer exposes library options and configurations in a much more obvious way, as you can see in Figure 5-36.

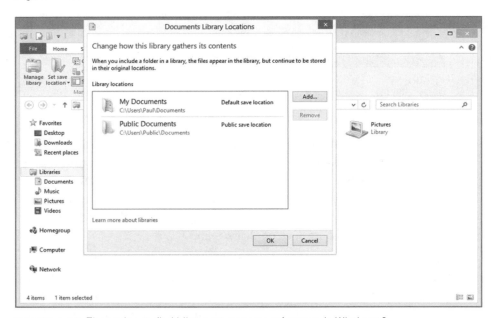

FIGURE 5-36: The easier-to-find Library management features in Windows 8

As before, you can configure which physical folders are used to populate individual libraries and you can, as before, make your own libraries, too. What's different in Windows 8 is that Microsoft is now providing SkyDrive apps for both the Metro and desktop environments (though only the former is available "in the box" with the OS). This means you can now access and use cloud-based SkyDrive storage as if it were part of your PC's hard drive, including with libraries.

Once you've downloaded and installed the SkyDrive application for Windows (apps.live.com/skydrive), it will sync the contents of your SkyDrive cloud storage to the location on your PC that you configured. Then, you can access your SkyDrive storage as you do with any other storage that's attached to your hard drive.

To add a SkyDrive-based folder to a library, simply right-click it in Explorer, as shown in Figure 5-37, and select Include in library and then the name of the library you prefer.

▶ The SkyDrive app for Windows caches the contents your SkyDrive cloud storage to the hard drive so that it's available when your PC is offline, too.

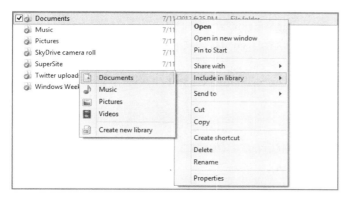

FIGURE 5-37: Adding a SkyDrive folder to a library

Then, you can even optionally make that cloud-based folder the default save location. To do so, open the library in question in Explorer and then select Set Save Location from the Library Tools – Manage tab in the ribbon. *Voila!* Now you have a file store that is replicated to the web and will survive a hard drive failure or operating system reinstall.

TIP This tip works with other cloud providers, too. For example, Google provides a Google Drive app that lets you access its cloud-based storage natively from File Explorer as well. If you use this service instead of SkyDrive, you could of course add Google Drive-based folders to your libraries instead. You can download Google Drive for Windows from the Google website: tools.google.com/dlpage/drive.

You could also take this tip to its logical conclusion and replace the default library locations with locations in SkyDrive. For example, you could create a Documents folder inside of SkyDrive, add it to the Documents library, and then remove the My Documents and Public Documents folders from the Documents library. Now a cloud-based folder will be your default save location for all of your documents and will be automatically replicated from PC to PC, and to the cloud.

POWER USER CUSTOMIZATION TIPS AND TRICKS

While personalizing the Metro and desktop environments is useful, we're particularly taken with customization tips that make the PC work the way you do. And with Windows 8, reaching that happy middle ground can be a bit more daunting since the new Metro environment isn't naturally efficient for power users, while the old-school desktop environment isn't necessarily a happy site for those less sophisticated users with tablets who would prefer to stick with Metro. (We're told those people exist. Bear with us.)

Here are a few tips for spanning the otherwise separate worlds of Metro and the desktop.

Easing the Transition Between Metro and the Desktop . . . with Wallpaper

If you've bet big on Metro and would like to stay out of the desktop environment as much as possible, you of course have our best wishes. And you can of course start by removing the tiles for the Desktop and any other desktop applications (like File Explorer) that may exist on your Start Screen. Good luck, seriously.

But anyone who uses Windows 8 will need to deal with the desktop from time to time, simply because Metro is an incomplete environment that doesn't offer all of the functionality that's present in the desktop. How could it? The Windows desktop is the result of over 15 years of improvements and tweaks, while the Metro environment is a 1.0 release. It's nice, sure. But it's always going to offer just a subset of the features you get in the desktop.

With that in mind, you can blunt the visually jarring effect that occurs when you switch between any Metro-based screen and the desktop by duplicating the Start screen background as your desktop background. There's no automated way to do this, but if you know the trick (and don't change your background too often), you can make it happen.

▶ This makes us wonder whether Windows 9 will feature some sort of cross-environment "themes" capability, since it's such an obvious need.

Here's how.

1. First, configure the Start screen with the theme—colors and background pattern—you prefer, as described earlier in the chapter. Then, click the small icon in the lower-right corner of the screen to enable the semantic zoom feature on the desktop. This will cause the tile groups to shrink down, as shown in Figure 5-38.

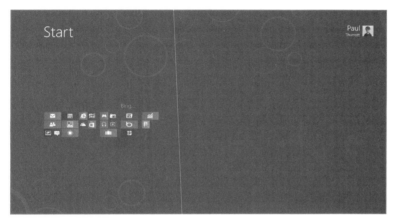

FIGURE 5-38: Semantic zoom on the desktop

2. Now, take a screenshot by tapping the Prt Scn key on your keyboard. This copies the onscreen image to the Windows clipboard.

3. Now, run Paint (Start Search, *paint*) and paste the screenshot image into the application (using Ctrl + V). Use Paint's magnification options to shrink the image a bit (using right-click) so that it resembles Figure 5-39.

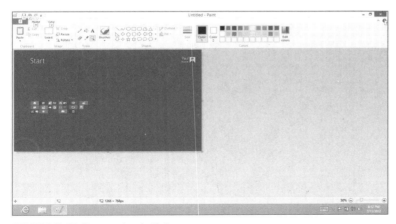

FIGURE 5-39: Screenshot in Paint

Two more steps.

4. Next, you must select the background color of the Start screen as the background color in Paint. To do that, select the Color picker tool and then right-click on a blank area of the background in the image. Then, cut out the tiles and the user tile with the Selection tool so that it resembles Figure 5-40.

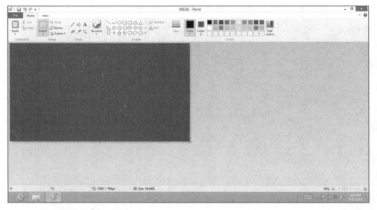

FIGURE 5-40: The edited background in Paint

5. Now, save the image to your Pictures library. And, from the File menu in Paint, choose Set as desktop background. Once you do, your desktop wallpaper will be changed to this new image (Figure 5-41).

Now, as you switch back and forth between the Start screen and the desktop (test this by tapping Winkey) you can see that the background remains the same, creating a fairly seamless experience.

FIGURE 5-41: The Start Screen background applied to the desktop

SUMMARY

While Windows 8 provides most of the same customization and personalization functionality from previous Windows versions, it also includes new capabilities. These extend from the expected Metro-based enhancements to new desktop customization features and, perhaps most interestingly, some features that make the Metro and desktop environments work better together. Now that you understand the basics of using both of these environments, and how to meld them to your needs, it's time to learn more about the Metro apps that make Windows 8 so special.

CHAPTER 6

Windows Store: Finding, Acquiring, and Managing Your Apps

IN THIS CHAPTER

▶ Understanding app stores and why Windows Store is important
▶ Understanding the rules for apps you download from Windows Store
▶ Launching and Browsing Windows Store
▶ Accessing content by category, list, or app
▶ Finding apps
▶ Downloading, installing, and updating apps
▶ Rating and reviewing apps and other reviews
▶ Uninstalling apps
▶ Configuring accounts and Windows Store preferences

With its Windows Store, Microsoft is following the app store model pioneered by Apple, sure, but it's also providing a unique approach to what is now considered a key part of any new platform. This approach establishes the very important rules that all apps available from the store must follow, providing users with the assurances they need to trust these apps. But it also plays into one of Windows 8's greatest strengths as a platform: These apps aren't just isolated islands of functionality, but they can also integrate deeply into the OS, extending the capabilities of Windows 8 well into the future.

As an app in its own right, Windows Store is beautiful to look at, easy to navigate, and a somewhat ideal way to discover, download, and manage Metro-style apps. It provides a rich environment with app categories and subcategories, lists of useful apps, app landing pages with detailed information, and an excellent set of feedback features that let you rate and review apps and other reviews.

This chapter examines Windows Store and how you can use this full-screen experience to find the apps that will matter most to you.

WHAT IS AN APP STORE . . . AND WHY DOES WINDOWS 8 NEED ONE?

While many associate app stores with Apple, the truth is that Microsoft got there years earlier with offerings such as Xbox LIVE Marketplace, Windows Marketplace, and other services. But Apple's begrudging entry into the app store space—remember, Apple originally wanted to keep the iPhone a closed system and only caved because of overwhelming customer pressure—ignited a revolution. To give the Cupertino consumer electronics giant credit where credit is due, Apple got its app store right, establishing rules for app submissions, purchasing, and management that are now essentially standard across the industry. Today, you can't launch or maintain a mobile or computing platform of any kind without offering an associated app store as well.

The app store in Windows 8 is called Windows Store, and it's modeled largely on the Windows Phone Marketplace, which Microsoft launched alongside its smartphone platform in 2010. And as with its Windows Phone offering, Windows Store is just part of a wider ecosystem of services that includes other online stores as well. For example, Windows 8 users may be interested in Microsoft's Xbox Music and Xbox Video Marketplaces as well.

▶ The Music and Video Marketplaces were previously collectively branded as the Zune Marketplace. With Windows 8, that brand is being phased out and is being replaced by the Xbox brand instead.

> **CROSSREF** The Xbox Music and Video Marketplaces are discussed in Chapter 9.

OK, so Windows Store is the app store for Windows. That's not a terrifically difficult concept, nor is the notion that Windows is supported by a surrounding ecosystem of related products and services. It's always been this way, of course, and with Windows 7, for example, we discussed how related products and services like Bing, Windows Live, and Zune "complete" the Windows experience. This sort of thing is absolutely still true today, though some of the brands have changed. But with Windows Store and the Windows 8 extensibility capabilities that its apps can take advantage of, things are a bit more nuanced today. They're also terrifically more exciting.

Consider the way applications have always extended the capabilities of Windows. In the past you could purchase full-featured applications like Microsoft Word or Adobe Photoshop to meet certain needs, such as creating and editing word processing documents or graphics art projects, respectively. The integration these applications offered with the underlying OS (still do, in fact) was pretty much relegated to snagging file associations. So you might open .docx files in Word instead of the WordPad utility that shipped with Windows.

Smaller applications, or utilities, such as a Zip utility or an antivirus solution, often supplied similar integration capabilities that lit up capabilities through the Explorer shell.

At a basic level, these classic Windows applications make Windows better, some-what generally, because they provide more capabilities than what is present solely in Windows. It's fair to say that no one uses Windows because of Windows itself, per se, but rather because of the utility of the amazing collection of applications that are available for this system.

None of this changes with Windows 8. Microsoft and third-party developers big and small will continue making traditional desktop-based applications to enhance that part of the Windows experience.

What changes in Windows 8, however, is that developers are now shipping Metro-style apps in addition to traditional Windows applications. Yes, some of them will simply be immersive, full-screen replacements for existing Windows applications. You'll see Metro-style word processors and graphics art apps, for example. But some will be much more than that.

Thanks to the extensibility features in Windows 8, developers can now create apps that make Windows 8 better in unique ways. In fact, they make Windows 8 almost future-proof in the sense that they can provide functionality to the OS that its makers didn't even know would one day be desirable.

▶ Remember, when we use the word app here, we are referring to Metro-style apps. Applications are traditional desktop applications.

Consider the Windows 8 share contract. Through this system-level service, apps can engage in two-way conversations without ever knowing what app is on the other side. The canonical example is sharing a web page via e-mail: Internet Explorer 10 for Metro supports one part of this contract—the ability to share an item, in this case a web page, with another app—and the Mail app supports the other part—the ability to receive a share request. This is a powerful feature because it's available to any Metro-style apps, and developers never need to know anything about the app that is on the other side of the equation. It's like copy and paste, but about a hundred times more powerful.

In a few years, some entrepreneur we've never heard of may launch a new online service we've never imagined. And while anyone could write a third-party app to support that service, with Windows 8, one could write an app that integrated with the OS's unique extensibility features. So this new Metro-style app for this new service could accept a share request from Internet Explorer 10 just like Mail does, but then do something completely different with it.

This is a simple (and purposefully vague) example. But the point is simple: Thanks to the massive and pervasive improvements to the underlying platform in Windows 8, apps aren't just something you install and use as standalone islands of activity. They will often be truly integrated experiences that make Windows 8 better. And that means that as time goes by, and more and more apps appear, Windows 8 is only going to get better. And it will do so even if Microsoft never lifts a finger to make that so.

Windows Store, then, isn't just a way to find new apps. It's a way to make Windows 8 better. That's just exciting.

FIRST RULE OF WINDOWS STORE: THERE ARE RULES TO WINDOWS STORE

If you're a developer targeting Windows 8 with a new Metro-style app, you've got a lot of work ahead of you, not just in writing that app, but in conforming to a long list of app rules that Microsoft has devised. These rules exist for simple reasons: Metro-style apps need to be safe, perform quickly, and work well, and they need to offer users a unique value of some kind.

For you, the Windows user, these rules are like the gold standard, ensuring that all of the apps you find on Windows Store—you know, the apps that are going to make Windows 8 better and better going forward—do what they're supposed to do. And while a rote list of these rules would be mind-numbingly boring, even to the most pedantic of developers, understanding what's required at a high level can be very informative. Here's what you can expect from the apps sold Windows Store:

▶ **Enterprises can get around this limitation, however, and "side-load" apps to their users through secure portals as well.**

- ▶ **Windows Store only:** Microsoft only allows Metro-style apps to be acquired and updated through Windows Store. Developers cannot offer these apps (or app updates) separately, from the web, or through other means. This allows Microsoft to control the quality of apps for Windows 8 and to enforce the rules that follow.

- ▶ **Free and paid:** Windows Store caters to both free and paid apps. Those paid apps can range in price from $1.49 on up (in the United States).

▶ **Trial versions:** App makers can optionally provide a trial version of a paid app. That trial version of the app has to provide a reasonable approximation of the full version and cannot simply be an ad for the paid app. Trial versions can be time-limited or feature-limited.

▶ **In-app purchases:** Apps can optionally offer in-app purchases, which are optional paid features.

▶ **Advertising:** Apps sold by Windows Store can contain advertisements. These ads can include offers for in-app purchases, offers for the full version of the game from the trial version, and so on. Apps cannot, however, exist solely to serve ads. And apps cannot serve ads on their live tile, app bar, or via the edge UIs.

▶ **PCs and devices:** The same Windows 8 apps can run on both traditional PCs (e.g., Intel x86) and new Windows RT-based (ARM) devices. However, app makers are not forced to support both, and you will see some apps that run only on one platform or the other.

> ▶ In this context, a PC is a PC based on an Intel or Intel-compatible chipset, and a device is a PC that's based on an ARM chipset and running Windows RT.

▶ **5 PCs/devices:** Apps you purchase or install from Windows Store can be installed on up to 5 PCs and/or devices.

▶ **Content policies:** Windows Store enforces strict content policies that can vary from region to region. No apps with a rating over ESRB (Entertainment Software Rating Board) Mature (or equivalent) are allowed, which excludes adults-only content (that which features prolonged scenes of intense violence or graphic sexual content).

> ▶ Apps must be rated and conform to rules set forth by the ESRB or equivalent rating system used in your locale.

▶ **One tile:** If you've ever installed an old-school Windows application like Office or Visual Studio on Windows 8, you know how awful it is to have numerous application tiles spewed onto your Start screen at the end. This won't happen with Metro-style apps: Developers are limited to adding just a single app tile to the Start screen.

▶ **Metro-style apps only:** Apps sold via Windows Store must be *real* Windows 8 apps—that is, Metro-style apps and not traditional Windows applications. That said, Microsoft is allowing developers to list their desktop applications in Windows Store, though directing users who wish to learn more, download the application, or purchase it, to do so from the developer's website.

▶ **No websites allowed:** An app must be a native Windows 8 app and not just a shell for a website. Windows 8 provides a facility for pinning favorite websites to the Start screen already.

▶ **Respect privacy:** If an app needs to publish your personal information to a third-party service, it must provide an opt-in mechanism so that you, the user, can explicitly OK this behavior before it happens. And the description provided must accurately explain how the information will be used or share and provide a way through which you can later rescind your permission. Apps that collect personal information must provide a privacy policy that explains how the developer is safeguarding your information.

▶ **Secure:** Apps cannot compromise the security or integrity of Windows. Put simply, they can't be malware or link to malware.

▶ **Reliable:** It sounds fairly obvious, but apps must be reliable and not stop working suddenly, end unexpectedly, or contain what Microsoft calls "programming errors." Ignore the irony of that statement for a moment and consider why this is truly important: When you download an application from the web, there's no quality guarantee at all, and if the application stops working or never works properly, you have no real mediation other than complaining to the developer. In Windows Store, there are community-based means of complaint—poor reviews and ratings in the store—and Microsoft, as the curator of the store, to complain to as well.

▶ **Performance:** Microsoft calls Metro-style apps fast and fluid, and it means that. Put in real-world terms, apps must start up in 5 seconds or less and resume in 2 seconds or less. Not impressed? Those scores must be obtained on a low-end, Atom-based PC. Chances are the Windows 8 device or PC you're using is much faster.

▶ **Windows 8 features:** Apps must support key Windows 8 features, including Snap, in which the app can share the screen with another snapped app. Apps must respect and utilize the system-level methods for app closing and not provide their own buttons or other mechanisms for closing. If an app uses notifications, it must support the system settings for these notifications so that the user can externally configure whether they work.

▶ **Network-friendly:** Thanks to a new emphasis on cellular connectivity in Windows devices and PCs—or what Microsoft calls metered Internet connections—apps must prevent users from unintentionally transferring large amounts of data over such networks. Typical examples include apps that provide streaming video or audio, both of which have specific transfer limits.

▶ **Multiple markets and languages:** Apps can be sold in multiple markets and in multiple languages if desired, though they must only support one of each.

LAUNCHING WINDOWS STORE

While Windows Store can be accessed like any other Metro-style app, the store is also central to other Metro experiences, so you'll find a few more entry points in Windows 8 as well. Here are some of the ways in which you can launch Windows Store:

▶ **Start screen tile:** The Windows Store tile, shown in Figure 6-1, is available by default on the Windows 8 Start screen. Just tap the tile to launch the app.

FIGURE 6-1: The Windows Store tile is the obvious entry point to this important app.

▶ **All apps:** If Windows Store isn't present on the Start screen for some reason, just enable the All Apps view (Right-click a blank area of the screen, tap Winkey + Z, or on a touch screen device, swipe up from the bottom of the screen). It will appear in this view as *Store*.

▶ **App Search:** You can also use Windows Search to search for Windows Store. Just tap Winkey + Q and type **store**.

▶ **From other apps:** Microsoft and third-party apps can provide front ends to Windows Store. The obvious example that's included with Windows 8 is Xbox Games, which provides access to, among other things, Metro-style games for Windows 8.

USING WINDOWS STORE

Of all the Windows 8 user experiences, Windows Store is perhaps the simplest and most obvious of all. Technology fans tend to toss around words like *intuitive* far more than is accurate, but in this case, it's close: You'd have a hard time getting lost in, or confused by, Windows Store. Shown in Figure 6-2, Windows Store is a model for the Metro-style fierce reduction of user interface that Microsoft seems very proud of these days.

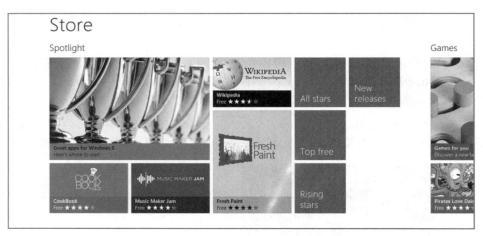

FIGURE 6-2: Awash in white space, it's Windows Store.

IT'S GOING TO CHANGE

Thanks to the dynamic nature of its new apps platform, the Metro-style apps that Microsoft includes with Windows 8/RT will change over time, so it's highly likely that this app will appear somewhat differently over time and will include additional features. This is normal, and as a general statement, it's probably fair to say that the version of Windows Store you use will provide a superset of the functionality we describe in this chapter.

Navigating the Store's Home Screen

As a true Metro-style experience, Windows Store offers horizontal rather than vertical navigation. That is, you scroll from left to right through the various app category sections that make up the home screen of this app, and not up and down as you would in a document-based application like Microsoft Word.

This navigation occurs logically enough as well: Users with touch-based devices will find that horizontal swipes work exactly as expected. Those with a mouse (or trackpad) can access the bottom-mounted scroll bar that appears when that pointing device is present, as shown in Figure 6-3, or use the mouse's scroll wheel.

FIGURE 6-3: Mouse users can navigate Windows Store with a scroll bar.

And if you're keyboard-bound, Page Up and Page Down will scroll the UI from category to category. Home and End will navigate directly to the front and rear of the app's home screen, respectively.

In fact, it's very similar to how the Start screen works. Windows Store even supports the semantic zoom feature that's also available in the Start screen. This feature lets you zoom out the display of the app and view it from afar, enabling you to gain a better understanding of its layout and navigate more quickly to a specific store category.

The semantic zoom view is shown in Figure 6-4.

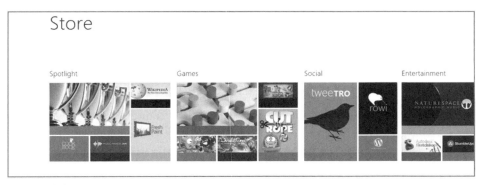

FIGURE 6-4: Windows Store in semantic zoom view

To achieve this effect, you pinch the screen if you're using a touch-based device. With a mouse and keyboard, hold down the Ctrl key and use the mouse's scroll wheel to move in and out of semantic zoom view.

Windows Store also provides an app bar, though it appears a bit differently than with other Metro-style apps, at the top of the app rather than the bottom, and using text-based links instead of normal buttons. Shown in Figure 6-5, the Store's app bar

lets you navigate quickly back to the Home screen from anywhere in the app—
a handy feature given how quickly you can get lost while spelunking for apps.

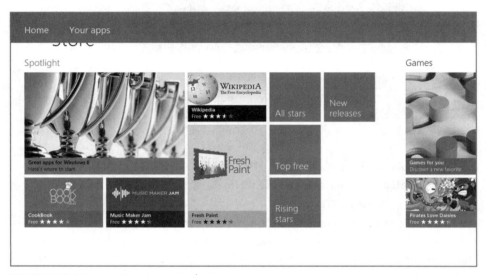

FIGURE 6-5: Windows Store's app bar provides a couple of handy quick links.

The Store's app bar also provides a way to jump quickly to Your Apps, a list of the
apps you've already downloaded or paid for. We discuss this latter feature later in
the chapter.

Understanding Windows Store Categories

As noted earlier, Windows Store uses a category-based design in which the various
app categories are represented visually by groups that are laid out from left to right,
much as Start screen groups can be. The following major groups are available:

▶ **Spotlight:** The first group provides a front-of-store experience, with the latest
and most highly reviewed apps, showcased apps, and other notable apps.

▶ **Games:** Expected to be the most popular app category as it is on Windows
Phone and other mobile platforms, this group gets preferential placement
and additional promotional space.

▶ **Social:** This group contains apps related to social network services, such as
Facebook and Twitter as well as blog-related apps, such as WordPress.

▶ **Entertainment:** This group covers entertainment related apps that often
cross over into music and video, including Flixster, Netflix, Xbox Companion,
and the like.

- ▶ **Photo:** Here, you'll find apps that extend the basic photo experiences in Windows 8 with support for editing capabilities and various online photo services.

- ▶ **Music & Video:** As with photos, Windows 8 provides only a basic multimedia experience, so this category will open up the platform's support for music, video, online radio, podcast, and other related services.

- ▶ **Sports:** Need an app to check up on the latest sports scores and gossip? It'll be in here.

- ▶ **Books & Reference:** Filled with apps for e-book reading platforms like Kindle and Nook, as well as more traditional reference material, this is the category to check out if you're looking to turn that Windows 8 tablet into an electronic bookshelf.

- ▶ **News & Weather:** If you wish to stay up to date with the news or weather, you'll find a plethora of apps here for newspapers like *The New York Times* and *Los Angeles Times*, TV, and online-based news shops, such as News360 and MSNBC, weather utilities, and the like.

- ▶ **Health & Fitness:** Need to track how many calories you've burned preparing for that dinner you made using an app from the next app category? You'll find an app for that in this category.

- ▶ **Food & Dining:** This category highlights cookbooks, restaurant review apps, and related apps.

- ▶ **Lifestyle:** A collection of apps related to lifestyle activities that are not covered by the other categories.

- ▶ **Shopping:** Here, you'll find apps for Amazon.com and your other favorite retailers as well as apps related to the shopping experience, including reviews-based apps.

- ▶ **Travel:** Travel apps, including currency converters, guides to international locales, and hotel, airfare, and auto rentals can be found in this category.

- ▶ **Finance:** Apps related to personal finance, taxes, and the stock market are available here.

- ▶ **Productivity:** Perhaps the broadest category aside from games, this category includes apps related to productivity, including note-taking solutions like OneNote and Evernote, word processors and other document editors, cloud storage, and much, much more.

- ▶ **Tools:** A collection of useful utilities which, like Security below, also includes a larger-than-usual selection of desktop applications in addition to Metro-style apps.

▶ **Security:** The most curious category because it will likely consist mostly of links to traditional desktop applications over time rather than Metro-style apps, this category houses PC security and personal protection apps.

▶ **Business:** This category includes the expected business-oriented titles, but also cloud-based storage services.

▶ **Education:** Here you'll find educational app titles of all types, from SAT preparation to star charts.

Within each group in the home screen, you will see a few promoted apps, tiled for top free and paid apps in that category, and other entries.

Diving a Bit Deeper

As you browse around Windows Store's virtual storefront, you'll eventually see something that strikes your fancy and you will want to dive a bit deeper. There are basically three paths you can take from the Windows Store home screen and arrive at a different type of landing page. These include landing pages for categories, lists, and apps. So let's look at each.

BROWSING BY CATEGORY

Each category has its own landing page that provides a list of the apps within that category that are sortable by subcategories, prices, and/or other criteria (noteworthy, newest, highest rating, lowest price, and highest price). Accessing a category landing page, curiously, isn't very obvious: You need to tap or click the category title on the Windows Store home screen.

The view is fairly consistent between categories, and you'll see the same basic user interface elements on each category landing page, as you can see in Figure 6-6.

These elements include the following:

▶ **Back:** A browser-style back button that persists throughout the Windows Store UI, letting you quickly navigate back to the previous screen. In the case of a category landing page, tapping this button will return you to the Windows Store home screen.

▶ **Category title:** A non-clickable title that indicates which category you're viewing.

▶ **App count:** Next to the category title, you will see an app counter listing how many apps there are in the current category. This number changes if you filter the list as described shortly.

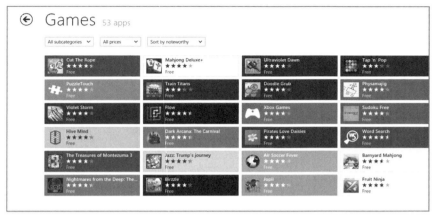

FIGURE 6-6: The landing page for the Games category.

▶ **Subcategory filter:** This widget lets you filter the current view so that it displays only apps of the selected subcategory. Available subcategories vary by category, of course. Games includes subcategories like Action, Adventure, Arcade, Card, Casino, and many, many more. A category view filtered with a subcategory will resemble Figure 6-7.

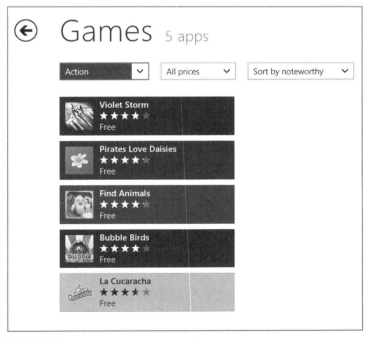

FIGURE 6-7: Viewing a subcategory only

► **Price filter:** With this widget, you can filter by price with available choices being free, free and trial, and paid.

► **Sort filter:** The sort filter is probably the least obvious but has some useful choices: Sort by noteworthy, newest, highest rating, lowest price, and highest price.

In case it's not obvious, you can filter the view by any combination of subcategory, price, and sort. So you could, for example, view only noteworthy, free, strategy games if that's what you're looking for. This is shown in Figure 6-8.

FIGURE 6-8: That's exactly the game I was looking for!

BROWSING BY LIST

In many of the category groups on the Windows Store homepage, you'll see colored tiles that represent app lists that are specially curated by Microsoft because they believe they'll be interesting to users. There are some regular lists that will often be available, such as Top free and Top paid, and then promotional lists that appear from time to time. It's not hard to imagine lists related to a holiday like Halloween, a major game release like the next Halo, or similar.

In Figure 6-9, you can see six such list tiles mixed in with tiles for individual games in the Spotlight group. These lists include Great apps for Windows 8, All Stars, New releases, Top free, Picks for you, and Rising stars.

When you view a list landing page, it looks a lot like the landing page for a category. There are Back, List title, and App count elements, as well as a grid of app tiles. Some of these list landing pages also include a nice textual description of the list so you can better understand what you're looking at, as shown in Figure 6-10.

What's missing here is any filtering: These list landing pages don't include the subcategory, price, and sort filters you see on a category landing page.

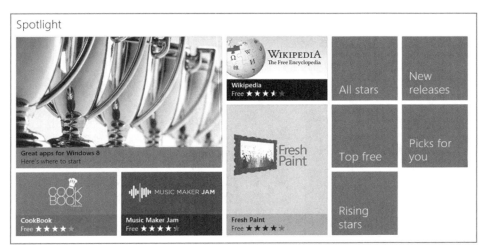

FIGURE 6-9: List tiles mixed in with tiles for individual games

FIGURE 6-10: A list landing page

BROWSING BY APP

Eventually, it all comes down to an individual app. You can reach an app landing page via a direct link on the Windows Store home screen or by tapping its tile on a category or list landing page. In Figure 6-11, you can see the landing page for an app.

FIGURE 6-11: An app landing page

These app landing pages, like those for categories and lists, feature some common elements. These elements include:

▶ **Back:** A browser-like Back button that will return you to the previous page.

▶ **App title:** Non-interactive title text providing the name of the app.

▶ **Navigational breadcrumbs:** Below the app title, you'll see two or more bread-crumb hyperlinks, providing you with both the exact location of the app in the store (like Home → Games → Puzzle) and a way to jump back to any location in the store above the app. That is, you can tap Home, Game, or Puzzle in the previously cited example and navigate directly to one of those locations.

▶ **Overview view:** The default view provides one or more screenshots, a description and feature list, and, optionally, other information such as links to the app website, app support, and feedback.

▶ **Details view:** Tap the Details header and the display will change to show you the app's release notes, supported processor(s) (x86, x64 and/or ARM), supported language(s), permissions, accessibility (if available), and terms of use. A typical app details view is shown in Figure 6-12.

▶ The permissions list is worth looking at. Many apps will require access to your Internet connection, but some of the other possible permissions include access to your home or work network, your music library, and the like.

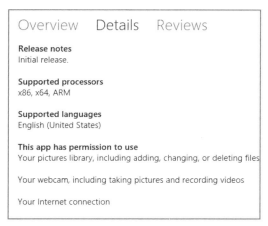

FIGURE 6-12: The Details view for an app

▶ **Reviews view:** Tap the Reviews header and you'll navigate to each of the reviews, and associated ratings, for the app. This list of reviews is sorted by newest by default, as shown in Figure 6-13, but it can be sorted by oldest, highest rated, lowest rated, or most helpful if desired.

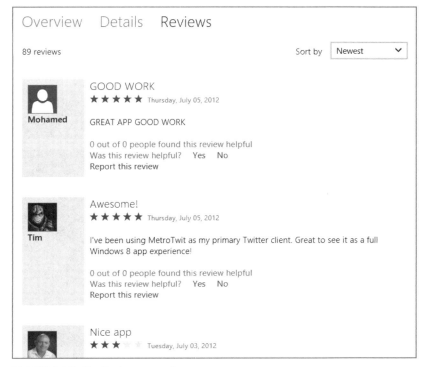

FIGURE 6-13: The Reviews page for an app

We examine app reviews and other feedback a bit later in the chapter.

▶ **Buy, Try, and Install button(s):** In the left pane of the default Overview view, you'll see one or more buttons related to downloading the app. These include Buy, Try, and Install. We look at app downloading and updating later in this chapter.

Other Ways to Find Apps

If you're content to simply browse around, the category-based layout of Windows Store is pleasant enough. But oftentimes you're looking for something specific. And Windows Store does provide a couple of other ways to find the apps you want.

FINDING APPS WITH SEARCH

The most obvious way to search for apps is to use the system-wide search functionality that's available to all Metro-style apps. This occurs via the Search pane, which can be summoned while using Windows Store by tapping Winkey + Q, or by invoking the Charms bar via touch or mouse and then selecting Search. The Search pane is shown in Figure 6-14.

The Windows Store search experience isn't bare bones. As you type, search suggestions appear at the top of the pane, as shown in Figure 6-15. And in addition to basic as-you-type suggestions, Search provides recommendations for particularly well-regarded apps when appropriate.

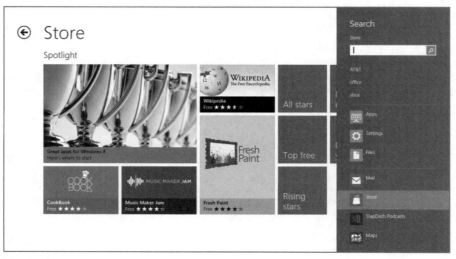

FIGURE 6-14: The Search pane

Search suggestions and recommendations appear as you type, in the Search pane. But if you tap Enter, a complete list of search results will appear directly in the app, as shown in Figure 6-16. These results can be fine-tuned much like other landing pages, and they provide widgets for category, price, and sort.

From here, you can tap the app you want, go back to the previous page with the Back button, or tap the subtle Home link to return to the Windows Store home screen.

FINDING APPS FROM THE WEB

Windows 8 users have a number of ways in which they can find Metro-style apps on the web. The first is via a developer-provided link. As it does with Windows Phone, Microsoft gives developers a way to link to Windows 8 apps from the web. So developers can create a website for their new app and provide a hyperlink that will actually cause the Windows Store app to launch when clicked, and then navigate to that app's landing page. This is similar to links you may have seen for iPhone/iPad and Android apps online.

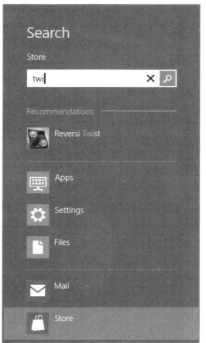

FIGURE 6-15: Windows Store Search supports search suggestions and recommendations.

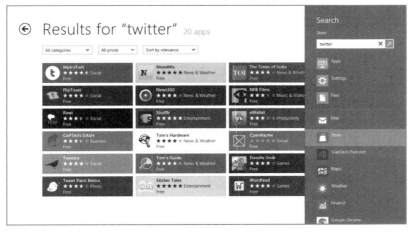

FIGURE 6-16: Search results appear in-app.

As an added nicety, Microsoft also publishes an HTML version of the Windows Store landing page for your app that developers can place on their own site. This landing page looks exactly like the app landing page in Windows Store except that the Buy/Try/Install buttons have been replaced by a View in Windows Store button. An example is shown in Figure 6-17.

FIGURE 6-17: A web-based landing page for a Windows 8 app directs users to Windows Store.

▶ The Store app catalog is literally indexed by search engines, so anything that's in the store is available from these services.

For you, this feature is useful because Windows 8 app listings are available to search engines. So you can visit Google Search, Bing, or whatever other search engine and find the apps you're looking for using the searching methods you're already familiar with. We suspect that many will do just that.

The final way in which you can find apps from the web is a bit more subtle—OK, a lot more subtle—and it requires you to be using the Metro version of Internet Explorer. When you browse to the website for a Windows 8 app, that site can optionally provide an entry in IE's Page Tools button menu, and can indicate this availability by placing a cute little plus ("+") sign on the button. When you click the Page Tools button, you'll see a menu item, Get app for this site, as shown in Figure 6-18. Clicking this item will cause the app's landing page to load in Windows Store.

FIGURE 6-18: An app switch button in IE 10 for Metro

If you already have the app installed on your PC, that menu item will let you open the app instead.

Downloading, Installing, and Updating Apps

OK, so you've found the app of your dreams. Now what?

DOWNLOADING AND INSTALLING APPS

As you may recall, Windows Store supports three basic types of apps: free, paid, and trial, the latter of which are a reduced functionality (or time limited) version of a paid app. These app types will be reflected in the button or buttons you see on the landing page of the app you intend to download. As an example, consider Figure 6-19. Here, we see a single Install button.

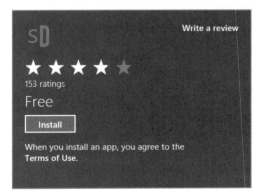

FIGURE 6-19: An app landing page can have buttons for Install, Buy, or Try.

Install is just one of several buttons that can appear here. The complete list included:

▶ **Install:** There are two reasons you might see an Install button. First, you have previously downloaded/purchased the app, so Windows Store is making it available to you now on another computer or device. Or second, the app is free.

▶ **Buy:** Click this to purchase a paid app.

▶ **Try:** Click this button to download a trial version of a paid app.

When you click any one of these buttons, the app begins downloading immediately. This is indicated in two ways: Windows Store navigates back to the homepage and displays a subtle installing message in the top right of the screen, followed by the notification shown in Figure 6-20.

FIGURE 6-20: Downloading and installing an app

If you're quick enough, you can click (or tap) that initial download message and view the Installing Apps screen. This screen, shown in Figure 6-21, provides a progress bar for the app download and install process.

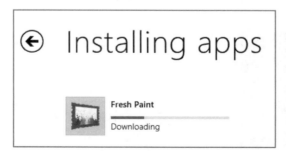

FIGURE 6-21: The Installing Apps screen

When the download completes . . . nothing happens. That is, if you stay on the Windows Store homepage, the installing message simply disappears. And if you do navigate to the Installing Apps screen, that's not much help either: It simply reports that you aren't installing any apps right now. Right.

As it turns out, the Metro-style app install process is so seamless that most installs take just seconds, and none require any hand-holding, User Account Control prompts, reboots, or the other nonsense that often accompanies a traditional Windows application installation.

On the other hand, a little guidance would be nice. But it's not difficult: To find your app, you need to visit the Start screen. When a new app is installed, it's placed on the end of the Start screen, so you may need to scroll to the right. In Figure 6-22, you can see our newly installed app, ready to go.

FIGURE 6-22: Newly installed apps appear at the end, or far right, of the Start screen.

UPDATING APPS

By default, Windows Store will automatically download any app updates in the background and then notify you—albeit in very subtle ways—when updates are ready for installation. There are two such prompts. The first appears on the Windows Store live tile. If you have one or more pending updates to install, this tile will display a number notification on its surface, indicating how many apps need to be updated, as shown in Figure 6-23.

> **CROSSREF** You can also manually check for updates, though this isn't usually necessary since the process is automatic. However, if you've disabled the automatic download of app updates, you can find out how to manually check for updates in the section "Configuring Accounts and Preferences" later in this chapter.

▶ Sometimes, if an app update is important and required, the app will actually notify you to download the update. The full-screen, modal notification will explain that a newer version of the app is required to continue using it.

When you navigate into Windows Store, you'll see a similarly subtle message in the top right of the screen indicating that updates are available. (See Figure 6-24.)

FIGURE 6-23: The Windows Store live tile indicates whether you have pending updates.

FIGURE 6-24: A subtle message indicating there are updates

Click this message to navigate to the App updates screen, where you can trigger the download and installation of these pending updates. You can see the available choices in Figure 6-25.

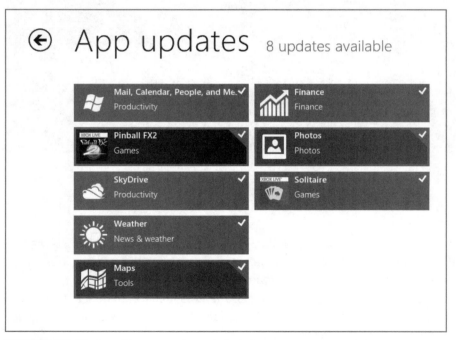

FIGURE 6-25: Windows Store prompts you to install one or more app updates.

To install all of the pending updates, simply click the Install button.

mylibraryrewards.com

sign-up to receive exciting
rewards and gifts simply
by reading!

Read-Reward-Redeem®

EXAMPLE REWARD
IN YOUR AREA

Graham Crackers
Comics: Three Free
Comic Books From 50
Cent Bins for ages 14
and under.

⊙ Plainfield
50 Points

FINDING YOUR APPS

Once you've used Windows Store for a while, or across a few PCs and devices, you may find it useful to view all of the apps you've downloaded and purchased. You can do this through the Your apps interface. To find this, display the Windows Store app bar and choose Your apps. After a bit of thinking, you'll see a display much like that in Figure 6-26.

FIGURE 6-26: The Your apps interface provides a handy front end to, well, your apps.

As with other areas of Windows Store, you can filter this view, in this case in two unique ways. You can view all of the apps you've downloaded or just the ones you downloaded on a particular PC. And you can sort by apps that aren't installed on the current PC, by date, or by name.

To install an app, simply select it and then click the Install button that appears in the app bar at the bottom of the screen as in Figure 6-27. You can also click View details to learn more about a selected app.

▶ Want to install all of your apps? Just click the Select all button in the bottom left of the screen and then click Install.

Getting the Core Microsoft Apps

Thanks to regulatory and antitrust-related agreements around the world, Microsoft is no longer free to bundle as many useful applications (or, in this case, apps) with Windows as it did in the past. For this reason, Windows 7 was often accompanied on new PC installs by related products like Windows Live Essentials and Zune that Microsoft said completed the Windows 7 experience. These applications didn't technically come with Windows, but they were available separately, for free, and PC makers were free to bundle the apps on their PCs alongside Windows. So the net effect for most users was the same as if Microsoft had included them in Windows 7.

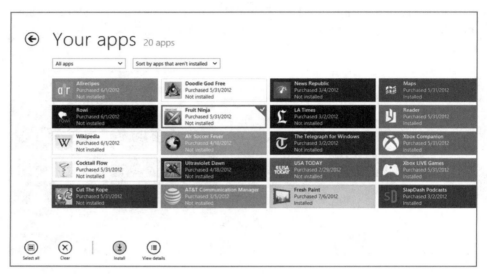

FIGURE 6-27: Installing apps from Your apps

Windows 8 faces similar scrutiny. So there are numerous Microsoft apps in this release that are not technically included with Windows 8. And though most PC makers are bundling them with Windows 8 as before, completing (or muddying, others would say) the experience, so to speak, many users will also acquire Windows on their own.

As discussed at the beginning of this book, we consider these apps to be a key part of the full, or complete, Windows 8 experience. The good news is that they're readily available from Windows Store. And all of them are free. So if they're not available in your copy of Windows 8 for some reason, you can find them here.

The app categories and the apps that fall within each are listed below:

- **Communications apps:** These include Calendar, Mail, Maps, Messaging, People, Reader, and SkyDrive, or what we call the productivity apps.

- **Entertainment apps:** Camera, Photos, Xbox Companion, Xbox Music, Xbox Video, and Xbox Games.

- **Bing apps:** Bing, Finance, News, Sports, Travel, and Weather.

Not surprisingly, this book assumes you have these apps installed, so if any aren't present on your PC, get cracking.

CROSSREF Microsoft's communications (productivity) apps are covered in Chapter 8. Microsoft's entertainment apps are discussed in Chapter 9.

Rating and Reviewing Apps and Providing Other Feedback

As you download and install apps, you may find yourself relying on the in-store reviews and ratings that other users have provided. And as you spend more time reading these often useful bits of feedback, you'll discover that you can optionally leave different types of feedback of your own, if you'd like and depending on what you're comfortable with.

Windows Store supports different types of feedback, listed here from simple and fast to more involved.

WAS THIS REVIEW HELPFUL?

As you read an individual review, you may feel that it was particularly helpful . . . or not. And in a nice bit of fair play—where the hunter becomes the hunted—you can review a review, so to speak. That is, you can indicate whether a review was helpful in getting you to decide whether to download or buy it.

To leave this kind of feedback, find the Was this review helpful? link that appears below each review, as shown in Figure 6-28. Simply click Yes or No to indicate your choice.

FIGURE 6-28: You can rate a review!

As more and more people rate reviews, these choices become very important as they indicate the relative trustworthiness of each review. If 19 out of 20 people found a review helpful, for example, chances are it's pretty good.

REPORT THIS REVIEW

Sometimes a review is so terrible it warrants special attention. Perhaps the author uses foul language or is complaining about something that has nothing to do with the actual app (a long-running pet peeve of ours). If so, you can report the review and a real, live human being at Microsoft will take a look. If they agree with you, the review could be removed from the store.

To report an app, click the Report this review link.

However, be careful when doing so: There's no confirmation and no chance to change your mind.

RATE AND REVIEW AN APP

If you're interested in opining on the quality of an app—for better or worse—you can write a review of your own. Reviews have a few components: a rating, which can go from 1 to 5 stars, a title, and then the review itself.

To write a review from within Windows Store, visit the app's landing page and click the Write a review link you'll see in the colored pane on the left side of the Overview view. In the next screen, shown in Figure 6-29, you're provided with stars for the rating and fields for a title and the review body.

You will need to have first installed the app for the Write a review link to appear. Obviously.

FIGURE 6-29: Windows Store app review form

Once you've written a review, the Write a review link on the app's landing page will change to Update your review.

Note that you are accountable for the reviews you write: The name and picture associated with your Microsoft account will accompany the review, for all the world to see. But with awesome responsibility comes awesome power: Your rating will impact the overall rating of the app, and your review is now open to the plaudits—or criticisms—of your fellow Windows 8 users.

Uninstalling Apps

If you're familiar with the horrific and unreliable method for uninstalling traditional Windows desktop-based applications, which in many cases does nothing to remove spurious files and registry entries, you'll be delighted to discover that uninstalling a Metro-style app is simplicity itself. Most surprisingly, perhaps, you uninstall these apps from the Start screen.

To uninstall an app, navigate to the Start screen and locate the tile for that app. If it's not present, you can use the Windows 8 All Apps list, or Start search to locate the app. Here's how:

▶ **All Apps:** From the Start screen, open the app bar. This can be done by swiping in from the top or bottom edge of the screen, by pressing Winkey + Z, or by right-clicking an empty area of the Start screen with the mouse. Then, select All apps from the app bar and locate the app you want to remove from the list.

▶ **Start Search:** From the Start screen, open the app search experience. This can be done by swiping in from the right edge of the screen and choosing Search from the Charms bar. (Alternatively, press Winkey + Q, or activate the Charms bar and choose Search with the mouse.) From this interface, type the name of the app you wish to uninstall until it becomes obvious in the filtered app list.

Whichever method you're using—the Start screen, All Apps, or Start Search—to uninstall an app you must select it first. This is done on a touch interface by tapping and holding and then dragging down until a selection border appears (Start screen tile) or the app tile is color-selected (All Apps, Start Search), and the app bar appears. With a mouse, simply right-click the tile. Keyboard selection is a bit trickier and less common, but you can use the arrows keys to highlight the correct tile or app, and then press Ctrl + Space to select it.

Figure 6-30 shows what a selected Start screen tile looks like.

FIGURE 6-30: A selected tile on the Start screen

Wherever you make this selection—from the Start screen, All apps view, or from Search, you will see an Uninstall choice in the app bar. To uninstall the app, simply select this button. As you can see in Figure 6-31, you will be prompted with a pop-up window and informed that Metro-style app uninstall is a complete wipe: not just the app but its data is removed from the PC.

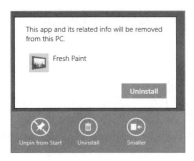

FIGURE 6-31: Are you sure you want to uninstall that app?

CONFIGURING ACCOUNTS AND PREFERENCES

► To do this, move the mouse cursor to the upper- or lower-right corner of the screen and then move the cursor along the right edge of the screen toward the center. It's a bit more natural to perform than it is to describe.

Like other Metro-style apps, Windows Store provides a simple Settings interface, and it is through this interface that you can access your account settings and other store-related preferences. Likewise, accessing this interface occurs as it does in other Metro experiences, through the Settings pane. You can access this pane from within Windows Store by typing Winkey + I, by swiping in from the right edge of the screen, or by using the mouse to enable the Charms bar and then choosing Settings.

The Windows Store settings pane is shown in Figure 6-32.

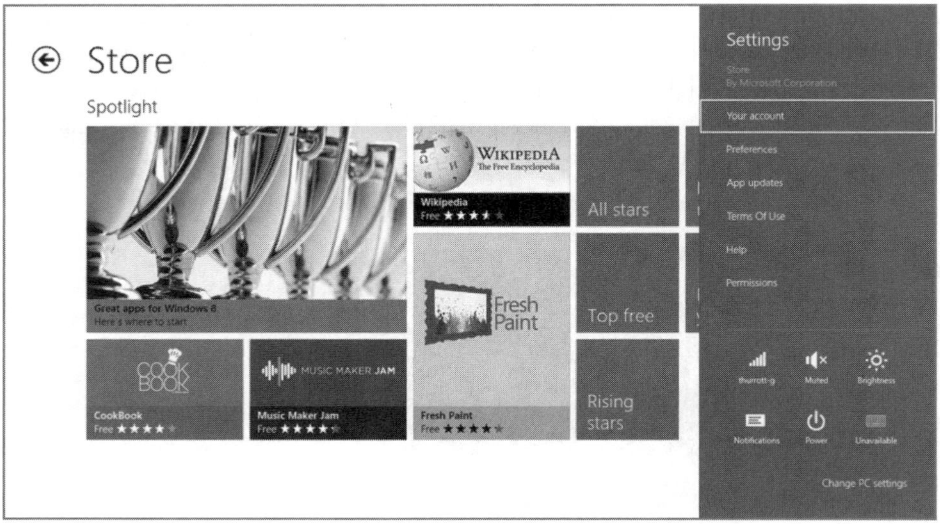

FIGURE 6-32: Windows Store settings

While the Preferences option may seem to be the most relevant, it leads to a screen with only two configurable choices—Make it easier to find apps in my preferred languages (which is enabled by default) and Make it easier to find apps that include accessibility features (which is not). Instead, click Your account. When you do, you'll see a full-screen interface like that in Figure 6-33.

▶ Click App updates to manually check for app updates.

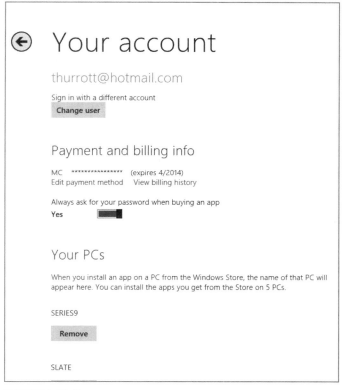

FIGURE 6-33: Your account

From here, you can configure some useful settings related to Windows Store. These include the following:

- ▶ **Your store account:** You can sign out of your current account and use a different account for store activities.

- ▶ **Payment and billing information:** Windows Store uses the credit card information that is registered with your Microsoft account for purchases by default, so this option is generally set to No. However, if you'd prefer to manually sign in to your Microsoft account every time a purchase is made for security reasons, you can make that change here.

▶ **Your registered PCs (and devices):** When you install any app (paid, free, trial) on a PC or device, it is added to the list of 5 PCs/devices to which you can install apps. These apps, of course, and the 5 PCs/devices list, are tied to your Microsoft account. Via this interface, you can remove a PC/device from the list of your registered PCs and devices, as shown in Figure 6-34. Doing so will prevent those apps from running on the deselected PC/device going forward.

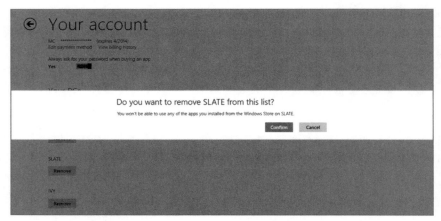

FIGURE 6-34: Removing a PC from your list of registered PCs and devices

SUMMARY

With Windows Store, you can feel secure that Microsoft's curated app store will provide you with the best possible experience, one that bridges the gap between the insecure Wild West of Google's Android platform and the overly controlling and nonintegrated Apple App Store. This best-of-both-worlds experience draws on the lessons Microsoft learned from Windows Phone Marketplace, as well.

Using the store is a breeze, thanks to its intuitive, Metro-style UI, logical category-based organization, and a plethora of app discovery and feedback tools. You can use Windows Store to find, download, try, and buy Metro-style apps, and then update them with new features as needed. Only app uninstall occurs outside the store, and that's a simple process that won't litter your PC with leftover files and registry entries.

With this experience under your belt, you can begin further exploring Windows 8's rich app landscape. And in the remainder of this section of the book, you'll do just that, as you examine Internet Explorer 10 and the various productivity and entertainment apps that make this OS the best Windows yet.

CHAPTER 7

Browsing the Web with Internet Explorer 10

IN THIS CHAPTER

▶ Understanding the relationship between the two versions of Internet Explorer that ship with Windows 8

▶ Using the Metro-style version of Internet Explorer

▶ Configuring IE 10 Metro

▶ Using the Desktop version of Internet Explorer

▶ Configuring IE 10 desktop

▶ Knowing when to use which browser

▶ Understanding the weird interaction between IE 10 desktop, IE 10 Metro, and third-party browsers

In keeping with the dual user experience nature of Windows 8 itself, Microsoft has reimagined Internet Explorer—and, really, web browsing in general as well—in this new operating system, creating a fascinating, dual-mode version of the most-frequently used Windows application. Internet Explorer 10 is, in many ways, the poster child for this Windows 8-based vision of the future, offering both a Metro-style user experience and a more traditional, desktop-based web browser version as well.

It's a model that other web browser makers, and perhaps other application makers, will emulate in their own solutions. But because web browsers play such a special role in Windows, having both Metro-style and traditional browsers available comes with some unique new constraints as well. So this chapter explores these changes, as well as the new features of both versions of Internet Explorer 10.

TWO BROWSERS, ONE BRAIN: UNDERSTANDING INTERNET EXPLORER 10

How you view Internet Explorer 10 will depend greatly on how you view Windows 8 and its two separate user experiences. That's because, like Windows 8 itself, Internet Explorer 10 offers two faces to the world: a full-screen, Metro-style version of the browser and a more traditional, desktop-based version.

Let's see what that means. In Figure 7-1, you can see the Metro version of Internet Explorer, with its normally hidden application user interface (or *chrome*) displayed for context. This version of IE offers a full-screen, touch-friendly, immersive user experience.

FIGURE 7-1: The Metro-style version of Internet Explorer 10

In Figure 7-2, meanwhile, you see the desktop version of Internet Explorer 10. This looks and works much like previous IE versions and is tailored for the traditional desktop environment. It offers a richer feature set, with full support for add-ons and browser extensions.

These two solutions are separate but also connected. That is, the Metro-style app and the desktop application are indeed two different executables, or programs. But they utilize the same rendering engine under the hood, share numerous features and data, and, most confusingly, interact with each other, and with other browsers and the underlying OS, in brand-new ways.

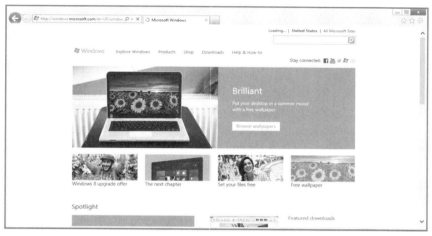

FIGURE 7-2: The desktop version of Internet Explorer 10

Microsoft describes these dual Internet Explorer applications as two different experiences, or skins, with one underlying browser engine. But that's a bit of a stretch. In reality, Internet Explorer 10 acts as two distinct applications, and that becomes more evident when you configure Windows to use a different default browser (like Google Chrome).

As a result, it's perhaps a bit fairer to say that Windows 8 offers two very different browser experiences, though each do share some underpinnings. Which one you use will depend very much on how you use Windows 8.

That is, if you find yourself using the Metro user experience a lot, perhaps because you're using a touch-based device like a tablet, you'll probably want to stick with Internet Explorer for Metro. But if you are using a more traditional mouse- and keyboard-based system, perhaps a desktop PC or laptop, the desktop version of Internet Explorer will be what you're looking for.

Or maybe things aren't so black and white. As it turns out, our devices, just like the OS they run, are changing. And as you read this, you could be using a tablet that docks and connects to a larger display and a keyboard and mouse, and other peripherals, while you're sitting at a desk. Or perhaps you'll opt for a hybrid laptop or Ultrabook that can work as both a traditional PC, with keyboard and mouse, or, with the flip of a screen, can be used like a tablet.

With such devices, your usage will vary not by the device type—since these new kinds of PCs are so versatile—but rather by the situation. They can change on the fly, in fact, and you can move between the different Internet Explorer applications as your usage changes. And because these two applications share browsing history, typed addresses, settings, and more, moving back and forth is fairly seamless.

▶ While we tend to use the term app to describe Metro-style solutions, and application for desktop solutions, this is just for convenience. Effectively speaking, both types of solutions are applications. (And, as it turns out, both are apps too!)

▶ IE 10 Metro and IE 10 desktop also share many useful security features, such as SmartScreen and InPrivate Browsing.

> **NOTE** IE 10 Metro and IE 10 desktop also share many (but not all) underpinning technologies, including hardware acceleration of web-based text, graphics, video, and audio, and compiled JavaScript—you know, if you're a web geek.

Another thing to consider, though this may be hard to believe: You may just end up liking Internet Explorer 10 Metro, and grow to prefer using it, even if you work mostly in the desktop environment. It can be said that the Metro version of Internet Explorer 10, with its chrome-free user interface and full-screen browsing experience, is like a gateway drug for the rest of Metro. It may, in fact, help convince you to ditch that aging desktop or laptop and head toward a more modern device with touch capabilities.

Either way, Internet Explorer 10 does offers what Microsoft loves to describe as a "no compromises" web browsing experience that works very well with both touch-screen devices and desktop-based machines, and also offers a way to move back and forth between them. Both experiences are available anywhere, from a powerful multi-display desktop all the way down to a svelte, 7-inch tablet.

But don't decide now. In the coming sections, we'll thoroughly examine the new Metro-style version of Internet Explorer. (IE 10 for the desktop hasn't changed much at all, from a user experience standpoint, since IE 9.) And then you can decide for yourself.

INTERNET EXPLORER 10 FOR METRO

▶ IE 10 Metro may be add-on free, but it does include an integrated version of Adobe Flash so it will work with many (but not all) popular Flash-based websites, including those for videos and games.

Internet Explorer 10 for Metro is a touch-friendly, Metro-style web browser that works pretty well with mouse and keyboard too. It offers an add-on free experience that is faster and safer but dispenses with some useful functionality you may expect if you've used previous IE versions.

Like other Metro-style apps, IE 10 Metro is immersive, or tailored for a touch-first device experience. That means no visual distractions—thanks to its lack of chrome—and the ability to use simple gestures to navigate the web and pan and zoom across individual web pages.

IE 10 Metro also changes the web in some crucial ways. On-screen controls like check boxes and radio buttons are styled differently so that they're touch-friendly. It's very similar to the experience offered by the Windows Phone version of Internet Explorer, in fact.

Some common browser activities are handled quite a bit differently in this version of Internet Explorer. For example, search and sharing occur from the system-wide contracts that are available from the Charms bar. And the Metro Devices interface is used to print, play video on other screens, and interact with other devices.

CROSSREF Chapter 3 describes Charms, contracts, and other common Metro features.

Some things, of course, are the same as with the desktop version of IE. Aside from the basic feature set, including features like InPrivate Browsing and Tracking Protection, you'll find that many keyboard shortcuts from desktop IE continue to work in the Metro version of the browser. And if you find a page that won't work in IE Metro—perhaps because of its lack of add-on support—you can easily open that page in the desktop version of Internet Explorer and get back to work.

The IE Metro User Experience

The Metro version of Internet Explorer 10 should be available via its live tile on the Windows 8 Start screen, as shown in Figure 7-3.

FIGURE 7-3: The Internet Explorer 10 live tile

IE METRO ISN'T ALWAYS AVAILABLE

Yes, that says *should*. Sadly, depending on how you acquired Windows 8—perhaps by upgrading an existing PC or from a PC maker who has modified the default settings—you may see a tile for the desktop version of Internet Explorer instead, as shown in Figure 7-4. Or, you may see a tile for a competing web browser.

FIGURE 7-4: See this tile instead? That's the IE 10 desktop tile.

continues

(continued)

Unfortunately, this is an important consideration, because when another browser or the desktop version of IE is configured as the default browser, Internet Explorer 10 for Metro won't even be available. It will literally be hidden from you, and unavailable. Because of this possibility, we explain exactly how and why this happens, and how you can fix it, in the final section of this chapter. So if you're not seeing what you should be seeing, jump ahead now. And no worries, it's easily fixed, if not easily understood.

The first time you launch the Metro version of Internet Explorer may be a bit surprising, and while Figure 7-5 is probably inadequate for explaining why, here it goes.

FIGURE 7-5: It's the touchable web: IE 10 for Metro.

> Yes, this is why Google named its own browser Chrome.

> To hide the edge UIs, simply perform the same swipe—or keyboard shortcut, or right-click, again. These things almost always work like a toggle.

What you may not be getting from that static screenshot is that Internet Explorer for Metro, like IE for Windows Phone, offers only a very minimal user interface, and one that is, in fact, hidden by default. So what you're looking at there is a web page loaded in a browser that has no surrounding user interface, or what browser makers call chrome. That is, you're seeing just the web page, and not the browser.

Like other Metro-style apps, Internet Explorer 10 does provide a so-called edge UI that is accessed by swiping toward the middle of the screen from the top or bottom edge. (Mouse users can right-click any blank area of the browser's surface to trigger this interface, while keyboard users should learn the Winkey + Z shortcut.) When you access this edge UI, the browser will resemble Figure 7-6.

FIGURE 7-6: The IE Metro edge UI

There's a lot going on here. In fact, one thing you may have noticed is that Internet Explorer 10 is fairly unique among Metro-style apps in that it not only offers a single app bar—that toolbar-like control at the bottom of the screen that in IE is called the navigation bar—but it also offers a second bar, called the tab switcher, at the top of the screen. Almost all Metro-style apps offer a single app bar. But very few go beyond that, as IE does.

The reason for this overloaded user interface is simple. Internet Explorer 10 is a fairly complex and certainly full-featured app, just like its desktop-based cousin. And it requires the additional space for commands that's afforded by the extra chrome.

> **NOTE** In some cases, only the navigation bar will appear, allowing you to type a URL into the address bar or perform other actions. If you don't see the tab switcher as well, simply swipe down from the top of the screen (or perform any other input action that will display an edge UI).

UNDERSTANDING THE NAVIGATION BAR

The Internet Explorer navigation bar has several main user interface components, which are called out in Figure 7-7 and described next.

▸ **Back:** This button functions like a simplified version of the Back button commonly found in desktop web browsers. However, in keeping with the Metro design philosophies, it lacks advanced features, such as the ability to tap and hold to access a menu of past pages and the browser History.

FIGURE 7-7: The IE navigation bar

> **NOTE** IE Metro supports other ways to go back to the previously loaded web page. We'll examine these capabilities in the "Navigating the Web with IE 10 Metro" section.

▶ **Site Icon:** A noninteractive button that displays the site's icon, if any.

▶ **Address bar:** This control works much like the address bar in the desktop version of Internet Explorer, but with some key differences. You can, of course, select the address bar to type any arbitrary URL, and then press Enter to start navigation. But IE Metro is unique because a full-screen view of Frequent and Pinned sites is displayed each time the address bar is selected. And as you type, these lists are filtered, on the fly. This feature is so cool, we discuss it more in the "Finding Favorites and Other Websites" section later in this chapter.

Sites with encrypted connections will include a lock badge in the address bar, just as with the desktop version of IE. This control also works as a progress indicator while sites are loading.

The address bar also *lacks* some features of the desktop IE's address bar, including a menu-based auto-complete list and Compatibility View.

▶ **Refresh/Stop:** This button works just like its desktop cousin: Tap it to refresh (reload) the current page or, if the currently loading page is stuttering or not completing for some reason, tap it to stop it from loading.

▶ **Pin to Start:** While old-school IE users probably cart around a folder full of Favorites—Internet Explorer's version of the browser bookmarks feature—the cool kids started pinning their favorite sites to the Windows 7 taskbar with IE 9. And now in IE 10, you can pin your favorite sites to the Windows 8 Start screen too. This is how you do it, and because it's such a great new feature with unique capabilities, we examine it in detail later in this chapter.

> **NOTE** The Favorites Bar is no longer available in IE Metro, because of screen real estate reasons.

▶ **Page Tools:** This useful tool displays a pop-up menu when tapped. From here, you can utilize IE Metro's Find on Page and View on the Desktop

▶ To search the web from the address bar, simply type your search query in the address bar. Internet Explorer will search the web using the configured search engine, which, by default, is Bing.

▶ You can still pin websites to the Windows 8 taskbar. But you will do this separately, from the desktop version of IE.

functionalities. The former helps you search the currently displayed web page for a specific search term. The latter, new to IE 10, loads the currently displayed web page in the desktop version of Internet Explorer. You will also occasionally see a Get app for this site option in the Page Tools menu; in such cases, the button itself will change a bit, adding a small gear graphic, indicating that a Windows 8 Metro-style app is also available.

▶ **Forward:** Yep, this works much like the Forward button in the desktop version of IE. But as with Back, it lacks advanced features, like the ability to tap and hold to access a menu of past pages and the browser History.

UNDERSTANDING THE TAB SWITCHER

Whereas desktop versions of Internet Explorer feature an always-visible row of browser tabs, IE Metro tries to do more with less, so it hides its new tab switcher and other UI chrome elements by default. But when enabled, the tab switcher, as shown in Figure 7-8, provides the UI elements described next.

FIGURE 7-8: The IE tab switcher

▶ **Active Tab(s):** The majority of the tab switcher is occupied with one or more thumbnails representing the currently open browser tabs, each with its own web page loaded. You will always see at least one tab thumbnail here—representing the current page—and if you open enough tabs, a second tab thumbnail row will appear.

▶ **New Tab:** This button opens a new tab and then provides a view of your Frequent and (if available) Pinned lists (offering your most frequently accessed sites as well as those you've pinned to the Start screen, respectively) and the address bar so you can manually type in a website URL—or a search term—if desired.

▶ **Tab Menu:** This button displays a small menu when tapped. It has two choices: New InPrivate tab and Close tabs. The former opens a new tab in Internet Explorer's InPrivate Browsing mode, which prevents anything that happens in that tab from making its way into the global browser History. (What happens in InPrivate Browsing mode stays in InPrivate Browsing mode.) Close tabs is exactly what it sounds like: it simply closes all but the currently displayed tab.

▶ IE Metro only supports two tab thumbnail rows in the tab switcher. If both rows are full, and you open yet another tab, the oldest tab is removed.

▶ Want to close just a single tab? Ctrl + W still works for the current tab. And you can use the little close icon on a tab if you prefer using touch or the mouse.

NAVIGATING THE WEB WITH IE 10 METRO

Now that you're up to speed on the major UI components of the Metro-styled version of Internet Explorer 10, you can turn your attention to actually using the browser. You'll also see some similarities with desktop IE versions, and some differences, which could prove to be vexing.

Key among these is right-click, or what we call "tap and hold" for touch users. This common action doesn't work in IE Metro the same as it does in the desktop versions of the browser, and in fact only offers up limited options, depending on what you've clicked (or tapped). Right-clicking also brings up the browser navigation bar if you're not selecting an on-page object.

What this means is that you can't right-click any element on a web page and access all of the advanced options you get with desktop IE. Instead, you'll have limited options depending on what you've selected:

- ▶ **Images:** Right-click an (unhyperlinked) image, and you'll see two useful choices in the context menu that appears: Copy, which copies the image to the clipboard, and Save to Picture library.

- ▶ **Hyperlinked Images:** Right-click a hyperlinked image, and you'll see Copy, Copy Link, Open link in a new tab, Open link, and Save to Picture library.

- ▶ **Text:** If you select a block of text on a web page, you can right-click to copy it to the clipboard.

- ▶ **Hyperlinked text:** Right-click hyperlinked text, and you'll see Copy Link, Open link in a new tab, and Open link.

But most actions will work as expected in IE Metro. You can tap hyperlinks to access the underlying page, scroll with your finger, and so on. Here are some key navigational concerns you'll want to know about in Internet Explorer for Metro.

HOME

As with mobile device browsers, IE Metro does not support the notion of Home, let alone allow you to configure multiple homepages, as does the desktop version of IE. Instead, the browser maintains state between sessions, and even between shutdowns, so that the last site you were visiting—all open tabs, really—are automatically reloaded the next time you open IE Metro.

BACK AND FORWARD

As noted previously, the IE Metro navigation bar sports both Back and Forward buttons for normal navigation, albeit without any advanced features. But when you consider that IE Metro will normally be used in a chrome-less mode in which the navigation bar and tab switcher are hidden, re-enabling the navigation bar just for basic purposes could get pretty tedious. Fortunately, there are other ways.

Keyboard users can utilize the standard Alt + Left Arrow and Alt + Right Arrow combinations for Back and Forward, respectively. But since Metro in general and IE Metro specifically are designed for multi-touch interfaces, it's more likely that you'll want to utilize some new gestures to navigate Back and Forward. To do so, simply tap and hold near the edge of the screen and then swipe toward the middle. If you do so from the left edge of the screen, you'll navigate back. Do so from the right, and you'll navigate forward.

But even mouse users have a new way to navigate. If you move the mouse cursor near the left edge of the screen, you'll see a new Back transport control appear, as in Figure 7-9. You can click this control to navigate Back without needing to first display the navigation bar. A similar control appears on the right side of the screen for Forward.

FIGURE 7-9: The IE Back tip lets you navigate back without having to first display the navigation bar.

VISITING SPECIFIC WEBSITES

As with any web browser, you can arbitrarily visit any website by typing its name into the address bar. As described previously, however, the address bar is hidden by default. So swipe up from the bottom edge of the display (or down from the top) to display the navigation bar, which includes the address bar.

FINDING FAVORITES AND OTHER WEBSITES

Since the Metro version of IE is focused on providing basic web browsing functionality in a package that is touch-friendly, it doesn't include all of the features of its

▶ Keyboard users will want to remember one of two quick keyboard shortcuts to more quickly bring up the address bar: Alt + D or Ctrl + L. Of course, with a mouse, you can simply right-click any blank area in IE Metro.

desktop cousin. Or in some cases, it hides functionality in order to keep the display minimalist.

One of the classic examples of this latter user interface miscue is Favorites. It's in there. In fact, IE Metro synchronizes your Favorites list with the desktop version and, if you've enabled it, with other PCs as well. But this browser offers absolutely no way to access your Favorites as a list or menu. And it provides no way to save a site as a Favorite. Instead, you must pin favorite sites to the Start screen.

But since IE Metro does at least synchronize with your list of Favorites, there must be some way to access these sites from the browser, right? Right. And there is. It's just not clear to us how anyone would ever discover this functionality on their own.

The only way to access Favorites in IE Metro is via search: Select the address bar and start typing. As you do, the navigation tiles at the top of the display change to display search results that match what you're typing. And these results comprise four things: frequently accessed sites, pinned sites, very popular websites, and . . . wait for it . . . your Favorites. You can see this effect in Figure 7-10.

FIGURE 7-10: Favorites are available only when you search through the address bar.

▶ Favorites, pinned sites, and your browsing history are all synced from PC to PC if you sign in to Windows 8 with a Microsoft account, as discussed in Chapter 2.

Why so opaque? It's pretty clear that Microsoft considers the Favorites list a legacy interface and would prefer users to start moving toward pinned sites. This will be fine for average consumers who only store a handful of frequently visited sites. But power users will need to know the workaround, or simply stick with the desktop version of IE.

You can access the Frequent list, as the list of frequently accessed sites is called, and your pinned sites—but not your Favorites—simply by selecting the address bar. This navigation list display is shown in Figure 7-11.

FIGURE 7-11: Frequent and Pinned sites are available when you just select the address bar.

WORKING WITH TABS

Tabs provide a convenient way to access multiple websites from the same browser window. And IE Metro, as a modern mobile web browser, offers decent tab functionality. As noted earlier, you can access the new tab switcher by using the top or bottom edge UI (or the Winkey + Z shortcut) and manage tabs from there. But your old tab skills work as well. You can use Ctrl + T to open a new tab, for example, and Ctrl + W to close one.

Internet Explorer Metro also provides access to InPrivate tabs, special tabs whose browser history will not be recorded as you go, providing a sense of privacy. InPrivate Browsing is available via a button in the tab switcher, but you can also use the keyboard shortcut Ctrl + Shift + P. However you choose to engage this feature, you'll see a display similar to that in Figure 7-12, indicating that InPrivate Browsing is on and you're safe.

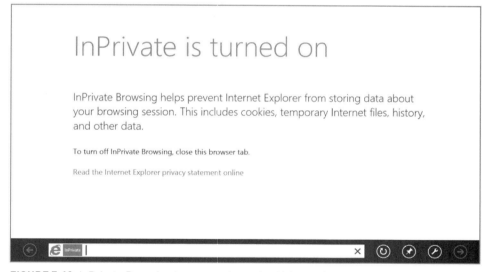

FIGURE 7-12: InPrivate Browsing keeps your browsing history private.

You can switch between open tabs most easily with the keyboard: The Ctrl + Tab keyboard shortcut from desktop IE works identically in IE Metro.

FUN WITH ZOOM

If you've ever used a mobile browser before, you know that most support a cool, touch-based system in which you pinch the screen or double-tap the screen to zoom in to and out of specific areas of a web page. Not surprisingly, IE Metro supports these gestures too. And they make a big difference in the way you'll read many web pages.

Consider a typically busy website like the one shown in Figure 7-13. While it is possible to read such a site on larger screens, the text is small and hard to read with smaller displays like those on a slate-based device.

FIGURE 7-13: Modern websites are often difficult to read on portable devices like those running Windows 8.

Internet Explorer 10 for Metro offers two ways to cut through the clutter. First, you can double-tap the screen to zoom in to the area you tapped, such as a column of text. This will resemble the screen shown in Figure 7-14.

To reverse the effect, just double-tap the screen again.

The second and arguably even more fun effect involves pinching the screen to zoom arbitrarily. Simply pinch the screen with two fingers to zoom out, and then "reverse the pinch" to zoom back in.

Actually, there's a third way. If you'd prefer to change the screen zoom permanently, you can configure IE Metro to do so. Please refer to the section "Configuring IE 10 Metro," later in this chapter, for details.

▶ Surprisingly, these features are touch-only. There's no way to pinch or double-tap zoom with the keyboard or mouse.

DOWNLOADING FILES

While IE Metro utilizes the same Download folder as the desktop version, the download experience is, naturally, a bit different. This browser utilizes a pane just above the navigation bar, asking whether you'd like to Run, Save, or Cancel the downloadable file. This is shown in Figure 7-15

FIGURE 7-14: You can zoom in to a text column or other on-screen area by double-tapping it.

FIGURE 7-15: The file download experience

You may be familiar with this process on the desktop version of IE, which offers advanced save options—Save and run, and Save as—in addition to the choices offered in IE Metro. But as it turns out, the Save option in IE Metro is identical to Save and run on desktop IE. That is, IE Metro will prompt you to run a downloaded file—assuming it passed the SmartScreen security screening—as shown in Figure 7-16.

FIGURE 7-16: You're prompted to run files downloaded from IE Metro.

▶ All files downloaded through the Metro environment are automatically scanned before you're allowed to open them.

SEARCHING THE WEB

Searching the web from a web browser has evolved over the years, with desktop versions of Internet Explorer first offering a dedicated search box and then integrating search directly into the address bar. In the Metro-style version of Internet Explorer, this capability has been refined yet again: This browser uses the integrated Search contract capabilities of Windows 8 to provide Internet search capabilities.

So you perform a search just as you do in any other Metro-style app: Open the search pane from the Charms bar and start typing.

Here's how:

▶ **Touch:** Swipe in from the right side of the screen to open the Charms bar and then tap Search.

▶ **Mouse:** Move the mouse cursor into the top right or bottom right of the screen and then move the cursor along the right edge of the screen; then, click Search.

▶ **Keyboard:** Press Winkey + Q to open the search pane.

However you do it, the search pane will resemble Figure 7-17.

FIGURE 7-17: To trigger an Internet search from IE Metro, you must use the search pane.

As we explained in Chapter 3, the Search contract that backs this functionality is available system-wide in Windows 8 to any Metro experiences that choose to support it. And many do: This interface is used to search for Metro-style apps, classic Windows applications, settings and control panels, and files, as well as many different Metro-style apps—including, as it turns out, Internet Explorer Metro.

Here are a few things to note about this functionality.

First, the default search engine is Bing. This choice is inherited from the desktop version of Internet Explorer and is extremely laborious to change. If you simply want to perform a one-time search via Google, or some other service, you're better off navigating to that service's website manually.

NO, REALLY, I WANT TO CHANGE THE SEARCH PROVIDER

Okay, so you *really* want to change the search provider? Don't say we didn't warn you. Here are the hoops you need to jump through:

First, open the desktop version of Internet Explorer, as you can't change search providers using IE Metro. Now open the Tools menu by clicking the gear icon in the upper-right corner of the window (or type Alt + T); then, click Manage Add-ons. This opens the Manage Add-ons window.

On the left, click Search Providers, then drill down to your preferred search service on the right; then, click the Set as default button.

Of course, you probably only have one search provider, Bing, installed on your PC. To install another search provider—the reason you're reading this— click the Find more search providers link at the bottom of the window. This will load the Internet Explorer Gallery website where you will then need to find and install a service provider.

One last hoop: Newly installed providers don't always show up in the Manage Add-ons window immediately. To make that happen, you may need to close the Manage Add-ons window and try again. It's surprisingly laborious.

Second, the search pane maintains a list of recent searches. So you may see these appear below the search box in the search pane. Click one to rerun that search.

SHARING A WEB PAGE WITH OTHERS

In addition to supporting the Search contract, Internet Explorer Metro also supports the Share contract, allowing it to share web pages with other apps.

To share a web page from IE Metro, open the share pane via the Charms bar. This works identically to the procedures detailed in the previous section, but you will choose Share instead of Search from the Charms bar. When you do, the Share pane appears as shown in Figure 7-18.

▶ Only a handful of built-in apps can act as receivers for share events from Internet Explorer Metro, including Mail and People, the latter of which connects to social networks like Facebook and Twitter.

Select the app you wish to share with and that app's Share interface will appear. In Figure 7-19, we're using the Mail app to share the current web page with others via e-mail. (This experience will vary from app to app.)

FIGURE 7-18: You can share web pages with others using the Share contract.

FIGURE 7-19: A few apps can act as Share receivers and accept your share request.

PRINTING WITH IE METRO

To print from the Metro-style version of Internet Explorer, you can access the Devices interface, which is also accessible via the Charms bar. This is the standard way to print from Metro-style apps. However, IE Metro also supports the traditional Ctrl + P keyboard shortcut.

▶ Not all Metro apps do.

Once displayed, the Devices pane should resemble Figure 7-20.

Select a printer from the list and you'll see a screen like that in Figure 7-21, with options that are specific to that printer. Tap Print to print the page.

FIGURE 7-20: Printing occurs via the Metro-style Devices interface.

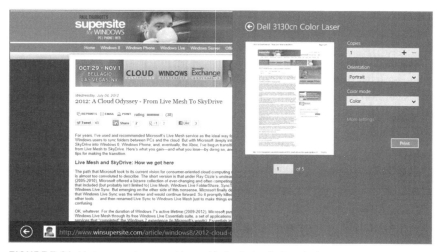

FIGURE 7-21: Metro apps have pretty sophisticated printing choices.

NOTE Some printers may not support showing all the advanced configuration options you're used to seeing via the Devices interface. But don't fret; you can still access those features via the print dialog shown in desktop applications, including the desktop version of Internet Explorer.

FINDING WINDOWS 8 APPS ON THE WEB

▶ If you already have the app in question, the item will read, Switch to app. Tap that and the app will run.

Finally, here's a fun Windows 8–specific feature you'll see from time to time. When you visit a website that offers a Windows 8 app, it can change the Page tools app bar button and menu. The button will display a small plus sign, and when you click it, a third new menu choice, Get app for this site, will appear, as shown in Figure 7-22.

FIGURE 7-22: Sites can advertise their Windows 8 Metro app through IE Metro.

Tap that item and the Windows Store will open and navigate to the app's landing page.

USING PINNED WEBSITES

If you're familiar with Internet Explorer 9, you know that Microsoft added a unique ability to this version of its web browser: The ability to pin websites to the Windows 7 Start menu and taskbar, alongside those for traditional Windows applications. These pinned sites work much like regular applications, and they appear in a special version of the Internet Explorer 9 browser frame that is color-coded to match the design of the underlying site.

The desktop version of Internet Explorer 10 provides this same capability in Windows 8, but the new Metro-style version of IE 10 offers a unique, Metro-based take on this functionality: You can now pin websites to the Start screen as well.

This makes sense when you consider that the Start screen is replacing the application-launching functionality of the Start menu and taskbar in Windows 8.

But there are some curious behaviors—and differences with taskbar/Start menu pinning—to know about.

To pin a website to the Start screen, load it in Internet Explorer Metro and then tap the Pin button in the navigation bar. (This bar may be hidden. If so, you can swipe up from the bottom of the screen or use your other new Metro skills to display it.) As shown in Figure 7-23, you're given a chance to rename the site before it's pinned. (Some websites have annoying long names.)

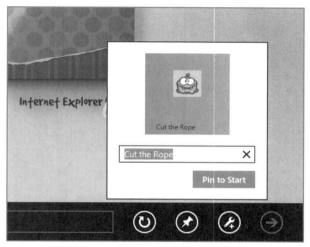

FIGURE 7-23: You're given the opportunity to rename the site before you pin it to the Start screen.

Once you tap the Pin to Start button, the site is pinned. You'll need to manually leave Internet Explorer to see this, however, so press the Windows key on your keyboard (or access the Start option in the Charms bar) to return to the Start screen. Since all newly pinned items are added to the end of the Start screen—on the far right—you'll need to scroll over there to see the pinned site. This can be seen in Figure 7-24.

From here, you can perform basically two different actions. You can move the pinned website tile to a new location or you can unpin it.

CROSSREF Start screen customization is discussed in Chapter 5.

Pinned site tiles can provide simple alphanumeric notification badges just like they can on the taskbar, with the canonical example being an e-mail service that displays the number of unread e-mails. But the tiles for pinned websites simply aren't as expressive as those for Metro-style apps can be.

FIGURE 7-24: All newly pinned items are placed at the end of the Start screen by default.

Within the browser, however, pinned sites also offer another feature borrowed from pinned taskbar sites: Jump lists. So if you tap that site tile, you'll notice that IE Metro loads with a slightly different user interface, assuming that the pinned site utilizes jump lists: The Pin to Start button in the navigation bar has been replaced by a new menu button. And if you click this button, you'll see whatever jump list the site provides, as shown in Figure 7-25. (The items in this menu will vary from site to site.)

FIGURE 7-25: A jump list displayed in IE Metro

If you're familiar with pinned sites in IE 9 and Windows 7, you know that they run in their own browser frame. But this isn't the case with IE 10 Metro and Windows 8. Instead, these pinned sites load inside the same IE Metro app as any other web pages, and they will load alongside whatever other tabs were already open in the browser.

Configuring IE 10 Metro

The Metro version of Internet Explorer 10 is configured just like all other Metro-style apps, via the globally available Settings pane. To activate this pane, swipe in from the right of the screen to display the Charms bar and then tap Settings. IE 10 Metro settings can be found at the top of the Settings pane, as shown in Figure 7-26.

▶ Mouse users can activate the Charms bar by moving the mouse cursor to the upper right (or lower right) of the screen and then moving the cursor along the right edge of the screen toward the middle. Then click the Settings charm.

FIGURE 7-26: IE 10 for Metro settings can be accessed from the Settings pane.

Internet Explorer Settings is accessed by tapping the Settings link. As you can see in the aggregated view of this unique interface shown in Figure 7-27, which most likely won't be completely viewable on your screen and will need to be scrolled vertically to see all the options, there's a lot going on here.

▶ Keyboard users can use the Winkey + I shortcut to go directly to Internet Explorer Settings.

Available settings include the following:

- ▶ **Delete Browsing History:** Deletes all temporary files, cookies, and saved passwords. Unfortunately, there's no way to delete the contents of just one; it's an all-or-nothing, one-click option.

- ▶ **Permissions:** Although this isn't a common feature yet, with more and more portable computing devices being sold every year, some websites are starting to request location information from visitors in an effort to offer a personalized, location-based experience (or, more nefariously, advertisements). By default, IE 10 will trigger a notification when such a request is made. But you can turn off this behavior—and thus allow all sites to automatically grab your location data—if you'd like. A separate Clear button lets you clear the list of sites for whom you've OK'd location data, once again triggering those notifications each time a location request comes in.

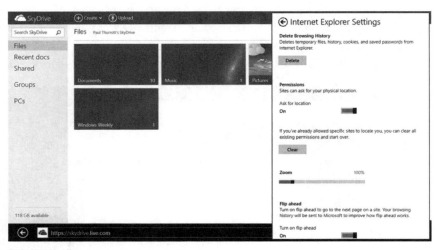

FIGURE 7-27: Internet Explorer Settings

▶ **Zoom:** By default, Internet Explorer displays web pages normally, at a zoom level of 100 percent. But depending on the resolution and size of the screen (or, with a tablet, the device itself), you may want to configure the browser to always display items a bit bigger, or smaller. That's where Zoom comes in. You can zoom as low as 60 percent, and as high as 260 percent, and thanks to Windows' amazing text rendering capabilities, the results will be readable and surprisingly clear regardless of which zoom setting you choose. But this feature is particularly useful for high DPI displays (smaller screens with very high resolutions, typically), because normally displayed websites will look too small.

NOTE Zoom is one of those features that makes IE 10 for Metro more palatable on a big screen display. Just set the zoom level to 140 or 160 percent and enjoy the big-screen goodness. You can see a typical zoomed website in Figure 7-28.

FIGURE 7-28: Internet Explorer can elegantly resize websites to fit the size and resolution of your screen: Here, 125% zoom is utilized.

▶ **Flip ahead:** This new IE 10 feature—also available separately in the desktop version of the browser—helps site navigation work faster by silently preloading page linked from the current page in the background. Because it requires sending some information to Microsoft to work, this feature is opt-in and disabled by default.

▶ **Encoding:** While you won't need to muck around with this option very much, you should head here if you visit websites where the text isn't displaying correctly (usually those in other languages).

USING THE DESKTOP VERSION OF INTERNET EXPLORER 10

The Metro-style version of Internet Explorer 10 is obviously big news because it's a key component of converting users over to the new Metro environment and its touch-first apps. For the majority of Windows users, however, or those with traditional desktop PCs and laptops, Internet Explorer 10 Metro is decidedly less well-optimized for the input devices they're using and are comfortable with.

More to the point, it's also lacking some key functionality, such as the ability to run in a floating window alongside other applications on the desktop. It can't run add-ons or browser extensions, including ActiveX controls. And while it supports pinning favorite sites to the Start screen, those pinned sites don't take on their own app-like identity, as do sites you pin (to the taskbar) with the desktop version of Internet Explorer.

So it's no surprise that IE Metro's less adventurous cousin is going to get the nod from a very large number of Windows 8 users. But that said, there's just aren't many new features in this version of IE. If you're used to Internet Explorer 9 already, IE 10 will be very familiar.

Under the hood, Microsoft has been thoroughly overhauling the engines that drive the browser's HTML, CSS (cascading style sheet), and JavaScript rendering: the three core technologies that enable today's more standards-compliant web. Where IE was once the laughing stock of the web standards world, IE 9, and now to an even greater degree, IE 10, is not only performing well, but it's leading the way.

Without getting too deep into the technical miasma that are web standards, this leadership takes two forms. The first is an ability to accurately render the various features that web standards bodies recognize as being key parts of the most relevant building blocks of modern web standards—those HTML, CSS, and JavaScript bits. A web developer should be able to target these standards—and not be forced to write to individual browsers and browser versions—and know that what they create will simply work.

The second form of Internet Explorer leadership over competing browsers is performance. One of the most amazing transitions we've witnessed in recent years is the methodical remaking of Internet Explorer's rendering capabilities from being software driven to being pervasively hardware accelerated. This means that any modern PC can offload the rendering of virtually any o-screen element in the browser from the PC's microprocessor to its graphics processing unit, or GPU. The result is better performance, better battery life, and less general overhead for the system. It's not just a win-win. It's a win-win-win.

> **NOTE** What's a "modern" PC? Basically, any PC that was manufactured to run Windows Vista or newer. So any PC that was made since 2006 qualifies for purposes of this discussion.

As far as you and other Windows 8 users are concerned, what really matters is that the browser starts up quickly, runs reliably and with good performance, and renders the sites you visit accurately.

CONFIGURING IE 10 DESKTOP

The configuration of the desktop version of Internet Explorer hasn't changed much over the years because it mostly still occurs through Internet Options, which is still accessible via Control Panel (try Start Screen Search) or from within IE itself via Tools, Internet Options. Either way, you'll see a window like the one in Figure 7-29.

FIGURE 7-29: Internet Options

> **NOTE** For some reason, this window is titled Internet Properties when you launch it from Control Panel and Internet Options when you do so from IE. Ah, Microsoft, thy name is consistency.

Since we're all adults here, we won't step through every single option in this complex and multi-tabbed window. But there are some new and/or important options that every IE user should at least be made aware of:

▶ **Better browsing history deletion:** While the Metro version of Internet Explorer 10 lets you delete temporary files, history, cookies, and saved passwords in one fell swoop only, the desktop version features a far more granular control in which you can choose which of the following to delete: temporary files, cookies, history, download history, form data, passwords, and more. It's far more powerful and useful. (Where: General tab, Browsing history, Delete.)

▶ **Tab options:** The desktop IE version offers a bewildering array of options related to tabs. (Where: General tab, Tabs, Tabs.)

▶ **Which version of IE to use:** If Internet Explorer is configured as the default browser—a feature we examine in a moment—you can choose which of the two IE 10 browsers to use for opening links in other programs. This can even override the default browser behavior, so you might configure IE Metro as the default but choose to open all external links in the desktop version. (Where: Programs tab, Opening Internet Explorer.)

▶ **Manage add-ons:** Unlike IE Metro, the desktop version can be extended with an amazing array of add-ons. You manage them through the logically named Manage Add-ons interface. (Where: Programs tab, Manage add-ons, Manage add-ons.)

> ▶ If you deselect the Open Internet Explorer tiles on the desktop option, the IE tile on the Start screen will utilize the IE Metro icon but, when clicked, will open IE desktop.

NOTE You can also launch Manage Add-ons from the Tools menu in IE.

WHERE IE METRO AND DESKTOP MEET...AND DON'T

As we discussed previously in this chapter, it's very easy to launch the desktop version of Internet Explorer from the Metro version: Just tap the Page tools button in the navigation bar, and then View on the desktop to load the currently displayed web page in the desktop version of the browser. You may want to do this when you run into a web page that won't work in IE Metro, perhaps because it expects an add-on of some kind.

In such cases, you'll see some content that isn't displaying correctly, along with a message like that shown in Figure 7-30 indicating that the site would load properly only if you downloaded the appropriate add-on. This happens most frequently with Adobe Flash (though many such sites do work in IE Metro) and (irony alert) Microsoft Silverlight based sites.

Don't be fooled by this. Yes, you can follow the supplied link and, yes, you can download and then install the appropriate add-on. (This will happen in the desktop environment, which is perhaps a clue to the futility of this action.) But when you do, the add-on is only installed in the desktop version of IE. When you return to IE Metro and reload the page, you'll get the same message about needing to download the add-on.

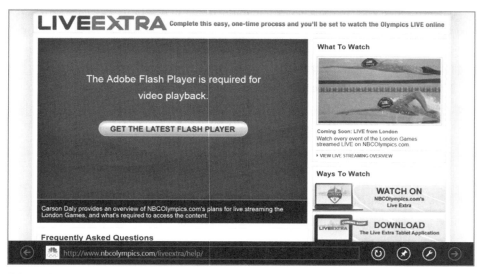

FIGURE 7-30: When good sites go bad: Browser add-ons won't run in IE Metro.

We wish IE Metro were a bit more sophisticated about this. But you'll quickly learn, and remember, that IE Metro can't work with add-ons. So you'll have to do something different, like load that page in desktop IE and see if it just works. Chances are it will.

OK, so you know how to handle the situations where you're in IE Metro and want (or need) to load a page from desktop IE. But what about launching IE Metro from desktop IE?

Unfortunately, there's no direct way to open a page you're viewing in IE for desktop in IE Metro. But if you really want to do this for some reason, the simplest way is to just copy the URL of the page, switch to IE Metro, and paste it into the IE Metro address bar. As always, keyboard shortcuts are your friend: Alt + D will select the One Box/address bar in either browser, and Ctrl + C and Ctrl + V can be used to copy and then paste, respectively.

IE 10 AND DEFAULT BROWSER SELECTION

Before moving on from our look at web browsing and Windows 8, there's a final, somewhat uncomfortable topic to discuss. And that's what happens when you change the default web browser in Windows 8 to anything other than the Metro version of Internet Explorer. Trust us; this is going to get weird.

First, understand that in a clean, unchanged install of Windows 8, the Metro-style version of Internet Explorer 10 is indeed the default browser. This means that anytime a web browser is needed by the OS, another Metro-style app, or a desktop application, IE 10 Metro is invoked.

Likewise, in this default configuration, you will find an IE 10 Metro tile on the Windows 8 Start screen. What you won't find, curiously, is an IE 10 desktop tile. And there is no way to add an IE 10 tile to the desktop when IE 10 Metro is the default. That's just the way it is.

Unfortunately, Windows 8 is oftentimes not configured in this way. And of course, you can change things yourself. So let's look at some of the scenarios in which IE 10 Metro is not the default browser, and see what happens.

You Change the Default Browser to IE 10 Desktop

If you'd rather use the desktop version of IE 10 as the default browser and not IE 10 Metro, you can do so by accessing Internet Options from within IE 10 desktop as described earlier in the chapter. Then navigate to the Programs tab and change the Choose how you open links option to Always in Internet Explorer in the desktop.

And if you want the desktop IE tile on the Start screen (and any pinned websites) to open desktop IE instead of IE Metro, also check the box titled Open Internet Explorer tiles on the desktop.

When you perform both of these steps, IE Metro, for all intents and purposes, is removed from your system. It's not literally gone, of course; it's just inaccessible. And it will remain so until you change those settings back.

You Configure a Third-Party Web Browser as the Default Browser

Like previous Windows versions, Windows 8 allows you to install your choice of third-party browsers. But when you do so, things can change with IE 10, depending on how the other browsers are configured.

▶ The only way to return IE Metro is to make IE the default browser in Default Programs again.

Specifically, if you configure a third-party browser—Google Chrome or Mozilla Firefox for example—to be the default browser in Windows 8, the Metro version of Internet Explorer disappears.

You can see the change on the Start screen: The tile for IE has changed to a tile for desktop IE, not IE Metro.

You Upgrade to Windows 8 from Windows 7 and Can't Find IE Metro

If you upgrade a Windows 7–based PC to Windows 8, you may notice that the IE tile on the Start screen is for the desktop version of IE 10 and not for the Metro version as expected. This is for the same reason as stated earlier, and you had configured a different browser as the default browser before upgrading. So Windows 8 hides IE 10 Metro. Again, to return IE as the default, you will need to access the Default Programs interface.

SUMMARY

If ever there were a poster child for the dual—one might say dueling—nature of the Windows 8 user experiences, it's Internet Explorer 10. As with the OS on which it runs, Internet Explorer 10 offers two separate but complementary user experiences: a standard Windows application that runs in the desktop environment and a touch-first, Metro-style app.

The Metro-style version of Internet Explorer 10 works best on tablets and other touch-based devices, offering all of the gesture support you'd expect combined with the best features of the desktop browser.

For users on traditional PCs, or those who prefer the more full-featured desktop versions, Internet Explorer 10 builds on the improvements of previous IE versions, offering better performance, better web standards support, and, of course, some great integration with the Metro browser.

The strangest part of this dual browser experience, perhaps, is understanding how each of these products works with the other and, more confusingly, with third-party browsers. Here, the dual nature of Internet Explorer becomes more confusing than complementary. But with a little bit of understanding, you'll be able to configure your PC to work with the browser or browsers you prefer.

CHAPTER 8

Get It Done with Windows 8's Productivity Apps

IN THIS CHAPTER

▶ Understanding the relationship between your Microsoft account and key Windows 8 productivity apps

▶ Using People to manage contacts

▶ Using Mail to manage e-mail

▶ Using Calendar to manage your schedule

▶ Using Messaging to communicate with others

▶ Using SkyDrive to store and access files online

▶ Using Windows Reader to view PDF files

▶ Using Bing Maps to get directions and find your location

▶ Understanding the Other Metro productivity apps

▶ Using Microsoft Office for advanced productivity tasks like document editing, spreadsheet creation, presentation making, and note-taking

Throughout its decades-long existence, Windows has been known primarily for its use as the basis for the PC productivity workhorse, and it has long included a suite of useful productivity applications. These applications have always ranged from marginally useful to truly useful depending on the version of Windows and the tool in question. But with Windows 8, you are given a truly impressive arsenal of useful Metro-style productivity apps and, of course, traditional Windows applications.

This chapter examines the new Metro-style apps that Microsoft includes with Windows 8 and RT, whether they're acquired with a new PC purchase or downloaded separately from the Windows Store. These include new contacts, e-mail, calendaring, and messaging solutions that replace legacy Windows Live applications, as well as useful new apps for cloud storage access, PDF reading and annotation, mapping, and more. This chapter also briefly examines the Office 2013 applications—Word RT, Excel RT, PowerPoint RT, and OneNote RT—which come exclusively with Windows RT, the ARM-based variant of Windows 8.

IT'S GOING TO CHANGE

Thanks to the dynamic nature of its new apps platform, the Metro-style apps that Microsoft includes with Windows 8/RT will change over time, so it's highly likely that the apps described in this chapter will appear somewhat differently over time and will include additional features. This is normal, and as a general statement, it's probably fair to say that the Metro-style productivity apps you use will provide a superset of the functionality we describe in this chapter.

A NOTE ABOUT THE WINDOWS PRODUCTIVITY APPS AND YOUR MICROSOFT ACCOUNT

Before we can discuss the individual productivity apps that are considered part of the full Windows 8 experience, you need to be aware that many of these apps—including the core People, Mail, Calendar, and Messaging apps—all rely on connectivity with your Microsoft account, or what used to be called a Windows Live ID. You may recall from previous discussions in this book that we strongly recommend using a Microsoft account for your sign-in with Windows 8 instead of an old-fashioned local account because that former account type provides such useful integration capabilities. But we realize that some of you will ignore this advice, either because you feel you know better or because you simply don't have a choice, perhaps because the Windows 8 PC you're using is supplied by work or for other reasons.

If that's the case, the first time you launch People, Mail, Calendar, or Messaging, you will be asked to sign in to your Microsoft account, as shown in Figure 8-1. There is no way to use these four apps otherwise, because they are, by nature, what we call *connected apps*, or apps that offer no disconnected-only experience. (Microsoft calls them communications apps.)

▶ Don't confuse "connected" with "online." Some of these apps do work when the PC is offline. But they all rely on online services, not local-only data.

Add your Microsoft account

We'll save this info so you can use your account with Mail, Calendar, People, and Messaging.

Email address

Password

Sign up for a Microsoft account

Save   Cancel

FIGURE 8-1: You will sign in to your Microsoft account. Oh yes, you will.

That is, they rely on online services in ways that are pervasive and necessary. So with People, you will not manage contacts that are local to that one PC. Instead, you will manage contacts that are stored in one or more cloud-based services. Ditto for Mail, Calendar, and Messaging. None of these apps works only with local data. (In fact, none work with local data at all.)

Microsoft first took this approach with Windows Phone back in 2010, and it was somewhat controversial at the time. Some users, familiar with local personal information stores like that provided by traditional Windows applications such as Microsoft Outlook didn't understand the benefits of centralized, cloud-based data storage, or were perhaps suspicious of such services or unwilling to change. With Windows 8, however—and with Windows Phone 8 as well, for that matter—Microsoft has leapt firmly into this connected future. And while you're still welcome to use old-fashioned applications that lock data to a single hard drive on a single PC, the software giant won't help you do so with its own Metro-style apps in Windows 8.

We recognize that this will still be somewhat controversial with an increasingly smaller group of people who resist change for whatever reason. But we also believe that Microsoft's approach with Windows 8 is correct. And having long ago adopted this cloud-based model, we're excited to access our data from anywhere now using Windows 8. We suspect most of you are as well.

PEOPLE

When you sign in to Windows 8 for the first time with a Microsoft account, a number of interesting things happen behind the scenes, including the ability to sync settings between PCs. But Windows 8 also provides this account information to apps, including the core productivity apps that one might want to use with an online account, like Mail, Calendar, Messaging, and People. That latter app, based on the People hub that appeared first in Windows Phone, is Windows 8's new contacts management app. And it provides a nice interface for aggregating the contact lists from multiple accounts, providing a single view into them all, and thus for all the people you know and interact with each day.

The People app is shown in Figure 8-2.

FIGURE 8-2: The People app helps you manage your contacts.

▶ This app is called the People hub on Windows Phone, but it looks and works similarly.

The People app also provides a nice, Metro-style view of all of the activities that your contacts are doing online, culled from the various feeds that are associated with their accounts. This can include sources such as Windows Live, Facebook, Twitter, and more, and includes the ability to comment on what others are doing.

Finally, you can also use the People app to view and edit your own online persona, which is the way other people view you out in the world.

Understanding the People App

Like all Metro-style apps, the People app is a full-screen experience with a nice layout that automatically flows according to the size and pixel density of your display. This app consists of the main view and several other views, including:

- **Social:** A timeline-like view of your contacts' activities across all of the connected online services.
- **Me:** Here, you can view and edit your own online persona.
- **Notifications:** A list of notifications from each of the connected online services.
- **What's new:** The latest activities from across the connected activities.

You can switch to the other views by clicking (or tapping) the appropriate headings or tiles in the People app's main view.

The People app also provides an app bar that is hidden by default. Its functionality varies by view and is described in the appropriate sections later in this chapter. But as always, this app bar can be enabled by right-clicking any on-screen empty space with the mouse, by swiping toward the center of the screen from the top or left edge, or by typing Winkey + Z.

The People app is also designed to be snapped, utilizing a new feature of the Metro environment that allows one app to be used as a secondary app next to another Metro-style app or the Windows desktop. As you can see in Figure 8-3, the snapped view of the People app provides a handy miniaturized version of the full app.

FIGURE 8-3: The People app in snapped view

Managing Accounts

While you may have many contacts and other information associated with your Microsoft account, it's as likely that you use other account types for e-mail, contacts, calendar, and task management too. And for this reason, the People app is one of a few places in Windows 8 from which you can configure other accounts as well. Configurable account types include:

▶ **Facebook:** The world's most popular social networking service, Facebook is a great way to keep up with your friends' and families' activities. In Windows 8, the People app will pull information from your Facebook friends list (that is, contacts) and provide a look at their activities in the What's new view.

▶ **Twitter:** This very popular micro-blogging service has emerged as a social networking wunderkind in its own right, providing numerous feed types, topic searching, and follower and following lists. Twitter posts, called tweets, will appear in the What's new view.

▶ **LinkedIn:** Popular with upwardly mobile, white collar wage earners, LinkedIn is the social network for those who wish to keep up with co-workers and professional contacts. The People app integrates with your LinkedIn contact lists.

▶ **Microsoft/Hotmail:** Microsoft's popular web-based mail service is the basis for most people's Microsoft accounts, and since Windows 8 uses this account as your sign-in by default, chances are you've already configured one. Hotmail provides e-mail, contacts, calendaring, and task services, and as with the Google account type, each surfaces in the appropriate Windows 8 apps. The People app, as you'd expect, integrates with your Hotmail contact list.

▶ **Exchange:** The People app can connect natively to Exchange and Exchange-type accounts, meaning those that utilize the Exchange ActiveSync (EAS) technologies, a de facto standard for mobile devices. Generally speaking, you will use this account type for any account that utilizes Exchange Server, Office 365, or something similar, all of which offer e-mail, contacts, calendaring, and task management. The People app provides integrated access to Exchange or EAS-based contacts.

▶ **Google:** The world's largest Internet company provides excellent e-mail and contacts (Gmail) and calendaring and tasks (Google Calendar) services, and this account type will connect each to the appropriate apps in Windows 8. The People app accesses your Gmail account's contact list.

▶ Microsoft is in the process of replacing Hotmail with a new web-based e-mail service called Outlook.com. It works similarly to Hotmail.

To configure an account, click the appropriate account type under Add people to your contact list and follow the steps requested. Each account addition occurs via a full-screen notification-type interface like the one shown in Figure 8-4.

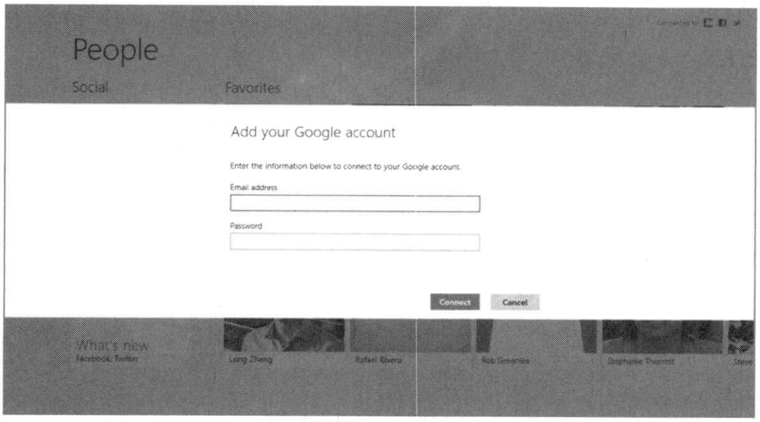

FIGURE 8-4: Adding a new account to Windows 8

If this account isn't present, you can access the Accounts interface from the Settings pane. Shown in Figure 8-5, this pane can be reached in a variety of ways, including by typing Winkey + I, swiping in from the right edge of the screen, and tapping Settings, or by using the Metro-style mouse hotspot for the Charms bar and then clicking Settings.

Click Accounts to view Accounts settings, which lets you access and add additional account types. The Accounts settings interface is shown in Figure 8-6.

▶ You can also delete accounts from here, though it's not particularly obvious. Just right-click the account you'd like to delete—or tap and hold—and choose Delete from the menu that appears.

FIGURE 8-5: People settings pane

FIGURE 8-6: Accounts settings

Managing Contacts

Managing accounts is usually a one-time thing. For the most part, you'll be interacting with contacts while using the People app. And the nice thing about this app is that all of your contacts, aggregated from multiple accounts, can be accessed in a single location. From here, you can perform a number of useful activities related to contacts.

INTERACTING WITH YOUR CONTACTS

If you manually launch the People app, you'll be presented with the app's main view, which lists all of your contacts in two groups. If you've configured any contacts as favorites, as described a bit later, those contacts will appear on the left.

The default view is pretty basic, and pretty obvious. But there is a fun hidden feature that makes it much easier to navigate through a huge list of contacts: Just tap any letter. To jump to the contacts that start with *F*, for example, just type **F**. The view will change, as shown in Figure 8-7.

FIGURE 8-7: You can quickly jump through the contact lists by typing a letter.

To view the details for an individual contact, simply select that contact from the list. What you see here will vary pretty wildly based on a number of factors, including which account(s) to which the contact is attached and what information you or they have provided, but it should resemble Figure 8-8.

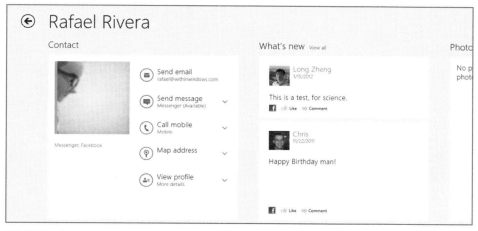

FIGURE 8-8: A typical contact card

Some of the information that can be associated with a contact includes:

▶ **Contact information:** Name, associated account(s), address, and so on, but also actionable options such as Send e-mail, Send message, Map address, and more.

▶ **What's new:** A list of the contact's activities, culled from one or more accounts.

▶ **Photos:** A collection of the contact's photos, culled from one or more accounts.

For both What's new and Photos, the views are not just read-only: You can comment on posts and photos, and even "like" items, just as you might if you accessed Facebook or Twitter manually.

> **NOTE** If you have duplicate contacts—two contact cards with the same information—you can also *link* them together. View one of the duplicates, display the app bar, and choose Link.

EDITING A CONTACT

To edit a contact's information, right-click anywhere while viewing a contact card and then choose Edit from the app bar. A new view called Edit contact info will appear, as shown in Figure 8-9.

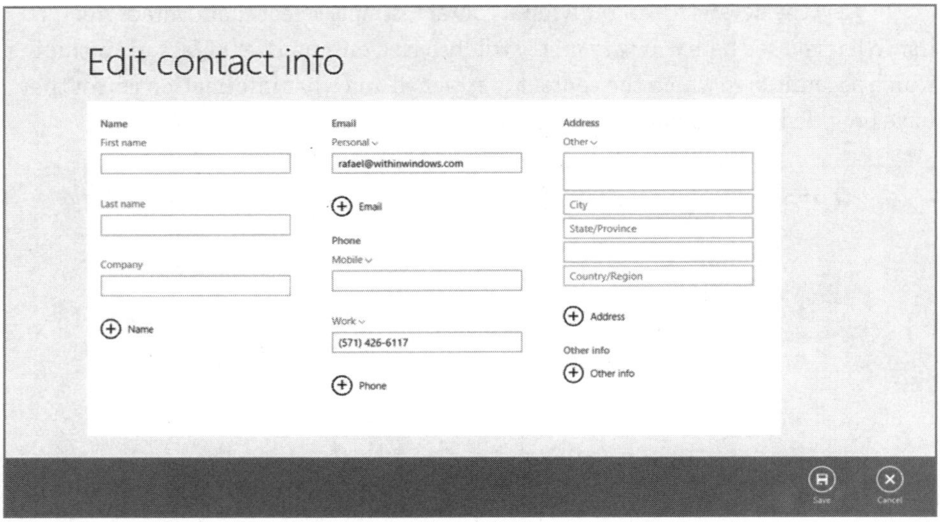

FIGURE 8-9: You can easily edit a contact's information.

Edit the information as needed and then click Save in the app bar to save the changes.

ADDING A NEW CONTACT

You can also add a new contact, of course. To do so, display the app bar while in the People app's main view and click the New button. (It resembles a "+" sign.)

This interface is fairly obvious and similar to the Edit screen mentioned previously, but the one area to call out is the Account drop-down list: This interface determines which account will store the new contact. By default, People will use your Microsoft account for all new contacts, but you can change that on the fly if you prefer to associate it with another account.

ADDING A CONTACT TO FAVORITES

The Windows 8 People app, like previous Microsoft contacts management solutions such as Windows Live Messenger and the Windows Phone People hub, supports the notion of favorite contacts. Favorite contacts, or Favorites, are provided a special and prominent location in the main view of the People app, so you can access them more easily.

To add a contact to favorites, open that person's contact view, display the app bar, and then click Favorite. When you return to the main view of the app, that contact will have been added to the favorites area on the left.

PINNING A CONTACT TO START

If you find yourself interacting with a certain contact frequently, you can pin that person's contact tile to your Start screen for quick access. To do so, open that person's contact view, display the app bar, and then click Pin to Start. You'll be shown a preview of the tile, as shown in Figure 8-10, and be provided with a chance to edit the tile name.

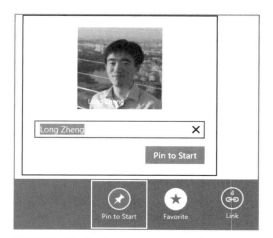

FIGURE 8-10: Pinning a contact to the Start screen

To view the new tile, return to the Start screen and navigate to the end (right side). As you can see in Figure 8-11, your contact now appears in live tile form on your Start screen.

And it is indeed live, and not just a static picture. By default, the contact's live tile will animate and will display recent activities culled from their What's new feed. You can, of course, disable that effect: Simply right-click the tile and choose Turn off live tile from the app bar that appears. (You can also unpin the tile from this interface.) Other possible configuration options include moving the tile to a new location, perhaps in a new or existing tile group.

FIGURE 8-11: A frequently-accessed contact appearing as a live tile on the Start screen

SEARCH: FINDING CONTACTS

Like many other Metro-style apps, the People app supports the system-wide Search contract, so you can use this capability to find a particular contact whether you're currently in the app or not.

To search from within People, type Winkey + Q. This displays the standard Search pane, with the People app selected. Now, just type part of the name of a contact you'd like to find. When you press Enter, the search results appear within the People app, as shown in Figure 8-12.

What's amazing about these new system-wide Metro features, of course, is that you don't even have to be using People to search for contacts. In fact, you can do so from anywhere in Windows 8: the Start screen, another Metro-style app, or even from the desktop.

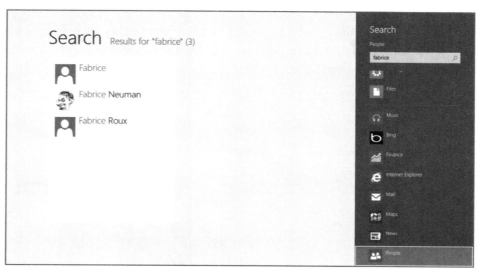

FIGURE 8-12: Search from within People.

To see this in action, return to the Windows desktop (Winkey + D) and tap Winkey + Q. The Search pane appears as expected, so start typing part of the name of a contact you'd like to find. But this time, instead of just typing Enter, select People from the list of apps. *Voila!* The search results are returned in the People app.

Seeing What's New with Your Friends, Family, Co-Workers, and Other Contacts

In addition to functioning as a super-powered address book, the People app also provides a What's new feed that aggregates content from Facebook, Twitter, and other accounts. It's a one-stop shop where you can find out what's going on with your friends, family, and other contacts, no matter where they're posting information. The What's new view is shown in Figure 8-13.

What's new provides a decidedly Metro-y take on this sort of information, with each post segregated into a tile-like space. Scrolling occurs horizontally—that is, left to right—and not vertically, as with document-based applications. And while the app will refresh this view periodically, you can refresh it yourself by enabling the app bar and clicking the Refresh button.

One of the neatest things you can do, of course, is interact with your contacts by leaving comments and other feedback to their posts. What you can do varies from account type to account type. For example, you can also choose to "like" a Facebook post, mark a Twitter "tweet" as a favorite, or "retweet" something you see on Twitter. To do any of this, find a post you like and click it. It will display full screen, as in Figure 8-14, providing a more complete view that includes others' comments as well as whatever actions are available.

FIGURE 8-13: The What's new view provides a way to easily keep up with your friends and other contacts' activities.

FIGURE 8-14: A contact's post shown in all its full-screen glory

Then, tap the Add a comment box on the bottom to add a comment. You can optionally click a Like, Favorite, or Retweet button if available, again depending on the account to which the post was made.

Viewing Your Digital Persona . . . And Creating Your Own Posts

In addition to your contacts and their aggregated activities view, People provides a handy front end for managing your own digital persona, or the online account or accounts that establish you as an entity that can perform tasks and establish relationships with others. Called Me and shown in Figure 8-15, this interface is to you as the What's new view is to others, a look at what's going on . . .with you.

FIGURE 8-15: The Me view is all about you.

In this view, you can see and edit your own contact information via the View profile link, view your own What's new feed, which is culled from whatever online accounts you've configured, view and deal with pending notifications, and view the photos you've recently posted to social networks and other accounts.

Most important, perhaps, you can also use this interface to post to supported social networks. If you have more than one configured, you'll see a drop-down letting you choose the service you want to use, and a text box labeled "What's on your mind?" where you can type in your new post.

MAIL

It's perhaps surprising that the Windows 8 Mail app is a big-screen version of the mobile Mail app that first debuted in Windows Phone, providing access to multiple e-mail accounts using an interface that's optimized for bigger, touch-enabled screens. It utilizes common e-mail features like attachments, CC and BCC support, and the reading of textual and graphical e-mails. It also works in either portrait or horizontal display modes, so you can manage mail the way you want to.

Understanding the Mail App

Mail provides a three-pane view, as shown in Figure 8-16, where you can see the major elements of the app's primary user interface.

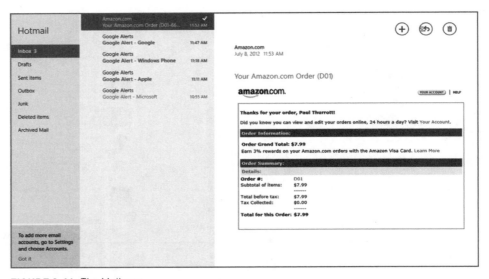

FIGURE 8-16: The Mail app

These elements include:

▶ **Accounts pane:** This leftmost pane provides access to each configured account and to the e-mail folders contained within each. (Only the folders for the currently selected account are shown.) The number of unread messages will appear next to the Inbox folder heading. Or, if you have multiple accounts, next to the link for that account. In Figure 8-17, you can see the accounts pane in Mail as it looks configured for three different accounts.

FIGURE 8-17: Multiple accounts in Mail

- **Messages pane:** Displays the contents of the current folder in the currently selected e-mail account. (The default is Inbox.)

- **Reading pane:** Displays the currently selected e-mail message.

- **New:** Click to create a new e-mail message.

- **Respond:** Click to reply, reply to all, or forward the currently selected e-mail message.

- **Delete:** Click to delete the currently selected e-mail message.

If you display Mail's app bar, you will reveal several other commands, including:

- **Sync:** Click this button to manually check for new e-mail messages at each configured account.

▶ To select multiple messages, right-click them in turn in the Mailbox folder pane. Once the messages you want are selected, you can apply actions such as Mark as Read, Mark as Unread, Move, and Delete to them. These all occur through Mail's app bar.

▶ **Pin to Start:** Click to pin the current mail folder view to the Start screen for fast access. This works much as it does for contacts in the People app: You can rename the tile as desired, and it will appear at the right end of the Start screen when first created.

▶ **Move:** Click this button to move the selected message to a new folder. When clicked, the Folders view will temporarily appear—with the rest of the app grayed out—so you can pick a new location for the message.

▶ **Mark as read/Mark as unread:** This button toggles the "read" state of the selected message. By default, a message is marked as read when it is selected.

> **NOTE** Mail is a modern and fairly efficient e-mail solution, but as a mobile app it's missing a few typical features one might be expecting. Key among these, perhaps, is the ability to drag and drop, such as you might do to move messages from one folder to another: This capability simply doesn't exist in Mail, and if you're used to managing mail in, say, Windows Live Mail, Outlook, or even web-based solutions like Hotmail or Office 365, it takes some getting used to. Remember: Metro-style apps work like—are, in fact—mobile apps, so they follow some usage patterns that may seem out of place on a full-featured PC.

Managing Accounts

While Windows 8 supports numerous account types as explained in the previous section about the People app, only a few of them—Hotmail, Google, and Exchange (which handles Exchange Server, Office 365, many other Exchange ActiveSync-based account types), and IMAP—provide e-mail support that works with the Mail app. Put another way, the Mail app functions much like a mobile device mail application and not like a full-featured desktop application such as Outlook. It's basically just an EAS e-mail app—Hotmail and Google use EAS behind the scenes to sync with mobile devices—though to be fair, it's more accurately described as a connected mail app, since it does also work with IMAP-based e-mail accounts too.

This design has its pros and cons, but the end result is that Mail, like Windows 8, is forward leaning, and not all that concerned with legacy e-mail solutions based on out-of-date technologies like POP3. If you need that kind of support, you will have to look elsewhere.

The first time you use Mail, you'll see a little box in the bottom of the Accounts pane that explains how you add accounts and provides a link for doing so. But you can add accounts at any time by visiting the Settings pane, as with other Metro apps.

To display that pane, press Winkey + I, or find it via the Charms bar, and then click Accounts. You will see a display much like that in Figure 8-18, listing the accounts you've already configured.

FIGURE 8-18: Mail accounts settings

To add a new account, click Add an account. Then, in the next screen, choose among the available account types; Hotmail, Google, Exchange, or Other Account. Account creation occurs as it does in the People app, via a full-screen Metro-style notification like the one in Figure 8-19.

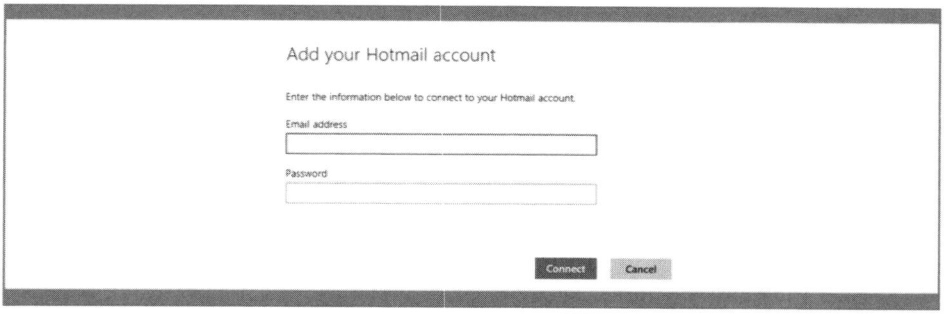

Add your Hotmail account

Enter the information below to connect to your Hotmail account.

Email address

Password

Connect   Cancel

FIGURE 8-19: Adding a new e-mail account

Note that if you need to configure an IMAP-type e-mail account, you will want to use Other Account as the account type and then click the Show more details link to enter the appropriate server information.

To manage an existing account, navigate to Settings, Accounts and then click the account you wish to edit. You'll see a pane like that in Figure 8-20.

FIGURE 8-20: Managing an existing account

Some of the key items you can configure here include:

▶ **Account name:** The name of the account as it appears in Mail. (Mail chooses generic names like Hotmail and Exchange by default.)

▶ **Download new email:** The schedule for e-mail retrieval, which for EAS-type accounts can be configured to As items arrive, Every 15 minutes, Every 30 minutes, Hourly, or Manual.

▶ **Download email from:** The range of pasted e-mail to download to your PC.

▶ **Automatically download external images:** Can be on or off depending on the security settings of your e-mail provider.

▶ **Show email notifications for this account:** Can also be set to on or off. If on, you will be notified with a "toast"-style notification each time you receive a new e-mail. These notifications resemble Figure 8-21.

▶ **Remove account:** This button lets you remove the account from Mail.

FIGURE 8-21: An e-mail notification toast

Managing E-mail

Once your various accounts are all configured, you can begin using Mail normally, as you would with any other mail application. Things work mostly as expected, though there are a few unique aspects to this application you should be aware of.

First, there's no centralized, linked inbox view as there is on Windows Phone and other mobile e-mail clients. Instead, each account is accessed separately, with its own inbox and set of folders. So if you are using multiple accounts, you can jump back and forth through the Accounts pane.

As a Metro experience, the Mail app makes it a bit ponderous to select multiple e-mails in the Mailbox folder pane and then act on them as a single unit. For example, suppose you want to select three e-mails and then move them to a new folder. To do so in Mail, you must right-click each e-mail to select them in turn—a small check box will appear in each e-mail header to indicate the selection, as shown in Figure 8-22—and then select the appropriate command—in this case, Move—from the app bar.

▶ You can multi-select contiguous e-mail messages as you would other objects in Windows, such as files in the filesystem—select the first message, scroll down to the last one you wish to select and, while pressing the Shift key, select the last. Voila!

▶ Want to select all of the messages in a folder? Select one and then press Ctrl + A.

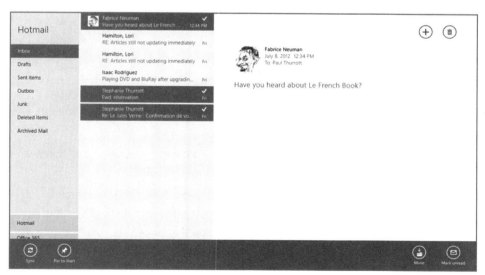

FIGURE 8-22: Selecting multiple e-mails

When you do select Move, most of the Mail app visually fades away, aside from the Folders view, so you can choose where you'd like to move the e-mail.

SENDING AND RECEIVING NEW MAIL

Mail retrieval happens automatically and, as noted previously, the schedule can be configured on an account-by-account basis. But you can always manually check for mail at any time if you're the disbelieving type: Display the app bar and tap Sync.

RESPONDING TO OR FORWARDING AN E-MAIL

Microsoft overloads the Respond button in the upper right of the Mail app with three related and useful commands: Reply, Reply all, and Forward. When you tap this button, a small pop-up menu appears, offering those options.

If you find this too ponderous—which it certainly can be—you can use keyboard shortcuts instead: Ctrl + R for Reply, Ctrl + Shift + R for Reply all, and Ctrl + F for Forward.

WRITING AN E-MAIL

When you write a new e-mail or respond to an e-mail you've received, Mail first provides the view in Figure 8-23.

FIGURE 8-23: A plethora of options are available for e-mails you write with Mail.

The following options are available initially:

▶ **Account:** If you've configured two or more e-mail accounts, you can choose from which to send the message, using a drop-down box.

▶ **To:** The e-mail recipient. Mail will use auto-complete as you type, comparing the name or e-mail address you're typing with the contacts in the People app. If you've configured an Exchange-type account, you can also use the drop-down that appears to search your workplace's user directory.

▶ **CC:** A "carbon copy" field reserved for recipients that are not the direct target of the e-mail but need to be included for some reason.

▶ **Show more:** Here, you can display BCC ("blind carbon copy") and priority choices, the latter of which lets you change from the default of Normal to High or Low priority, depending on the needs of the message.

▶ **Subject:** The subject of the e-mail.

▶ **Message body:** The body of the e-mail message, including, optionally, the pre-populated signature (which can be configured in account settings).

▶ **Send:** Click this button to send the message.

▶ **Cancel:** Click this button to save a draft of the message or delete it.

The default set of options provided by Mail here are, of course, decent. But if you display the app bar in this view, you'll find many more options. These include:

▶ **Save draft:** Click this button to save a draft of the current message.

▶ **Attachments:** This most interesting of commands triggers a Metro-style file picker view, providing you with a way to select one or more files from common filesystem locations—Documents, Pictures, Music, and the like—and apps that surface files from online services, including Camera, Photos, and Sky-Drive, which is shown in Figure 8-24.

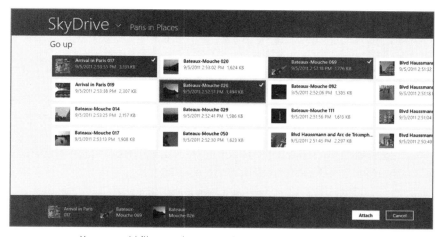

FIGURE 8-24: You can add file attachments using a standard Metro-style file picker.

▶ **Copy/Paste:** This button, which will read Copy/Paste or Paste depending on whether anything is selected and/or in the Windows Clipboard, lets you perform common Copy and Paste operations.

▸ **Font:** A simple font picker with several fonts and font sizes from which to choose.

▸ **Bold, Italic, and Underline:** Three common text-related commands, each with its own button.

▸ **Text color:** A simple font color picker with just several colors.

▸ **Bulleted list:** A way to start a bulleted list or select text and then change that to a bulleted list.

▸ **Emoticons:** This opens a pane with a surprisingly diverse and voluminous collection of high-resolution emoticons across categories like people, activities, food and things, travel, nature, and symbols. As you can see in Figure 8-25, this pane slides in from the left side of the screen and stays open so you can add multiple emoticons if needed.

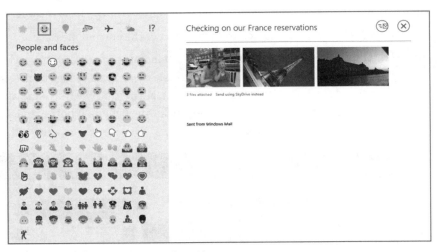

FIGURE 8-25: An amazing array of emoticons

▸ **More:** This button triggers a pop-up menu with more choices, including Bulleted list, Numbered list, Undo, and Redo.

Searching for E-mail

As with the People app, you search your e-mail using the system-wide Search capability, or contract. Put more succinctly, you search for content in the Mail app. This works as it does everywhere else in Metro: Just type Winkey + Q from within the Mail app, or do so from anywhere in the system and then choose Mail from the list of apps on the right. This displays the standard Search pane.

Now, just type in a search term. This can be part of an e-mail message or subject line, or the name of a person who has sent you e-mail (or received e-mail from you). When you tap Enter, the search results appear within the Message pane of the currently selected account in the Mail app, as shown in Figure 8-26.

FIGURE 8-26: Search for e-mail from anywhere in Windows 8.

Note that Search provides a history list of previously performed searches, and that this history is app-specific. So when you search from Mail, this Mail-specific history list appears below the Search box so you can re-do the search at any time.

Configuring the Mail App

Aside from the accounts settings discussed previously, the Mail app offers only a handful of other interesting configuration choices. You can configure the following features through the Permissions choice in this pane:

▶ **Notifications:** This toggle determines on an app-wide basis whether Mail can trigger "toast"-style notifications every time a new e-mail arrives.

▶ **Lock screen:** By default, the Windows 8 lock screen will provide a simple Mail icon with a number indicating how many new, unread e-mails are available. (It is similar to the behavior in Windows Phone, actually.) For this feature to work, of course, Mail has to be running in the background. And if you'd prefer for that not to happen, you can disable it here.

▶ Note, however, that when this is enabled, you can still determine whether each account triggers these notifications individually. (You do so through the settings for each account.)

CROSSREF You can configure which of the available lock screen icon spots is used by Mail by visiting PC Settings, Personalize, Lock screen. We discuss this and other personalization features in Chapter 5.

Snap: Sharing the Screen with Mail App

As with other Metro apps, Mail supports the Metro Snap view, by which you can dock, or snap, the app to the left or right side of the screen and use it alongside another Metro-style app or the Windows desktop. Frankly, it's not horrible when you consider the amount of information this app displays normally. But because of the thin, 320-pixel-wide area afforded to snap apps, Mail can only show a single pane at a time in this view. You can see this effect in Figure 8-27.

FIGURE 8-27: Mail in snapped view

You can navigate between the Accounts, Messages, and Reading pane views, though many e-mail messages are difficult, if not impossible, to read in this view because of the horizontal space limitations. The best reason to consider snapping Mail is for those times when you're working in another app, or on the desktop, but you want to keep an eye on Mail for some reason. When the e-mail you want does arrive, you can simply unsnap the app and view it full screen instead.

CALENDAR

Microsoft provides several excellent calendaring services through its Hotmail and Exchange technologies, with the latter surfacing not just in traditional, enterprise-based versions of Exchange Server but also in the far more affordable and accessible

Office 365 service. Powering these services on the back end is a Microsoft technology called Exchange ActiveSync (EAS), which provides push-based support for e-mail, contacts, tasks, and, yes, calendaring. EAS is a de facto industry standard, it's used even by Microsoft competitors such as Apple and Google, and it's at the heart of Microsoft's new Calendar app.

Like the Windows Phone app on which it is based, Calendar is a *connected* calendar, one that is designed to work in concert with one or more online calendars, in this case calendars that are provided using EAS technologies. So it works with Microsoft calendars such as Hotmail Calendar and Exchange/Office 365, of course, but also calendars from other companies, such as Google Calendar.

If you set up Windows 8 to sign in with a Microsoft account as we recommended early on in the book (and you did, right?), then you already have a Hotmail Calendar. And that calendar is automatically available through the Calendar app. You can, of course, configure other calendars as well.

Understanding Calendar

Calendar offers a simple, full-screen, Metro-style interface. The default display, shown in Figure 8-28, provides a look at your schedule using a month view.

To see more options, as always, you right-click any empty space on the screen (or, with touch, swipe toward the middle of the screen from the top or bottom edge of the screen). When you do so, Calendar's app bar appears as shown in Figure 8-29.

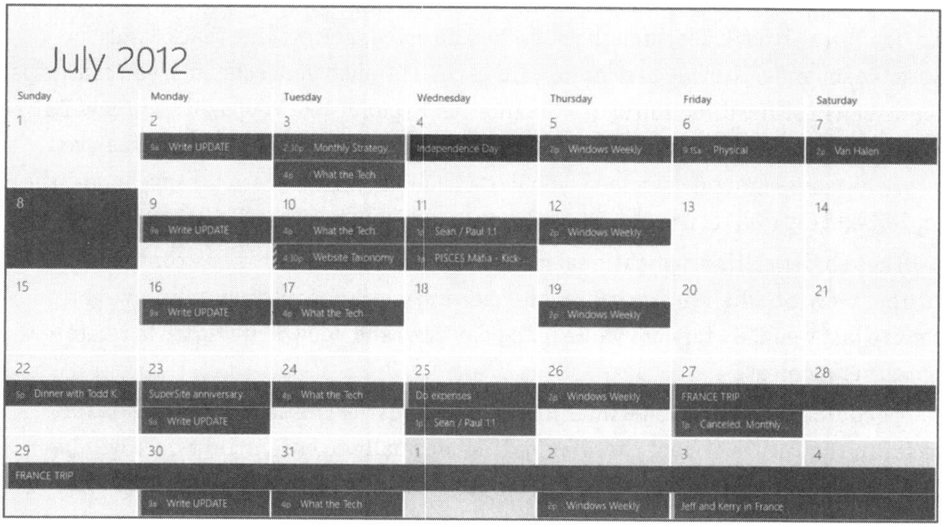

FIGURE 8-28: Calendar app

The Day, Week, and Month app bar buttons are used to change the view. For example, the week view will resemble Figure 8-30.

FIGURE 8-29: Calendar's app bar

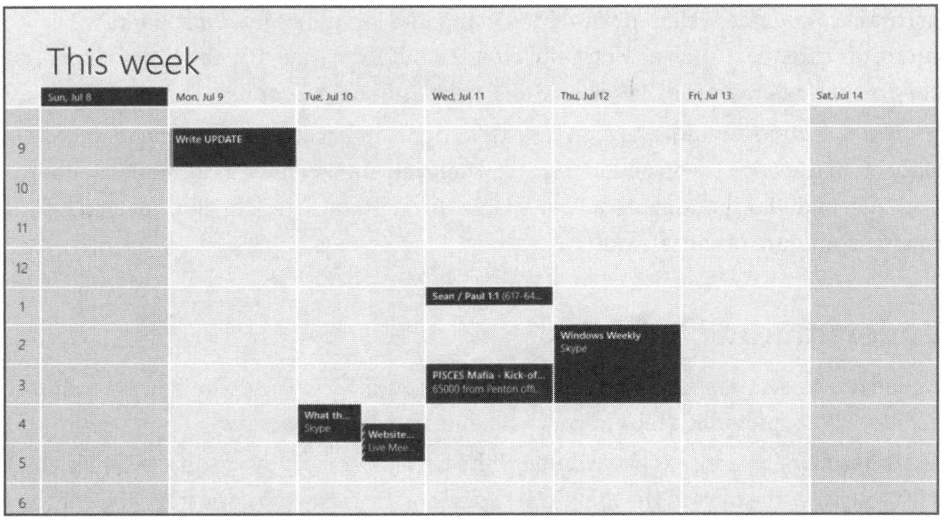

This week

	Sun, Jul 8	Mon, Jul 9	Tue, Jul 10	Wed, Jul 11	Thu, Jul 12	Fri, Jul 13	Sat, Jul 14
9		Write UPDATE					
10							
11							
12							
1				Sean / Paul 1:1 (617-64...			
2					Windows Weekly Skype		
3				PISCES Mafia - Kick-of... 65000 from Penton offi...			
4			What th... Skype	Website... Live Mee...			
5							
6							

FIGURE 8-30: Calendar's week view

You can also navigate through your schedule using browser-like "back" and "forward" commands. To move back or forward in time through your schedule, you can swipe the screen in either direction or use the Internet Explorer-like keyboard shortcuts Ctrl + Left Arrow and Ctrl + Right Arrow (for back and forward, respectively). Or, when you move the mouse around on-screen, you'll see small navigational arrows appear near the top left and top right of the screen. Click one to navigate in either direction.

These browser-like navigational movements take place within the context of the current view. So when you go back while viewing your schedule in week view, you go back to last week. Go forward while using day view and you will navigate to tomorrow. It's all very logical.

Of course, you may sometimes find yourself lost in the schedule, or at least so far in the future or past that navigating manually to the current date will be tedious. Fortunately, in this case, Calendar provides a handy Today button in the app bar. Just click that to return to the current day, week, or month, depending on the view you've chosen.

Managing Accounts

A calendar is only valuable to you if it holds your schedule, so the first order of business is getting this app connected to the calendar service you use. The choices are somewhat limited because Calendar supports EAS-based calendars only.

To access the account management interface, you must display the Calendar settings pane. As with any Metro-style app, you do so by typing Winkey + I, or by activating the Charms bar with the mouse or touch and then choosing Settings.

The Calendar settings pane, provides only a few options, including Accounts, which is what you're concerned with here. (Another useful entry, Options, will be discussed later in the chapter.)

In the Accounts view that appears, you'll see a list of configured accounts—just Hotmail by default—and an Add an account link, as in Figure 8-31. Click that, and you'll be offered the supported account types.

Since this works as it does in Mail, there's no need to belabor the point, and indeed, accounts you configure here will be configured for you in Mail (and People), and vice versa.

Calendar lets you configure multiple accounts, of course, and the events associated with each account will be color coded in the application. (You can change these colors through Settings, Options, as described later in the chapter.) Additionally, you can configure multiple accounts of the same type. So if you have two Hotmail accounts, for example, you can easily configure Calendar to display the schedule from both.

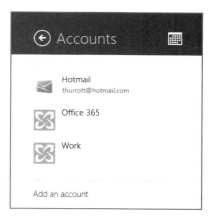

FIGURE 8-31: Calendar account management

> **NOTE** When you configure an EAS-type account in People, Mail, or Calendar, that account is automatically made available to the other apps as well. So if you added a Gmail account to Mail earlier, its corresponding Google Calendar-based schedule will already appear in Calendar too.

Working with Events

Once you start viewing your various calendars in the Windows 8 Calendar app, you'll probably want to use this interface to manage your various events as well. And as you

▶ Some calendar solutions refer to events as "appointments." The terms are interchangeable.

might expect, Calendar offers some useful functionality around creating and viewing events, as well as how you can be reminded about pending events.

To create a new event, open the Calendar app bar and tap New. (This button resembles a "+" sign.) You'll see the view in Figure 8-32, which provides a plethora of items to configure.

▶ You can also use the Ctrl + N keyboard shortcut to create a new event.

FIGURE 8-32: The new event view

These items, which have been nicely simplified using plain language, include:

▶ **When:** A number of Metro-style fields that let you configure a date for the event.

▶ **Start:** A number of Metro-style fields that let you configure the start time for the event.

▶ **How long:** Here, you can choose a length of 0 minutes, 30 minutes, 1 hour (the default), 90 minutes, 2 hours, all day, or custom. That latter option changes the Details pane of the new event view to include an End date area where you can configure the exact date and time the event will end.

▶ **Where:** Really just a plain text field that can contain any text, this field lets you enter a location for the event, like *Las Vegas*, *Home*, *Phone*, or whatever.

▶ **Calendar:** If you've configured more than one calendar, you can choose which calendar gets associated with this event.

▶ **Show more:** This link provides access to additional event items, including How often, Reminder, Status, Who, and Private.

▶ **Title:** On the right side of this display is a title area, which allows you to provide a name, or title, for the event.

▶ **Message:** Also on the right side is an expansive message area that lets you copy and paste or write details about the event.

▶ While some calendar solutions support rich text and even graphics in the message field, Microsoft apparently never got that memo: You can only use plain text here.

Oddly, unlike the New Mail screen in the Mail app, this screen doesn't provide an app bar or any options related to formatting.

To save the event, just click the Save button. Or cancel it by clicking the Cancel button.

Dealing with Reminders

Like other Metro-style apps, Calendar provides notifications using the standard, system-level notifications that you see from time to time. As you may know, Windows 8 offers two basic notification types, full-screen warnings and pop-up *toast* notifications that appear in a thin strip near the top right of the screen. Calendar uses the latter type, and at the configured time, you'll see a Calendar notification toast appear, as in Figure 8-33. Click the toast and Calendar will load so you can view more details about the event.

FIGURE 8-33: Calendar notification toast

Configuring Calendar Options

Calendar offers some useful configuration options. To view and modify them, visit Settings, Options, and you'll see an Options pane like that in Figure 8-34.

Here, you can determine on a calendar-by-calendar basis whether to display that calendar's events in Calendar and what color you wish to use to display that calendar. Note that calendar sources with multiple cal-endars will show an entry for each calendar.

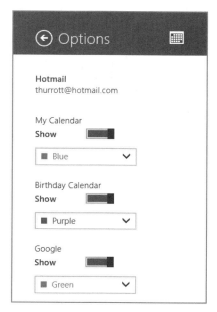

Snapping Calendar

Like other Metro-style apps, Calendar supports the Metro Snap capability, so you can snap it in a subordinate position on-screen next to

FIGURE 8-34: Calendar Options.

another Metro-style app or the Windows desktop. Unlike some Metro-style apps, however, Calendar works quite well in this arrangement, providing a customized layout that matches the thin area provided quite nicely.

As you can see in Figure 8-35, the snapped Calendar app provides a thumbnail view of the month as well as any events that are occurring today. You can also click other days in the month view to see the events for those days.

FIGURE 8-35: Calendar snapped next to the desktop

▶ You can always type Ctrl + T to "go to today" in Calendar, whether it's in snapped view or the normal full-screen mode. Ctrl + N works in snapped view, too, for creating a new event.

Two additional commands are available via the snapped Calendar's app bar: Go to today in the calendar and Add a new event. When you choose the latter, you get the nice snapped version of the new event screen shown in Figure 8-36.

FIGURE 8-36: The new event view, snapped

Lock Screen and Live Tile Use

Because of the nature of the Calendar app and the underlying calendar services it utilizes, this is a very interesting example of where the Windows 8 integration strategy makes a lot of sense. That is, while you can absolutely open the Calendar app to view your events and manage your schedule, oftentimes you simply won't need to. And that's because the Calendar app is very deeply integrated into Windows 8.

In the previous section, we discussed how the Calendar app can provide notifications that alert you to pending events no matter where you are in the system—Start screen, Metro-style app, or the Windows desktop—or what you're doing. But Calendar also provides at-a-glance calendaring information in other key places in the Windows 8 user interface, such as the Lock and Start screens.

LOCK SCREEN

The expressive new Windows 8 lock screen provides a ton of useful information at a glance, including the date and time, the number of pending e-mails, your network connectivity, and so on. But Calendar is awarded a special capability on the lock screen: When configured properly, you can see the title, location, and duration of your next event, as shown in Figure 8-37.

Let's review the three configuration interfaces you could access to change this behavior.

The first is the Calendar settings pane. If you access this interface (easiest way: Winkey + I from within the app) and click Permissions, you'll see an option there that allows this app to run in the background and display information on the lock screen. This option must be set to On for this functionality to work.

FIGURE 8-37: Calendar event information on the lock screen

The second place is in PC Settings, the new Metro-style control panel. If you access this interface (Winkey + C, Settings, More PC settings) and navigate to Personalize, Lock screen, as shown in Figure 8-38, you will see some pertinent settings for Calendar.

FIGURE 8-38: In PC Settings, you can configure how Calendar works with the lock screen.

Under the Lock screen apps area, you'll see that Windows 8 allows you to configure up to seven Metro-style apps that can run in the background and provide quick status and notifications. But below that is a very interesting option: You can configure a single app to display detailed status information. If Calendar isn't chosen here, click the "+" icon and choose Calendar from the pop-up list.

If you're *still* not seeing Calendar events on the lock screen, there's one last place to check. In PC Settings, navigate to Notifications and then ensure that the option Show app notifications on the lock screen is set to On.

> **CROSSREF** Windows 8 offers far too many ways to customize the system, but we cover this functionality in Chapter 5 if you can't get enough.

LIVE TILE ON THE START SCREEN

If you're using the Start screen as a dashboard of sorts, you know that most Metro-style apps provide live tiles that provide ongoing, app-related updates. In the case of Calendar, this functionality is quite useful, as the app's live tile will animate through the day's pending events as you watch. The Calendar live tile, shown in Figure 8-39, is quite expressive.

Of course, if you misconfigure things, the live tile could be very static. But you can check the live tile properties easily enough to make sure it's configured to your liking. To do so, right-click the Calendar live tile and consider the commands that appear in the app bar at the bottom of the screen, as in Figure 8-40.

FIGURE 8-39: The Calendar live tile

FIGURE 8-40: The Calendar live tile settings

- **Unpin from Start:** Here, you can remove the Calendar live tile if you don't wish to use it anymore.

- **Uninstall:** This option lets you uninstall Calendar.

- **Smaller/Larger:** Calendar can only display live updates when it's set to the larger (rectangular) tile size. If you set it to the smaller (square) size, it will simply animate between static displays.

- **Turn live tile off/on:** You can use this command to toggle whether live updates appear on the tile's surface. By default, this is set to on.

MESSAGING

If you're familiar with Windows Phone, you know that Microsoft's smartphone platform sports an excellent unified messaging client called—wait for it—Messaging that lets you communicate with others via services such as SMS, MMS, Windows Live Messenger, and Facebook, all via a single interface. That Messaging client uses color-coded *threads* to differentiate between conversations you have, regardless of the service used, and you can switch back and forth between the available services depending on which services your contacts use as well. It's a nice little app that integrates well with the underlying OS, popping-up notification toasts if you're doing something else and a new message arrives.

> **NOTE** SMS stands for Short Message Service and is used for text messaging, while MMS stands for Multimedia Messaging Service and can be used for sharing video, photos, and other multimedia content.

The Messaging app for Windows 8 works in much the same way, though there are some key differences between the two. The biggest is that the Messaging app for Windows 8 does not support cell phone/smartphone services such as SMS and MMS, since these occur over carrier networks and almost always incur additional fees.

Though these the two apps work similarly, those who are familiar with Windows Live Messenger for Windows might consider Messaging to be its Metro-styled equivalent, or even replacement. That's because Messaging works with the same basic two services as does Windows Live Messenger: Windows Live and Facebook.

Understanding Messaging

Messaging provides a simple, full-screen interface like that shown in Figure 8-41.

On the left, you will find a Threads pane that contains the various threads, or conversations, you have (or are currently having) with others. Each contact will have their own thread, so each time you communicate with the same person, the new conversations will be appended to the previous ones.

FIGURE 8-41: Messaging

The Threads pane also includes a prominent New message link which lets you start a new conversation with a contact.

On the right of the application window is the large Messages pane, which shows you the conversations that have occurred in the currently selected thread. At the bottom of the window is a box in which you can type a message. When you tap Enter, that message is added to the currently selected conversation and thread.

When you activate the Messaging app bar—by right-clicking a blank area of the screen, tapping Winkey + Z, or swiping toward the center of the screen from the top or bottom edge—a few additional commands are revealed.

► **Status**: This button allows you to set your online status, which is how you will appear to other contacts in their own messaging applications. Available choices in the pop-up menu that appears when this button is clicked include Available (what we used to call "online") and Invisible ("appear offline").

► **Invite:** This button triggers a pop-up menu with two choices, Add a new friend and View invites.

► **Delete:** This command lets you delete the currently selected thread. It will delete the entire thread, and not any individual part of the thread.

Managing Accounts

Messaging is primarily a Microsoft Messaging (formerly Windows Live Messaging) client, and as such it will be automatically configured to access this service if you sign in to your PC using a Microsoft account as we recommend. That said, you can also connect to Facebook's messaging service (as you can from Windows Live Messenger), and we suspect other services will come on board over time, thanks to the Windows 8 extensibility features.

Accounts are added and managed in Messaging as they are in other Metro-style apps like People, Mail, and Calendar, through Settings, Accounts. Unlike other apps, however, Messaging does not support multiple Messaging or Facebook accounts: You get only one of each.

Working with Threads

To start a new messaging thread, click the New message link. The unique People chooser interface will appear, as shown in Figure 8-42.

FIGURE 8-42: The People chooser lets you pick a contact to communicate with.

The People chooser is very interesting, because it connects to whatever Metro-style apps that have registered with the system to provide access to contacts, or the People app by default. But as more such apps become available, you'll be able to choose contacts from those apps, too, using the drop-down control to the right of the People title in the chooser.

The chooser is also smart about which contacts to show you. That is, it doesn't provide you with a rote list of every single contact you have. Instead, it only shows you those contacts that are connected to a compatible service. You can optionally toggle the view between all of these contacts and only those who are currently online.

Once you've selected a contact, you return to the main Messaging view. If you've not yet communicated with the selected contact, a new thread will be created. If you have, the new messages you'll exchange will be appended to the end of your existing thread.

Messages within a thread follow a logical form, using rectangular conversation "bubbles" that are similar to those in other messaging apps, such as the one in Windows Phone. Each time you hit Enter, that message—contained in its own bubble—is completed and sent to your contact.

Handling Notifications

Since most people won't want to stare at the Messaging screen and wait for a new message to arrive, Messaging supports the standard Windows 8 notifications capabilities and will provide pop-up notification "toasts"—along with a corresponding notification sound—whenever a new message does appear. These toast notifications will appear briefly on-screen, near the top-right corner, no matter where you are in the system, on the Start screen, while using a different Metro-style app, or on the Windows desktop. A typical Messaging notification can be seen in Figure 8-43.

FIGURE 8-43: Messaging notifications appear over other Windows 8 experiences.

NOTE This is probably obvious, but Messaging notifications will not appear when you're using Messaging. If you receive a message from another contact outside of the thread you're currently viewing, Messaging will do one of two things:

▶ If a thread already exists for that contact, the thread is moved to the top of the threads list.

▶ Otherwise, a new thread is created and added to the top of the threads list.

To deal with a Messaging notification, just click it and you'll be brought into the Messaging app where you can read the entire message and reply if necessary.

Of course, notifications are, by definition, interruptions and you may want to configure the way the system deals with notifications globally or for Messaging particularly.

As with other apps, you can configure some notification settings in Settings, Permissions, including whether Messaging notifications are enabled in Windows and on the lock screen.

Notifications can also be globally and temporarily toggled on or off using the Settings pane. To access this interface, type Winkey + I or open the Charms bar and then select Settings. From this interface, you can select the Notifications icon near the bottom of the pane to toggle this functionality, as shown in Figure 8-44.

That functionality is nice from time to time, such as when you're busy working and don't want to be disturbed. But as you use

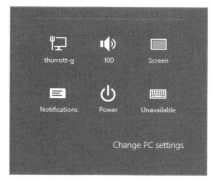

FIGURE 8-44: Notifications can be toggled globally, on the fly, using this icon.

Windows 8 more and more, you may find that you want to change the way Messaging notifications work going forward. This happens via the new PC Settings interface. (You can reach PC Settings at any time by accessing the Settings pane and selecting More PC settings.)

A few relevant options here include:

▶ **Notification sounds:** We happen to find the chime that rings each time a notification appears to be annoying. If you do too, change the option titled Play notification sounds to Off.

▶ **Show individual app notifications:** You can determine whether individual Metro-style apps, including Messenger, can even display notification toasts. Given the nature of this app, we recommend leaving notifications on for Messaging. But if you're not interested, you can disable this behavior.

Snapping Messaging

Messaging provides a reasonably useful snapped experience by which you can snap the app to the left or right side of the screen alongside another Metro-style app or the Windows desktop. In this mode, only one of Messaging's panes can be seen at a time, as shown in Figure 8-45.

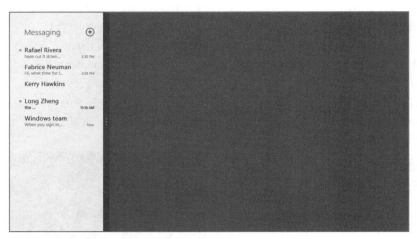

FIGURE 8-45: Messaging app in snapped mode

Most Messaging functions work just fine in this mode. You can view individual message threads, add messages to an existing thread, and, via the hidden app bar, change your status or start a new message thread.

SKYDRIVE

For years, Microsoft has offered a cloud storage service called SkyDrive that has offered an industry-best allotment of free online storage—7 GB most recently—but few ways to use it effectively. As a result, SkyDrive had been largely ignored by the computer-using public, while competing offerings from Apple (iCloud), Amazon (Cloud Player and Cloud Drive), and Google (Google Play and Google Drive) have grabbed all the headlines.

That's changed. And while there are many reasons why SkyDrive is central not only to Microsoft's vision for Windows 8 specifically, but also for all of its consumer-oriented offerings generally, here's one pertinent fact that may drive this home nicely. Windows 8 doesn't provide a way to browse the local filesystem from the new Metro environment. But it does offer a way to browse your SkyDrive storage, and the SkyDrive app is a neat little solution for those of us with our heads—well, our data at least—in the clouds.

▶ SkyDrive has had a few names over the years, including Windows Live SkyDrive. Today, however, it's referred to as Microsoft SkyDrive, or simply SkyDrive.

SKYDRIVE REQUIRES A MICROSOFT ACCOUNT SIGN-IN

There is one important consideration with the SkyDrive app. We mentioned early in the chapter that the People, Mail, Calendar, and Messaging apps require you to sign in with a Microsoft account, though you can do so even if you're signing in to the PC with a traditional local account. The SkyDrive app does not allow this: To use this app, you must sign in to the PC with a Microsoft account. To change how you sign in, you can visit PC settings, Users, and then select Switch to a Microsoft account. (Or, if you're using a domain account, you can connect a Microsoft account to that domain account.)

Understanding the SkyDrive App

The SkyDrive user interface, shown in Figure 8-46, replicates the folder structure of your SkyDrive storage.

To understand how this is so, compare it to the web-based view of the same SkyDrive account, which is shown in Figure 8-47. Restyled to resemble the Metro app, the SkyDrive web interface also utilizes Metro-style elements to represent folders and files, providing a more consistent experience.

▶ You can also install the SkyDrive application for the Windows desktop and view and manage your SkyDrive-based storage from there.

FIGURE 8-46: The SkyDrive app

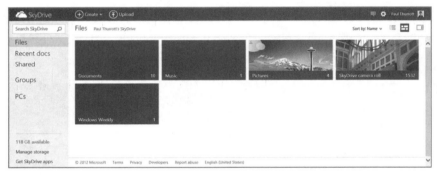

FIGURE 8-47: SkyDrive on the web now resembles the Metro SkyDrive app too.

Navigate inside one of the folders in the SkyDrive app and you'll see a similar Metro treatment applied to documents as well. In Figure 8-48, you can see a SkyDrive-based folder that contains both subfolders, on the left, and documents and other files, which are displayed on the right.

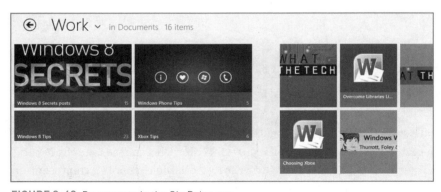

FIGURE 8-48: Documents in the SkyDrive app

Beyond that, SkyDrive offers browser-like navigational controls, including a large, obviously placed "Back" icon in the top left of the screen. Keyboarders can also use the browser-based Alt + Left Arrow shortcut to navigate back if they'd like.

As with other picker-style Metro user experiences, there's a subtle widget next to the SkyDrive title. Click this widget, which resembles a downward-facing arrow, and a small menu, or jump list, appears, as shown in Figure 8-49. This menu lets you jump to frequently needed locations, including the root of your SkyDrive storage as well as virtual views such as recent documents and shared documents.

FIGURE 8-49: SkyDrive's jump list

Opening and Editing Documents and Other Files

To open a document, simply tap (or click, or otherwise select) it. Some document types, like PDF files, will open in the Metro-style app, or Windows desktop application, that is associated with that file type. However, some behave a bit differently than expected. For example, Office documents—Word documents, Excel spreadsheets, and PowerPoint presentations—as well as OneNote notebooks open in the SkyDrive-based Office Web Apps instead. This can be seen in Figure 8-50.

▶ Would you prefer to open that document in Microsoft Office on your PC? You'll have to download it first, as discussed next.

When viewing a folder full of photos, as shown in Figure 8-51, SkyDrive provides a more compelling and panoramic view of the folder contents.

But there's still little you can do beyond viewing individual photos: No slideshow is available, and you can't even manually switch from photo to photo in a pleasant full-screen view.

Copying Files from SkyDrive to the PC

To copy (or download) a document, photo, or other file from your SkyDrive storage to the PC, simply select it and then display the app bar (Winkey + Z is quickest). Then, select the Download button, which can be seen in Figure 8-52. You can perform this action on individual files or multiple files.

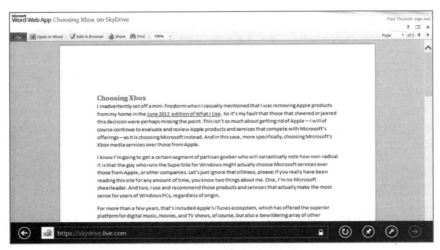

FIGURE 8-50: A SkyDrive-based Word document will open in the Office Web Apps.

FIGURE 8-51: Viewing a folder full of photos on SkyDrive

Copying Files from the PC to SkyDrive

To copy (or upload) a document, photo, or other file from your PC to SkyDrive, navigate to the destination location in SkyDrive, display the app bar and then select the Add button. A File picker screen will appear, allowing you to select one or more files from your local filesystem, as well as from various Metro-style apps that are connected to online services of their own.

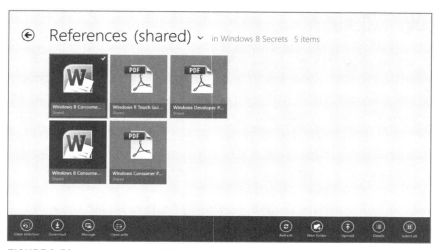

FIGURE 8-52: You can download SkyDrive-based files using the app bar.

As you select files to upload, they are added to the File picker's basket, which runs along the bottom of the screen. This basket lets you collect files from various locations and then upload only when you've gotten all the files you want, no matter where they're found throughout your PC's filesystem and potentially on other storage services in the cloud.

Sharing Files from SkyDrive

To share files from SkyDrive, you use the system-wide, Metro-style sharing mechanism that's available to all apps. Simply open the Share pane (via the Charms bar, or with the Winkey + H keyboard shortcut) and you can share the currently selected document, photo, or other file via any apps that are configured to offer this capability. In Figure 8-53, you can see that Mail and People are available for sharing the currently selected document.

FIGURE 8-53: Sharing a file from SkyDrive

WINDOWS READER

> ► Windows Reader
> also works with
> Microsoft's aborted
> XPS document
> format.

After fighting against the tide of Adobe's popular PDF document format for years, Microsoft has finally given in and created its own Windows PDF reader app. Dubbed Windows Reader, this great little app works as expected and is a lightweight and fast alternative to Adobe's bloated Reader application, even for those who prefer to stick largely with desktop applications.

Windows Reader presents a very simple full-screen interface, like many Metro-style apps, but some interesting features are revealed, as always, by activating the app bar (Winkey + Z, swipe toward the center of the screen from the top or bottom edge, or right-click anywhere). Windows Reader is shown in Figure 8-54 with its app bar displayed.

FIGURE 8-54: Windows Reader with its app bar displayed

Windows Reader provides the following features related to PDF document viewing:

▶ **Zoom:** In any of the available view styles, you can zoom in and out to better see the document. Zooming works as it does elsewhere in Metro: Via pinching on touch-based systems, with Ctrl + - (zoom out) and Ctrl + + (zoom in) keyboard shortcuts, or by holding down the Ctrl key and using your mouse's scroll wheel.

> **NOTE** Zoom out enough and you'll see a nice thumbnail view.

▶ **View styles:** The Two pages, One page, and Continuous buttons in the Reader app bar work like toggles so that only one can be on at a time. In Two pages view, Reader will display two pages of the current document side by side. In

One page view, only one whole page will be seen at a time and you must use the app's navigational controls (discussed next) to move from page to page. In Continuous view, only one whole page will be seen at a time, but you can scroll through the document continuously, with the start of the next page being visually attached to the end of the current page.

▶ **Navigation:** In Two pages and One page view, you can swipe left and right, use the left and right arrow keys, or click the pop-up navigational controls that appear to move through the document.

In Continuous view, navigation works differently. That is, instead of behaving like a standard Metro-style app with horizontal navigation, it behaves like a traditional document-based Windows application and utilizes vertical navigation instead. In this mode, you can move through the document by swiping up and down, by using the up and down arrow keys, or by utilizing the scroll bars that appear on the right side of the application.

▶ **Find:** By using the Find button in Reader's app bar, you can search for text within the current document. This interface supplies Previous and Next buttons so you can find individual references to the search text, and an optional results pane, that calls out each instance of the search text in the document for quick navigation.

▶ **Annotations:** You can make annotations (but not edits) to a PDF document with Reader by selecting a block of text, right-clicking, and choosing Highlight (to add a colored highlight to the text) or Add a note (to embed a note in the PDF). You can then save the changes to the original PDF or to a copy.

> ▶ *This right-click menu also lets you copy the text to the Windows clipboard.*

▶ **Rotate:** If you've ever gotten a PDF file that seems to be visually sideways, you know how useful this command can be.

> ▶ *Reader won't save rotation changes you make to the document, for some reason.*

▶ **Print:** Since Windows Reader is a document-based app, you may actually want to make a hard copy from time to time. That works as it does elsewhere in the Metro environment: You access the Devices charm (Winkey + C, Devices) and then select the appropriate printer from the list. Or, access the printer list directly with Ctrl + P.

THE BING APPS

In Windows 8, Microsoft has adapted many excellent Bing services into Metro-style apps. And while some of them are worth only a passing mention, one app in this group, Bing Maps, is quite useful.

Bing Maps

As it does for Windows Phone, Microsoft provides an excellent Bing Maps app for Windows 8 that brings the beautiful and useful Bing location and directions functionality to a new generation of Windows PCs and devices. You're welcome to use Maps on any PC, of course, but it works best on highly mobile devices such as tablets and hybrid portable computers that have pervasive Internet connectivity, perhaps via a cellular-type connection, and of course a GPS sensor.

> **NOTE** We'll often refer to Bing Maps simply as Maps, and it is that latter, simpler name that is used in the user interface.

It won't be surprising, perhaps, that Bing Maps prompts you to access your location information before running for the first time, as shown in Figure 8-55.

FIGURE 8-55: Bing Maps needs access to your location for fairly obvious reasons.

Once your location is available, Maps will then zoom into your current location, using a nice animation that's the hallmark of Bing Maps across the web and various mobile implementations.

ALL OVER THE MAP: NAVIGATING WITH BING MAPS

Maps works much as expected, and much like other Metro-style apps, with a clean interface and most options hidden in an app bar. You can swipe around on-screen to move the view in various directions, or, on a mouse-based system, simply "grab" the map with the mouse cursor and then move the mouse in any direction to achieve the same effect.

For keyboard users, there's a neat navigational shortcut that's not immediately obvious. Simply tapping the arrow keys does nothing. But if you hold down the Ctrl key and then tap an arrow key, the map will navigate one-half-screen's worth in that direction. Type Ctrl + Left Arrow, for example, will navigate a bit to the west. (How much will depend on the current zoom level.)

Speaking of zoom, this functionality works as expected as well. On touch-based systems, you can pinch to zoom out and reverse-pinch (or double-tap) to zoom in. Mouse users can access the on-screen zoom controls that appear in the left side of the screen, as shown in Figure 8-56. You can also use the mouse's scroll wheel to zoom in and out.

Keyboard users can zoom with Ctrl + - (zoom out) and Ctrl + "+" for zoom in (which is to say, Ctrl, Shift, and "+").

If you get lost, you can always find your current location by selecting the My Location button on the app bar. (If it's hidden, you can display the app bar by tapping Winkey + Z, right-clicking, or by tapping and holding.)

FIGURE 8-56: No touch? No problem: You can still zoom with a mouse!

CHANGING THE LOOK OF MAPS

You can change the look of the Maps presentation in two ways:

- **Show Traffic:** By default, Maps doesn't muddy up the view with traffic indications—roads that are colored green, orange or red depending on the traffic level—but this is obviously useful information if you're using the app on the go. To enable this display, activate the app bar if necessary and tap Show Traffic in the app bar. The view will change to reflect the current traffic conditions, always excellent in the Boston area. To disable this display, simply toggle Show Traffic again.

- **Map Style:** Maps supports two display styles, Road View, which is the default, and Aerial View. You can toggle this view with the Map Style button in the app bar.

FIND YOUR OWN LOCATION

If Maps gets lost for some reason, you can use the My location button in the app bar to find yourself again. Simple.

FINDING A LOCATION

To find a particular location with Bing Maps, you use the system-wide Search contract functionality, available from the Search pane. There are many ways to display this pane, but the simplest, perhaps, is to type Winkey + Q; mouse or touch users can display the Charms instead and then choose Search.

To search, simply type a location name into the search box and press Enter (or select the Search button). When you do, Bing Maps will likely navigate to the exact location, unless you've been too vague. A direct hit can be seen in Figure 8-57.

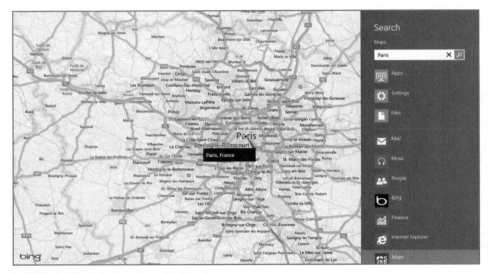

FIGURE 8-57: Find a location with Bing Maps.

Bing Maps utilizes Bing's search technologies on the back end, so you might expect searching to be fairly granular. It's not. Yes, you can use *paris france* to find Paris, France. And if you type in *las vegas*, Bing Maps will zoom right to Las Vegas, Nevada. But if you meant Las Vegas, New Mexico—or Paris, Texas, for that matter— you'll need to be more specific. Or, you can use a neat option that appears in the app bar after a location has been found: You'll see a new More results button that will display other possibilities. (You can also use the Refine button to refine your search, or the Clear button to start over.)

GETTING DIRECTIONS

Where Bing Maps really shines is in its ability to help you find your way. If you want to get directions, click the Directions button in the app bar to display the Directions pane shown in Figure 8-58.

Then, you can enter starting and ending locations in the provided boxes. The first will default to *current location*, which is exactly what it sounds like. And if you want to reverse the directions, tap the directional button at the right of the top box.

When you're ready to get the directions, click Enter (or tap the right arrow icon to the right of the bottom box). Bing will think for a bit and then provide its attractive, full-screen driving directions as shown in Figure 8-59.

FIGURE 8-58: Bing's Directions interface

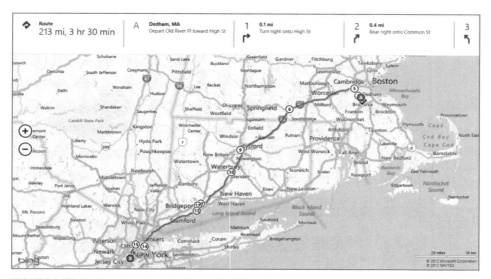

FIGURE 8-59: Getting from here to there with Bing Maps

You can zoom into parts of the route by clicking, tapping, or otherwise selecting individual parts of the route display at the top of the screen. And the printed version of the Bing Maps directions is particularly nice: You access this interface, as always through Charms, Devices, and then the appropriate printer. The Print pane can be seen in Figure 8-60.

You can also use the Clear Map button to exit from this display.

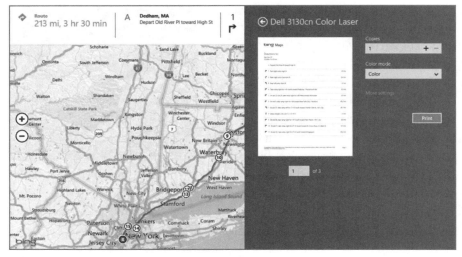

FIGURE 8-60: Bing Maps makes beautiful printed directions.

Bing

The Bing app is a Metro-based version of the Bing website, with a beautiful full-screen interface sporting Bing's beloved "picture of the day," a prominent search box, and links for searches that are popular right at this moment. You can see the Bing app in Figure 8-61.

FIGURE 8-61: The Bing app

Click the prominent More button in the bottom right of the screen, and you can view a more visual, Metro-like take on the day's biggest happenings, as in Figure 8-62.

FIGURE 8-62: Bing's more visual view of today's big searches

Bing Finance, News, Sports, and Weather

Microsoft also provides four very similar looking apps, Bing Finance, News, Sports, and Weather, which take the notion of a news aggregator and turn it into something truly beautiful and useful. Each obviously focuses on its own core topic, with Finance providing a gorgeous front end to the stock market and financial news and topics, News providing a general purpose news experience, Sports taking on locale-specific sports news of note, and Weather doing its best to make the weather look gorgeous, no matter how ugly it gets outside.

Since each is so similar from a presentation perspective, let's just look at one, Sports, to see how something basic can be made to look so beautiful. In Figure 8-63, you can see the Sports landing page, which provides beautiful, magazine-style photography and layout.

Scroll over to the right and you'll see other top stories from the day, highlighted again in a highly visual style with a nice layout as in Figure 8-64.

Each of the apps is fully customizable in some way. In Sports, for example, you can follow your favorite sports, teams, or players. And in Weather, of course, you can configure the weather display for your favorite places, and even pin individual weather tiles for each on the Windows 8 Start screen.

FIGURE 8-63: The Sports app

FIGURE 8-64: Top stories in Sports

MICROSOFT OFFICE COMES TO WINDOWS . . . SORT OF

Over the years, we've been struck by how many people seem confused by the relationship between Microsoft's two most successful product franchises, Windows and Office. That is, many people believe that Office is "part" of Windows and that these two very separate software solutions are thus one. And some are surprised when they reinstall Windows, or get a new PC, to discover that Office is no longer present. So we've spent a lot of time trying to educate people about the differences between Windows and Office, and how they are separately acquired.

To be fair, the reason so many people believed that Windows and Office came together is that, for many, they did. Most people acquire both Windows and Office together with a new PC purchase and thus don't draw a distinction between the two. The problem is, if you're not paying attention at the time of that PC purchase, you may not get Office at all, or you may get a version of Office that you don't want.

Also, during the life cycle of Windows 7, many PCs came with a stripped-down Office version called Office Starter that included two very basic Office applications, Word Starter and Excel Starter. This solution came free with many PCs and was designed to be electronically upgraded to higher-end, paid versions of Office.

With Windows 8—and a new family of Office products branded as Office 2013—Microsoft is completely changing the equation. The ARM-based versions of Windows 8, called Windows RT, actually do come with a special version of Office 2013, and while this freebie Office version doesn't offer all of the power and flexibility of the high-end Office 2013 suites, it's a far cry from the basic experience previously offered by Office Starter. (Office Starter is no longer available.) Office 2013 for Windows RT version includes Word, Excel, PowerPoint, and OneNote, and if you purchase any Windows RT-based device, you'll get these powerful applications for free.

▶ Windows PCs that do not include these full-featured Office applications will almost certainly include, or offer, some form of Microsoft Office. Check with your retailer or hardware maker for details.

As you may recall, with Windows 8 and RT, Microsoft has divided the PC market somewhat with two complementary Windows 8 families of products, one of which runs on traditional PCs (and, confusingly, device-like tablet PCs) based on familiar Intel x86/x64 and compatible chipsets. But there are also versions of Windows 8 that run on the ARM platform, which is typically used on very thin, light, and elegant portable devices similar to Apple's iPad. Those Windows 8 versions, collectively called Windows RT, do include the Microsoft Office applications Word, Excel, PowerPoint, and OneNote. So that's something to consider when you're shopping for a device.

▶ Windows RT devices come with some significant downsides, however, as well, including one key issue: A lack of compatibility with traditional third-party Windows-based applications. We discuss these issues in Chapter 1.

NOTE Why do Windows RT devices include Office you ask? Though Windows RT looks and works much like traditional x86 versions of Windows 8, it is not compatible with traditional Windows desktop applications like Office. So Microsoft has made a special version of Office just for Windows RT, while focusing mostly on Metro-style apps going forward on that platform.

There is some precedence for this product bundling. As long ago as 1995, when Microsoft launched the first version of Windows CE, a specially made version of Windows designed to run on non-PC devices of the day, it also bundled basic versions of its Office applications, then called Pocket Office, with the tiny machines that ran that OS. And through the years, subsequent updates to that product line, including Pocket PC and Windows Mobile, also included these Pocket Office applications as part of the platform.

And in the modern Windows Phone platform, which is today now based on the PC version of Windows 8, Microsoft continues to bundle Office. Windows Phone 8 includes what's now called Office Mobile 2013, with portable versions of Word, Excel, PowerPoint, and OneNote that provide not just document compatibility and basic editing functionality, but also interoperability with Microsoft's cloud-hosted Office document repositories, SkyDrive and SharePoint. So it should be no surprise that Windows RT devices—that is, those machines that sit logically between phones and "true" (or at least traditional) PCs—would also offer similar functionality.

Expectations for Office on a highly mobile device like a tablet are, of course, somewhat reduced compared to those one might have for a solution that runs on a full-featured PC. But since many Windows RT and Windows 8-based devices can be docked or otherwise transformed into more powerful PCs with keyboards, mice, and external screens, the bundling of these applications is all the more interesting for those of us who want one device that does it all.

In any event, the bundled version of Office includes the following solutions:

▶ **Word:** When you think about word processing, you think about Microsoft Word, and while there have been many pretenders throughout the years, none have approached the power and utility of Microsoft Word, nor its amazing reading experiences. In fact, Word is so good, we used it to write this book.

▶ **Excel:** Excel is Microsoft's spreadsheet solution, and like Word, it dominates the market in which it competes. Excel offers all of the number crunching functionality you expect and lets you analyze and visualize data in amazing, graphical ways.

▶ **PowerPoint:** Microsoft's presentation package is a staple in offices and schools around the world, offering professional features, support for amazing embedded multimedia, and the ability to broadcast to any Internet-connected PC or device.

▶ **OneNote:** Less well known than the other Office applications, perhaps, OneNote is ideal for portable devices, offering amazing, cloud-connected note-taking capabilities.

▶ Microsoft is also providing two Metro-style Office apps with Office 2013, OneNote and Lync. These work with both Windows 8 and Windows RT.

SUMMARY

As this chapter ably demonstrates, Windows 8 is a productivity whirlwind, with an amazing array of Metro-style apps and traditional desktop applications that will keep you up to date, efficient, and working through any conditions. From the new Metro-style People, Mail, Calendar, Messaging, SkyDrive, Reader, and Bing offerings like Maps, Bing, Finance, News, Sports, and Weather, and more, Windows 8 includes enough in the box to keep you busy for a long, long time. Of course, Windows 8 isn't just about work. And in the next two chapters, we'll examine the fun side of Windows 8, examining its entertainment and game capabilities, respectively.

CHAPTER 9

Relaxing with Windows 8's Photo and Entertainment Apps

IN THIS CHAPTER

▶ **Viewing photos from your PC and** multiple online services with the Photos app

▶ **Using the Camera app**

▶ **Understanding your options** for more sophisticated photo needs

▶ **Enjoying your music collection** and accessing Microsoft's Music Marketplace with the touch-friendly Xbox Music app

▶ **Understanding your options** for more sophisticated music needs

▶ Buying and **renting** movies and TV shows online and watching them with the Xbox Video app

▶ **Understanding your options** for more sophisticated video needs

In the old days, users would manage their media collections on their PCs and then sync a subset of their photo, music, and video content with devices and share a further subset via discs, USB devices, and online services. While these activities are still possible in Windows 8, and will no doubt be quite popular for some people, Microsoft is embracing a new way of doing things that more closely mirrors related changes in the tech industry.

The new way of doing things was triggered by a technological advance called *cloud computing*. In this new model, your data isn't stored on a single hard disk on a single PC, where it's inaccessible from other PCs and devices and could potentially suffer from data loss because of a catastrophic hardware failure. Instead, the data is stored in the cloud—in

powerful, geographically redundant data centers run by major corporations we actually trust—and is always accessible from any PC or device.

In this new cloud computing model, all of your data is always available on your
PC, just like before. But now you can pick up almost any other PC or device and still
access your data seamlessly, because it's automatically synced for you. Microsoft
pioneered this new approach with Windows Phone back in 2010, and it's finally going
mainstream with Windows 8.

You can see cloud computing's impact on Windows 8 in many places, from the new
Microsoft account sign-in to the synced settings and the mobile device–like productivity apps discussed in the previous chapter. But the system's photos and entertainment capabilities, related to digital photos, music, and video, are an interesting case.
This is because Microsoft had previously spent over a decade delivering an increasingly powerful but complex series of applications and services through its Windows
Media and Zune product lines, to which hundreds of millions of Windows users have
grown accustomed.

Today, those services are being reorganized under the Xbox entertainment
brand. Previously, Xbox meant one thing and one thing only, video games. But Xbox
is evolving into a more general purpose entertainment platform, adding digital
music and video to its stable of capabilities. (Photos remain separate because users'
photos are their own and are not acquired from a central location.)

If you're not ready to move forward and utilize online services like SkyDrive to store
your music collection, or rent and buy movies and TV shows from Microsoft's Xbox-based
marketplaces, no need to worry; all of the local-based digital media capabilities in
Windows 7 are still present in Windows 8. But as with the rest of this book, this chapter
focuses solely on the new capabilities. And in this specific case, that means enjoying
digital photo, music, and video content in new ways through new Metro experiences.

IT'S GOING TO CHANGE

Thanks to the dynamic nature of its new apps platform, the Metro-style apps
that Microsoft includes with Windows 8/RT will change over time, so it's highly
likely that the apps described in this chapter will appear somewhat differently
over time and will include additional features. This is normal, and as a general
statement, it's probably fair to say that the versions of the Photos, Camera,
Xbox Music, and Xbox Video apps you use will provide a superset of the functionality we describe in this chapter.

A NOTE ABOUT THE WINDOWS 8 ENTERTAINMENT APPS AND YOUR MICROSOFT ACCOUNT

In Chapter 8, we discussed how many of Windows 8's productivity apps are simple clients for online services provided by Microsoft and other companies. As such, you must sign in to your Microsoft account to access many of these apps, even if you've elected—against our advice—to not automatically do so by signing in to the PC with a Microsoft account.

Photos and Camera actually work fine without a Microsoft account, go figure, but as you'll see, you will need to sign into various online services to use Photos to its fullest. But Microsoft's new Metro-style entertainment apps, Xbox Music and Xbox Video (and the related Xbox Companion) do require you to sign-in with a Microsoft account to be used effectively.

If you have signed in with a Microsoft account, these apps will automatically sign into that account as well, tying your PC or device to the Xbox entertainment services in the cloud. But if you've configured a non-Microsoft account and attempt to run one of these apps, you'll be asked to sign-in with a Microsoft account. You can retain your current domain or local account if you'd like, and just sign in to app and app groups with a Microsoft account. Or, you could follow our advice from Chapter 12 and do the right thing: Sign in with a Microsoft account. Or, if you have a domain account, connect it to a Microsoft account. Signed in with a local account? Convert it.

Both Xbox Music and Xbox Video provide a similar experience for non-Microsoft account users. You'll just see a non-threatening Sign In prompt in the upper-right corner of the screen, as shown in Figure 9-1.

> ▶ These apps rely heavily on online services, are less full-featured when you're offline; you'll only be able to use content stored on the machine, your own PC-based photos, music, and videos, and any rented movies or purchased TV shows or movies.

FIGURE 9-1: Xbox Music and Video both require a Microsoft account to be used fully.

If you don't sign-in, you'll only see a tiny subset of the functionality described in this chapter. But you're not going to go through any of that, right? Right.

ENJOYING PHOTOS

Windows 8 includes tools for enjoying digital photos on your PC or device, no matter the source. That means basic photo-viewing experiences for both Metro and the desktop, and ways to acquire (or download) photos from a digital camera, smartphone, memory card, or other device. But most Windows 8 PCs and devices will also include more advanced tools for editing photos, uploading them to your favorite online service, and more. Don't worry: If you don't have these tools, we'll tell you how to get them.

> **NOTE** As with elsewhere in the book, we focus only on new features in Windows 8, and not on functionality that remains unchanged from previous Windows versions. Again, the assumption is that you know how to use Windows and want to get up to speed on the new stuff.

Here we look at the photo features in Windows 8, starting with the new Metro-style Photos app.

Using the Photos App

The new Photos app is a great way to view your photos, whether they are on the PC, in SkyDrive, on your other PCs, or on various third-party online photo sharing services. It also provides photo acquisition features, so you can acquire, or "download" photos from a digital camera, memory card, or other device.

The Photos app, shown in Figure 9-2, is a typical, full-screen, Metro-style experience, with large tiles representing the photos on your PC, in various online services, and on your other connected PCs.

These sources can include some combination of the following:

▶ **Pictures library:** Here, you'll find all of the photos stored in the Pictures library on your PC.

▶ **SkyDrive:** Microsoft's cloud storage service, SkyDrive, provides 25 GB of free storage plus paid annual tiers for those who need even more.

▶ **Facebook:** The most popular social network on earth is also an increasingly common way for people to share photos with friends, family, co-workers, and other contacts.

▶ **Flickr:** Yahoo!'s popular Flickr remains the number one photo-sharing service on earth.

▶ **Connected PCs:** If you've downloaded and installed the SkyDrive desktop application from www.skydrive.com on each of your PCs, you will see the photo collections from those PCs listed here as well. In Figure 9-2, for example, Ivy-1 and Series9 represent other connected PCs.

FIGURE 9-2: Photos app

ABOUT LIBRARIES

Microsoft introduced libraries in Windows 7, providing a new way to collect related content—documents, music, photos, and videos by default—in virtual folders that are really views to two or more physical folder locations on the PC. Libraries continue in Windows 8 largely unchanged, and Microsoft provides the same four default libraries—Documents, Music, Pictures, and Videos—as it did in the previous OS version. Likewise, each library aggregates the same two physical folders as in Windows 7, in default. So in the case of the Pictures library, that means the My Pictures folder that's part of your user account and the Public Pictures folder.

This is all a long way of saying that Windows 8's basic photo management features haven't changed since Windows 7.

Depending on how you've configured your Microsoft account, some of these sources will and will not be immediately available. The Pictures library is always available, online or off, and will include whatever photos and other pictures you store in your Pictures library. And your SkyDrive source should be automatically configured since your Microsoft account comes with access to SkyDrive storage.

But the other sources, Facebook, Flickr, and your connected PCs, may or may not be configured and available. If you took the time to associate your Facebook account with your Microsoft account, this source will be set up and ready to go. But if not, you can do so now from within Photos. And the process for configuring this account to work with Photos is similar to that for Flickr, which has to be performed manually regardless of how you've configured your Microsoft account. So let's examine that first.

CONFIGURING FACEBOOK OR FLICKR PHOTOS

To manually configure Facebook—remember, the process is also very similar for Flickr—to work with the Photos app, you will need to visit the app's Settings pane. To do so, tap Winkey + I. (Or, with a touch or mouse interface, display the Charms bar and then select Settings.) The Settings pane should resemble Figure 9-3.

FIGURE 9-3: Photos Settings

Select Options to display various options related to Photos. Next to both Flickr and Facebook, you will see a link titled Options. Click the link for the service you wish to configure. (We're using Facebook in this example, but the process is very similar for Flickr.)

Photos will pass you through to the web-based Facebook authentication site using Internet Explorer. Here, as shown in Figure 9-4, you will authorize Photos to use your Facebook account.

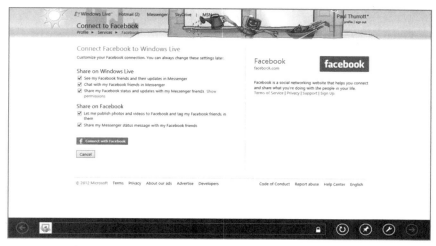

FIGURE 9-4: Configuring Photos to work with Facebook

Click Connect with Facebook to connect the Facebook service to the Photos app. Once you've provided your Facebook credentials, Microsoft will link the two accounts and you can return to the Photos app. When you do, you'll see that a new Facebook tile has been added to the app, providing you with access to the photos from that service (see Figure 9-5).

FIGURE 9-5: Facebook is now available in Photos.

Again, the way you configure Photos to work with Flickr is identical to what we just discussed. So if that's required, you can connect to your Flickr account in the same fashion.

► If you don't use Facebook or Flickr, you can actually remove these tiles from the Photos home screen. We describe this process a bit later in the chapter.

USING SKYDRIVE TO CONNECT TO OTHER PC PHOTO LIBRARIES

By this point, you should have Photos configured to work with some combination of your local photos, SkyDrive-based photos, and possibly your Facebook and Flickr-based photos as well. That's a lot of photos. But most people have two or more PCs, and if you configure these PCs a certain way, you can actually access the photo collections on your other PCs—or what we call your connected PC—from any of your PCs.

This assumes that the PCs in question are online, of course. If a connected PC is off or asleep, you won't be able to access its pictures from the Photos app. On the good news front, these other PCs don't have to be on your home network to work: One could be in Singapore, for example, and one in Boston, Massachusetts, and you'd still be able to make the connection as long as they're both online.

So how do you connect PCs? There are two requirements:

► **Microsoft account:** You must configure each PC to sign in with the same Microsoft account.

► **SkyDrive application for Windows:** You must install the SkyDrive application for Windows (not to be confused with the Metro-style SkyDrive *app* for Windows 8) on each PC and configure that application to use a feature called Remote Fetch. This feature makes that PC's files available to you on your other PCs and devices. You do this through the SkyDrive application's Settings window, which can be seen in Figure 9-6, and accessed through the app's system tray icon.

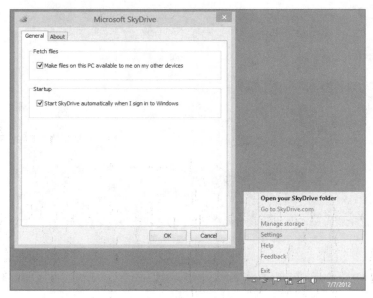

FIGURE 9-6: Make sure the SkyDrive application is configured to share its files with other connected PCs.

When you do configure your PCs to use SkyDrive's Remote Fetch feature, the photo libraries from those PCs will appear in the Photos app on your other PCs. It's like magic!

NAVIGATING THROUGH YOUR PICTURES LIBRARY, SKYDRIVE, FACEBOOK, AND FLICKR

Once all of your photo sources are configured, you can use the Photos app as it is intended: to view *your photos*, regardless of their location. Well, assuming you're online, that is: When you're offline, only the Pictures library tile will respond.

Navigation in each source is similar: You're presented with a horizontally arranged list of tiles, each of which represents a folder, file, depending on the source. These tiles are in alphabetical order, from left to right, with folders appearing before actual files. Consider the view shown in Figure 9-7, which displays the contents of the Pictures library.

FIGURE 9-7: Viewing folders in the Pictures library

In this view, you can see two folders, which are represented as tall, rectangular tiles and a single photo, which appears in its native aspect ratio. If you find this view constrictive, you can view more folders (and files) simultaneously by using semantic zoom to pan back the view, resulting in the grid-like layout shown in Figure 9-8. Obviously, this option—which is available in virtually all Photos views—is more effective (and even necessary) when you have a lot of pictures.

FIGURE 9-8: You can zoom out to view more photos on-screen at once.

You can enable semantic zoom in a variety of ways. With a touch-based system, you use the suddenly common pinching gesture, with two fingers, directly on the screen. With a mouse and keyboard, you can hold the Ctrl key and use your mouse's scroll wheel. Or, with just the mouse, click the small minus ("-") symbol in the bottom right of the screen.

And if you zoom enough in the correct direction, you can even use this feature to zoom into a photo! (If you do, you can use the small plus ("+") symbol that appears in the lower right to zoom back out as well.)

These basic views are true of all the photo sources, but of course each is a bit different in its own way. So here's some information to consider about each:

► **Pictures library:** By default, the Pictures library consists of the contents of two locations, My Pictures and Public Pictures, but you can add and remove locations as well. Files and folders in a library are mixed together and arranged as one. So if you have folders named *Alpha* and *Gamma* in your My Pictures folder and then one folder named *Beta* in Public Pictures, they will be arranged alphabetically as *Alpha, Beta,* and then *Gamma* in the Pictures library in both File Explorer (on the Windows desktop) and in the Pictures library view in the Photos app.

► **SkyDrive:** When you access SkyDrive from its normal web interface at skydrive. com, you're given the opportunity to configure the "type" of each folder. One of those types is Photos. And only folders that are configured as type Photos will appear in the Photos app in Windows 8. So if you're not seeing certain SkyDrive photos appear, make sure they're in a properly configured folder.

▶ **Facebook:** Everyone's favorite social networking service organizes photos into albums, and what you'll see in the Facebook view in Photos will correspond to that. You'll see common Facebook locations like Cover Photos, Mobile Uploads, Wall Photos, and so on, as well as whatever albums you've manually created. The order here, however, is not alphabetical. Instead, they're arranged by which most recently were accessed.

▶ **Flickr:** Yahoo's popular photo-sharing service provides users with a Photo-stream, which is basically just every photo you've ever uploaded. But it also provides folder-like containers, including sets, which can be further grouped into collections. So you might consider these folders and sub-folders, respectively. Looking at the Flickr view in Photos, you'll see a tile for your Photo-stream and then tiles for each collection and set.

▶ **Connected PCs:** As with your own Picture library, your connected PCs will present an aggregated list of folders, sorted alphabetically.

VIEWING PHOTOS AND PHOTO SLIDESHOWS

Each of the supported photo sources provides nearly identical features related to viewing photos and photo slideshows. So you can browse into any source, and eventually you'll be presented with one or more actual photos, in a folder. At this point, you can perform some basic activities related to individual photos or groups of photos.

To view a photo full-screen, simply select it. This works exactly as expected, but if you open the app bar (Winkey + Z) while viewing an individual photo, you'll see some interesting options, as shown in Figure 9-9.

These options include the following:

▶ **Set as ... Lock screen:** While you can always use the PC Settings interface to select a favorite photo for your lock screen image, oftentimes you'll think to do this while actually viewing photos. This menu item, found by tapping the Set as button, lets you do so.

▶ **Set as ... App tile:** By default, the Photos app tile will shuffle through photos, presenting an animated view. But you can configure a single picture to be the permanent tile image if you'd like.

▶ **Set as ... App background:** As you've seen, the Photos app provides a nice photographic background image in its main view. But you'll probably want to change that to a favorite photo of your own. When you do, this view will change to resemble Figure 9-10.

▶ Note that this delete button is not available when viewing photos on connected online services or PCs.

▶ **Delete:** This button deletes the file from your PC, after a quick confirmation.

▶ **Slide show:** This button triggers a slideshow of the photos contained in the folder that contains the picture you're currently viewing.

FIGURE 9-9: A single photo viewed full-screen

FIGURE 9-10: Customizing the Photos app with your own picture.

Of course, you can also trigger slideshows from a folder view, and when you access the app bar from this view, you get a different set of buttons, and thus capabilities. A few are notable.

The first is a Browse by date button, though it only appears in the Pictures library view. When you activate this button, the view switches so that each "folder" tile now represents a month, as in Figure 9-11. (And there's now a new Browse by album button in the app bar so you can switch back.)

FIGURE 9-11: The Pictures library, viewed by date

> ► In this Browse by Date view, you can also reverse pinch to zoom out and see more on-screen at once.

There's also a power-user feature of sorts that lets you collect photos from different folders (within a single photo source) into a basket, like that in the Metro-style File Picker, so that you can run a slideshow of photos from different locations.

To use this feature, enter a folder or view that contains photos. Then, select individual photos, as you would when selecting Start screen tiles: by right-clicking them, tapping and dragging down a bit, or by pressing the Spacebar; as you select a photo, a selection rectangle will indicate success. Or you can select every photo in a folder by opening the app bar and pressing Select All.

> ► This is a neat feature, but it works only within a single source. You can't mix photos from, say, Facebook and Flickr into a single slideshow. You'll be prompted to that effect if you try.

Either way, as you select photos, you'll see two new buttons in the app bar as you go: a Clear Selection button for clearing the selection and a selection thumbnail that indicates how many photos you've selected; these can both be seen in Figure 9-12. Once you've selected all the photos you want—again, from multiple folders—you can tap the Slide show button to start this more advanced slideshow type.

SHARING, PRINTING, AND SEARCHING

Many common photo-related activities work consistently with similar features in other Metro apps, thanks to the new system-wide capabilities in Windows 8. For example, when viewing a photo, you can print it by accessing the Devices interface (Winkey + K) or, more directly, the Print interface (Ctrl + P). Or you can use the Share interface (Winkey + H) to share the photo with others using a compatible Metro-style app, such as Mail.

FIGURE 9-12: Multi-selecting photos from different folders.

▶ There's no way to search all sources simultaneously, though that would be very useful.

Likewise, the excellent Search functionality in Windows 8 can be used in Photos to find particular pictures. If you access the Search charm (Winkey + Q) while viewing a photo or from within a particular folder, the Search pane that appears will search only that folder. Search at the source level and it will search just that source.

If you open the Search charm from outside the Photos app and then select Photos from the list of apps in the Search pane, you get a grid-based view of your Pictures library, filtered to the search term, as shown in Figure 9-13.

FIGURE 9-13: A Photos search results list

ACQUIRING PHOTOS FROM A CAMERA, MEMORY CARD, OR OTHER DEVICE

If you've ever connected a digital camera, a camera's memory card, or another device (like a smartphone) that contains pictures to Windows in the past, you know that

Microsoft's desktop OS has long supported basic photo acquisition (or what some people think of "downloading") capabilities through desktop apps like Photo Gallery. You can still do this, if you'd like. Or, you can use the new Metro-based photo acquisition interface that's available through the Photos app.

When you plug in a compatible device that contains photos, you'll see a Metro-style notification flyover, or "toast," like that shown in Figure 9-14.

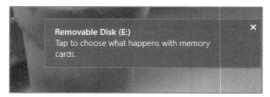

FIGURE 9-14: Windows 8 asks what you'd like to do when you plug in this sort of device.

If you select this notification, you'll see a window similar to that in Figure 9-15; like the notification, this display can appear anywhere in Windows, including Photos or other Metro-style apps, the Start screen, or the Windows desktop.

FIGURE 9-15: Choose what you'd like to do with devices that contain photos.

You may want to use Photos as the default choice when such a device is plugged into the PC, though we feel that you should examine your choices before making such a decision. Remember that you can always change what happens later using the AutoPlay control panel, though. So if you make a mistake, or want to change your selection later, you can do so.

▶ The easiest way to find AutoPlay is to use Windows Search: Type autoplay, select Settings, and then choose AutoPlay from the results list.

For now, let's just use Photos to manually acquire photos from an attached camera, memory card, or other device. To do so, launch the Photos app and then display the app bar. On the far right side of this app bar, you'll see an Import button. Click this, and Photos will prompt you to choose a device, as in Figure 9-16.

Do so, and you'll be presented with the full-screen interface shown in Figure 9-17. Here, you can determine which photos to acquire and what the folder name that contains them will be.

FIGURE 9-16: Choosing a device with photos.

What you can't do, of course, is configure other photo acquisition options, and this is why we noted previously that you may want to review your options first. Photos doesn't let you name the acquired photos to your liking (unless you happen to like the default, which is to use awful, camera-based names). And it doesn't let you choose whether to delete the photos from the device once they're acquired. (They are not deleted.)

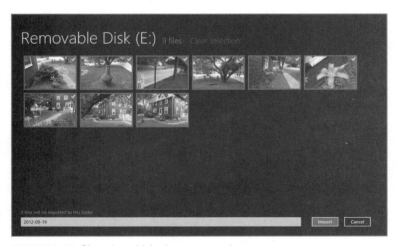

FIGURE 9-17: Choosing which photos to acquire.

Click Import to acquire the photos.

When you're done, you're prompted to open the folder containing the photos you just imported. This will happen in Photos, of course, not in File Explorer on the desktop.

Put simply, the photo acquisition capabilities in Photos are, well, basic. And if you want more control over this process, as we do, you should consider using the free Photo Gallery desktop application instead. We look at this useful tool a bit later in the chapter.

Using the Camera App

As with other mobile, touch-based systems, Windows 8 includes a simple Camera app that works with the camera (or, in the case of some modern devices, the *cameras*) that is included in (or attached to) your PC or device. This app lets you capture still pictures and short movies. It's not quite as useful as, say, a camera in a smartphone, but it's there if you need it.

The first time you run the Camera app, you'll be prompted to allow the app to use your webcam and microphone. Obviously, you must allow this for the app to function. If you block this access, the app will simply quit.

The Camera app, shown in Figure 9-18, is simplicity itself. There's an app bar, always visible in this app, with just a handful of buttons.

FIGURE 9-18: Dashing! The Camera app

Available app bar buttons include:

▶ **Change camera:** On PCs or devices with multiple cameras, the Change camera button will let you choose which camera to use. For example, many Windows 8 and RT devices include both front- and rear-facing cameras. This button works like a toggle: Tap it once to change the view to the next camera.

▶ **Camera options:** Click this button to see a pop-up display with three options that will be consistent across all Windows 8 PCs: Photo/Video resolution, Audio device, and Video stabilization, though not all options will be configurable on all PCs. You can also click a More link here to view additional camera options. What you see in that interface will vary from PC to PC, but some of the more common options include Brightness, Contrast, Flicker, and Exposure.

▶ **Timer:** This button acts as a toggle. When selected, the next photo or video you take will be preceded by a 3-second countdown, giving you time, perhaps, to jump into the frame.

▶ **Video Mode:** This button also works as a toggle. By default, Camera is set up to take still photos. But if you enable this button, it is set up to take videos instead. Tap it again to return to camera mode.

▶ *Keyboard users can tap Space to take a photo or start/stop video recording.*

To take a photo with Camera, simply tap (or click) anywhere on-screen. If you're in video mode, this will start video recording instead. To stop recording, tap (or click) the screen instead.

Photos and videos taken with Camera can be found in the Camera Roll photo, which is added to the default save location for the Pictures library (My Pictures, by default).

Doing More with Your Pictures

The Photos app is fine for what it is. But it doesn't have any photo editing features at all. Its photo acquisition features are lackluster at best. And if you want to share photos via an online service that's not supported by a Metro-style app that's savvy to the Share contract, you're out of luck on that count as well.

For these and other slightly more advanced scenarios, you'll need to turn to the Windows desktop. Here, you'll find some features that are built into Windows 8 directly, and a few that will require some optional and free Microsoft applications that may or may not be installed on your PC or device.

Since these capabilities haven't changed since Windows 7, we won't go into great depth here. But we'll provide you with a rundown of the applications you can use, and for what activities, and help you find any missing applications that may not be included with your Windows 8 install.

BUILT INTO WINDOWS 8: PHOTO VIEWING ON THE DESKTOP

Windows 8 includes an admittedly well hidden desktop application called Windows Photo Viewer that lets you view individual photos and perform other photo-related functions. Windows Photo Viewer is odd in that you can't actually find the application via normal means—it doesn't appear in the All Apps view or even via Start Search. But you can access Photo Viewer by right-clicking an image file from the desktop and choosing Open with and then Windows Photo Viewer.

As you can see in Figure 9-19, this application provides print-, e-mail-, and disc burning-based ways to share photos and a handy but simple slideshow feature courtesy of that large button in the lower middle of the window.

FIGURE 9-19: The Windows Photo Viewer application provides basic features related to viewing and sharing photos from the Windows desktop.

You could also make Windows Photo Viewer the default photo-viewing application if you wanted. To do so, right-click an image file and choose Open with then Choose default program, and then pick Windows Photo Viewer from the list that appears. Or, use the Default programs control panel (via Start Search).

Or don't. Because there's a better option for desktop users . . .

COMPLETING THE WINDOWS 8 PHOTO EXPERIENCE WITH PHOTO GALLERY

If you're looking for a more versatile tool that can do it all when it comes to photos—photo acquisition, viewing, editing printing, e-mail sharing, burning to disc, tagging, captioning, geotagging, advanced slideshows, sharing with numerous online services including SkyDrive, Facebook, YouTube, Flickr, panoramas, and more—look no further than Photo Gallery. This amazing application, shown in Figure 9-20, is everything you need, all in one place.

▶ Photo Gallery used to be called Windows Live Gallery, and it was previously available as part of a suite of apps called Windows Live Essentials. The application carriers forward, minus the Live branding.

FIGURE 9-20: Photo Gallery

▶ If you're in a pinch, Microsoft Paint, included in Windows 8, also provides some basic photo-editing features.

Photo Gallery is the full meal deal, and because it provides a superset of the features available in a basic Windows 8 install, we recommend using it over the built-in tools.

HOW TO FIND PHOTO GALLERY

The only problem with Photo Gallery is that you may not find it on your PC or device. If that's the case, browse to `windows.com`, where you'll find this and other useful Windows applications.

BUYING, MANAGING, AND PLAYING MUSIC

Microsoft has supported music lovers with various Windows-based applications and platforms for over a decade, beginning with its first true jukebox, Windows Media Player, which debuted in Windows Millennium Edition (Me), way back in 2000. In Windows 8, well, things get a little Metro-y.

Yes, Windows 8 includes Windows Media Player, which you may remember from Windows 7. And Windows 8 Pro users (only) can optionally buy and install Windows Media Center, which was also available in Windows 7. So the range of functionality provided by these applications is still available in Windows 8, if not improved. (In fact, as far as we can see, they *are* the versions of Windows Media Player and Media Center from Windows 7, carried across unchanged.)

Over the past several years, Microsoft also cultivated a separate and somewhat incompatible media platform called Zune, which included software, device, and music and video service components. Zune was meant to be a one-stop-shop solution that could compete head-to-head with Apple's dominant iPod/iTunes, but suffice it to say that never happened despite some interesting advantages on the Microsoft side. So Zune has been discontinued as a brand.

The trouble is, just declaring Zune dead doesn't magically erase the parts of this tragic platform that are still out in the world. Millions of people still use the Zune PC software, which offers some interesting advantages over both Microsoft's own Windows Media Player and competing applications such as Apple iTunes. The Zune software and services were integrated into the first two versions of Windows Phone, as well, also in use by several million people around the world. And key parts of the Zune platform, including the music and video marketplaces, are good enough to survive the death of this brand. And, as it turns out, they're continuing forward, minus the Zune name.

So in addition to carrying forward its legacy music applications for old-timers, Windows 8 also provides a Metro-style music experience, called Xbox Music, which while based on Microsoft's Zune efforts, now accesses Xbox-branded services on the back end. Not coincidentally, it looks and works much like the Music experience on the Xbox 360, and it accesses the back end Xbox Music Store that used to be part of the Zune platform (as Zune Music Marketplace). Since this is the biggest change, music-wise, in Windows 8, we'll focus largely on that app and its supporting services here.

▶ Note that Windows Media Player and Media Center are not available in Windows RT at all.

Using the Xbox Music App

Microsoft's new Xbox Music app is a front end for your own content—which you store on your own PC or in the cloud-based SkyDrive service—as well as content that's found in the Xbox Music Store. Shown in Figure 9-21, Xbox Music provides a basic but attractive Metro-style app that uses different functional groups across its horizontally scrolling interface.

FIGURE 9-21: The Xbox Music app

Oddly, the first group, My Music, is found off to the left of the main view, while the other groups can be found by scrolling more normally to the right. Available groups, from left to right, include:

▶ **My Music:** Here, you'll find some of your own music, arranged as a grid of albums, as in Figure 9-22.

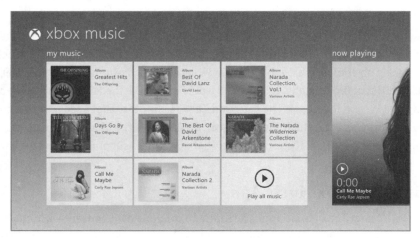

FIGURE 9-22: Your own music collection, or as much of it as will fit in this display

However, if your collection is empty—most likely, since most people don't have gigabytes of music content sitting on their PCs—this interface will more closely resemble the barren wasteland shown in Figure 9-23.

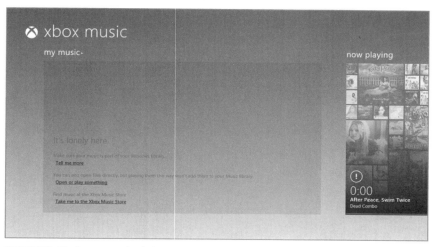

FIGURE 9-23: A more typical view of the My Music group

▶ **Now Playing:** This group, which is the default view for the app, provides a large Now Playing tile if you've been playing music, and a music promotional pane if not, along with a handful of smaller promo panes.

▶ **Spotlight:** This group works much like the identically-named group in Windows Store: It's a place for Microsoft to highlight artists, digital albums, and the like. There's even an annoying advertisement.

▶ **Most Popular:** Here, you'll find a rundown of the albums and artists that are most popular in the Xbox Music Store right now.

Put simply, there may be multiple groups in the Xbox Music app, but there are really only two basic activities occurring here. You're going to access your own music collection, or you're going to browse, potentially buy, and, if you have an Xbox Music Pass, even play music online.

Naturally, we'll look at both.

ACCESSING AND PLAYING YOUR OWN MUSIC

To access your music collection, scroll over to the My Music group and tap the My Music heading. You'll be presented with the full screen My Music view shown in Figure 9-24, which provides a nice if somewhat inefficient album-based view of your music collection by default.

FIGURE 9-24: My Music

This view is about as simple as it looks, but there are some navigational components worth noting. These include the following:

▸ **Back:** As with many multi-screen Metro-style app experiences, the Xbox Music app provides a browser-like Back button for returning to the previous screen.

▸ **View menu and Arranged by:** You can change the view between Albums, Artists, Songs, and Playlists. Each has a similar presentation, though you can also choose to sort each a bit differently. For example, in Figure 9-25, you can see the Artists view sorted alphabetically.

FIGURE 9-25: The Artists view, alphabetically

The Music app includes an app bar, but it doesn't do much beyond allowing you to open an individual music file unless you're already playing music. We'll examine that functionality in just a bit.

First, however, let's dive into the collection a bit deeper. If you're using the Albums or Artists view and select an item (that is, an album or artist, respectively), it provides a pop-up display providing more information about that item. In Figure 9-26, you can see this effect for a particular artist.

FIGURE 9-26: Selecting an artist or album provides a pop-up instead of opening a new screen.

This unique approach displays the information about the artist or album in this new area, but it will typically require more space than the area provides. So this view also enables you to scroll within the area, vertically, to see more information. In either view, for example, you can scroll down (within this pop-up) to see more songs.

This pop-up also provides prominent Play all, Add to now playing, Explore artist, and Play on Xbox 360 buttons. But you may be surprised to discover that tapping an individual song here won't trigger immediate playback. Instead, this expands the view in-line yet again, providing separate Play and Add to now playing buttons, just for that song, as shown in Figure 9-27.

Here's a rundown of the actions you can trigger from these pop-ups:

▶ **Play:** This button plays the current selection, which can be a song, an album, or an artist, and triggers the app bar-based Now Playing experience shown in Figure 9-28. Here you'll find useful on-screen playback controls and other buttons.

▶ If you click Play, the selected song is added to—and does not replace—any other songs that may already be in the Now Playing playlist.

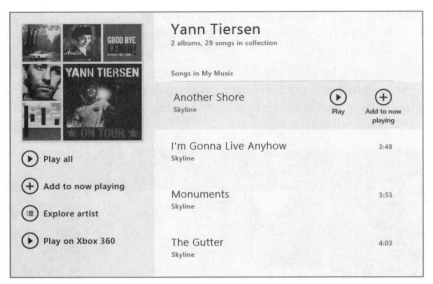

FIGURE 9-27: Selecting a song will expand a new area with unique buttons for just that song.

FIGURE 9-28: The app bar-based Now Playing experience

To see the full-screen Now Playing experience, click or tap the album art view in the app bar. When you do, the screen will change to resemble Figure 9-29. Here, you can see an animated Now Playing area on the left with more information, like artist biography and discography, which can be viewed by scrolling to the right.

FIGURE 9-29: The full-screen Now Playing experience with additional information showing

Or, you can simply click the little Full Screen widget, in the bottom right of that Now Playing area, to see only the Now Playing view full screen. This can be seen in Figure 9-30. This screen should be familiar to anyone who's played music via the Zune PC software or Xbox 360.

FIGURE 9-30: The full-screen Now Playing experience showing only the Now Playing area

Note that most of the playback controls you see on this screen will disappear if you stop interacting with the PC. Wiggle the mouse, tap the screen or a keyboard key, however, and they'll return.

Available controls on this screen include:

▷ **Back:** Tap here to return to the previous view.

▷ **Rewind:** Rewind the currently playing track.

▷ **Play/Pause:** Play or pause the currently playing track.

▷ **Forward:** Fast forward the currently playing track.

▷ **Now playing:** Display the Now Playing list.

▷ **Full-screen toggle:** Toggle between the truly full-screen view and the previous full-screen view, which includes additional biographical and discography information about the currently playing artist.

▶ **Add to Now Playing:** You can add songs to the Now Playing list at any time by expanding an album, artist, or song, and then clicking the Add to Now Playing button.

▶ **Explore Artist:** This button displays the full-screen artist details screen described earlier and provides access to the artist's biography and discography.

▶ **Play on Xbox 360:** This button launches the Xbox Companion app, which will connect you to an Xbox 360 console in your home (it needs to be powered on first) and play the selection there, instead of on the PC or device. Two things happen when this connection is made. On the Xbox 360, a familiar (and Music app-like) Now Playing screen appears for playback and, in fact, gives you additional playlist editing features you don't even get in the Music app, such as the ability to clear the queue and add and remove songs. And on your PC or device, the Xbox Companion app provides a remote-like experience called Xbox Controls that provides playback buttons, as shown in Figure 9-31.

▶ Microsoft will be replacing the Xbox Companion app with a similar but more powerful app called Xbox SmartGlass, which should be available by the end of 2012. You may want to look for this app, too.

▶ If you don't already have the Xbox Companion (or SmartGlass) app installed, you'll be prompted to get it from Windows Store.

There's one more aspect of music playback that needs to be addressed. While Play to Xbox 360 is useful and interesting, it's not the only solution that Windows 8 provides for playing music from your PC (or device) to another device in your home. That is, in addition to supporting Play to Xbox 360, Windows 8 (and thus the Metro-style Xbox Music app) also supports the Digital Living Network Alliance (DLNA) "Play To" technology, which works with a wide range of devices, including, go figure, the Xbox 360.

> **NOTE** This Play on Xbox 360 functionality is a bit more sophisticated than the Play To feature that's been in Windows for years. To work, however, Play on Xbox 360 requires that the content you're playing be found in the Xbox Music (or Video) Store, whereas Play To simply streams music from the PC or device to the console.

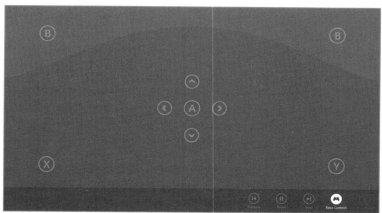

FIGURE 9-31: The Xbox Companion app lets you push music playback to your Xbox 360 and use your Windows device like a giant remote.

▶ The playback controls persist as you navigate through the music Marketplace, unlike with some online stores.

So why support both Play on Xbox 360 and Play To? Play on Xbox 360 is, of course, Xbox-specific, and it requires that the content you're playing is found in Microsoft's Xbox-based online stores. That's because while using Play on Xbox 360, Xbox Music isn't streaming the content, it's handing it off and letting the console play it instead. Play To, meanwhile, is more basic in that you're just streaming content from the PC (or device) to a compatible set-top box. So if you were to shut down the PC, the music playback would stop. On other hand, Play To lets you play music through the console that isn't found in the Xbox Music Store.

To utilize Play To, start music playback and then bring up Xbox Music's app bar. Click the Play To button on the right of the app bar, and then choose the appropriate device from the Play To pane that appears, as in Figure 9-32.

FIGURE 9-32: Using Play To

From here, playback control works as it does when you play music locally on the PC: You simply use the Xbox Music's playback controls (in the app bar) to control playback.

USING THE XBOX MUSIC STORE

Microsoft isn't shy about its attempts to sell you music via its Xbox Music Store (formerly Zune Music Marketplace), which can be accessed from the Spotlight and Most Popular groups on the Xbox Music home screen as well as through various links like the Artist information interface in your own collection.

Clicking the title of the Spotlight or Most Popular group will provide a view similar to that of My Music. This is a rather paltry front end to what Microsoft claims is an online storefront of approximately 30 million tracks either way, but as you can see in Figure 9-33 it is, at least, simple.

FIGURE 9-33: Most Popular view of the Xbox Music Store

Since this interface is so similar to that of My Music and provides the same ways to filter and view information, drill down into various artists, albums, and genres, there's no need to cover basic navigational information here. Instead, let's look at some of the unique things you can do in the Xbox Music Store.

BUYING SONGS FROM XBOX MUSIC

To purchase an album or song, click the Buy Album (or Buy Song) button you'll find in the pop-up for that item. Xbox Music will display a full-screen notification interface like that in Figure 9-34, and step you through the process of purchasing the music.

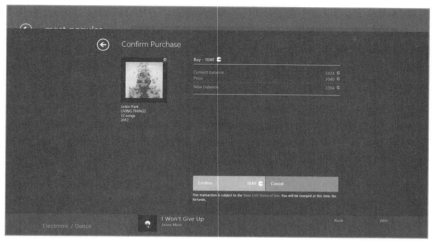

FIGURE 9-34: Buying a song from the Xbox Music Store

One important note about the music purchasing experience: You must use Microsoft Points. Microsoft doesn't use your local currency for purchases as do other online music stores like Amazon MP3 and Apple iTunes. Instead, Microsoft uses a system called Microsoft Points, which works across its other online stores, including the Xbox Video Store and Xbox Game Store.

The Microsoft Points system exists for one reason and one reason only: to save Microsoft money—since you must buy points in batches, sparing the company per-transaction credit card fees—but its biggest effect is to make online purchases needlessly confusing for consumers.

For your edification, 80 Microsoft Points is worth $1.00 US, so you can see how the math gets fairly convoluted. But Microsoft sells points, online and via gift card-like cards in retail stores, in bundles of 400 ($5), 800 ($10), 1600 ($20), 4000 ($50), and 6000 ($75) points. So if you're interested in giving Microsoft an interest-free loan, you can stock up.

PLAYING MUSIC WITH XBOX MUSIC PASS

Microsoft has an interesting music subscription service called Xbox Music Pass—formerly Zune Music Pass—which provides you with almost unlimited access to its online music collection for a monthly fee. (In the United States, this fee is $10 per month, but if you sign up for a year upfront, you will receive 12 months for the price of 10, or about $8.33 a month.) Depending on how you feel about owning music and the quality of Microsoft's Xbox Music Store, this is either a tremendous bargain or something to avoid all together.

Maybe we're just getting old, or perhaps we're simply tired of micromanaging a locally saved music collection, but we've come to really appreciate and enjoy Xbox Music Pass. But instead of trying to sell you on this service, we'll simply explain what you can do with (almost) unfettered access to the Xbox Music Store music collection.

First, you can use the Play album, Play song, Play top songs, and other similar buttons you'll see as you navigate around the Xbox Music Store to stream virtually any music in its entirety. If you were not an Xbox Music Pass subscriber, you'd only get a 30-second preview. (This streaming functionality is also available on Windows Phone handsets, Xbox 360 consoles, and via the web.)

Second, you can arbitrarily download any of this music to your PC and, while your subscription is in place, play it (online or off) on your Windows-based PCs and devices (and Windows Phone handsets). It's like having 30 million songs in your own music collection—you know, as long as you're a paying customer. You'll see a handy Add to my music link, like that in Figure 9-35, letting you copy Store music to your own PC.

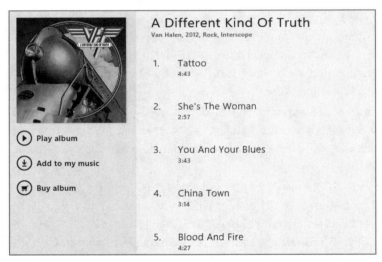

FIGURE 9-35: Using Add to my music to copy music from the Store to your PC

Xbox Music Pass has other advantages, but the point here is that with this service, the Xbox Music Store is suddenly open to you in ways that it isn't otherwise. You can find out more about the service at www.xbox.com/music.

SEARCHING THE STORE FOR MUSIC

Of course, even finding music to buy can be difficult. And while the navigational facilities in the Xbox Music Store are, at best, basic, your best bet is to search for the music you want. And in this one case, Xbox Music Store actually works really well (assuming you know what you want, of course), thanks to its integration with the system-wide Windows 8 search functionality.

Search works as it does throughout Windows 8, and you can trigger a search of the store from within Xbox Music or at any time from elsewhere in the OS. To do so, display the Search charm (Winkey + Q) and, if you're not already using Xbox Music, be sure to select Music from the apps list in the search pane.

Then start typing in a search term, perhaps an artist, album, or song name, and the Search experience will often supply suggestions as you type. You can see an example of this in Figure 9-36, and search results appear right in the Xbox Music app, giving you a way to dig deeper into your favorite music.

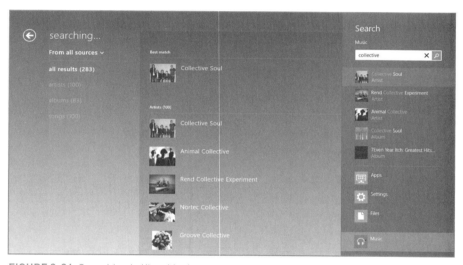

FIGURE 9-36: Searching in Xbox Music

WHAT ABOUT PODCASTS?

While the Music + Videos app on Windows Phone fully supports podcasts, the Xbox Music app in Windows 8/RT doesn't, so there's no way to find, subscribe to, or listen to/view podcasts. Instead, you'll need to try a third-party app. One that's emerged as an early favorite is SlapDash Podcasts, which you can find in Windows Store.

Doing More with Music

While the Music app provides a handy, consumption-only interface for music, those who have more advanced needs will need to turn to some classic Windows applications that have been kicking around for several years.

All versions of Windows 8 include Windows Media Player, which is shown in Figure 9-37. This application has historically been used as a media management system, but it hasn't really changed since Windows 7, for better or worse.

▶ Note, however, that neither of these options are available to Windows RT users: Only Windows 8 provides any support for these legacy desktop-based music applications.

FIGURE 9-37: Windows Media Player

Windows Media Center, meanwhile, started life as a consumption-only application, like today's Metro-style apps, though it picked up more sophisticated capabilities over time. It features large, touch-friendly controls, works well in full-screen mode, and has a particularly nice Now Playing interface, which is shown in Figure 9-38.

Unfortunately, finding Media Center is a bit problematic.

First, Media Center is not available on Windows RT or the base version of Windows 8, which is called Windows 8 Core. Instead, you must have Windows 8 Pro before you can get Media Center.

Second, even if you have Windows 8 Pro, Media Center isn't free: You can buy it for a small fee from Microsoft using the new Add Features to Windows interface. (You can easily find this through Start Search.) Why bother? If you have to ask, you don't want Media Center. And frankly, the world has moved on anyway.

FIGURE 9-38: The full-screen Media Center music playback experience

BUYING, MANAGING, AND PLAYING MOVIES AND TV SHOWS

The Windows 8 video experience revolves around a new Metro-style app, called Xbox Video, and some traditional Windows applications—Windows Media Player and Windows Media Center for playback and Movie Maker for video editing and sharing—which carry over from Windows 7.

So it shouldn't be surprising that the video experience is similar to that of music: The Metro-style Xbox Video app works well enough for video playback on tablets, other portable devices, and PCs, and for browsing Microsoft's new Xbox Video Store online, but doesn't offer any advanced features. If you want to do more with videos, like edit your own home movies and share them via online services like Facebook or YouTube, you'll need to stick with the more productive desktop environment and those more mature Windows applications.

> ► The Xbox Video app is a bit more limited than that, actually. It can't play DVD- or Blu-ray-based movies either.

> **NOTE** You'll also need to stick with Windows 8, and not Windows RT. Note that Windows RT does not include or support Windows Media Player, Media Center, or Movie Maker.

Of course, what we're most concerned with here is the new stuff. And that means the Xbox Video app.

Using the Xbox Video App

If you've used the Xbox Music app described earlier in this chapter or are familiar with the video playback capabilities of the Xbox 360 video game console, the Xbox Video app will be immediately familiar. As you can see in Figure 9-39, this app is a typical, Metro-style full-screen experience that extends horizontally and looks and works much like the Xbox Music app.

FIGURE 9-39: The new Xbox Video app

And like the Xbox Music app, the Xbox Video app pushes Microsoft's online store experiences over your own local video collection, offering Spotlight, Movies Store, and Television Store groups up front, somewhat obscuring your own media.

Frankly, with the prevalence and usefulness of online video stores like Microsoft's, and the fact that most people simply don't have massive collections of TV shows and movies as they do music, this isn't as bothersome as it may be with the Xbox Music app.

NAVIGATING YOUR OWN VIDEOS

▶ You can find Handbrake at handbrake.fr.

If you do have a PC-based video collection for some reason—perhaps you've ripped DVDs to the PC's hard drive using Handbrake or similar tools—or you've rented or purchased TV shows or movies from Microsoft—which we describe a bit later—this content will be found by navigating left to the My Videos group on the Xbox Video home screen. This group, shown in Figure 9-40, will show a selection of videos found in your Videos library.

You can click the My Videos title to view your own video collection in a full-screen view like that in Figure 9-41. Here, your collection is divided into All, Movies, TV, and Other categories, and you can sort the view in various ways.

FIGURE 9-40: The My Videos group is a front end to your own collection.

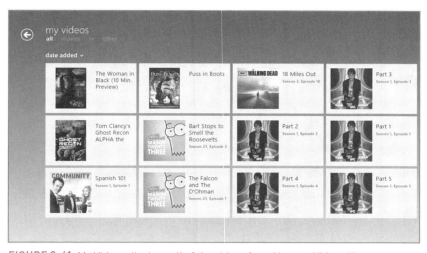

FIGURE 9-41: My Videos displays all of the videos found in your Videos library.

As you dive into your collection, by selecting a category and then an actual video, the Xbox Video app will display a pop-up for selected video, as shown in Figure 9-42, that offers a variety of options which includes some combination of the choices Play, Play on Xbox 360, Explore movie/series, Play trailer, and more.

FIXING THE VIDEO CATEGORIES

The Xbox Video app, like the Zune PC software on which it is based, often misfiles videos, assigning many of them to the nebulous Other category. The only way to fix this that we've found is to install the legacy Zune PC software (`www.zune.net`) and use that application's Edit capability to change the video type of each file to the appropriate value (usually TV Series or Movies). Unfortunately, the Xbox Video app doesn't provide any editing capabilities of its own.

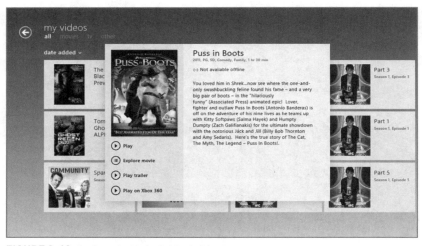

FIGURE 9-42: Options for an individual video

These options work as they do in the Music app, of course, and will vary from video to video. For example, some videos will not have the Play on Xbox 360 button available because of compatibility issues.

PLAYING A VIDEO

Playing a video works as expected. When you click or tap the Play button, the full-screen playback experience appears, and will look something like Figure 9-43.

These simple controls should all be pretty familiar. The timeline scrubber is a big, touch-friendly control that takes the guesswork out of finding the right place in a video, even on a tablet. And Play/Pause works exactly as expected.

▶ Anyone who's fiddled with the iPad video playback controls will appreciate this.

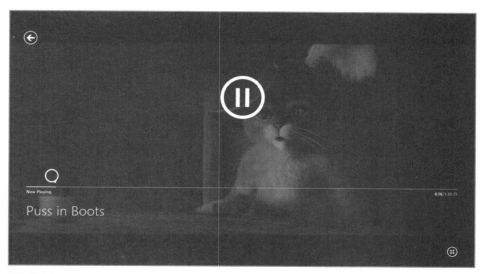

FIGURE 9-43: The Xbox Video playback experience

In addition to the onscreen controls, you can display the app bar during playback to access more playback controls and other options. This app bar is shown in Figure 9-44.

FIGURE 9-44: The Xbox Video app bar-based controls

Available buttons can include:

▶ **Download:** This button will appear only on content you've purchased from Xbox Video Store. You're free to stream this content at any time for the most part (there are exceptions related to "video window" issues, in some cases) and if you'd like to play this content offline, this button will make that option available.

▶ **Delete:** This will delete the currently selected video (if in your collection).

▶ **Repeat:** When toggled, the current video will play on an endless loop.

▶ **Previous:** This button rewinds the current video by 15 seconds.

▶ **Play/Pause:** Toggles video playback.

▶ **Next:** This button fast forwards the current video by 15 seconds.

▶ We describe
Play on Xbox 360
and the related Play
To experience back
in the Music section.

▶ **Play on Xbox 360:** In this scenario, you can hand off the playback of Store-based content from your PC to your Xbox 360, over the same home network only. That is, the content you play *to* the Xbox doesn't have to come *from* Windows 8. Instead, it can be located online, in the Xbox Video Store.

Accessing Store Content

Most people who use the Xbox Video app aren't going to have large video collections they've ripped from optical media. Instead, and in keeping with the modern design of the Metro environment in which it runs, Xbox Video operates as a front end for Microsoft's Store back end, in this case with the TV and Movie Stores in particular.

You're probably familiar with how such stores work thanks to previous experience with Apple iTunes and other e-commerce destinations. But Microsoft's online efforts, perhaps not surprisingly, offer some advantages.

First, the basics. Microsoft offers both TV shows and movies for purchase, and movies for rent. Some of this content is available in a choice of standard definition (SD) or high-definition (HD) formats, where the latter is more expensive but looks better on higher resolution screens. Videos rented or purchased from Microsoft work with the Xbox Video app, Windows Media Player, and Media Center in Windows 8/RT, with the Xbox 360, and on Windows Phone, too. And, as with music, Microsoft unfortunately uses Microsoft Points for its video sales, so you'll be doing some math.

Intriguingly, you're given some choices when you buy or rent videos. That is, you can stream the video directly to the current PC or device, bypassing the need to download it before watching it. But if you do want to watch the video later offline (say, on a plane), you can choose to download if you prefer. But you can also simply just make the purchase and then not watch the rented or purchased video at that time. Later, you can access the video content from a Windows 8/RT PC or device, or the Xbox 360, or Windows Phone, and begin watching as you please.

This choice is pretty liberating, and you may find yourself queuing up a few movie rentals for the weekend on your Windows 8 tablet but then watch them at home via your Xbox 360 and HDTV. Or you could stream part of a purchased movie on the 360 and then finish watching it in downloaded form on your Windows 8 tablet on the way to work the next morning (assuming you commute by bus or train, of course).

▶ This content
is also compatible
with Windows
Phone.

And in case it's not obvious, content you purchase is yours forever, for the most part. This content is associated with your Microsoft account, and anytime you access the Store—from Windows 8 or the Xbox 360—you can browse through your previous purchases, or simply go to an item directly in the marketplace and start streaming it immediately: Instead of a Play/Rent button, you'll just see a Play button.

The Movies and Television Stores work as expected, offering different navigational schemes—Featured, New releases, Top selling, Genres, and Studios for movies and Featured, Last night's shows, Free TV, Top selling, Genres, and Networks for television—and, in some views, different filtering and sorting capabilities.

The Movies and Television Stores work a bit differently than does the Music Store in Xbox Music, providing you with a true front end to the whole store experience. But content selection works as it does in Xbox Music: When you select a movie, for example and as shown in Figure 9-45, you'll see buttons related to buying and renting the film, movie information, Play on Xbox 360 (when available), and to playing the trailer.

FIGURE 9-45: Options associated with movies in the marketplace

Because TV shows feature multiple episodes across multiple seasons, the Store provides a slightly different layout. When you select a TV show in the Television Store, you'll only see a few choices, including View seasons and Explore series. When you select the former, a new full-screen view appears, offering information about the show plus links to each of its seasons, as shown in Figure 9-46.

When you select a season, a pop-up appears, as is common in the Xbox Music and Video apps, providing links for each episode in the season. Select an episode and you'll see buttons related to buying the episode and, depending on the content, playing it on the Xbox 360. This can be seen in Figure 9-47.

The renting and purchasing experiences differ a bit, and for reasons that are best left to the imagination, not all video content is available in both HD and SD formats, so you may not have that choice. When you do, you'll see a screen like that in Figure 9-48, letting you choose between both quality sizes and either streaming or download.

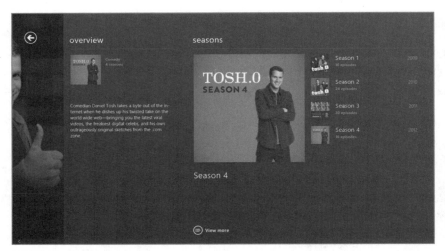

FIGURE 9-46: A set of tiles related to a TV show's different seasons

FIGURE 9-47: TV show episode options

When buying such a movie, your choices are between HD download and stream, and SD download and stream.

When you purchase a TV show, you will also see different choices. There are no TV show rentals, but you can choose to purchase shows in SD or HD (when available), and you always get both download and stream availability. You can also choose to buy a Season Pass, which provides all of the episodes in the given season in a batch, including those seasons that are still in progress. You will see the same HD and SD choices as you do with movies, assuming those options are available for the title you selected.

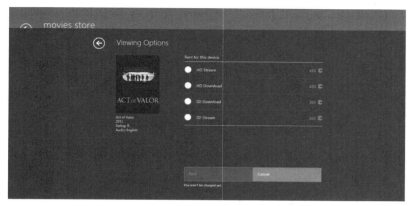

FIGURE 9-48: You will often see choices between HD and SD, and between downloading and streaming.

Doing More with Videos

As we discussed in the Music section, the old-school Windows Media Player application is available to all users of Windows 8, and this solution provides decent, desktop-based video playback. You can also purchase and download the Windows Media Center solution if you're running Windows 8 Pro only. Again, neither application is available to users of Windows RT.

Frankly, we think you can do better. If you want to play videos on the Windows desktop, check out VLC Media Player from videolan.org. It provides all of the video playback features from both Windows Media Player and Media Center but offers some significant advantages over either. First, unlike Media Center, VLC is free. And it also supports all kinds of subtitles and captioning, something that's decidedly lacking in Microsoft's video playback applications.

Movie Maker is another useful video tool that's been kicking around for over a decade in one form or another. The current version is tuned, somewhat, to editing home videos and then sharing them online via YouTube, Facebook, and other services. Movie Maker is shown in Figure 9-49.

HOW TO FIND WINDOWS MOVIE MAKER

As with Photo Gallery, Movie Maker may not be preinstalled on your Windows 8-based PC or device. And the solution is the same: Browse to windows.com and download it.

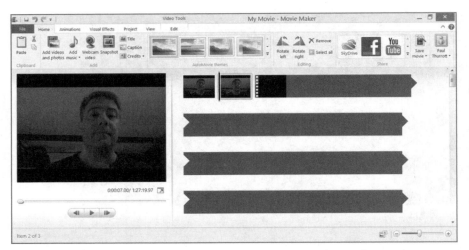

FIGURE 9-49: Movie Maker helps you edit home videos and post them online.

SUMMARY

While the new Metro-style digital media experiences in Windows 8 are almost purely consumption-based, they nicely complement the already rich and mature digital media applications that Microsoft has included in Windows for years. Photos is a simple and attractive, and touch friendly, way to enjoy your photos, no matter where they're stored. Xbox Music provides a device-like interface for playing music online or off. And Xbox Video integrates nicely with Microsoft's online marketplace, providing a handy way to access TV shows and movies, at home or on the go. It even lets you play videos through your Xbox 360, using the handy Xbox Companion app.

Together, these apps provide a decent set of basic consumption capabilities. But over time, Windows 8 will be improved both with updates to these apps and by new Metro-style apps that provide additional digital media functionality. As with everything else in this pioneering new OS, what you get in the box, so to speak, is just the beginning.

CHAPTER 10

Xbox Games with Windows 8

IN THIS CHAPTER

▶ Understanding Windows 8's new game-related features

▶ Finding and acquiring Metro-style games for Windows 8

▶ Learning about the features of Xbox LIVE

▶ Understanding how Microsoft has integrated Xbox LIVE with Windows 8

▶ Using the Xbox Games app to discover Xbox 360 and Windows 8 games

▶ Using the Xbox Companion app to find content and play it on the Xbox 360 video game console

If the rise of touch-based devices like the iPad and smartphones has taught us anything, it's that people love to play casual games. And while some hard-core gamers will cling to their high-end gaming devices—say, the Xbox 360 video game console or Windows-based PCs—this audience is a minority. Most people enjoy games but don't have the time or energy to devote to all-night death-match contests in virtual worlds. And the changes Microsoft has made to Windows 8's built-in games functionality reflects that fact.

Windows has always included at least a handful of casual games, most notably the now-classic Minefield and Solitaire. But with the switch to immersive, full-screen, Metro-style experiences in Windows 8, Microsoft is likewise moving its game efforts into this environment. So the new game experiences in this release are tailored to Metro and are largely designed around the multi-touch interactions that will be common on tablets and other touch-screen devices.

This chapter examines the game-related functionality that is new to Windows 8 and covers what you need to do to get up and running with this new generation of touch-based gaming experiences. We don't focus on the legacy features that carry forward from previous versions.

IT'S GOING TO CHANGE

Thanks to the dynamic nature of its new apps platform, the Metro-style apps that Microsoft includes with Windows 8/RT will change over time, so it's highly likely that the apps described in this chapter will appear somewhat differently over time and will include additional features. This is normal, and as a general statement, it's probably fair to say that the Metro-style Xbox apps you use will provide a superset of the functionality we describe in this chapter.

GAMES AND THE METRO ENVIRONMENT

▶ Windows 8 can, of course, run traditional Windows games that run under the desktop and provide full-screen experiences as well. The capabilities listed here are in addition to legacy features.

In Windows 7, Microsoft bundled several fun games that ran within the Windows desktop environment, as one might expect, as well as a container for games, if you will, called Games Explorer. This time around, Windows 8 instead integrates with Microsoft's popular Xbox LIVE games and entertainment services. It includes a new app called Xbox Games, a central location for discovering, downloading, and buying new Xbox LIVE games for both Windows 8 and the Xbox 360. And of course, you can find and download more casual Metro-style games through the Games area of Windows Store.

The differences between Xbox LIVE games and other games can be important if you're a bit more serious about gaming than the casual gamer. But we'll discuss the vagaries of the Xbox LIVE service—and what it means to be an Xbox LIVE game title— later in the chapter. For now, let's examine how Metro-style games differ from their predecessors in earlier versions of Windows.

▶ Note, however, that Windows RT cannot run traditional Windows games that run under the desktop.

▶ **Full-screen, immersive experiences:** Like all Metro-style apps, Metro-based games are full-screen, immersive experiences. They provide a so-called chrome-free experience with no visible OS-based user interface elements such as toolbars, window handles, and so on, and feature smooth, flicker-free performance with adaptive layout capabilities that ensure that these games look great on any PC or device, regardless of the screen size or resolution.

Consider the game shown in Figure 10-1. Here, you can see a game in which the entire screen is literally used for one purpose only: for the game itself. No other UI intrudes on this experience.

FIGURE 10-1: Windows 8 Metro-style games are full-screen, immersive experiences.

▶ **Multi-touch and sensor compatible:** As with games on smartphones and other tablet-based systems like the iPad, Windows 8 Metro-style games integrate with underlying system capabilities such as multi-touch and the gyroscope and other sensors and devices. This opens up a whole new realm of possibilities, such as driving games in which you physically move a tablet in space to steer, accelerate, and brake, or interactive games in which the device's cameras are used to interact with the outside world.

On the flip side, these games are also generally designed to be used with other input devices. So if you're using a mouse- and keyboard-based PC instead of a tablet, you can still play.

▶ **Integrated with Metro experiences:** Like any other Metro-style apps, Metro-style games fully integrate with the wider Metro experiences. This means that edge and corner UIs such as the Charms bar, Back, Switcher, and Start are all available during gameplay. For example, in Figure 10-2, you can see the Charms bar being displayed over a game.

Furthermore, you can receive notifications during gameplay. This can be helpful if you're whittling away a few minutes before a meeting or other event, and you wish to be alerted when it's time to get back to work. A typical notification, again being displayed over a game, can be seen in Figure 10-3.

FIGURE 10-2: Metro experiences such as the Charms bar are still available while playing a game.

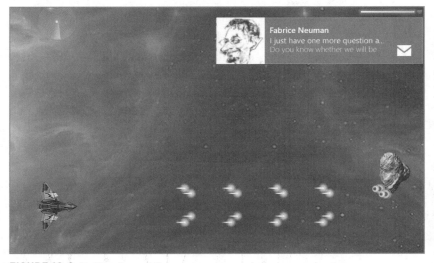

FIGURE 10-3: Notifications still pop up onscreen during gameplay, too.

Metro-style games also use the standard Metro-style Settings interface, which is available via the Winkey + I keyboards shortcut or through Settings in the Charms bar. This consistency means that you will always know where to go to access game options, permissions and ratings capabilities, as shown in Figure 10-4. That said, many games will opt to use their own interface for in-game options.

FIGURE 10-4: From Settings, you can access game permissions and ratings capabilities.

Finally, Metro-style games can utilize any common Metro-style user interfaces that are available to other apps, including edge-triggered app bars, file pickers, and the like. (That said, many games will choose to use more customized experiences, but that's up to the developer.)

▶ **Acquiring and updating happens through the Windows Store:** Like other Metro-style apps, Metro-style games can only be acquired from Windows Store, and that includes free games, trial games, full games, and Xbox LIVE games. Ditto for software updates: When a game needs to be updated, you'll see an alert badge on the Windows Store live tile on the Start screen and a notice about pending updates inside the Store app. No Metro-style games can be offered elsewhere, for security and reliability reasons.

▶ **Rights for up to five PCs and/or devices:** One of the many upsides to Microsoft's Windows Store requirements for Metro-style games is that you have the right to install a purchased game on as many as five Windows 8 PCs and/or devices, each of which needs to be associated with your Microsoft account. This is in sharp contrast to retail video games, which are almost always licensed for use on just one PC.

▶ **Compatible with both Intel-compatible PCs and ARM-based devices:** Most Metro-style games are designed to be compatible with both Intel-compatible PCs as well as ARM-based Windows RT devices. Not only that, but they are also engineered to perform similarly on both types of machines, regardless of the underlying architectural differences.

▶ You can find and acquire Xbox Games through the Xbox Games app, too, but it is utilizing Windows Store on the back end.

That said, you'll want to be careful about choosing games that work on both, and as you can see in Figure 10-5, the Windows Store landing page for each game will describe which platforms are supported.

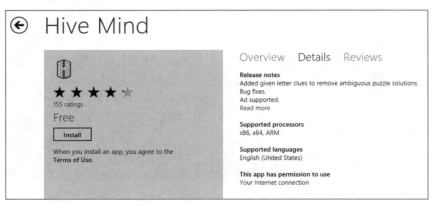

FIGURE 10-5: You can discover which platforms a game is compatible with in the Windows Store.

▶ **In-app purchases:** Metro-style games can provide in-app purchases, which can include new content or functionality, such as unlocking the next level of a game, a new weapon, or other trinket. In-app purchases have proven to be very popular on other casual game platforms like smartphones and, no doubt, will prove to be so in Windows 8 as well.

▶ **Not just for simple games:** While there is no shortage of simple, casual games like Checkers and Hangman, Windows 8 Metro-style games can be as photo realistic and exciting as anything on the Xbox 360 or other dedicated game platforms. The system supports advanced DirectX capabilities for both 2-D and 3-D experiences that take advantage of every ounce of processing muscle your PC can provide. Will there be a future version of *Call of Duty* or *Halo* in a Metro-style version? There's no (technical) reason why not.

▶ **Multiplayer online games:** You're not (necessarily) alone when you game on Windows 8. Metro-style games can support full multiplayer capabilities as well, letting you compete with others online in real time.

▶ **Optional integration with Xbox LIVE:** As noted earlier and described later in the chapter, developers can choose to release their games as is or integrate them into the Xbox LIVE service. This requires additional work on their part, but Xbox LIVE also provides additional capabilities as you'll soon discover. Xbox LIVE games are also available separately through the Xbox Games app.

FINDING AND ACQUIRING GAMES FOR WINDOWS 8

In Chapter 6, we discuss Windows Store, Microsoft's new online marketplace for Metro-style apps. And as previously discussed, this is the place where you can discover, download, and purchase new Metro-style games as well. Given the popularity of games, especially casual games, it's no surprise that this type of app is prominently offered in the Windows Store.

As you can see in Figure 10-6, the Games group is the first actual category of apps displayed in the main screen of the Windows Store.

FIGURE 10-6: The Games group figures prominently in the Windows Store.

Finding games in Windows Store is straightforward, and this process is documented elsewhere in the book. As a quick refresher, Windows Store is the only distribution point for (Metro-style) games, which can be offered in free, paid, and trial versions, with or without in-app purchasing and advertisements.

The Games group in the Windows Store supports more subcategories than any other category: Action, Adventure, Arcade, Card, Casino, Family, Kids, Music, Puzzle, Racing, Role Playing Shooter, Simulation, Sports, and Strategy. As you can see in Figure 10-7, filtering the view to show just a single subcategory really cleans up the display.

The landing page for an individual game features the same views provided for other apps including Overview, Details, and Reviews pages, which are generally stocked with information. Figure 10-8 shows a typical game landing page.

▶ Again, you can find Xbox LIVE games in the Xbox Games app.

FIGURE 10-7: Filtering the Games category by subcategory

FIGURE 10-8: A game landing page in Windows Store

As with installation for other apps, game installation is nearly instantaneous and happens in the background; though if you're quick enough, you can view the Installing apps page to view the install progress. Windows 8 will display a toast notification when the game is installed, and if you view the end (right side) of the Start screen, you'll see that a single tile for the new game has been added, as shown in Figure 10-9.

FIGURE 10-9: A tile for a newly installed game is added to the end of the Start screen.

FINDING GAMES WITH SEARCH

As with other Metro-style apps, Windows Store fully supports the Windows 8 Search contract, which means that you can search for individual game titles from within the store, or from anywhere in Windows 8. To do so, type Winkey + Q to display Search, or open the Charms bar and then select Search. If you are outside of Windows Store at the time, be sure to select Store from the list of apps in the Search pane when searching.

If the Windows Store has a problem, it's that it gets overloaded pretty quickly. Curiously, it's lacking a subcategory called Xbox LIVE, which would show both full-featured Xbox LIVE game titles as well as the smaller, indie-type Xbox LIVE Arcade games that many users are looking for. Fortunately, Windows 8 provides another sneaky way to peek into Windows Store and find only those types of games. We'll discuss that in the next section after a brief explanation of the Xbox LIVE service and why it's so important.

FINDING AND ACQUIRING DESKTOP GAMES

▶ Desktop games (and applications) cannot run on Windows RT. They are designed only for Windows 8 (and perhaps older versions of Windows, too).

Oddly enough, Microsoft does allow developers to advertise legacy desktop games and applications in Windows Store alongside Metro-style games and apps. These games do not necessarily offer any of the formal capabilities provided through true Metro-style games, and, because of this, Microsoft doesn't let you download those games from the Store. Instead, you'll be directed to visit the developer's web site.

Let's quickly see how this works.

When browsing through Windows Store, you'll come across some game and app tiles that include the notation "desktop app," as seen in Figure 10-10. This indicates that the game (or application) is for the desktop, and not the Metro environment, so you will not see a rating or price, as with Metro-style apps and games.

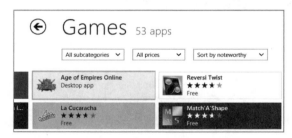

FIGURE 10-10: Desktop games (and applications) will include a "desktop app" note on their tiles in Windows Store.

View the game's landing page, as in the example in Figure 10-11, and you'll see that desktop games and applications cannot be downloaded from Windows Store. Instead, you can click the link, Get app from developer, to visit a website and proceed from there.

FIGURE 10-11: The landing page for a desktop game

XBOX LIVE AND WINDOWS 8

Xbox LIVE began in 2002 as a feature of the original Xbox console. It was an offshoot of the multiplayer features in the first *Halo* game, and essentially formalized those features across an online network that other games could then use. But the Xbox LIVE service as we now know it appeared in 2005 alongside the Xbox 360, Microsoft's second video game console. At that time, Microsoft greatly enhanced Xbox LIVE, providing the core capabilities and experiences that Xbox 360 gamers—and Windows Phone and now Windows 8 games gamers—still enjoy today.

> **NOTE** Video game historians will note that the first video game console Microsoft contributed to was the Sega Dreamcast. But when the Windows CE-based environment in that console proved unpopular with game developers, Microsoft took things into its own hands and created the Xbox.

Microsoft also offers two types of Xbox LIVE accounts: a free account that's simply called Xbox LIVE and a paid account called Xbox LIVE Gold. Xbox LIVE Gold members pay about $50 a year and are rewarded with some unique features. Looking just at the Xbox 360 console, gamers who opt for the Gold subscription get online multiplayer gaming, party and party chat functionality, and video chat capabilities. But they also get access to many multimedia services, including Netflix, Hulu Plus, HBO GO, Sky Player (UK only), Last.fm Internet music streaming, Xbox Music and Video services, and a lot more.

▶ *Many of these third-party services, of course, require a separate subscription as well.*

> **CROSSREF** Microsoft's Xbox entertainment services, Xbox Music and Xbox Video, used to utilize the Zune brand. Windows 8 includes apps for these services, too, which we discuss in Chapter 9.

Signing up for Xbox LIVE is one of many ways in which you can create a Microsoft account. (Other popular methods include signing up for Hotmail or the Xbox Music Pass subscription.) Xbox LIVE, like other Microsoft services and, now, Windows 8, uses the same underlying identification service. So at the time of sign-up, you can use your own e-mail account, no matter where it's from, and Xbox LIVE will convert that e-mail address into a Microsoft account. Or, if you already have a Microsoft account through Hotmail, MSN, or wherever, you can simply use your existing account. For purposes of this discussion, we'll assume that you've created a Microsoft account, since you'll be using this same account for gaming purposes on Windows 8, just as you do on the Xbox 360 (and Windows Phone).

▶ *Microsoft account used to be called Windows Live ID.*

Next, let's examine what your Xbox LIVE account provides.

Xbox LIVE Accounts

► Microsoft's Xbox LIVE service is always changing, so it's possible and even likely that there will be additional features offered in addition to what's outlined here.

Your Xbox LIVE account is your online persona on that online service, the thing that represents you in whatever virtual worlds you decide to use. Each Xbox LIVE account consists of the following general features:

▶ **Gamertag:** This is your identity, or name, on Xbox LIVE, and it will be the same name you previously established for your Microsoft account. If you're not happy with this name, you can change it at any time, but Microsoft charges $10 each time in order to prevent kids from constantly changing their names while playing games. Yes, really.

▶ **Gamer Zone:** This item describes what type of gamer you are and can be set to Recreation, Pro, Family, or Underground.

▶ **Gamer Picture:** This is a small, usually simple picture that represents you online. Subscribers to the free Xbox LIVE service have one Gamer Picture, which is shown to all users, while Xbox LIVE Gold gamers can have two: one for friends and one for the general populace. (See? That $50 annual fee *does* make sense.) If you have a video camera add-on for the Xbox 360 console, you can use that to take a still photo of yourself as a gamer picture, but only for friends to see.

▶ **Motto:** This is a 21-character textual representation of who you are and what you stand for. I've used such bon mots as *The end is listless* and *Pwned*.

▶ **Avatar:** Based largely on the Nintendo Wii's similar Mii characters, an avatar can be designed to look (somewhat) like you, albeit a slightly rotund and cartoonish you. A typical avatar is shown in Figure 10-12.

FIGURE 10-12: Cartoonish avatars are now used to represent your Xbox LIVE identity online.

- ► **Name:** This can be your real name or a nickname.

- ► **Bio:** A text box providing up to 499 characters for describing your history or other relevant information.

- ► **Location:** A text field with up to 40 characters of space for describing your general location.

- ► **Privacy Settings:** You have fine-grained control over various privacy settings, including those related to voice and text, camera, profile, online status, video status, friends list, game history, member content, Xbox marketing, and partner marketing.

- ► **Profile:** Your Xbox LIVE profile consists of the Gamertag, Gamer Zone, Gamer Picture, Motto, Avatar, Name, Bio, Location, and privacy settings information described previously.

- ► **Rep:** This is your rep, or reputation score, on a scale of one to five. Every Xbox LIVE member starts with a rep of 3, but it can go up or down from there based on your experience (where the more you play, the higher the rep) and whether any other gamers complain about you online (the more you misbehave, the more people complain, and the more your rep declines).

- ► **Gamerscore:** Each Xbox LIVE game can assign Gamer Points to individual achievements, as we'll soon discuss. These points are applied to your Gamerscore, which starts at 0 when you open the account. The higher your Gamescore, the more experienced you are, generally speaking, though many hard-core gamers only play in multiplayer matches that don't provide multiplayer achievements and thus might have deceptively low Gamerscores. Likewise, those with higher Gamerscores could be achievement point addicts, or even cheating.

- ► **Gamercard:** Your Xbox LIVE Gamercard combines your Gamertag, Gamer Picture, Rep, Gamerscore, and Gamer Zone into a single, easily viewable overview of your Xbox LIVE account, or gamer persona.

- ► **Messages:** Using an e-mail-like system, Xbox LIVE members can send messages to each other using text, audio, and video. These messages aren't ever broadcast via normal e-mail systems (via the e-mail associated with your Microsoft account), but you can view and respond to received messages, and create new ones, on the Xbox 360 and via the Xbox website, as shown in Figure 10-13.

- ► **Friends list:** As with Facebook and other social networking services, you can "friend" other people online, send and receive friend requests, see what your friends are doing online in real time, send messages to friends, and more. The Xbox LIVE Friends list is sorted by online status, so that online friends are listed first.

► Just a common sense bit of advice: Don't be too specific with your location.

FIGURE 10-13: You can access the Xbox LIVE Messages functionality via the web.

▶ **Players list:** Xbox LIVE tracks the players you've most recently played against so you can find them again later and request a rematch, send feedback (positive or negative), or send a friend request.

▶ **Games list:** Xbox LIVE also tracks the games you've most recently played on the Xbox 360, Windows Phone, and Windows 8, as well as the achievements you've most recently earned, including all of the achievements earned in each played game. Friends can examine your account to see which games you've played, and which achievements you've earned, and compare them to their own results.

Xbox LIVE and Xbox LIVE Arcade Games and Achievements

If you're an avid game player, one of the best reasons to join Xbox LIVE is, well, the games. And among the cream of the crop are those games that get people together so they can compete against each other online.

On the Xbox 360, the most common of these types of games, the multiplayer games, are online shooters, such as those in the *Call of Duty*, *Gears of War*, and *Halo* series. But there are many other wildly popular online game types on Xbox LIVE as well, including real-time strategy, racing, and, Kinect titles, the latter of which use that device's motion-sensing and voice technologies to provide unique experiences.

Aside from facing off against your friends and others, Xbox LIVE also offers an achievements system in which games can offer between 200 and 1,000 achievement points, usually via a large number of individual achievements. When you do trigger an achievement—perhaps by completing an in-game level or other task— the console displays the ever-popular Achievement Unlocked notification, providing the name of the achievement. You can tap a button on the Xbox 360 controller to learn more, including how many achievement points you've earned and the description of the achievement. You can also view your overall Gamerscore to see how the achievement points affected things.

HOW MANY POINTS?

Although 200 to 1,000 achievement points seems like a wide range, it is, in fact, even wider than that.

Xbox LIVE games for Windows Phone, and Xbox LIVE Arcade titles, which tend to be shorter and much less expensive than normal Xbox LIVE titles, typically provide 200 achievement points that can be spread out over up to 12 individual achievements. Retail Xbox LIVE games for the Xbox 360 and Windows 8 typically provide 1,000 achievement points, which can occur over as many as 50 individual achievements. But Microsoft has also expanded the achievement points system for those game makers that wish to support their games with add-on packs that extend gameplay and provide new features. For those games, it's possible to have as many as 1,750 achievement points, over as many as three separate add-on packs.

Xbox LIVE games also support a feature called leaderboards, which are ranked lists that are relevant to the individual game. In a shooter like those in the *Call of Duty* series, for example, there are leaderboard lists for most overall points, most overall victories, most victories per game type, and so on.

Xbox LIVE Comes to Windows 8

While Xbox LIVE was originally conceived as an online service for the Xbox video game consoles, Microsoft ported it to Windows, poorly, as Games for Windows – LIVE in 2006. Games for Windows – LIVE is pretty lackluster, only offering a subset of the capabilities you get with Xbox LIVE on the 360. But it still exists and Microsoft has pledged to continue supporting it in Windows 8, even though it supports only those games that run via the legacy Windows desktop. We won't examine it in more detail here because nothing has changed.

In the years since creating this weird offshoot of Xbox LIVE, Microsoft also created the Windows Phone platform, which debuted in 2010. One of the major features of that platform was an integrated version of Xbox LIVE.

Unlike Games for Windows – LIVE, Xbox LIVE for Windows Phone wasn't a horrible compromise, and it provided access to great Xbox LIVE games, with achievements and other Xbox LIVE features. Xbox LIVE on Windows Phone was so successful, in fact, that Microsoft decided to bring it to Windows 8 as well.

▶ Windows 8 also includes apps for Xbox entertainment services, including Xbox Music and Xbox Video.

So what's the difference between Xbox LIVE (for Windows 8) and Games for Windows – LIVE? It's two-fold. First, Xbox LIVE works with Metro-style games on Windows 8, not desktop-based games. Second, Microsoft has created new Xbox LIVE user experiences for Windows 8 that mirror those it created first for Windows Phone. These experiences take the form of two apps, for now, called Xbox Games and Xbox Companion.

> **NOTE** Like so many Metro-style apps in Windows 8, Xbox Games and Xbox Companion are connected apps, meaning that they require you to sign in with a Microsoft account. As always, it's easiest if you simply sign in to your Windows 8 PC or device using a Microsoft account. But if you are using a local account type, you can sign in to a Microsoft account the first time you run either of these apps.

Xbox Games

▶ The Xbox Games app is identified only as Games on the app's live tile and in All Apps.

Xbox Games is the front end to all of your Xbox LIVE game activities on Windows 8, and oddly enough that includes a ton of Xbox 360-related functionality, too. If you're familiar with the Games hub in Windows Phone, you will see the functional similarities, though the Windows Phone interface lacks the links to Microsoft's dedicated gaming console. And if you're familiar with the Xbox 360, you'll immediately recognize that the Metro-style Xbox Games app is very much based on the console's Dashboard user experience. You can see this app in Figure 10-14.

Xbox Games is a standard, horizontally oriented, Metro-style user experience, but with one twist. Yes, it's divided into a series of groups that extend from left to right, like other Metro experiences. As with the Xbox entertainment apps, Music, and Video, Xbox Games does not start up oriented at the left edge of its extended, multi-screen user interface. So while you can scroll to the right when you first enter the app, you can also, oddly, scroll to the left.

When you do, you'll see that there are two small groups, Gamercard and Friends, to the left of the starting point of the app, at the Spotlight group, as shown in Figure 10-15.

FIGURE 10-14: Xbox Games

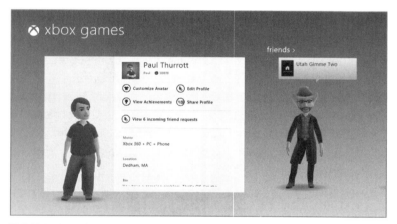

FIGURE 10-15: Look to the left of Spotlight and you'll see two semi-hidden groups.

The following groups are available in Xbox Games.

GAMERTAG

This interactive group provides a ton of editable information related to your Gamertag, including your first name, Gamerscore, motto, location, and bio, plus links to customize your avatar, edit your profile, view your and achievements. You can also share your profile and view incoming friend requests.

The achievements interface lets you view your Xbox 360, Windows Phone, Games for Windows – LIVE, and Windows 8 game achievements by game or date, with the ability to sort between all achievements and unlocked achievements (those you've actually achieved). As you can see in Figure 10-16, as you scroll to the right, you will see that every Xbox LIVE game you've ever played, regardless of platform, is accounted for.

FIGURE 10-16: Bask in the glory of your past achievements.

You can also click on individual games—using the box art or Game Details button—to see the full-screen landing page for that game in what's called the Games Store (as described later in this chapter). This interface scrolls off to the right and provides different capabilities depending on the title, but you'll see such things as a trailer movie, Buy Game for Xbox 360 and Play on Xbox 360 buttons, lists of game achievements, extras, and related games, and more. A typical game landing page is shown in Figure 10-17. (We'll examine the Buy Game for Xbox 360 and Play on Xbox 360 buttons a bit later in the chapter.)

FIGURE 10-17: A game landing page for an Xbox 360 title

The Customize Avatar option brings up a paper doll-like interface where you can dress up your avatar with new tops, headgear, glasses, wrist wear, gloves, rings, and other silliness. The Customize Avatar interface is shown in Figure 10-18.

▶ It's up to you, of course, but real men don't play dress-up with their avatar. Just saying.

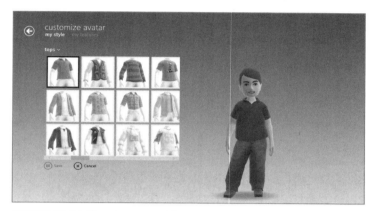

FIGURE 10-18: Play dress-up with your avatar.

FRIENDS

In the Friends group, you'll see the avatars of the first several of your friends who are currently online. Tap on the Friends title to see the full list of your online (and recently online) friends, also in avatar form. Or, tap on a friend's avatar to view their Gamertag information, as in Figure 10-19, and compare how they're doing against you.

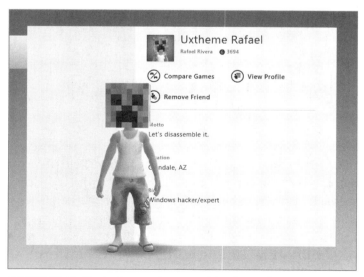

FIGURE 10-19: Find out more about your friend's gaming activities.

SPOTLIGHT

The Spotlight group is the default view in Xbox Games and functions as it does in Windows Store. It's a place for Microsoft to highlight and promote games and other offers that it thinks you'll find interesting. It's also, sadly, stocked with a couple of outright advertisements, which we find a bit insulting, having recently renewed our Xbox LIVE Gold subscriptions at $50 a pop.

GAME ACTIVITY

The Game Activity group, shown in Figure 10-20, provides a grid of the games you most recently played across all of the platforms on which Xbox LIVE is supported, in reverse order.

FIGURE 10-20: Your most recently played Xbox LIVE games

If you tap on the Game Activity title, it will present the entire list of Xbox LIVE games you've ever played, dating all the way back to 2005. In keeping with the game activity theme here, the games—each represented by box art—can display messages about the activities that friends have done with each. So you may see something like *1 beacon*, *2 online*, or similar noted on individual games, indicating that you're friends are busy having fun online while you're reading this dry, humorless tome.

When you tap on an individual game, a display pops up to show more information about the game, much like the interfaces in the other Xbox apps, Music and Video. This can be seen in Figure 10-21.

CROSSREF The Xbox Music and Video apps are discussed in Chapter 9.

What you see here will depend on the platform of the game that you've selected. Most games will provide at least some descriptive text about the title. But you can also see a number of buttons, including:

▶ **Play:** This button appears next to Windows 8 Metro-style games. If you click this button, the game will begin playing immediately.

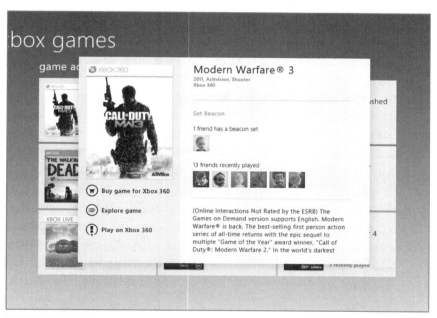

FIGURE 10-21: Viewing more information about a recently played game

▶ **Play on Xbox 360:** This button appears next to Xbox 360 games. If you click this button, the Xbox Companion app, described a bit later in this chapter, will open and attempt to connect to your Xbox 360 console and start the game.

▶ **Buy game/Buy game for Xbox 360:** This button triggers a full-screen Confirm Purchase experience. If you've selected this option for an Xbox 360 game, the game you're purchasing will be installed on the first console to which it's downloaded, so be careful if you own more than one. (Hey, it happens.) Note that the Buy Game for Xbox 360 option is only available for those Xbox 360 games that can be purchased electronically; some games are retail-only and require physical DVD-based media.

▶ **Explore Game:** This button launches the game landing page discussed earlier.

▶ **Play Trailer:** This button launches the video playback of the game's trailer.

WINDOWS GAMES STORE

Now, we can guess what you're thinking. We just told you that the Windows Store was the *only* place you could find, download, and update Windows 8 games, and yet here we are in the Xbox Games app and there's a group called Windows Games Store. What's up with that?

It's a fair question.

Behind the scenes, all of Microsoft's online entertainment services—Xbox LIVE Marketplace, Windows Store, Windows Phone Marketplace, the old Zune Music and Videos Marketplaces (now called Xbox Music and Xbox Videos, respectively), and so on—utilize the same back end. You might think of this back end as Microsoft Marketplace, though to be honest that's not really the name. But you get the idea. Microsoft really has just one online marketplace. But it's exposed in different places differently.

So, yes, Windows Store is the go-to place for all Windows 8 apps. But if you're just looking for Xbox LIVE games for Windows 8—that subset of Windows games that utilize the Xbox LIVE service and thus provide unique features like achievements—then Windows Games Store does that, and without any distractions. It includes featured games, picks for you (based on previously played games), genre lists, and more. To be fair, it's not an actual marketplace; it's just a group within Xbox LIVE games, and a window, if you will, into a very specific subset of Windows Store.

XBOX GAME MARKETPLACE

When you consider that Microsoft's online marketplace for the Xbox 360 is actually called Xbox Marketplace, the Xbox Games Store group seems a bit misnamed. But let's not quibble. This group, like Windows Games Store, is really just a view into an actual online store—in this case, the Xbox Marketplace—and like the Windows Games Store, it provides different views, such as Games on Demand, Demos, Indie, Arcade (for Xbox LIVE Arcade), and All Games. You can also sort by genre and arrange the view by best-selling today, release date, best-selling all-time, top rated, and title.

The Xbox Games Marketplace is shown in Figure 10-22.

FIGURE 10-22: Xbox Games Marketplace

What makes Xbox Games Store unique is that it's basically a place to browse, find, and purchase games for the Xbox 360. You do this from Windows presumably because it's a better experience than doing so on the console itself. Like the Game Activity group discussed previously, you'll see buttons such as Play on Xbox 360 and Explore Game, and they work just as they do elsewhere in this app. But you'll also see new options like Buy game for Xbox 360. And that means you'll eventually find yourself pushed over to the Xbox Companion app, which happens when you make a game purchase or select the Play on Xbox button. So let's examine that app next.

Xbox Companion

The Xbox Companion app is based on a similar app for Windows Phone. As its name suggests, it's designed as a companion to the Xbox 360, and as such it is a key part of Microsoft's strategy to better integrate its previously separate Windows and Xbox platforms.

The Xbox Companion app is often triggered from other Metro-style apps, including Xbox Games, Xbox Music, and Xbox Video. But it can also be run independently.

Before doing so, however, you will need to configure your console to work with the Xbox Companion app. To do so, boot the Xbox 360 into the Dashboard and then navigate to Settings, System, Console Settings, and then Xbox Companion. There, change the setting from Unavailable to Available.

Next, run Xbox Companion in Windows 8 or RT. The app will connect to your console and then present a UI similar to the one shown in Figure 10-23, with a number of groups laid out in a horizontal, Metro-style UI that should be familiar by now. (Like Xbox Games, it features a hidden, leftmost group that you can scroll over to find.)

▶ *Xbox Companion will eventually be replaced by a similar but more full-featured app called Xbox SmartGlass. This app, due by the end of 2012, will offer a superset of the functionality in Xbox Companion.*

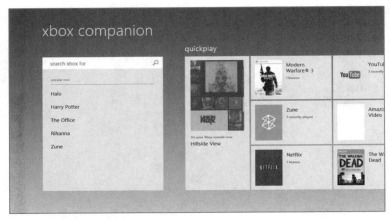

FIGURE 10-23: Xbox Companion

Xbox Companion provides the following groups.

SEARCH

The Search experience, shown in Figure 10-24, is similar to the Bing group on the Xbox 360 Dashboard. (And no, we can't imagine why Microsoft doesn't use consistent naming.)

FIGURE 10-24: Xbox Companion Search

You can type virtually anything Xbox related—a game, movie, or TV show name, for example, or perhaps an actor or musical band name—and the app will then show search results in a graphical Metro-style interface that is sorted by videos, games, and music. For example, a search for *Van Halen* reveals a number of relevant results in the music category. *The Office*, however, will be most relevant under videos, since it's a hit TV show.

Search results work like so many other Metro-style experiences, providing options like Play on Xbox 360, Explore Game, Play Trailer, Series Details, and so on, which will vary by content type. Since the point of this app is to act, literally, as an Xbox Companion, the assumption here is that you're sitting in front of your Xbox 360 and HDTV and using Windows 8 or Windows RT as a large, intelligent remote, looking for content that you'll then play to the console (and thus to your HDTV and/or home theater system).

We'll examine Play on Xbox in just a bit. But the end game for all of the options in this app, when you think about it, is to play the selected or found content on the console.

QUICKPLAY

The Quickplay group is an interesting collection of Xbox 360 content—games, entertainment experiences such as Netflix, and the Dashboard itself. When you tap one, the Xbox will navigate to that experience (for example, playing on Xbox) and you'll be provided with the full-screen Play on Xbox experience, described at the end of this section.

VIDEOS

The Videos group provides a front end to the Xbox 360's movies and TV shows experiences, which consists of video apps such as ESPN, Hulu Plus, MLB TV, Netflix, Vudu, Xbox Videos, and more. As you can see in Figure 10-25, there are tiles for promoted individual movies and TV series, but also Explore Movies and Explore TV tiles that will load the appropriate Store in the Metro-style Xbox Video app.

FIGURE 10-25: The Videos group in Xbox Companion

GAMES

The Games group provides a similar treatment for Xbox 360 video games, with some tiles for individual games that link to landing pages for those titles, as well as a Discover Games tile that loads the Xbox Games Store in the Xbox Games app.

MUSIC

The Music group works similarly to the Videos and Games group; a Find Music tile loads the Xbox Music interface in the Metro-style Xbox Music app.

PLAY ON XBOX 360: THE XBOX COMPANION'S REASON FOR BEING

What each of the groups in the Xbox Companion app has in common is that all of them lead you to one unavoidable outcome: Eventually, you're going to come across music, or a game, TV show, or movie that you will want to play on the Xbox 360 console. And while the experience differs slightly from content type to content type, in general the effect is the same: You click the Play on Xbox 360 button and Xbox Companion connects to your console, after asking if you mind interrupting your current (Xbox 360) session if you're currently running an app or game on the console.

When this happens, the Xbox Companion app switches to the full-screen display shown in Figure 10-26. (This will of course vary depending on the content type you've chosen.)

FIGURE 10-26: While handing off playback to the console, the Xbox Companion displays a full-screen interface.

From here, you could use your Xbox controller to control the action. But the Xbox Companion can also function as a basic controller. To enable this mode, display the app bar and press the Xbox Controls button. The display will change to resemble Figure 10-27, letting you navigate through menus by using sliding gestures and tapping on virtual buttons to make selections. (You can tap on the middle of the screen to emulate the green "A" button.)

You can't play games with this virtual controller. After all, it only emulates a handful of buttons and some simple navigation controls. But with the Xbox 360 being used more and more for entertainment experiences of all kinds, Xbox Companion is a great way to interact with that content on the console, and to find games, videos, music, and more.

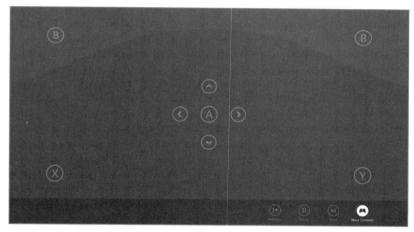

FIGURE 10-27: The Xbox Companion virtual controller

SUMMARY

With Windows 8 aimed squarely at a Metro-styled future, it's no wonder that the new Windows 8 game experiences are Metro-based as well. This version of Windows offers a stunning array of games of all kinds through the Windows Store, provides handy organizational features for those who wish to access their favorite games from the Start screen, and of course it integrates with Microsoft's market-leading Xbox LIVE service for the first time, offering access to the full range of gaming and entertainment services that Microsoft previously provided only on its Xbox 360 console. There are also fun hooks in Windows 8 for controlling the Xbox 360 and finding content that can be played to the console, with your Windows 8 device acting like a big and sophisticated remote control.

CHAPTER 11

Storage, Backup, and Recovery

IN THIS CHAPTER

▶ Understanding Windows 8 storage basics

▶ Discovering, configuring, and using Storage Spaces

▶ Enabling File History for automatic file backup and versioning

▶ Using Storage Spaces and File History together

▶ Using the Windows Recovery Environment

▶ Creating a Recovery Drive

▶ Using Push Button Reset to reset or refresh your PC

▶ Accessing hidden system image backup and recovery functionality

In Windows 8, Microsoft has dramatically recast its storage and backup and recovery technologies while offering a familiar selection of other related tools that have appeared in Windows for years. This melding of the old and the new is, of course, a theme that runs throughout Windows 8, as is the notion of reimagining Windows itself. So while previous Windows versions included ways to recover data and the entire OS in the event of a disaster, in Windows 8 these tasks are more logically linked together. Because, after all, when you do have to resuscitate a PC, you want to resuscitate it all—your data included—and not just the OS.

To this end, Windows 8 includes technologies such as Storage Spaces, which keeps your data safe through hardware redundancy, and File History, a far more useful new take on the Previous Versions feature from older Windows versions that makes document and data backup and recovery automatic and highly graphical. Best of all, you can even combine Storage Spaces and File History into a single cohesive solution that not only backs up your crucial data but does so in a way that will survive hardware failures. It's brilliant.

Windows 8 also reimagines PC recovery in ways that will astonish you. Thanks to the new Push Button Reset functionality that can return your Windows 8 install to its factory-fresh condition, complete with a new car smell, you can also quickly recover all of your data, settings, and Metro-style apps as well. And this process generally takes just minutes, not the half or full day such procedures would require with Windows 7 or the typical PC maker recovery solution. It's night and day.

This chapter examines these technologies. In some cases, you will need to learn some new skills. Trust us, however; it's worth doing.

> **NOTE** We're all about "new" here. But many Windows 7 recovery features do carry forward, mostly unchanged, in Windows 8. These include Windows Troubleshooting, the Problem Steps Recorder, System Protection, and System Restore.

STORAGE BASICS: NTFS TODAY, REFS TOMORROW

While the details have changed fairly dramatically, PCs still interact with storage devices—hard drives, solid state storage (SSD), USB memory keys, and the like—the same as they ever have. That is, to enable the use of storage, the devices must be formatted with a filesystem and then assigned a drive letter so that Windows, or the apps and applications that run within this environment, can access their contents.

> ▶ And go figure, FAT lives on today with a version of the system called exFAT that is used almost exclusively on flash storage devices.

Over the years, Microsoft's filesystem technologies have evolved dramatically, first with MS-DOS–based filesystems built around the FAT (file allocation table) architecture that debuted in Microsoft Stand-Alone Disk BASIC *way* back in 1977. Originally designed for 5.25-inch floppy disks, FAT was evolved over the years to support different floppy disk formats and then hard drives of ever-increasing sizes.

When Windows NT debuted in 1993, it included a new filesystem called NTFS that had numerous advantages over the FAT-based filesystems Microsoft was still using in then-mainstream Windows versions. Without getting into the technical details, suffice it to say that it was more reliable, efficient, manageable, and, eventually even offered better performance though that certainly wasn't true of the first few versions. It also supported much bigger storage devices than the FAT filesystems.

With Windows XP in 2001, Microsoft made NTFS the default filesystem for its OS, and in the intervening years, this filesystem has been regularly updated with new features and functionality, including support for encryption, quotas, file versioning, and much more. And in Windows 8, NTFS is still the default filesystem for storage devices, especially hard disks and SSDs. But that's all about to change.

Concurrently with Windows 8, Microsoft developed a new filesystem that will one day replace NTFS. Dubbed the Resilient File System, or ReFS, this new filesystem is currently available only in Windows Server 2012, and then only for the file server workload. Moving forward, however, Microsoft will extend ReFS first to work elsewhere in Windows Server, including as a boot disk. And it will then move ReFS to the Windows client as well.

Microsoft has not yet revealed how or when that could happen. So it's equally possible that ReFS support will debut in a future Windows 8 service pack or other update, or that it will simply be included in Windows 9.

Compared to NTFS, ReFS is an evolution, not a brand-new filesystem. So it retains complete compatibility with NTFS while offering automatic data correction and support for even larger partition/disk, file, and folder sizes, among other things. ReFS also works with the storage features discussed in this chapter, including Storage Spaces.

For now, just know that you will be using the NTFS filesystem almost exclusively in Windows 8 when it comes to large capacity storage devices like hard drives and SSDs, even though it's possible in some cases to format them with FAT-based filesystems.

STORAGE SPACES

NTFS and other filesystems have their advantages, but the reliability of any filesystem is ultimately tied to the weakest link in the chain, the underlying storage hardware. It's a simple fact of life that hard drives (and related storage devices) fail, and that when they do so, they often bring your data down with them.

Windows has used various technologies over the years to help overcome the inevitability of data loss. For example, Windows 7 includes a feature called Previous Versions that automatically stores document revisions so that you can later go back and resuscitate an older document version when needed. It also includes a Windows Backup utility that does a decent job of backing up important files, or even the entire PC.

▶ Storage Spaces works only with Intel x86/ x64 versions of Windows 8, not with ARM-based Windows RT systems.

These and other recovery solutions are reactive, meaning they provide help in the event of a worst-case scenario, be it the accidental deletion of a file, the overwriting of a file with an older, less correct version, or whatever. But they don't solve the underlying problem of relying on a single hard disk (or other device). They don't, for example, replicate your critical data across two or more disks automatically so that if one drive fails, your data is still safe.

Windows 8 includes such a feature. It's called Storage Spaces, and it works with both NTFS- and ReFS-formatted disks, providing a safe, secure, and redundant way for you to provision, manage, and use storage that spans multiple disks, replicating your data automatically.

Storage Spaces provides two basic services:

▶ **Data redundancy:** Storage Spaces utilizes data mirroring technology to ensure that there are at least two copies of data, each of which lives on a different disk, to help prevent data loss in the event of a hard disk failure. Storage Spaces lets you configure up to three disks for redundancy purposes. (It also supports a parity feature, which provides you with two different copies of your data but requires three physical disks; the third disk is used for parity purposes.)

▶ **Single pool of storage:** You can organize the storage on your various hard disks in one or more storage pools that are managed as a single entity—called a storage pool, or simply *pool*—despite having storage that could span many disks. And unlike complex technologies such as RAID, these disks can be of multiple different sizes and types, and can include fixed disks (SATA) and external storage (like USB). You're free to mix and match as you like, and adding storage to a storage pool is as simple as plugging in a new disk and adding it to that pool using a very simple interface.

Storage Spaces is easy to set up and configure, and once you do that, you can pretty much just get on with life and not worry about it anymore. Storage Spaces also integrates with File Explorer, much like libraries do. This means you get a normal view of the storage from Explorer, and it uses a normal, widely understood drive letter, appearing to look and work just like a simple hard drive. This is useful for users, but also for the OS and any applications, since they'll expect such things. This means the compatibility of Storage Spaces is excellent.

Storage Spaces also lets you create a space that is bigger than the total amount of physical storage. This feature, which is called *thin provisioning*, lets you preconfigure a space to a large size and then add physical storage later, when it's actually needed. Likewise, physical storage is only allocated as it's needed. (You'll be prompted when needed through Action Center, which uses a Windows Troubleshooting notification.)

▶ Storage Spaces is conceptually related to a technology called Drive Extender, which debuted in a product called Windows Home Server. That said, Storage Spaces is the superior solution and is technically unrelated to Drive Extender.

Finally, in addition to working with normal NTFS-based disks, Storage Spaces is also compatible with ReFS-based disks. This means that today on Windows Server 2012, you can optionally mix and match NTFS and Resilient File System (ReFS)-based disks. And in the future, you'll be able to do so on Windows as well.

As is always the case with new technology, Storage Spaces brings with it some new terminology. Where a storage pool can consist of the storage on one or more disks—though of course you'd need two or more for redundancy—you access this storage via a new entity called a *storage space*, or *space*. To understand what this means, consider how libraries work in Windows 7 and 8. In these operating systems, you have physical folders such as My Pictures and Public Pictures, and the combined, virtual view of these folders is called the Pictures library. Spaces work the same way. You may combine your E: and F: drives into a single pool of storage. But you will access that pool through the filesystem using a virtual view called a space, and that space will be given a name. In this case, it could be called the Pictures space.

So storage spaces have names and drive letters. But they also have an assigned resiliency type. This determines how (or whether) the data stored in the space is synced automatically across two or more disks, or what is called redundancy. The available resiliency types include:

▶ **None:** In this configuration, the space works exactly like a normal hard drive. Data is not mirrored on two or more disks but is instead stored on just a single disk. This configuration requires a storage pool with at least one physical disk.

▶ **Two-way mirror:** Here, your data is mirrored on two physical hard disks, protecting that data from a single hard disk failure. This configuration requires a storage pool with at least two physical disks. However, the available storage in the pool will be halved, assuming both disks are the same size.

▶ **Three-way mirror:** In this configuration, your data is mirrored on three physical hard disks, protecting that data from the failure of two hard disks. This configuration requires a storage pool with three physical disks. However, the available storage in the pool will be one-third the total, assuming all three disks are the same size.

▶ **Parity:** In this advanced configuration, your data is mirrored alongside additional parity information that could help Windows recover data in the event of a hard drive failure.

▶ A parity configuration is notably good for storing very large files, like videos.

Because spaces have this unique capability to reserve more storage than is physically available in the attached disk(s), the feature lets you plan for the future by pretending that you have more storage than you do. If the data stored in the space begins exceeding your physical capacity, you'll be notified to add more physical storage.

Meanwhile, because Storage Spaces uses thin provisioning to allocate only a small amount of physical storage when a new space is created, even if you create a space of multiple terabytes, only 1 GB of space is actually taken right away.

Getting Ready for Storage Spaces

To use Storage Spaces, you will need at least one additional hard disk or similar storage device. It can be an external device (typically USB-based) or internal (SATA, perhaps). But if you want to take advantage of Storage Spaces' redundancy features, you will need two or more hard disks. These can be different sizes and types, and any mix of internal and external devices. Storage Spaces is very flexible.

When you attach a new hard disk to your PC, it will usually show up in File Explorer accompanied by a new drive letter. We assume anyone reading this book at least understands this basic Windows functionality.

Of course, things aren't always this simple. Most PCs need to be shut down before internal hard disks can be installed, and sometimes when you add an internal or external storage device, it simply doesn't show up in Explorer. If this is the case, you must use the Disk Management tool to format or otherwise enable the disk. The quickest way to run Disk Management is to mouse into the lower-left corner of the screen, from either the Start screen or the Windows desktop, right-click to display the new Windows 8 power user menu shown in Figure 11-1, and select Disk Management.

▶ The Windows system and boot partitions, which are typically both the C: drive, cannot participate in Storage Spaces.

▶ You can also display this handy menu by typing Winkey + X.

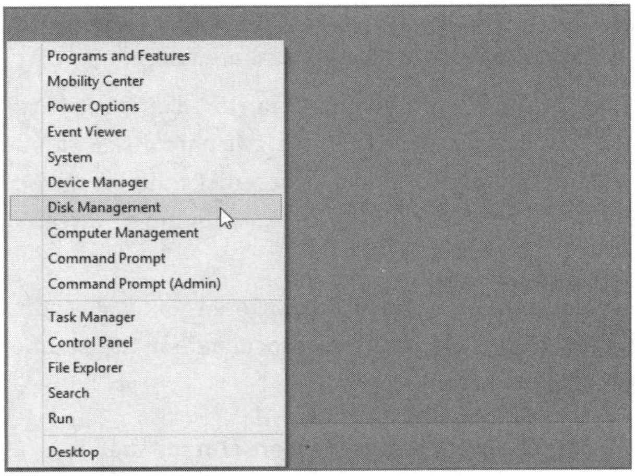

FIGURE 11-1: A new power user menu provides quick access to useful but infrequently needed tools.

Disk Management, shown in Figure 11-2, shows the various physical disks that are connected to your PC and graphically displays how each is partitioned. For example, Disk 0 in this PC was partitioned by Windows Setup into a system reserved partition, which doesn't get a drive letter and second, larger boot and system partition that's been assigned to drive C:.

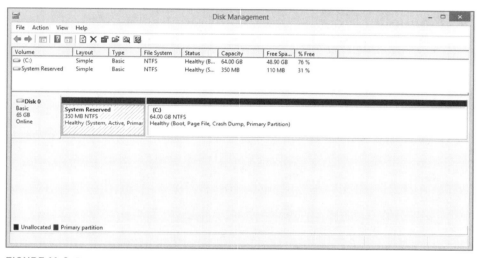

FIGURE 11-2: Disk Management

Disk Management has been around since the earliest days of NT, so we won't belabor its use here, but the important thing to note is that this is the first place you should look when you add a hard disk to your PC and it doesn't show up in Explorer. From this interface, you can do such things as format a disk, activate a disk, assign a drive letter, partition a physical disk into separate logical disks, and shrink and expand existing partitions. If it relates to storage, Disk Management is the place to start.

The Most Basic Storage Spaces Configuration of All: One Disk, One Space, No Resiliency

The simplest possible Storage Spaces configuration involves just one (additional) disk, which you will use to create a single storage pool that can then be divided into one or more storage spaces; we'll use one to keep things simple.

After you've added the disk and verified that it's working in File Explorer, you need to access the Storage Spaces control panel, the Windows 8 user interface for managing this feature. As a classic Control Panel, Storage Spaces is well hidden, but you can find it easily enough by using Start Search (look under Settings, not Apps) or, if you're more of a desktop kind of person, by using the power user menu or some other means to launch Control Panel and the search from there.

However you do it, Storage Spaces will resemble Figure 11-3 when launched the first time, regardless of how many additional disks are attached.

FIGURE 11-3: The Storage Spaces control panel

▶ The new pool creation process is destructive, meaning that any data on a non-pooled (that is, normal) disk will be deleted as part of the process. You can think of this as formatting the pool, if that helps it make sense.

Click the link titled Create a new pool and storage space. After a User Account Control prompt—you don't want the commoners mucking around with storage, now—you'll be presented with the display shown in Figure 11-4. Here, Storage Spaces has found a single viable disk and is offering to let you use this device to create a new storage pool.

▶ The Take offline link removes the drive letter from that storage device. You can do this to recover that drive letter, which you may wish to use for the space you're about to create.

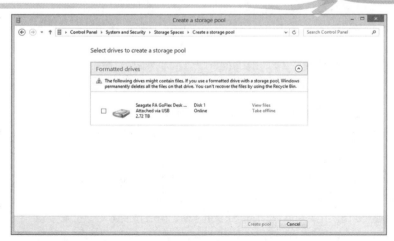

FIGURE 11-4: Creating a new storage pool with just one physical disk

To add the disk to a new pool, select it (by clicking the empty check box next to the disk) and then click Create pool. A new pool is created and then you are prompted to create a storage space that will exist in that pool. Unlike a pool, a storage space has a name, a drive letter assignment, and a resiliency type, and it can reserve more storage than is physically available. All of these capabilities are configured in this screen, which should resemble Figure 11-5.

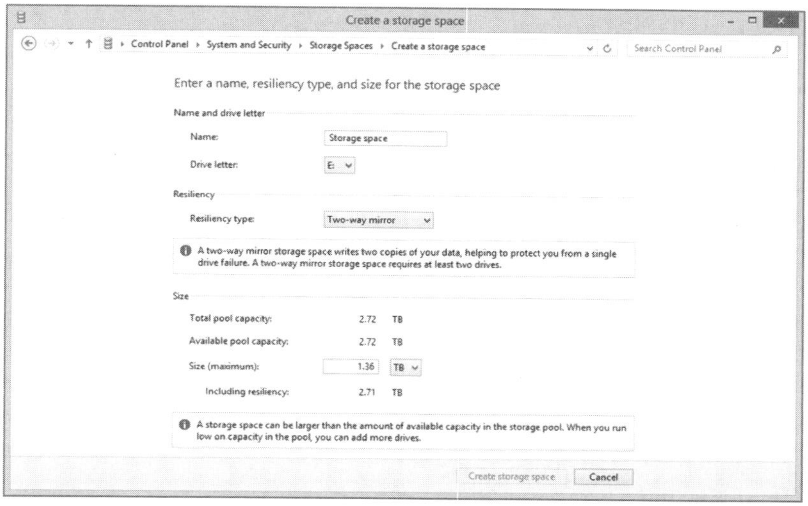

FIGURE 11-5: After the pool is created, it's time to create a space within that pool.

For a one-disk configuration, the choices are fairly limited: You can assign a name and drive letter of your choosing, but the only resiliency type you can use is "Simple (no resiliency)," which for some reason is not automatically selected. (The other options require two or more attached disks.)

So select "Simple (no resiliency)" from the Resiliency type drop-down and then click the Create storage space button. Storage Spaces creates your new storage space and returns to the main Storage Spaces' control panel view, which will have changed, as shown in Figure 11-6, to include the details about your new storage pool and the single space it contains. (Additionally, a new Explorer window will open, showing the virtual partition that represents your new space.)

You can also expand the physical drives area to see the one-to-one representation between the actual drive and the space for which it is being used. Obviously, this capability gets more interesting—and useful—when you create a space with two or more physical disks.

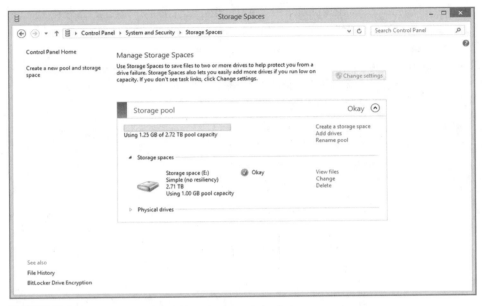

FIGURE 11-6: One storage space with a single contained storage pool

Storage Pool Configuration Options

Once you have configured at least one storage pool, there are a few new options that present themselves. All of these are available from the main Storage Spaces control panel view, and all but the first three are found within the Storage pool area:

- ▶ **Create a storage space:** Every storage pool will contain at least one storage space. But once you have a storage pool, you can keep adding additional spaces as needed. To do so, click the link titled Create a storage space. You'll see the same interface discussed in the previous section, and your options will be limited only by the available storage types attached to the PC.

- ▶ **Add drives:** If you've already created a pool and would like to add one or more drives to that pool, you do so through the Add drives link. Drives added in this fashion will automatically be made available to any spaces within the pool. (But note that Storage Spaces does not provide a way to change the resiliency or size configuration of a space after the fact, as is discussed a bit later in the chapter.)

- ▶ **Rename pool:** By default, a storage pool is silently given the imaginative name Storage pool by Windows. You can change this with the Rename pool link though, to be fair, this isn't something you'll need to deal with unless you're creating multiple pools for some reason. That's a fairly advanced configuration and, in our opinion, pretty crazy for even an advanced PC user.

▶ **Create a new pool and storage space:** This link on the left side of the Storage Spaces window will allow you to create other storage pools, and their contained spaces, assuming you have the additional disk capacity to support such a thing. Honestly, a single storage pool with multiple spaces is probably complex enough for most people. But if you have the urge to really overthink things, go nuts.

Storage Space Configuration Options

You can also configure various options related to a storage space. These include:

▶ **Change:** You can change various aspects of a storage space after it's created using this link. These include three key storage space options: Its name, its drive letter, and its maximum storage space size.

▶ **Delete:** You can delete a storage space as well. This will remove the space only; the containing pool is retained along with any attached storage.

▶ **Remove (drive):** If you have two or more disks being used for a storage space, you will see a Remove link next to each. If you click this, the drive is removed from the pool and the space, is formatted, and will reappear in File Explorer with a new drive letter. If you remove the last drive associated with a pool, that pool will be removed as well.

▶ Any data stored on a space is deleted when the space is deleted. So be sure to back up anything important before continuing.

▶ Note that this option will not appear when there is only one drive in a space.

A More Resilient Space: Two Disks, Two-Way Mirroring

While a single-disk storage space has some value, the inability to add resiliency at a later date seriously hampers that kind of configuration. As far as we're concerned, the real value of Storage Spaces begins when you have two or more disks you can use in a mirrored setup. This configuration will automatically replicate data between two disks, providing you with some measure of protection in the event of a hard disk failure.

Consider the screen shown in Figure 11-7. Here in the Storage Spaces interface, you can see that the PC has two additional 3 TB drives that it can use as the basis for a storage pool and one or more contained storage spaces.

To get started, select both of the disks and then click Create pool. As before, the storage pool is created and you are shown the screen in Figure 11-8, where you select options related to the first contained storage space. This time, you can select a two-way mirror for some hardware resiliency. In fact, that resiliency type is selected by default.

FIGURE 11-7: Two additional disks will open up additional configuration options.

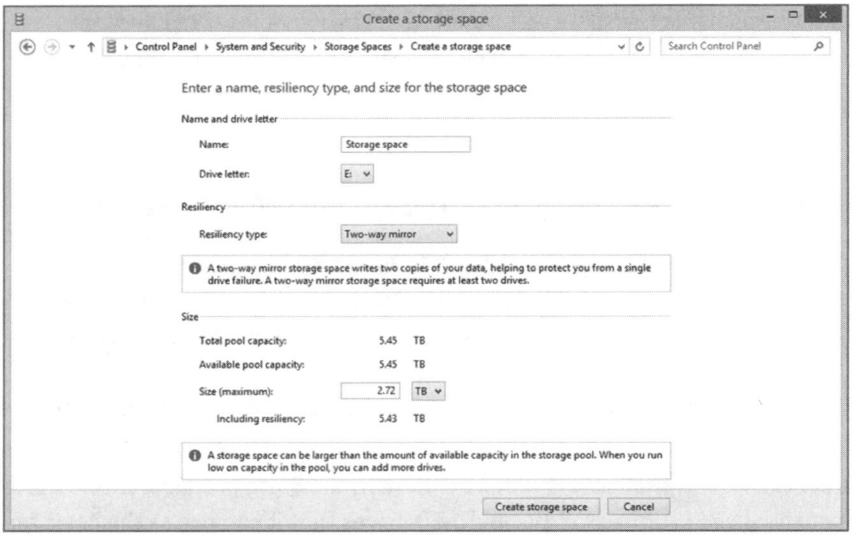

FIGURE 11-8: Now you can choose a two-way mirror.

Note that by default, Storage Spaces selects 2.72 TB (or roughly 3 TB) for the maximum size of the space, even though the total pool capacity is twice that. That's because that's the natural size of the mirrored disks: the combined size halved, so that each bit of data will be equally replicated across both physical disks. You can of course increase the logical size now and add physical storage later if and when it's needed. In fact, you can basically make it as big as you want. (You can also increase or otherwise change the space's maximum size later if needed.)

Click the Create storage space button to initialize the space. A new Explorer window opens, too, displaying this new space. But as you can see from the Explorer view that opens, it appears as a normal 3 TB disk to the system, even though under the hood it is using about 6 TB of actual physical storage spread across two disks. Mirroring reduces the available storage, but offers better resiliency. That's the trade-off.

▶ Everything about the space is normal from an Explorer perspective. You can even protect it with BitLocker if you want.

Back in the Storage Spaces control panel, you can see that once again the new pool has been created, along with a single space. But this time the space includes two hard disks, as you can see when you expand the Physical drives view as shown in Figure 11-9.

FIGURE 11-9: A two-way mirrored space, as seen in Storage Spaces

Under the hood, of course, a mirrored storage space is far more powerful than a single drive. Anything stored within is being replicated across the two physical disks, automatically. You could add more spaces to the pool, rename the pool or its contained spaces, and perform other management tasks. In fact, if you return to the Storage Spaces control panel, you'll see a number of details about the pool and space you've created.

Storage Space Tom Foolery: What Happens When … ?

Storage Spaces is a pretty amazing feature, and it's not hard to imagine tying together multiple high-terabyte hard drives to create a single pool of redundant storage for a massive video collection, music library, or any other data. But such a configuration seems to require a desktop computer, and unless you've been living under a rock for the past few years, you know that most people are turning to laptops, tablets, and hybrid portable computers, not traditional desktop computers. Is Storage Spaces only a toy for that niche audience of power users that still use desktop PCs? Not quite.

First, it is worth noting that many users with big media collections may indeed want to invest in a desktop PC solely so they can use this feature and then share their media around the home using the home network. In this way, a fairly pedestrian Windows 8 PC—albeit one with a ton of storage—could be used as a replacement for a Windows Home Server machine or, more likely, network attached storage. It's just so versatile.

But even for users of portable PCs and devices, Storage Spaces can make plenty of sense. Remember, this feature works equally well with internal and external storage, so there's no reason you couldn't link multiple external drives off your portable PC—or better yet, off a dock or USB port extender—and simply use the contained spaces when you're sitting at the desk. When you're out and about with the PC, it will still work normally. But when you're home, or at the office, the space(s) will be available.

▶ In fact, all of the Storage Spaces examples used in this chapter were done on a Windows 8-based tablet computer connected to a dock that had several USB 3.0-based hard drives chained to it through a USB 3.0-based extender.

OK, but what happens when you start removing disks? Does Storage Spaces freak out? It depends.

If you detach all of the storage used by a space at once, the space will simply disappear. But when you reattach the storage, the space comes back immediately and all is well.

A more slippery slope is encountered when you remove one of the disks being used by a space that is configured with two or more disks. In this case, the space still exists in Explorer and functions normally. You can read and write to it and access it like any other disk. But under the hood, some error messages are being generated, and if you look at the Storage Spaces control panel, you'll see the beginnings of a hissy fit developing, as in Figure 11-10. Spaces has detected that a drive is missing and, thus, the space's resiliency is compromised.

Eventually, you'll receive an Action Center-based notification warning you to reconnect the drive. But the system will continue working properly and, if you do reconnect the drive, all will return to normal. (This happens almost immediately, though Spaces will repair things, meaning it will ensure that the replication between drives is accurate and complete.)

But here's where things get really weird.

FIGURE 11-10: A drive is missing from a mirrored space.

What happens when you use the drive or drives from a space with another Windows 8-based computer? That is, you bring home a different laptop from work, or whatever, plug in the drives that make up a space on some other machine. What then?

Amazingly, incredibly...it just works. Windows 8 will take a moment to install the devices the first time, but after a few seconds, you can open Explorer and see not the separate drives, but rather the exact same storage space, just as you had configured it on the original PC. (With one difference: It won't necessarily retain the same drive letter between PCs.)

This is true regardless of how many of the configured disks you attach, and it has amazing repercussions for those who need to blow away a PC configuration but retain all the data. By putting your valuable data in spaces, you can be sure it's all immediately available after the fact when you reinstall Windows 8 or simply buy a new PC.

▶ Ready for your head to explode? This works with Windows Server 2012 as well.

Amazing.

> **NOTE** We probably shouldn't be putting this idea in your head, but it's even more amazing than we suggest. You could actually change the configuration of the space on the second PC—say by adding a new disk—and when you go back to using the space with the first PC, that configuration will carry back as well.

Advanced Storage Spaces: Three-Disk Configurations

There are two final, extreme Storage Spaces configurations, both of which involve using three disks with either mirroring or parity. In a three-way mirrored configuration, Storage Spaces works just like two-way mirroring, except, of course, that your data is replicated on three physical disks. With parity, again, additional redundancy information is written to each disk, which could help with recovery in the event of a hard drive failure.

Creating either configuration works much as before, however, this time you will need three additional disks. After selecting each in the Create a Storage Pool window, you'll be presented with the screen in which you provide a name, drive letter, resiliency type, and logical size for the first space in the pool, as shown in Figure 11-11.

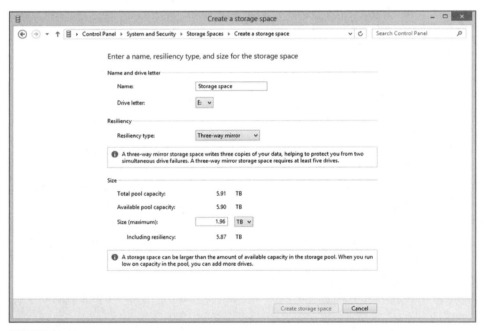

FIGURE 11-11: This time, the Storage Spaces configuration uses three drives.

In a three-way mirror, the total storage pool capacity is of the total capacity of the three drives added together, so in this example, with two 3 TB disks and one 512 GB disk, it's roughly 6 TB. But a parity configuration, shown in Figure 11-12, is a bit different.

Here, the total storage pool capacity is again roughly 6 TB, but the maximum pool capacity usage is different than that of a three-way mirror configuration because of the way parity works.

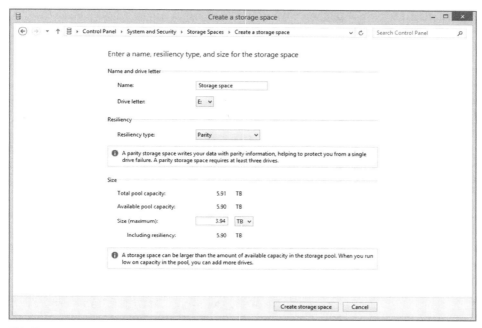

FIGURE 11-12: Using parity eats up a bit more space but is more resilient.

When Drives Fail: Storage Spaces Recovery

Earlier, this chapter described the situation where you remove a disk from a storage space and then later plug it in again, repairing the space and bringing everything back to normal. That's nice when it happens. But what if a disk goes bad?

Just as you can easily remove disks from a space as noted previously in this chapter, you can also add new disks. But since disks are added to pools, not to spaces, you'll need to remove the old, potentially damaged disk first. And then the space will simply claim storage on another disk in the pool for its own. Here's how it works.

Suppose you have a pool that consists of one space, called Space (we know, inventive), that's been configured as a two-way mirror with a logical size of 20 TB, and two physical disks, each of which are 3 TB. Over time, the space fills up with content—perhaps you've been busy ripping your DVD collection to the PC in anticipation of an optical disc-less future—and you're getting close to the 3 TB physical space limit. And then disaster strikes: One of the disks goes down for the count, so your content is no longer being replicated.

When this type of thing happens, Action Center will trigger a notification like the one shown in Figure 11-13. Click it and you will navigate immediately to Storage Spaces so you can fix the issue.

FIGURE 11-13: An Action Center warning about low disk capacity in your storage space

In the Storage Spaces control panel, you will see warnings next to the space itself as well as the injured disk. If you attempt to remove the bad disk, you may see an error message related to data that has to be reallocated. Instead, click the Add drives link, select the disk or disks you'd like to add to the pool, and then Storage Spaces will do the rest. Eventually, you'll be able to remove that bad disk from the control panel and get back to work.

Note that this would also work if you wanted to replace existing disks with larger capacity disks. So when those 4, 5, or 6 TB hard drives come to market, you'll be ready.

FILE HISTORY

Windows 7 included a decent but well-hidden feature called Previous Versions that allowed you to recover an older version of a document or other data file, perhaps because you made an editing error and then inadvertently saved over the correct version. Previous Versions was a first stab at creating a front end for a service called Volume Shadow Copy that debuted in Windows Server 2003. And it was fine if you knew it was there. But most users didn't. That's because you had to right-click on the document, choose Properties, navigate to the Previous Versions tab, and hope that the appropriate previous version of the file was there.

In Windows 8, Previous Versions has been replaced by a vastly superior feature called File History. This feature works much like Previous Versions did, and utilizes updated versions of the same back-end technologies. But there are three major differences between Previous Versions and File History. First, File History isn't enabled by default, so you'll need to turn it on. Second, File History uses a lot less disk space to perform its backups, thanks to new compression technologies in Windows 8 and its ability to cache backups on your system disk. And third, File History is about a million times easier to use than Previous Versions. OK, we exaggerate. Maybe it's just a thousand times easier.

What File History Backs Up

By default, File History automatically backs up everything in your libraries, on your desktop, in your Favorites, and in Contacts. That's a lot more stuff than it perhaps sounds like; remember that your libraries consist of eight locations by default: My Documents, Public Documents, My Music, Public Music, My Pictures, Public Pictures, My Videos, and Public Videos.

You can also configure File History to automatically back up other locations of your choice or, to not back up certain locations too. If you have a home network with a home server, a network attached storage (NAS) device, or a PC with lots of storage, you can even configure File History to work across the network, and then automatically recommend that location to others on the homegroup, creating a central location for all file backups.

> ▶ Not impressed? Well, if you create your own libraries, file versions in those locations will be backed up too, and automatically. Come on, that's downright impressive.

> CROSSREF Chapter 13 discusses homegroups, which is a networking feature that makes home-based sharing easier than ever.

To better understand File History, let's see it in action.

Enabling and Configuring File History

File History, like Storage Spaces, is implemented as a classic control panel. So the fastest way to access its configuration interface is to use Start Search. Or, display Control Panel via the new power user menu (mouse into the lower-left corner of the screen, right-click, and select Control Panel) and then search for File History using the preselected search box.

The File History control panel is shown in Figure 11-14. As you can see, it's disabled by default.

On a single disk PC or device, like your typical portable computer, File History will recommend using a network location.

> ▶ File History actually caches a subset of your file backups to your system disk. So this feature will often work just fine even when you're away from home with a portable computer.

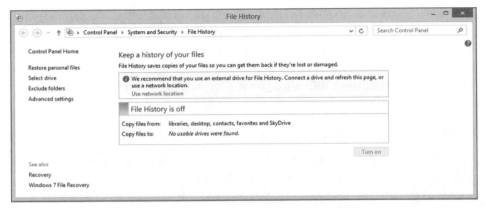

FIGURE 11-14: File History is disabled by default and will recommend a network location on a single disk system.

Alternatively, you can use any other disk, including a removable, USB-based hard drive. If you have such a disk attached to the PC, File History will resemble Figure 11-15, where the other disk is preselected.

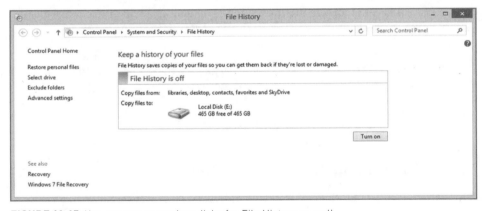

FIGURE 11-15: You can use secondary disks for File History as well.

To enable File History, simply click the Turn on button. However, some configuration options are available and should be considered first:

▶ **Change drive:** If you're not happy with the drive that File History selected, click this link to select a new one. The resulting page will help you select a new disk, if one is available, or a network location.

▶ **Exclude folders:** If you would like to exclude certain folder locations from being backed up, you can do so here. Remember that everything in your libraries, desktop, Favorites, and Contacts is backed up, so be sure to pick a folder inside one of those locations, since other locations are already omitted.

▶ **Advanced settings:** This important interface, shown in Figure 11-16, provides some fine-grained control over key File History functionality. You can change how often files are backed up, the size of the offline cache (which is the size of the File History backups replicated on your system disk), and the length of time to save backups. You can also use this interface to clean up (that is, delete) older backups and advertise your backup location to others on the homegroup.

▶ You can also manually run a File History backup at any time by revisiting the control panel and selecting Run now.

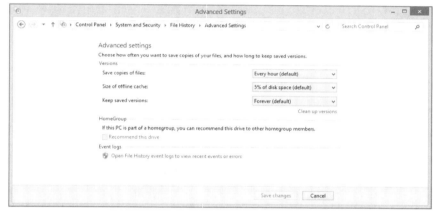

FIGURE 11-16: Be sure to spend some time examining these options.

Once you've configured File History to your liking, click Save changes to return to the main File History screen and then click Turn on. File History will indicate that it is saving copies of your files for the first time, but you are free to close the window, get back to work, and do other things. You can pretty much forget about File History until you need it.

Recovering Documents and Other Data Files with File History

When the time comes to recover a lost or previous version of a file, you have two basic ways to access the new File History restore functionality. You can relaunch the File History control panel and click the Restore personal files link. Or, you can use the far more discoverable method that's available right in File Explorer. This latter option makes more sense for two reasons. Oftentimes when you're looking for the previous version of a file, you're staring at that folder anyway. And when you trigger File History restore from File Explorer, it will navigate automatically to that location for you. So you won't need to hunt around for the file.

Since the second method makes so much more sense, we'll examine that. Navigating in File Explorer to the scene of the crime—a folder in which a file was deleted or overwritten, perhaps—you will find a History command in the Home tab, as shown in Figure 11-17.

▶ Since the Explorer ribbon is minimized by default, you may need to expand it before you will see the History command.

FIGURE 11-17: The History command opens File History restore for the current folder.

Click History to display the File History restore interface shown in Figure 11-18.

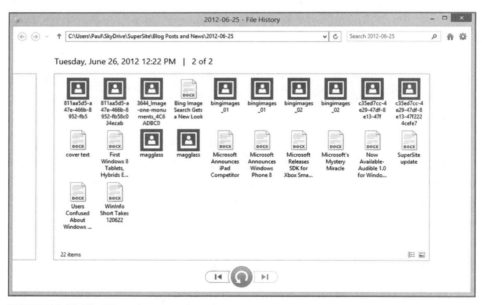

FIGURE 11-18: File History's restore interface

This window includes some interesting features. First, the current view shows the most recent file revisions, typically from the same day, and generally from a fairly recent time period. (If you left File History's Save copies of files feature on the default setting, these versions will be less than one-hour old.) There are navigational elements similar to those in File Explorer that allow you to go Back and Forward, and up one level, and you can type an arbitrary Explorer location into the address bar if you'd like.

The Options icon (which resembles a gear) in the top right provides numerous options related to icon view styles as well as some restore links. And the Windows Media Player-like control at the bottom of the window will let you restore any selected files and folders, or all of them. Or you can click the Rewind button to see earlier versions of the backed-up files. In fact, if you keep clicking this button, you'll travel back in time (not literally), seeing multiple revisions of frequently-accessed documents as you go.

If you find something you'd like to recover, you have two options: You can recover them directly to the same folder, overwriting whatever's there now; or you can recover them to a different location.

To recover files and folders to the same location, just select what you want and then click the big blue Recover button. The wizard will ask you if you'd like to replace the current files, skip any duplications, or choose which files to keep in the current folder; this interface, shown in Figure 11-19, is identical to the normal file remediation window one sees when copying files with Explorer.

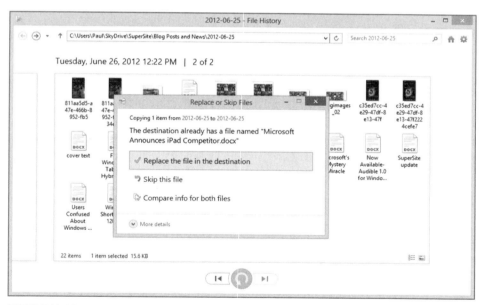

FIGURE 11-19: File History will ask you what to do with recovered files.

If you'd rather restore files to a new location so you can compare them side-by-side with the current version, click Options and then Restore to instead. A standard Save As dialog will appear, letting you pick the location you prefer.

> **NOTE** Yes, File History looks a lot like the Time Machine feature in Mac OS X, minus the ridiculous animations and graphics. To be fair, however, Microsoft implemented the underlying technologies behind File History several years before Apple copied *them* with Time Machine.

Better Together? Storage Spaces + File History

File History is an excellent way to ensure that your most valuable documents and other files are backed up regularly and available in different historical versions. Likewise, Storage Spaces is an amazing Windows 8 feature that provides redundant storage for your most valuable data, protecting them from a potential hard drive failure. Since File History works with secondary (or network-based) disks by default, you may be thinking that there's no benefit to using these two features together. That's crazy talk.

For the ultimate in data protection, consider creating a storage space with two or more disks in a two-way mirror configuration. Then, you can configure File History to back up your files to the space, instead of to a normal disk. In fact, you might want to advertise this location to other PCs in your homegroup so they can back up over the network to this new, super-reliable disk mirror. This will enhance the resiliency of all of your backups, no matter which PC you use on the home network.

Like peanut butter and chocolate, File History and Storage Spaces are two great tastes that go together. And they form the basis for an amazing centralized home network backup solution you can use with multiple PCs. Just a thought.

USING THE WINDOWS 8 RECOVERY TOOLS

Like previous versions of Windows, Windows 8 includes a full suite of system recovery tools that can help fix a non-booting PC and correct other system issues. Some of these tools are available from within Windows 8, but since you often need them most when Windows won't boot, they're also available outside of Windows as part of the Windows Recovery Environment, or WinRE. This environment can be accessed from the Windows Setup media (DVD or USB flash drive), from a dedicated system recovery disc (or drive) you can (and should) create, or at boot time when your PC first turns on. To start, let's examine how you can create a dedicated system recovery disc.

Creating a System Recovery Disc (or Drive)

Because these tools are so important and are usually needed when something horrible happens, we strongly recommend taking the time to make a system recovery disc (or USB-based drive) just in case. You can do this from the Recovery control panel. (To find it, open Control Panel and search for **recovery**. Then, choose Recovery, and *not* Windows 7 File Recovery.) This interface, called Advanced recovery tools, should resemble Figure 11-20, providing you with access to a few additional tools.

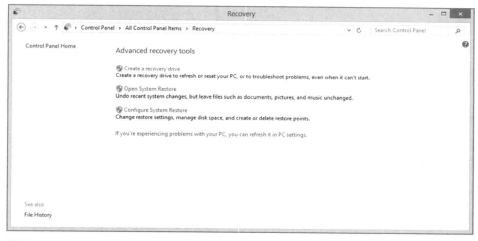

FIGURE 11-20: Recovery control panel

Click the link titled Create a recovery drive. After a User Account Control prompt, the Recovery Media Creator will run. This tool helps you create a bootable USB flash drive or, if you prefer, CD or DVD. (The flash drive must have a capacity of at least 256 MB, and its contents will be erased during the creation process.)

Which to choose? USB is faster and more reliable, but some PCs can't boot from a USB device, so you will want to test this before committing. We recommend starting with USB and going from there.

> ► The Recovery control panel won't even provide an option for optical disc media if a USB flash drive is inserted. So if you intend to make a disc, be sure to unplug any USB media first.

> ► The similar tool in Windows 7 could only create optical disc-based recovery media.

Booting to the Windows Recovery Environment

With Windows 8, you now have a wealth of riches when it comes to booting into the Windows Recovery Environment, or WinRE. Of course, you may not be feeling all that positive about things if you have to use these tools. Here are the various ways in which you can access WinRE.

... WITH THE SYSTEM RECOVERY DRIVE

If you created a system recovery drive, you can boot from this USB flash drive or disc, instead of from the PC's hard drive as usual, and load the Windows Recovery Environment. (Interrupting your PC's normal boot process varies from machine to machine, so study the firmware screen that appears when the PC restarts for clues or consult your PC's documentation for the answer.)

... WITH THE WINDOWS SETUP MEDIA

Your Windows 8 Setup media can also be used to run the Windows Recovery Environment. (Interrupting your PC's normal boot process varies from machine to machine, so study the firmware screen that appears when the PC restarts for clues or consult your PC's documentation for the answer.) When you boot from the Setup media, you will first be presented with a screen in which you select the language, time and currency format, and keyboard or input method. Click Next to skip this screen. When you do, you will be shown the Install now screen. Instead of clicking Install now, however, click the link titled Repair your computer. On the Choose an option screen that appears next, click Troubleshoot.

... BY INTERRUPTING THE NORMAL PC BOOT

In previous Windows versions, you could interrupt the Windows boot process by holding down the F8 key immediately after the BIOS screen and before the Windows loading animation. If you did it just right, you'd enter the Windows Recovery Environment.

Windows 8 makes this much easier. Instead of trying to interrupt the boot manually—somewhat impossible on touch-screen tablets in particular, but difficult on all Windows 8 PCs because the OS boots so fast—simply navigate into the Metro-style PC Settings interface and visit the bottom of the General area. There, under Advanced startup, you'll see a Restart now button, as in Figure 11-21. Click that to enter the Windows Recovery Environment.

... FROM THE WINDOWS 8 BOOT MENU

If you have a PC configured for dual-boot (that is, you can choose between two or more operating systems at boot time), you can access WinRE from the boot menu that's already in place. From the main menu, titled Choose an operating system screen, click Change defaults or choose other options. Then, in the Options screen, click Choose other options, and then Troubleshoot.

FIGURE 11-21: A new way to boot into the recovery environment

Using the Windows Recovery Environment

However you access these tools, you will eventually reach a Choose your option screen that has a Troubleshoot option. From the Troubleshoot screen—the heart of WinRE—you will find the following tools, many of which are accessible via the Advanced options:

▶ **Refresh your PC and Reset your PC:** These tools collectively make up a new Windows 8 capability called Push Button Reset. It's so important, that it's examined in the next section.

▶ **System Restore:** This is a legacy recovery capability from previous Windows versions that lets you reset the PC configuration to an earlier time, usually because you've installed a bad hardware driver that has made the system less stable. This feature is discussed later in the chapter.

▶ **System Image Recovery:** Another legacy feature and part of Windows Backup, this option lets you recover Windows using an image-based backup. Generally speaking, most users will not use Windows Backup with Windows 8, but you can use this option to recover a Windows 7- or Windows 8-based install if needed.

▶ **Automatic Repair:** This useful option should be your first stop if you are having issues booting into Windows. Simply click Automatic Repair and WinRE will diagnose your PC, check for disk errors, and attempt a repair. More often than not, this will simply work and you'll be up and running in no time.

▶ *This tool is analogous to Startup Repair from the Windows 7 version of WinRE, though it fixes other errors as well.*

> **NOTE**   If you sign in with a local account, you may be prompted to sign in here as well.

> ▶ **Command Prompt:** Designed for advanced users that know their way around a DOS-style command prompt, this interface provides access to a full slate of useful command-line tools, including diskpart.exe, recover.exe, and more.

> ▶ **Startup Settings:** This will apply many common troubleshooting configurations to Windows—a low-resolution video mode, Safe Mode, and so on—to ensure you can boot into a balky install and fix problems from the OS itself.

Push Button Reset

When you encounter a problem with your PC, be it performance related or otherwise, you can now undergo a surprisingly fast process in which Windows 8 is quickly wiped out and reinstalled in a factory-fresh condition. This doesn't require mucking around with a Setup DVD or USB media, and it won't take half the day as it did with Windows 7. Instead, Windows 8 includes a new feature called Push Button Reset, and it very well may be the single greatest new feature in this operating system.

Push Button Reset is exposed as two separate tools called Reset your PC and Refresh your PC, respectively. Both are available from the Windows Recovery Environment, as discussed previously. But you can also access both from the Metro-style PC Settings interface and from the desktop-based Recovery control panel. Microsoft clearly wants to make these capabilities readily available to everyone.

> ▶ **Reset Your PC** deletes all of your personal data, apps, and settings from the PC, and then reinstalls Windows to its factory-fresh, day-one condition. During the process, everything on the PC hard drive will be erased, so you may need to back up crucial documents and other data first.

> ▶ **Refresh Your PC** performs similarly, but this amazing utility retains all of your personal data, settings, and Metro-style apps (but not legacy desktop applications), reapplying them to Windows after it has been reinstalled.

▶ To be clear, desktop-based applications like Microsoft Office and Adobe Photoshop will need to be reinstalled after using Refresh your PC.

In either configuration, Push Button Reset is amazingly fast. According to Microsoft's own performance analysis, most PC Reset operations will finish in roughly 6 minutes, and a PC Refresh will take a bit over 8 minutes. These figures have been borne out in our own usage. In fact, they're conservative.

The impact of this tool cannot be overstated. With Windows 7, you could perform a clean install of the operating system in about 20 minutes, a major improvement over previous versions. But that didn't include the time and effort required to first back up your data, install updates, install applications, copy the data back, and then reapply all of your personal settings. With Windows 7, you typically spent the better part of day restoring a PC in this fashion. And it's a time-consuming and boring process with lots of downtime.

But it gets better. Push Button Reset is also vastly superior to the old ways of wiping out a PC because you can do it at any time. If something goes wrong, just Refresh the PC and all will be well. With the Windows 7 tools, you really had to be prepared, and then had to go through great time and effort to do it properly.

Critics and conspiracy theorists will point out, correctly, that Push Button Reset isn't a complete PC recovery solution because it doesn't help at all with traditional, Explorer-based applications like Microsoft Office and Photoshop. And that's a fair enough statement, though if Windows 8 is truly successful, these types of applications will soon only be used by power users and business users for the most part. So Push Button Reset, combined with other data backup features in Windows 8, does present a fairly complete solution for most average users, especially as they replace their old applications with new Metro-style apps over time.

Regardless, even those who do need to install and update a handful of traditional Windows applications after the fact will still experience an amazing reduction in the time it takes to complete the entire process. This one feature has revolutionized the way users restore Windows and get back to work. You're going to love it.

The following two sections discuss how you can use PC Reset and PC Refresh, respectively. As you may recall, these tools are available from the Windows Recovery Environment, but also from PC Settings (in the Metro environment) and the Recovery control panel. Because these interfaces are simpler and easier to reach, you will often proactively use Push Button Reset, and not as the result of a calamity that renders your PC non-bootable. But you can always use these tools from WinRE if you prefer.

FINDING PUSH BUTTON RESET (METRO VERSION)

To access the Metro-style interface for Reset your PC, visit PC Settings and navigate to General. Near the bottom of the list of General PC settings, you will see the options Refresh your PC without affecting your files and Remove everything and reinstall Windows. These represent Refresh your PC and Reset your PC, respectively.

Now, follow the instructions in one of the following two sections, depending on which you'd like to accomplish.

USING PC RESET: WIPING OUT WINDOWS AND STARTING OVER

When you click the Get Started button under Reset your PC and start over, a full-screen Metro-style notification like the one in Figure 11-22 will appear.

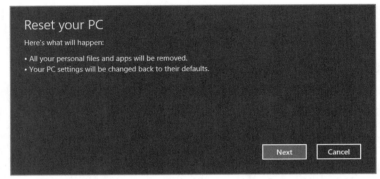

FIGURE 11-22: The Reset your PC screen explains what's about to happen.

▶ Again, PC Reset is about reinstalling Windows from scratch and starting over. Nothing else will be retained. So be sure to back up first.

This notification alerts you that the PC Reset process will delete all of your personal settings, files, and apps.

Click Next to continue.

If you have more than one drive, PC Reset will ask whether you'd like to remove all files from all drives, or just from the drive on which Windows is installed. Make a choice, and then PC Reset will ask you to choose between quick and thorough file removal types, as shown in Figure 11-23. The second, more thorough option is useful if you wish to sell or give away the PC to others, but the first, quicker version is what you'll want when you're simply resetting the PC for your own uses.

▶ The thorough option will dramatically slow the reset process. Microsoft tells us that this PC Reset version uses a Department of Defense-style, three-pass disk wipe to do its thing.

Next, PC Reset declares that it is ready to reset the PC. Click the Reset button to continue.

FIGURE 11-23: Do it quick ... or do it right.

PC Reset will reboot the computer and quickly reinstall Windows. Your customized settings, data, and apps will all be deleted. After a few minutes and a few reboots, you will be presented with a shortened version of the Windows Setup procedure, during which you will agree to the Windows license terms and then complete the out-of-box experience (OOBE), where you configure some features and sign in for the first time. (Chapter 2 describes this procedure.) This makes sense, as you are essentially configuring this PC as if it were brand new.

Once this process is complete, you will sign in and arrive at the Start screen.

USING PC REFRESH: RESTORING WINDOWS ALONG WITH SETTINGS, DATA, AND METRO-STYLE APPS

When you click the Get Started button under Refresh your PC without affecting your files, a full-screen Metro-style notification will appear, alerting you that the PC Refresh process will retain all of your personal settings, files, and apps. However, traditional Windows desktop applications will be removed.

Click Next to continue.

PC Refresh is now ready to reset the PC while saving your personal settings, data, and Metro-style apps. Click the Refresh button to continue.

Your PC will restart and undergo the process of setting aside your personal settings, data, and apps, reinstalling Windows, and reapplying those items back to the new install. This will occur over your device's firmware screen or, on a traditional PC, on a screen that resembles the Windows boot animation.

After a few reboots, Windows 8 will simply return to your familiar lock screen. Sign in as before and Windows will indicate that it is preparing for a few moments. Then you'll be returned to the Start screen, just as you left it.

You should then navigate to the Windows desktop, where you'll find a web document listing the (classic) applications that PC Refresh removed. This list will help you get started reinstalling, as many web-based apps will be helpfully hyperlinked.

▶ *Obviously, you should still ensure that your data has been backed up before using Refresh your PC. Better safe than sorry.*

ACCESSING SYSTEM IMAGE BACKUP AND RECOVERY FUNCTIONALITY WITH WINDOWS BACKUP

In Windows 7, the backup and recovery story centered on a very useful tool called Windows Backup, which offered two basic features: It could be used to back up certain locations and their contained data to another hard disk, optical disc, or network share, and it could make system image backups of the entire PC, which could be used to recover Windows, its data and customizations, and applications and application states.

Windows Backup seems like the full-meal deal, so you may be surprised to discover that it's been relegated to also-ran status in Windows 8. Yes, it's still there. But Microsoft went to great pains to hide it. So naturally, we're going to tell you how to find it.

First, though, a short discussion about why this happened. If you've been reading this chapter, you know that Windows 8 includes amazing new tools related to storage, backup, and recovery. And that these tools separately allow you to fully recover a PC, and, optionally, all of your data, settings, and Metro-style apps in just minutes (Push Button Reset). Further, they let you recover not just backups of your most important documents and other data, but also an extensive collection of data file revisions (File History). Both of these tools separately answer different needs. But collectively, they accomplish almost all of what most people used Windows Backup for, and more important, they do so far more quickly.

This reasoning won't matter very much to you if you have a collection of Windows Backup-based backups from Windows 7 that you still want to access. Or perhaps you're simply just familiar with Windows Backup, like how it works, and wish to continue using this solution.

You can. But, boy, does Microsoft make it difficult.

Try to find Windows Backup from Start Screen Search, or by searching the classic Control Panel, and you'll come up blank. The term *backup* yields results for File History only, and a search for *windows backup* will actually come up empty. It's almost like they don't want you to find it.

> But seriously, you should be using the new tools in Windows 8, and not Windows Backup. The only real exception is that you have to access a previously created backup for some reason. That's really why this tool is still in Windows 8.

But fear not, it's there. Just search for *recovery* instead—from the Start screen or Control Panel—and you'll see a result called Windows 7 File Recovery. This, as it turns out, is both the way to access Windows Backup and a none-too-subtle reminder that Microsoft really wants you to consider using something else.

Say the magic words correctly and you'll see the Windows 7 File Recovery control panel shown in Figure 11-24. From this window, you can do everything you used to do in Windows Backup.

Just don't tell Microsoft we told you about this one.

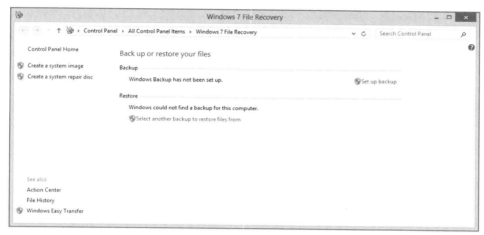

FIGURE 11-24: Windows Backup lives in Windows 8 as the Windows 7 File Recovery control panel.

WHAT'S MISSING: CLOUD BACKUP

While Windows 8 offers a fairly complete selection of backup and recovery tools, many of which are discussed elsewhere in this chapter, there is one key piece of the puzzle missing, and that's cloud-based backup. That is, in addition to backing up key data locally to another drive attached to your PC or, better still, to a completely different PC or device on your home network, you should consider having an off-site data recovery solution in place. This will provide that final measure of safety should a real-world disaster occur, such as a fire or theft.

To better understand the scope of this issue, consider how Windows 8's various backup and recovery tools work together to keep your PC and its contained data safe. At the most basic level, you can use the Push Button Reset functionality to quickly recover the operating system and, optionally, your data, settings, and Metro-style apps. So even in the worst-case scenario, software-wise, all you'll lose are your traditional Windows applications, which will need to be reinstalled.

Of course, recovering the operating system is only one layer of safety and this won't help with your precious data—documents, photos, and so on—if the PC's hard drive fails. So Windows 8 also offers a nice File History feature, which backs up not just your data, but the various revisions of your data as well. And it does so to secondary storage—another hard drive attached to your PC—or to a network location, further enhancing resiliency with physical separation.

You can enhance data storage in general, or File History specifically, with Storage Spaces as well. This amazing feature lets you mirror data across two or three disks, again providing protection in the event of hardware failure.

Old-timers, or those who simply can't let go of the previous ways of doing things, can take advantage of Windows 7-era backup and recovery features too, including various troubleshooting tools, System Restore for repairing bad driver installs and other issues, and even Windows Backup, for complete end-to-end PC image backups.

But none of these solutions will help if your home is destroyed, or the PC and its hard disks are stolen. What you need to complete this end-to-end backup and recovery picture is off-site storage. You need cloud backup.

Sadly, this is the one backup and recovery solution that Microsoft doesn't explicitly provide in Windows 8. You could, of course, pay for SkyDrive additional storage, use the SkyDrive application or a third-party solution to provide Explorer-based access to Microsoft's cloud service, and then back up data in that fashion. We happen to like using SkyDrive for this purpose, since it keeps valuable documents, photos, and other files synced between PCs and the cloud. The SkyDrive app's folder structure can be seen in Figure 11-25.

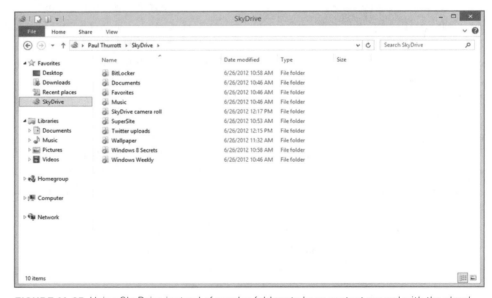

FIGURE 11-25: Using SkyDrive instead of regular folders to keep content synced with the cloud.

Or you could use a third-party service such as CrashPlan—which we're both using because of its low cost and excellent performance—Carbonite, or similar.

While we wish that Windows 8 completed the picture, there are certainly enough cloud backup services out there to satisfy anyone's needs. Just be sure to use one of these services, as ultimately, the responsibility to protect your data is yours alone.

SUMMARY

On the face of things, a topic like storage, backup, and recovery doesn't seem very exciting. But here's an amazing fact: Of all the new features and functionality in Windows 8, our two favorite, by far—Storage Spaces and Push Button Reset—are covered in this chapter. What a turn of events.

It all starts with the new storage features in Windows 8, the key of which is Storage Spaces, a way to elegantly and easily mirror multiple disks of multiple types and sizes, creating redundant pools of storage you can use as you see fit. Building on this is File History, an improved take on the Previous Versions feature from Windows 7 that automatically backs up multiple versions of your most important data files so you can always find the one you want.

Windows 8 also improves on the Windows recovery toolset and in a dramatic fashion. There are new and improved versions of legacy recovery tools, of course, but also brand-new tools like PC Reset and PC Refresh, components of a Push Button Reset functionality that lets you very quickly take a balky Windows install and make it new again.

Put this all together and you see a version of Windows that is safe and reliable and easily and quickly made right should something go wrong. This alone is an amazing achievement. That it is but a small part of the list in improvements in Windows 8 suggests that this is a mighty new OS release indeed.

CHAPTER 12

Accounts and Security

IN THIS CHAPTER

▶ Understanding accounts and account types in Windows 8

▶ Managing accounts with PC Settings

▶ Using advanced account management with Control Panel

▶ Using Microsoft Account features with other account types

▶ Understanding the new security features in Windows 8

▶ Protecting your PC from malware and viruses with Windows Defender

▶ Protecting your PC when Windows isn't running

▶ Preventing malware downloads with Windows SmartScreen

▶ Understanding the Windows 8 improvements to Action Center and other security features

Everyone who uses Windows knows that you typically sign in, or "log in" as we used to say, to the PC using an account with which unique settings, documents and files, and even applications are associated. The types of accounts we've used in Windows have certainly evolved over the years, but for the most part, there have been two basic kinds of sign-ins: domain accounts, which are used exclusively by corporations, and local accounts, which are specific only to the PC on which they are used; home users and most individuals have always used this latter account type.

In Windows 8, Microsoft is introducing a new type of sign-in that is tied to a Microsoft account, or what used to be called a Windows Live ID. (With Windows 8, Microsoft is eliminating Windows Live as a brand, but is continuing its most popular products and services, often with new names.) As you'll discover, this new account type is really just a formalization of a capability that debuted in Windows 7, but it takes on new prominence in Windows 8 thanks to this system's pervasive PC-to-PC sync capabilities.

Windows 8 also provides interesting new choices for signing in, augmenting the long-lived password system with some new choices that may make more sense on today's modern Windows devices and PCs. As always, securing your PC against electronic and human attack is job one for Windows 8, and in this version of Windows, you have more tools than ever to help ensure that your PC and its valuable data are safe.

But it all begins with your user account. So let's look at that first.

USER ACCOUNTS

Once relegated only to the corporate market, where they have always made sense because of their security and permissions boundaries, user accounts are central to today's PC experience—so central, in fact, that you establish your user account when you first install Windows or set up your new PC.

Of course, user accounts aren't generally as restrictive at home as they are at work. It's your PC, after all, and most people rightly feel that they should be able to do anything they want on their PC. So that first user account you create, during Windows Setup, is automatically an administrator-class account, providing the permissions and access control that one would expect.

▶ Families can further manage accounts using parental controls, which we'll examine later in the chapter.

These local user accounts, or what we used to call workgroup accounts, work well enough for what they are. And they allow for some niceties, even at home. You can create multiple accounts on a single PC, giving users their own sign-in identity, along with its associated custom settings (desktop wallpapers and so on) and Windows and application configurations.

But local user accounts are starting to show the strain of time, and as our PC usage changes, so do the needs we place on them. For example, most people don't bother to protect their own user accounts with a password, which can have huge ramifications in the event of a stolen PC. Local accounts are literally local to that one PC and thus hard, if not impossible, to replicate across machines; if you have more than one PC, as so many of us do now, making each one look and work the same is tedious. Local accounts make home network sharing difficult, too, which is why Microsoft created the homegroup sharing technique for Windows 7.

What's interesting is that Microsoft basically solved these issues over a decade ago when they instituted the Active Directory domain services scheme in Windows Server. This system, which is used by corporations around the world, provides a more centralized approach to user accounts (and other things). So instead of signing in to a single PC and locking all of your personalized settings to that one machine, you sign in, instead, to the domain. And if you need to access a different machine, your customized experience can travel with you, so to speak, from PC to PC. With this scheme, the settings you typically think of being associated with an account are no longer locked into a single PC.

Active Directory is powerful and interesting, but it's also far too complex for a home network and of course requires expensive and complex servers in addition to the PCs that people actually use each day. So this system isn't well-suited for regular users at home.

So for Windows 8, Microsoft has created a new type of user account, based on your Microsoft account (previously called Windows Live ID) that provides many of the niceties of Active Directory but with none of the complexity. In fact, for most people, signing in to a Windows 8 PC with a Microsoft account is just as easy as doing so with a traditional local account. But there are numerous advantages to doing so.

So let's examine them as part of a wider discussion about the types of accounts you can use with Windows 8.

Understanding Account Types

Windows 8 lets you sign in using three different types of accounts: domain, local, and Microsoft.

DOMAIN ACCOUNTS

Domain accounts are used by corporations that utilize an Active Directory infrastructure running on top of Windows Server. The account is centrally managed by your employer, as are whatever permissions and capabilities you may be able to enjoy.

You connect Windows 8 to a domain as you did with previous Windows versions, using the advanced system control panel. Once the domain is configured, you reboot the PC and then sign in with your domain account's username and password. In use, Windows 8 works almost identically to a local user account, but you lose some of the integration pieces that are special to Microsoft account sign-ins. As we'll see in just a bit, there is a simple way to mitigate that issue.

LOCAL ACCOUNTS

In Windows XP, Vista, and 7, most home users signed in to their PC using a local account, or an account that is, literally, local to that one PC. Local accounts are typically one of two account types, administrator or standard. An administrator essentially has complete control of the system and can make any configuration changes

► You can bypass this limitation by entering the credentials for an administrator account. You do so using a feature called User Account Control, which we'll examine later in this chapter.

they want. A standard user can use most application software and many Windows services, but is prevented from accessing features that could harm the system. For example, standard users cannot install most applications, change the system time, or access certain Control Panel applets.

In previous Windows versions, most people simply used an administrator-type account because standard user accounts were so limiting and annoying. But with the move to multi-PC households and the PC-to-PC sync capabilities one gets with using a Microsoft account instead of a local account, our expectation is that the vast majority of Windows 8 users will no longer use local accounts. It's still supported, of course, but it's just depreciated.

MICROSOFT ACCOUNTS

Signing in to a Microsoft account is now the default, and preferred, way of doing things. A Microsoft account provides you with all of the benefits of a local account—simplicity and the ability to have both administrators and less privileged users—plus the benefits of the multi-PC settings replication of a domain account, and, of course, integration with Microsoft's online services and third-party services like Facebook, Twitter, and more.

But the Microsoft account is more than a nicety. It's required for many of the Metro-style apps that are built into Windows 8, including the productivity apps—Mail, Calendar, People, and Messaging—the digital media and Xbox apps—Xbox Music, Xbox Video, and Xbox LIVE Games—and more. Windows 8 was designed to integrate deeply with a Microsoft account, much like Windows Phone before it. And a Microsoft account is super easy to use.

For these reasons, we believe that signing in with a Microsoft account is the obvious choice for most Windows 8 users. Furthermore, we pretty much assume that you're using a Microsoft account throughout this book because of the advantages of doing so.

There's just one problem. In some cases, you can't sign in to your PC with a Microsoft account the first time you set up Windows 8. For example, if your PC is offline the first time you use Windows 8, a Microsoft account won't even be offered. But the more obvious example, perhaps, is a work PC: There's no way that corporate will let you or other users bypass the built-in security features of their carefully crafted policies and sign in with your personal Microsoft account.

If only there was a way around this limitation.

Making the Most of a Domain or Local Account

If you are signing in to a PC with a domain or local account, there are some changes you can make to provide you with the best possible experience. Which you do will depend somewhat on whether you're currently signing in to Windows 8 with a local account or a domain account. These changes include:

▶ **Switch a local account to a Microsoft account:** If you opted out of the Microsoft account sign-in when you first set up Windows 8, perhaps because you were confused by this new account type and simply wanted things to be as close as possible to the way it was in Windows 7, Microsoft actually lets you change your local account after the fact and switch it to a Microsoft account.

▶ *You cannot do this with a domain account. Only a local account can be switched to a Microsoft account.*

To make this change, navigate to PC Settings and then Users. Then, under Your account, click the Switch to a Microsoft account button, as shown in Figure 12-1. *Voila!* Problem solved.

▶ *You can also use this same interface to switch from a Microsoft account to a local account. And no, we can't think of a single reason why you'd want to do this.*

FIGURE 12-1: You can convert your local account to a Microsoft account at any time.

▶ **Connect a domain account to a Microsoft account:** If you're using a domain account, you can't switch it to a Microsoft account. But you *can* link your domain sign-in with your Microsoft account, achieving the same benefits as you'd get by simply signing in with a Microsoft account. In the business, this is what we call a "best of both worlds" solution.

To do so, navigate to PC Settings and then Users. Under Your account, click the Connect your Microsoft account button. When you do, the screen shown in Figure 12-2 appears. Here, you choose which PC settings you'd like to sync with your domain account.

FIGURE 12-2: You can connect a domain account to a Microsoft account and even choose which settings to sync.

After choosing which settings to sync, you will sign in to your Microsoft account and confirm or enter your security verification information, just as you do when you sign in with this type of account normally. And from now on, you can use Microsoft's account services—and the bundled apps in Windows 8 that take advantage of them—seamlessly, without needing to sign in with each app. Actually, it's even better than that: Some apps simply won't work unless you sign in with a Microsoft account. This linking process makes them work.

WHY THIS MAY NOT WORK

Okay, there's a huge gotcha to this scheme. (You had to sort of expect there was going to be one.) It goes like this: Your domain administrators simply may not allow it. Whether they do will depend on a number of factors, but it all boils down to whether your environment is highly controlled. So all you can do is try and hope for the best.

▶ **Sign in to app groups with a Microsoft account:** There is a third approach, one that provides a more limited way to access some Microsoft account goodness, but without changing your domain or local account in any way. That is, instead of linking or switching your existing sign-in account, you can simply try to run one of the connected apps in Windows 8 and then sign in when prompted by a screen that will resemble Figure 12-3.

FIGURE 12-3: If you can't or won't use a Microsoft account, you can instead sign in to various app groups.

This approach isn't as sophisticated as using (or linking) a Microsoft account. You'll need to sign in a few different times, to different app groups—Microsoft considers the productivity (or what it calls "communications") apps to be one group, for example, and the Xbox (media and games) apps to be a separate group. And you don't get the PC-to-PC settings sync functionality that's available with a real Microsoft account sign-in. But if you don't have a choice—or are just really, really stubborn—this will at least let you use the built-in Metro apps to their fullest.

Managing Accounts

In previous Windows versions, we managed local user accounts in Control Panel, a desktop user interface that dates back to the earliest days of Windows. But in Windows 8, basic user account management tasks now occur within the Metro-based PC Settings instead, while, confusingly, a few more advanced or esoteric features can still be found in legacy control panels. So you may find yourself moving back and forth between the two environments depending on your needs.

Let's start with the basics.

MANAGING ACCOUNTS IN PC SETTINGS

Like many Metro interfaces, the Users section in PC Settings is almost disarmingly simple. As you can see in Figure 12-4, this UI lets you manage features related to your own and other user accounts. (This figure displays the version of this screen that most users will see, since it depicts a Microsoft account.)

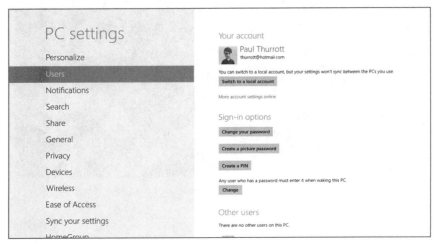

FIGURE 12-4: PC Settings provides a new user management interface.

These features, which vary somewhat depending on the type of account you use to sign in, can include:

▶ **Switch to a local account/Switch to a Microsoft account:** If you're signed in with a Microsoft account, there is a Switch to a local account button that will let you do just that, albeit at the expense of losing all of the included functionality one gets with such an account type. If you are signed in with a local account, however, you will see a Switch to a Microsoft account button instead.

▶ **Connect your Microsoft account/Disconnect your Microsoft account:** Those who are signed in with a domain account (used only in corporations and other businesses) will see a button, Connect your Microsoft account, as described earlier in this chapter. If you've already connected your domain account to a Microsoft account, you will see a Disconnect your Microsoft account button instead.

▶ **Change your password:** Those with local or Microsoft account sign-ins can change their password at any time using this button. Domain users will not see this option; instead, you can type Ctrl + Alt + Del and choose the Change a password option from the full-screen menu that appears. However, your ability to actually change your password will be based on corporate policy. (And, in fact, many businesses may require you to change passwords on a regular schedule, whether you want to or not.)

▶ **Create a picture password/Change a picture password:** With the advent of touch-based Windows devices, including tablets and other touch screen devices, Windows 8 now offers two fun and efficient new ways to sign in to your computer: picture password and PIN (the latter of which is described next). Neither replaces your normal password. Instead, you can use either to implicitly sign in to the system using your actual password, but using a method that is simpler (and, in this case, a bit more fun) than a normal password. This is especially useful because tapping out a long password on a touch screen can be tedious.

A picture password is essentially a photo over which you trace any combination of three circles, lines, and/or taps, using the device's touch screen. You might imagine a picture of a family member where you "poke" them in each eye and then draw a smile over their lips as an example of this type of sign-in (though not necessarily one you would want to choose to use, since such a combination of swipes is fairly obvious and could undermine the security of your PC).

Creating a picture password requires completing a short wizard. After providing your password to prove that this is your account, you're prompted to choose the photo you'll use. Obviously, you can use any photo of your choosing.

Once you've selected the picture and the wizard has verified this selection, you'll be prompted to set up your gestures, as shown in Figure 12-5. Here, you choose the three gestures you want to use—again, any combination of three circles, lines, and/or taps—as your sign-in.

FIGURE 12-5: Creating a picture password

The wizard will make you repeat the gestures to ensure that you've got the sequence memorized correctly, and then you're good to go. You can later change the picture password or remove it.

COMMON SENSE SECURITY TIPS FOR PICTURE PASSWORD

With the understanding that common sense is a key aspect of anyone's personal security regimen—and, on the flip side, that human error is almost certainly the number one factor behind most security mishaps—we feel compelled to remind readers that picture password, like any other authentication scheme, is only as secure as you make it. So use some common sense when creating a picture password, keeping the following tips in mind:

▶ **Complexity:** It's not hard to guess that a picture password that uses a person's headshot as the picture most likely involves poking both eyes and making a smile across the lips. Be more creative than that and use a photo that is more complex, with less obvious points of interest.

▶ **Use different gestures:** Three identical straight lines do not secure a picture password make. Consider mixing it up, using a combination of taps, straight/curved lines (in both directions), and circles that move in both directions (clockwise and counter-clockwise).

▶ **Physically shield the screen:** You wouldn't let strangers watch you enter your bank card's PIN at a cash machine. Don't let onlookers see your picture password . . . no matter how cute you think it is.

▶ **Clean the screen:** Today's touch-screen devices leave indelible smudges each time you tap or gesture. So be sure to keep your screen clean, reducing the chance that someone could tilt the device in the light and quickly guess which gestures you use to sign in.

▶ You're not locked into using this or any other sign-in type. You could have a password, a picture password, and a PIN all configured for the same account and then choose which to use at sign-in time.

▶ **Create (or change) a PIN:** If you've ever used a smartphone, you know that four-digit PINs, or personal identification numbers, are the norms for securely signing in on such devices. This sign-in option allows you to use the same convenient sign-in type on your Windows PC or device, and while it's particularly nice for touch-screen devices, we've both switched to using this sign-in type on our traditional desktop PCs, too, since it's so fast. Setting up a PIN is very straightforward, and each digit must be a number.

NOTE Oddly enough, you can use the picture password and PIN sign-in types
even with a domain account. However, some corporations have very strict password policies, so as is the case with other options in this chapter, you may not
be able to use these features with a work-based domain account.

▶ **Add a user:** If you select the Add a user link under Other users, you'll be presented with the new full-screen interface shown in Figure 12-6. It's set up for
a Microsoft account by default, but you can click the link titled Sign in without a Microsoft account to configure a traditional local user account instead.

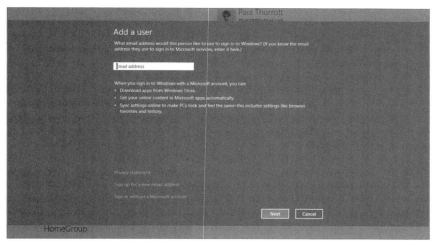

FIGURE 12-6: Add a user, Metro-styled

So, yes, you can mix and match Microsoft and local accounts (and even domain
accounts) on a single PC, though our general rule about using Microsoft accounts
exclusively when possible still applies for your own PCs.

ADVANCED USER MANAGEMENT WITH CONTROL PANEL

PC Settings is cute and everything, but if you want to dive into the nitty-gritty of
user account management, you'll need to visit the old-school Control Panel interface
instead. And yes, you still want to know about this interface even if you're not particularly interested in advanced features. And that's because there are certain things
related to account management that you can only do from Control Panel.

For example, the very first account you create with Windows 8 is always an
administrator-class account, and that's true whether that account is a Microsoft

account, as recommended, or a traditional local account. But when you create other accounts, as explained earlier, those accounts are not administrator-type accounts. And the Metro-style PC Settings interface doesn't offer any way to change them.

But Control Panel does. In fact, Control Panel provides so much additional functionality with regards to user accounts that it seems a shame to ignore it.

Of course, you need to find it first. The easiest way is via Start Search: Display the Start screen, type **user**, select the Settings filter in the right pane, and then choose User Accounts in the results list. This displays the old-school User Accounts control panel, as shown in Figure 12-7.

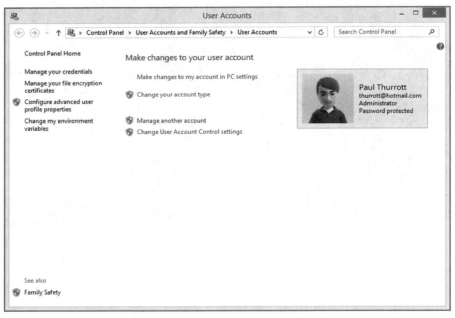

FIGURE 12-7: User Accounts control panel

▶ If you have only configured one user account, you cannot, however, change it from an administrator-type account to a standard user account. You must always have one administrator configured on the PC.

Here are some of the user account–related tasks you can only complete using Control Panel:

▶ **Change an account type:** As noted previously, the first account you configure on your PC—whether it's a Microsoft account or a local user account—is an administrator-type account. But what about subsequent accounts? As it turns out, all subsequent account additions—be they Microsoft or local accounts—are created as standard users, not administrators. This may be desirable, but if you'd like to change an account from one type to the other, you can do so.

To change an account's type, click the link Manage another account in the User Accounts control panel. This will change the display to resemble Figure 12-8, where you can choose an account to change.

FIGURE 12-8: The Manage Accounts interface lets you configure user accounts.

Select the account you wish to modify to display a screen like that in Figure 12-9. Here, you can see a secondary Microsoft account that was automatically configured as a standard account type when it was added to the system.

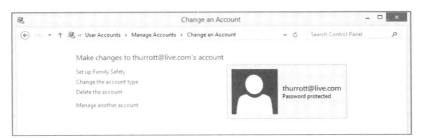

FIGURE 12-9: If it doesn't say Administrator above "Password protected," it's not an administrator.

Click the Change the account type link, choose Administrator, and then click the Change Account Type button. Now, you can see as in Figure 12-10, that this other Microsoft account is an administrator too.

▶ When working with a local account, you can also use this screen to change the account name, create or change the password, set up parental controls, or delete the account.

▶ When working with a Microsoft account, you can also use this screen to set up parental controls or delete the account (from the PC).

FIGURE 12-10: The secondary Microsoft account has been transformed from peasant to lord.

▶ **Manage User Account Control:** In Windows Vista, Microsoft introduced what was then a very controversial feature called User Account Control, or UAC, which took advantage of Microsoft's efforts to *componentize* Windows by dividing each of the system's functional entities, or components, into one of two groups: those that require administrative privileges and those that don't. Those that don't would just work and you could just go about your day and not really think about the security implications of anything underpinning the system.

But then there are those other components that do require an administrator-class account to actually work. Those components are a bit trickier. These components will trigger a UAC dialog, or prompt, that must be bypassed before you can continue whatever task you are trying to complete.

UAC is theoretically annoying, but it's been refined over the past two Windows versions to be, well, less noisy. That is, it doesn't rear its head very often any-more, and if you're logged in with administrator privileges—and chances are, you are—it will rarely do more than interject a small "Are you sure?" type dialog to interrupt your workflow.

This interruption will vary according to what you're trying to do—a UAC prompt appears when you try to install an application, for example—and according to what type of user account you're using. But the important thing to note is that the presentation of UAC prompts hasn't really changed since Windows 7. So unless you've been using Windows XP for the past few years, you already get the drill. It works much as it did in Windows 7 and is much less annoying than it was in Windows Vista.

Configuring User Account Control works as it did in Windows 7, via the User Account Control Settings control panel. So there's no need to waste time on it: UAC works as before, isn't annoying, and shouldn't be messed with.

NOTE Okay, there is one interesting side note about UAC in Windows 8: One place you'll never see this prompt is in any of Windows 8's Metro experiences. That's because UAC is a desktop technology, and the Metro environment has its own more pervasive protections built in and designed to protect the OS from exactly the kinds of issues that UAC, too, is aimed at.

▶ **Enable and configure Family Safety:** Microsoft first provided pervasive Windows-based parental controls functionality in Windows Vista, providing parents with a way to create and enforce settings related to computer usage, including a web filter (for allowing and disallowing individual websites and downloading), time limits, games, and applications (including which can and cannot be used).

In Windows 8, Microsoft is carrying forward the parental control functionality from its predecessor, and it works almost exactly the same way, with a few useful improvements. Parental controls, called Family Safety in Windows 8, can be applied only to non-administrator accounts—including Microsoft accounts, which is indeed new to Windows 8—and is administered one account at a time.

▶ Parental controls are not available when you sign in as a domain user.

There are two ways to add parental controls to an account. You may recall that when you add a new account to the system, it's silently created as a standard user account, and not as an administrator. So as an added nicety, Windows 8 provides a check box option, shown in Figure 12-11, which lets you enable Family Safety right when the account is created.

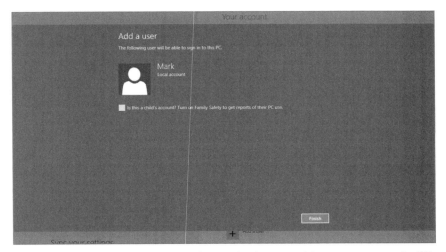

FIGURE 12-11: You can enable parental controls when you add a new account to the PC.

Or, you can add parental controls to an account after it has been created. To do so, select Manage another account from the main User Accounts control panel, select the account you want to manage, and then select Set up Family Safety. The Family Safety interface resembles Figure 12-12.

FIGURE 12-12: Family Safety helps you protect your children online and on the PC.

If you're familiar with the parental controls functionality that was included in Windows 7, all of the functionality from that release carries over into Windows 8. But there are a few useful additions in this release, too. For example, where the Windows 7 parental controls allowed you to specify the hours of each day that the child could use the PC—this feature is now called "curfew"—Windows 8 adds the ability to limit how many hours they can use the PC each day as well. Additionally, Family Safety integrates with Windows Store so you can see and control which Metro-style apps and games your child downloads, based on country-specific ratings; in the United States, we use ESRB (Entertainment Software Ratings Board) ratings.

▶ **Enable the Guest account:** While you can go to great lengths to protect standard user accounts with parental controls, sometimes all you're looking for is a single, temporary user account with standard user privileges that anyone can use. As with previous Windows versions, Windows 8 includes such an account, called the Guest account, and it's a safe and easy way to let others use your

PC without worrying that they're going to view, modify, or delete any crucial data, uninstall or change an application, or perform other dangerous tasks.

To enable the Guest account, select Manage another account from the main User Accounts control panel. Then, in the Manage Accounts screen, choose Guest. (Its icon will note that the Guest account is off.)

The control panel will ask you whether you're sure you wish to enable this account, noting that password-protected files, folders, and settings are not accessible to guest users. Click Turn on to enable the Guest account.

Now, when you leave the computer, you can lock your account (easiest way: Winkey + L). And then your children or actual guests can browse the web, run apps, and perform other common duties using the Guest account while you're away: A new Guest option will appear on the lock screen.

Remember that the Guest account is temporary to each sign-in. So when the user signs out of the Guest account, any settings changes or documents they've created will be deleted. Each time you sign in to the Guest account is like the first time that account is used, and nothing is retained.

▶ **Reset EAS Policies:** When you sign in to a Windows 8 PC or device with a Microsoft account, you're using a technology called Exchange ActiveSync (EAS) under the covers to provide push-based access to your Hotmail-based e-mail, calendar, contacts, and other data. EAS is a Microsoft-created corporate standard that is used by Hotmail and Microsoft's Exchange- and Office 365-based services, and also by competing services from Apple, Google, and other companies. (In this way, it's a de facto standard for all modern mobile devices.) And one of its big advantages is that it supports the notion of EAS policies, which can set restrictions on the device—smartphone, tablet, or PC— that you use to access the underlying services. For example, your workplace may want to ensure that you sign in with an account that has an acceptable password (from a length and complexity standpoint) and then auto-locks after a certain period of inactivity.

When you sign in with a Microsoft account, whatever restrictions Hotmail enforces are automatically applied to your PC. But this is only required if you are using Microsoft's bundled Mail app. If you access Hotmail's e-mail, calendar, and contacts from a Windows application, or from the web, you can decouple Hotmail's EAS policy requirements from your PC. And, oddly enough, you do this from the User Accounts control panel: Just click Reset EAS Policies on the left, and you'll see a window like the one shown in Figure 12-13.

FIGURE 12-13: You can reset EAS policies on·your PC.

THE USER ACCOUNTS CONTROL PANEL AND DOMAIN ACCOUNTS

The User Accounts control panel experience described in this chapter applies only to those who sign in with a local or Microsoft account. If you sign in with a domain account—or on a PC for which a domain account has been configured—you're going to see some different options in the User Accounts control panel.

While many of these options are only of interest to domain administrators, it's worth pointing out one of the common tasks we mentioned earlier is managed using this interface: changing an account type. To change an account type, click Manage User Accounts. Instead of opening a new view in the User Accounts control panel window, you will see the old-school windows in Figure 12-14.

FIGURE 12-14: User Accounts management on a domain-based system.

Now, select the account you want to change—and if you see two entries for one account, as you will for Microsoft accounts, choose the top one—and click Properties. Then just choose Standard user or Administrator from that window.

The easing of restrictions will apply until and unless you run the Mail, Calendar, People, or Messaging app(s) again. At that time, the EAS policies required by Hotmail will be simply be silently reapplied. If you sign in with a corporate account, however, it won't be so silent: You'll be prompted to accept the policies change.

SECURITY AND WINDOWS 8: KEEPING YOUR PC SAFE

While Mac partisans and tech pundits like to present a tortured view of how difficult it is to secure a Windows PC, the truth is far less dramatic. Previous to Windows 8, there were a few simple steps you could take to technically secure your PC—enabling automatic updates and installing an antivirus solution—and that, combined with some good old-fashioned common sense was all that was required.

In Windows 8, you'll be ecstatic to know, it's even easier.

Under the hood, of course, Microsoft's decades-long commitment to system security continues. This version of Windows includes the same anti-malware technology, firewall, User Account Control, and other security features that made Windows 7 the most secure version of Windows yet. And then they turned it up a notch by adding two crucial new features: Antivirus is now included in the OS, finally, so you won't need to add that separately. And the SmartScreen protection feature that the company debuted in Internet Explorer 9 is now part of Windows, so you're protected even if you use competing browsers.

You'll still want to employ common sense. But that's not a focus of this book.

Windows Defender

Microsoft has included an integrated anti-spyware and anti-malware solution called Windows Defender since Windows Vista. Defender was good at what it did—in fact, most Windows users simply aren't even aware of its existence, which is proof of its efficiency—but it's always been lacking one crucial feature: It didn't include antivirus functionality. So we recommended an external and free utility called Microsoft Security Essentials (MSE) for this purpose: MSE looked and worked just like Defender, but it added that one crucial feature, completing the Windows security picture.

Now, Windows Defender includes the same antivirus functionality that used to be part of Microsoft Security Essentials. It's built into Windows 8, it's enabled by default, and you get it for free, just for buying into Windows 8.

This is exciting because both of us have used MSE for years, and we trust it to protect not only our own PCs, but more crucially those of our families and friends. And we've experienced no major issues yet. Not once.

So our advice is simple. Assuming you're not spending your time in the nether regions of the web, downloading illegal software and goodness knows what else, Windows Defender is enough. It's lightweight and quiet, and it won't bother you with annoying pop-up dialogs. You won't need other security applications or even more expensive security suites. You know, assuming that common sense is employed.

> **TIP** Okay, there is one more thing you can continue doing from time to time: Use a second anti-malware utility. (You should never use two antivirus solutions, however, because they will interfere with each other.) It's not necessary to leave the second anti-malware utility running in real time, but it's a good idea to run it once in a while, just to make sure something hasn't slipped by.

But we know you want to know a bit more about Windows Defender.

Shown in Figure 12-15, Windows Defender has a simple interface. From here, you can trigger a malware and virus scan, check for updates, view the history of Defender's activities, or access various options. It works just as Defender did in Windows 7, except that it's now checking, in real time, for viruses as well as spyware and other malware.

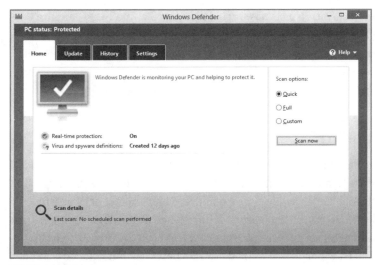

FIGURE 12-15: Windows Defender

There's not a heck of a lot to do here. Configured properly, Defender's real-time protection against viruses and malware will be enabled, and its virus and malware definitions—part of its ability to detect errant software—should be up to date. You can manually update the definitions from the Update tab, but it's unlikely there's an issue here unless the PC has been offline for weeks or longer.

Potentially harmful items that have been found are cataloged on the History tab. Here, you'll see different buckets for quarantined, allowed, and all detected items. If there are any items here, you can further remediate them if you'd like—perhaps by removing them entirely—but there's usually no reason to bother.

The Settings tab has, as expected, a number of configuration options and is worth looking at. For example, you can configure Defender to scan removable drives during a full scan. This is desirable if you regularly use an external disk, like a USB hard drive, when you're home. You can also configure Defender to automatically remove quarantined items after a set time period—by default it does nothing—and determine whether to participate in Microsoft's Active Protection Service, or MAPS, which is used to make Defender more effective for everyone. Do your part: We recommend at least a basic membership.

Boot-Time Security

Windows Defender, like its predecessor, is great at what it does. But there's one problem with an integrated antivirus and anti-malware solution like Defender, and that is that Windows 8 must be running for it to work. There are certain situations in which you may wish to secure your PC's hard disk—just as when it's booting—or need to run a security scan against the hard disk when Windows isn't running. And while one might argue that these capabilities aren't technically Windows 8 features per se, you need to know about them.

First, as PCs have become more sophisticated, the architecture on which Windows runs has evolved. And one of the biggest changes that Windows 8 has been designed to accommodate is the long overdue switch from the primitive BIOS (basic input/output system) environments that have graced (disgraced?) PCs since the 1980s. BIOS is a type of firmware, a tiny bit of software that runs before Windows when the PC first powers on. And while it's possible to run Windows 8 on a BIOS-based computer—basically every single PC made before 2012—a new generation of more sophisticated PCs and devices are instead using BIOS's replacement. It's called UEFI, or the Unified Extensible Firmware Interface.

UEFI provides many advantages over BIOS, but from a security perspective the big deal is that PCs based on this firmware type can support a new technology called

Secure Boot. Based on industry standards, Secure Boot ensures that a system hasn't been tampered with while offline. (That is, while Windows isn't running.)

It sounds Orwellian but the purpose of Secure Boot is valid: It targets a growing class of electronic attacks that insert code before Windows boots and try to prevent the OS from loading security software like Windows Defender at boot time, leaving the system vulnerable to further attack. Secure Boot ensures that only properly authorized components are allowed to execute at boot time. It is literally a more secure form of booting.

All Windows 8 PCs and devices will be configured from the factory to support Secure Boot and have this firmware feature enabled. But if you are going to install Windows 8 on a previous PC, you can check to see whether this feature is supported and then enable it before installing the OS.

As a feature of the PC firmware, Secure Boot isn't configured in Windows; it's configured in the UEFI firmware interface. This interface will vary from PC to PC, but it's generally available via a Boot or Security screen in the firmware and is toggled via an option that will be labeled UEFI Boot. This can be set to Enabled or Disabled.

The other security issue that arises at boot time occasionally is the need to scan an offline system. That is, you may want to run a Windows Defender security scan against a Windows 8 hard disk, but when Windows isn't running. This can be a vital capability if your system is infested with a *bootkit* or *rootkit*, malicious forms of software that are both hard to detect and almost impossible to remove . . . when Windows is running. But if you can attack bootkits and rootkits while Windows is offline, then *voila!* Problem solved.

Fortunately, Microsoft makes a standalone version of Windows Defender called the Windows Defender Offline. As you might expect, it is based on Windows Defender, and looks almost identical to that tool. But you install it to a bootable optical disc or USB memory stick and then boot the PC from that. Windows Defender Offline is shown in Figure 12-16.

Strictly speaking, there's no reason to run Windows Defender Offline unless you know you have a problem. But don't wait to create a bootable Windows Defender Offline disc or USB key until you have a problem: This is a tool you should have at the ready, just in case. You can download Windows Defender Offline from the Microsoft website at tinyurl.com/defenderoffline.

CROSSREF Some related security features, BitLocker and EFS, can be used to protect the contents of a Windows PC's hard drive. These are discussed in Chapter 14.

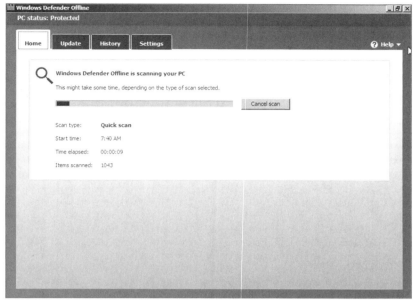

FIGURE 12-16: Windows Defender Offline can clean an offline PC.

Windows SmartScreen

Microsoft added an interesting and useful security feature to Internet Explorer 9 called SmartScreen that helps guard your PC against malicious software downloads. IE 9's SmartScreen feature works very well, but of course it can't help you if you use a different browser, such as Google Chrome or Mozilla Firefox, or if you download a malicious file through another means, such as an e-mail application or USB storage device.

To help protect you against malicious software more globally, Windows 8 includes a special version of SmartScreen, called Windows SmartScreen, which protects the filesystem against malicious files, no matter where they come from. Windows Smart-Screen works exactly like IE 9's SmartScreen feature, meaning it utilizes both holistic sensing technologies and an Internet-hosted service to determine whether files are malicious or at least suspected of being so.

▶ SmartScreen uses a Microsoft hosted "reputation" service that uses actual user feedback to help determine whether files are trustworthy. So that means you can help make the service more useful for everyone simply by using this feature.

CONFIGURING WINDOWS SMARTSCREEN

To configure Windows SmartScreen, you'll need to launch Action Center, which is available via the system tray (it's the icon that resembles a cute little white flag) or through Start Search.

Using the Action Center route, you'll see an option on the left of the window called Change Windows Start Screen settings. Click this option to display the window shown in Figure 12-17.

FIGURE 12-17: Windows SmartScreen settings

We recommend using the default setting, which is "Get administrator approval before running an unrecognized app from the Internet." Unless you're regularly hanging out in torrent sites or other gray areas of the Interwebs, you'll find this isn't too annoying.

USING WINDOWS SMARTSCREEN

When Windows SmartScreen fires up, you'll know it: The full-screen notification shown in Figure 12-18 displays, interrupting whatever you were doing.

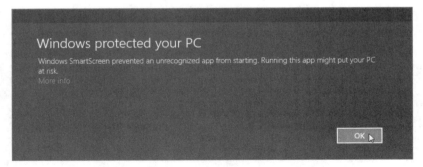

FIGURE 12-18: Windows SmartScreen notifications are a bit hard to miss.

As with any full-screen notification, you'll want to deal with this before proceeding. And while SmartScreen can certainly suffer from false positives, our advice is to think very carefully before just dismissing this. It's warning you for a reason.

Action Center Improvements

If you're familiar with Action Center from Windows 7, you know that it's an improved version of the Security Center that dates all the way back to Windows XP with Service Pack 2. In Windows 8, Action Center carries forward largely unchanged in that it still performs the same function of tracking security and troubleshooting items in the OS and popping up notifications when something goes wrong.

What's changed is that Action Center now tracks far more items than it did in Windows 7. And while many of the items it tracks are, as you might expect, related to new features in Windows 8, some aren't. It's just fleshed out better.

In Windows 8, Action Center now tracks these additional items:

► **Windows SmartScreen:** This security feature, described earlier, debuted in Windows 8 and provides anti-malware protection directly through the Windows filesystem.

► **Windows activation:** While activation is hardly new to Windows 8, Microsoft has created an Action Center experience in this release that tracks whether your copy of Windows is activated, and thus valid. You can see this interface in Figure 12-19.

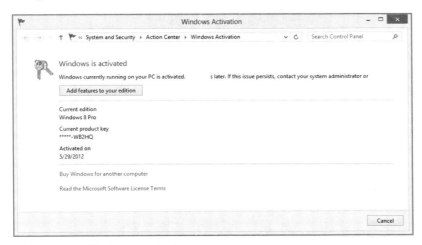

FIGURE 12-19: Windows is activated

► **Microsoft account:** The ability to sign in to Windows 8 with a Microsoft account is obviously new to this version of the OS, but the underlying technology that Action Center is actually tracking here is whether your account is working properly and syncing settings from the PC to SkyDrive (and thus to other PCs) and vice versa.

▶ **Automatic maintenance:** Like previous Windows versions, Windows 8 will automatically run a scheduled maintenance routine at a set time, 3:00 a.m. What's changed in Windows 8 is that this activity is now tracked by Action Center to ensure that it completes successfully. But you can use the Start maintenance link to run a manual check or Change maintenance settings to configure a new time.

▶ **HomeGroup:** Action Center now checks to see whether you're part of a homegroup. This is important because signing in with a Microsoft account breaks the normal workgroup-style home network sharing we used to use.

> **CROSSREF** We examine networking issues in Chapter 13.

▶ **File History:** The new File History feature works with the Push Button Reset functionality in Windows 8 to create a more flexible way of restoring lost data than the old method, a combination of Previous Files (which no one even knew existed) and Windows Backup (which was ponderous and slow).

▶ **Drive status:** Action Center now checks to see whether all of the fixed disks attached to your computer are working properly.

When Action Center detects an issue, it provides notifications via its system tray icon. Clicking these, or the associated warnings that appear in the Action Center control panel, brings you to the user interface you need to mitigate the issue. For example, as part of its overall system performance and reliability tracking, Action Center could eventually warn you to disable app[lication]s to help improve performance. This slightly off-base recommendation—it really means, "disable startup applications to improve boot-time performance" and has nothing to do with Metro-style apps—links to the Task Manager. In Windows 8, the Task Manager now provides a Startup tab that lets you enable and disable applications (but not Metro-style apps) that are configured to run at boot time. This can be seen in Figure 12-20.

But Wait, There's More

In addition to the features discussed previously, Microsoft has improved a number of security features that debuted in previous Windows versions, too. Most of the features don't require any user interaction. They simply work in the background, ensuring that Windows 8 is as secure as it can be.

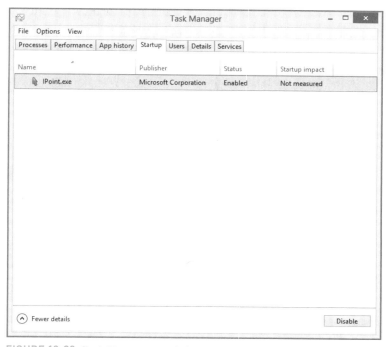

FIGURE 12-20: Task Manager now helps you disable boot-time applications.

A small sampling includes the following:

▶ **Credential Manager:** Windows has long included a Credential Manager inter-face—previously called Windows Vault—that helps you combine the usernames and passwords for the local network and for websites with your Windows user account. New to this release is that you can now tie these other sign-ins with your Microsoft account for the first time, since most people will be signing in to Windows 8 with that account type.

▶ **Windows kernel:** The innermost part of Windows has been shored up with protection technologies that were curiously available only to other Windows components in previous OS versions.

▶ **ASLR:** Since Windows Vista, Windows has employed a technique called address space layout randomization (ASLR) to randomly load code and data into different memory addresses at run time, cutting down on an entire class of memory-based attacks. In Windows 8, ASLR has been improved with even more randomness. And it's been extended to even more Windows components.

▶ **Memory:** Modern Windows versions have of course always included various forms of protection against memory-based attacks, and the move to isolated Metro-style apps will help in this and other regards. But Windows 8 also includes new protections against "use after free" vulnerabilities, where rogue or malicious applications are able to examine and exploit freed up memory that still includes valuable data or other code.

There's still more, but you get the idea. While many Windows 8 security features are in your face when required, some simply work behind the scenes, tirelessly keeping you safe without you doing a thing. What's missing is the "security theater" that used to dog older Windows versions, where the security features were purposefully made to be overly chatty and interruptive, providing you with a sense that something good was happening.

SUMMARY

With Windows 8, Microsoft offers the first major change to user accounts since, well, it added user accounts to Windows. Now, home users can get the same kind of settings-roaming functionality that was previously available only in expensive and complex corporate environments, tied to the online ID—the Microsoft account—we all already use. Of course, those using traditional workgroup-type local accounts or domain accounts won't be left behind either, and you can mix all three account types on the same PC if desired.

From a security perspective, Microsoft has finally closed the loop and silenced the critics by adding an excellent and effective antivirus solution to the OS. That, combined with new boot-time security protections, new security features like Windows SmartScreen, a host of new Action Center-based reliability and security tracking functionality, and, of course, all the excellent security features from Windows 7, makes Windows 8 the most secure Windows yet.

But then you expected nothing less, right?

CHAPTER 13

Networking and Connectivity

IN THIS CHAPTER

▶ Understanding which Windows 7 networking features carry over to Windows 8

▶ Connecting to and managing wired networks

▶ Connecting to and managing Wi-Fi wireless networks

▶ Understanding how cellular data networks work and how they are different from other network types

▶ Connecting to and managing cellular data networks

▶ Using Airplane Mode

▶ Using HomeGroup to share resources on a home network

▶ Using Credential Manager to share with older Windows-based PCs

After making major improvements to its networking infrastructure in Windows XP with Service Pack 2 a decade ago, Microsoft has been evolving this technology in subsequent Windows versions. In Windows 8, you see the most refined version of this technology yet, with new Metro-based interfaces for connecting to wired and Wi-Fi wireless networks. Windows 8 also includes a Metro-based front end to the HomeGroup network sharing scheme, which takes on all new importance in this release thanks to Windows 8's Microsoft account sign-in capabilities.

More revolutionary, however, is Windows 8's support for the cellular data networks that are becoming more and more ubiquitous thanks to the rise of smartphones, tablets, and other modern computing devices. Windows 8 treats this network type specially, with an understanding of their metered nature that will help users avoid overage charges and automatically switch to more efficient—and less costly—networks when available.

WHAT WAS OLD IS NEW AGAIN

All of the networking functionality you're familiar with from Windows 7 is present in Windows 8, though some of these interfaces have been updated to accommodate the new Metro environment that sits at the core of this new OS. Features that carry forward to Windows 8 include the following:

- ▶ **HomeGroup sharing:** In addition to older, traditional network-based resource sharing techniques from previous versions of Windows, Windows 7 added a simple new scheme called HomeGroup sharing. This makes it easy to share digital media content, documents, and printers on a home network. Because of the move to Microsoft account-based sign-ins in Windows 8, HomeGroup sharing is more important than ever in this release, so we explore this topic in more detail later in the chapter.

- ▶ **Network and Sharing Center:** This complex interface provides a single place to go to view, configure, and troubleshoot networking issues, and access new and improved tools. It's still there, virtually unchanged in Windows 8. If you're lucky, you will never need to use it.

  If you're unlucky, you can access Network and Sharing Center via Start Search. Or, right-click the Network notification icon in the Notification Area and choose Network and Sharing Center from the pop-up menu that appears.

  The Network and Sharing interface also includes a feature called Network Map that visually shows how your PC is connected to the Internet and other devices, an issue that is particularly important to understand when troubleshooting.

- ▶ **Seamless network connections:** In Windows XP, unconnected wired and wireless network connections would leave ugly red icons in your system tray, and creating new connections was confusing and painful. Now Windows connects to secure networks automatically. Windows will also automatically disable networking hardware that isn't in use, a boon for mobile computer users on-the-go who want to preserve battery life.

  The interface for managing wireless networks is now a Metro experience. Since it's new, we'll discuss that in the next section.

- ▶ **Network explorer:** The old My Network Places explorer from previous versions of Windows has been replaced and upgraded significantly with the new Network explorer. This handy interface supports access to all of the computers, devices, and printers found on your connected networks, instead of just showing network shares, as XP did. You can even access network-connected media players, video game consoles, and other connected device types from this interface.

▶ **Network locations:** Windows 7 featured a Set Network Location wizard that would appear whenever you connected to a new wired or wireless network for the first time. This wizard let you set multiple complex network characteristics under the hood by providing a simple list of choices for the type of network you were connecting to: Home, Work, or Public. Home and Work were essentially the same, in that both opened up sharing between your PC and other PCs and devices on the network. Public, meanwhile, was for public network connection, like the Wi-Fi connections you might run into at cafés, airports, and similar locations.

In Windows 8, network location is handled differently and, believe it or not, it's even easier than before. Now, there are only two states, and instead of forcing the user to think about the network type, you choose between whether you want to share or connect to devices. We explain this functionality and how to configure it on a per-connection basis in the next section.

CONNECTING TO AND MANAGING WIRED AND WIRELESS NETWORKS

With the move to a Metro-based infrastructure in Windows 8, many core system tasks now occur within that interface rather than in the classic desktop environment. So while many of the advanced networking features from Windows 7 are still present, largely unchanged, in Windows 8, the most frequently-needed features for connecting to and managing networks—both wired and wireless (Wi-Fi/802.11-style)—have changed.

Using Wired Networks

A wired Ethernet network is the simplest type of network to connect to, from the perspective of Windows at least. That's because Microsoft is making a big—and usually correct—assumption with this type of connection. And that's that anyone who signs in to Windows using a local or Microsoft account and then connects a network cable to the PC is doing so on their own home network. And that network, by definition, is trusted, a private network type, and one in which being able to share with other PCs and connect to devices is not only safe, but desirable.

Connecting to a wired network is as easy as plugging an Ethernet cable into your home router on one end and the appropriate port on your PC on the other. When you do, a few things happen. Under the hood, Windows establishes the connection and enables sharing and device connections. Then the Network icon in the Notification Area (of the Windows desktop) changes to indicate that you're connected, similar to the way it did in Windows 7.

If you click this Network icon, a new Metro-style interface, the Networks pane, will appear. This interface, shown in Figure 13-1, will help you manage not only wired networks, but also wireless (Wi-Fi) and cellular data networks.

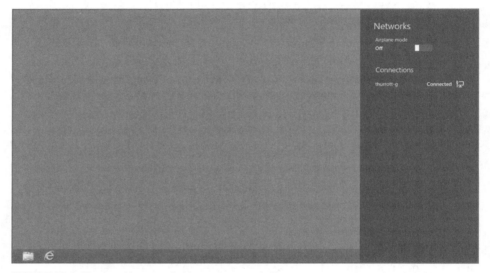

FIGURE 13-1: The new Metro-style Networks pane helps you manage networks of all kinds.

> **NOTE** The Networks pane is important enough that you may need or want to access it from the Start screen or a Metro-style app. To do so, you must first enable the Settings bar (Winkey + I being the easiest way) and then select the Network icon at the bottom of that pane.

There isn't a lot of configuring you can do with a wired network from this interface, but there is one bit of functionality: You can disable (or enable) PC sharing and device connections. To do that, right-click the wired connection in the Networks pane and choose Turn sharing on or off from the little pop-up menu that appears. This won't be hard since that's the only choice, as you can see in Figure 13-2.

In the resulting display, you'll be confronted with a question, part of Microsoft's never-ending attempts to turn something technical into child's play: Do you want to turn on sharing between PCs and connect to devices on this network?

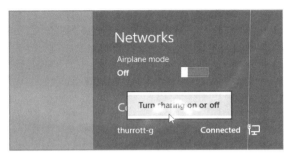

FIGURE 13-2: If you're looking for lots of options, look elsewhere; this is all you get for a wired network.

There are two possible answers:

▶ No, don't turn on sharing or connect to devices. For networks in public places.

▶ Yes, turn on sharing and connect to devices. For home or work networks.

In case it's not obvious, the first choice—for public places—maps to the old Public network location type from Windows 7. And the second choice, for home or work networks, maps to the Home and Work network location types, respectively.

Using Wi-Fi Networks

Wireless networks, of course, require a bit more finesse. Unlike wired networks, they're not assumed to be safe, since you could be connecting to the Internet from a café, airport, or other location where electronic predators are lurking, waiting to steal your valuable personal information directly from the airwaves. Furthermore, not all wireless networks were created equal: There are wide-open, unprotected wireless networks and protected networks that offer various levels of security. But even the various types of networks aren't completely safe, so it's best to err on the side of safety, which is exactly what Windows 8 does.

To connect to a wireless network, you display the Networks pane. As described previously, you can do so by clicking the Network icon in the Notification Area or by typing Winkey + I and then clicking the Network icon in the Settings pane that appears. As you can see in Figure 13-3, when you're within in range of one or more wireless networks, those networks will appear listed in the Networks pane under the heading Wi-Fi.

You will see two types of wireless networks here: unprotected and protected. An unprotected network is noted with a small exclamation point emblem to indicate that it could be unsafe. And as shown in Figure 13-4, when you select this type of warning, Windows provides a final warning before you connect.

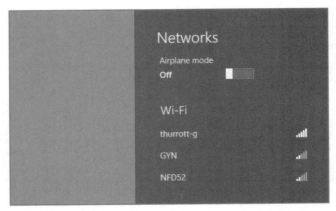

FIGURE 13-3: Available wireless networks are displayed in the Networks pane.

FIGURE 13-4: Windows 8 warns before letting you connect to an unprotected wireless network.

▶ Connect automatically is deselected by default for open, unprotected networks and selected for password-protected networks.

Regardless of the protected status of the network, you'll see two other choices when you select a wireless network in the Networks pane: Connect and Connect automatically. If you check the latter option before connecting, Windows 8 will automatically connect to this network whenever it's within range. (If there are two or more such networks, Windows 8 will intelligently select the one with the best connectivity.)

Once you click Connect, one of two things can happen.

For a password protected network, you'll be prompted to enter the password, as shown in Figure 13-5, and then Click Enter.

FIGURE 13-5: You need to enter a password for a protected network.

If you are accessing an open, unprotected network, the Networks pane will ask you whether you want to turn on sharing between PCs and connect to devices on this network. (For protected networks, this is the next step.) As with any other network type, there are two possible answers:

▶ No, don't turn on sharing or connect to devices. For networks in public places.

▶ Yes, turn on sharing and connect to devices. For home or work networks.

Choose accordingly, and you'll be connected to the network. In the Networks pane, the connection will be accompanied by a Connected notation.

Wireless networks provide many more configuration options than do wired networks. If you right-click a wireless network to which you're connected, you'll see a number of options, though it should be noted that not all of them are relevant to Wi-Fi networks. (Some are more applicable to cellular data connections, as described in the next section.) These options include:

▶ **Show/Hide estimated data usage:** This option is actually a toggle. When it's enabled, you'll see a data usage estimate whenever you select the connection, as shown in Figure 13-6.

Using this information to keep track of usage is, of course, valuable for cellular data connections, which are always metered. You can click the Reset link in the Networks pane to reset the data usage estimate to 0.

▶ Mouse over a connected network and Windows will provide information about the type of the network (for example, 802.11g or similar for wireless networks) and the type of security it uses, if any.

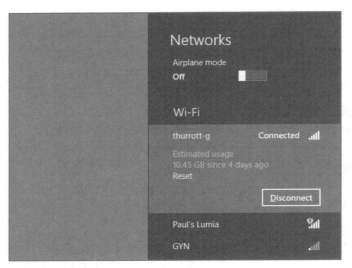

FIGURE 13-6: Keep track of your data usage.

▶ **Set as metered/non-metered connection:** This option changes the behavior of certain connected Windows features when enabled. Since it's more typically needed for cellular data networks, we'll discuss this feature in the next section.

▶ **Forget/Remember this network:** If you've configured Windows 8 to remember a wireless network and thus reconnect to it automatically, you can change that behavior using this option (and vice versa).

▶ **Turn sharing on or off:** This option displays the same interface described previously, letting you choose between enabling and disabling PC sharing and device connections.

▶ **View connection properties:** Choosing this option displays an old-school desktop-type configuration window like the one shown in Figure 13-7. This interface lets you configure advanced settings for obscure, non-typical wireless networks and isn't generally needed.

CONNECTING TO CELLULAR DATA NETWORKS

Over the years, the support in Windows for different network types and networking technologies has of course evolved. And in Windows 8, finally, Microsoft is explicitly supporting the 3G and 4G/LTE cellular data networks that are now becoming ubiquitous.

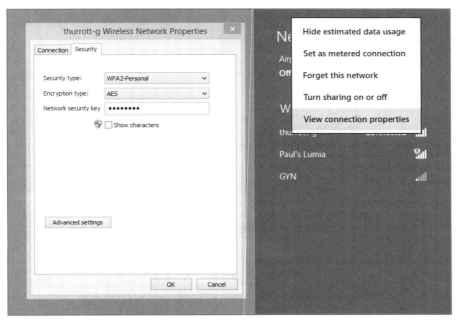

FIGURE 13-7: Back to the Stone Age

UNDERSTANDING CELLULAR DATA NETWORKS

3G refers to the third-generation cellular data networks that are now considered the baseline—that is, the slowest—for such networks.

4G, confusingly, refers broadly to a range of cellular network types, including pseudo-4G data networks such as HSPA (high-speed packet access) and HSPA+ that are really based on the older 3G standard.

LTE, or long-term evolution, is, for now at least, the "true" standard for 4G cellular data connectivity and offers the best performance of these network types.

Prior to this release, you could connect to such networks using third-party software, which was generally acquired from the wireless carrier or device maker that provided the connectivity, perhaps through a USB-based add-on peripheral or internal SIM card interface in a laptop or other device.

> **NOTE** A SIM (subscriber identity module) card is a small integrated circuit on a plastic card that is used to authenticate your device, and thus you, the wireless subscriber, to the cellular data network. These cards are used in smartphones, tablets, and modern PCs, and while they come in various sizes, they are functionally identical.

But now, in Windows 8, this capability is just built-in. And that integration into the OS isn't just a convenience. In addition to providing the functionality that used to require third-party software installation, the built-in cellular data connectivity that's available in Windows 8 is also more intelligent. It will use your Wi-Fi or other network connectivity whenever possible, switching off of cellular as frequently as possible in order to save you money. That's because cellular data is notoriously expensive and almost always metered, with a set monthly or per-use allotment of data.

Put simply, Windows 8 treats cellular data just like your smartphone does, neatly bridging the connectivity gap between those small and highly portable devices and the monolithic PCs of the past.

Choosing a Cellular Data Connection

To use a cellular data connection with the integrated Windows 8 capabilities, or what Microsoft calls mobile broadband, you must have a Windows PC or device that includes a built-in SIM port. If you don't have such a thing, you utilize external methods for connecting to the Internet via a cellular data connection. Some of the more obvious choices include the following:

▶ **Portable wireless router:** Many wireless carriers sell tiny wireless routers that access their data networks and then broadcast a Wi-Fi network that you can use with multiple devices and PCs. From the perspective of Windows 8, connecting to such a device is no different from connecting to any Wi-Fi wireless network. A typical device, such as the Novatel MiFi, is resold by a number of wireless carriers and shown in Figure 13-8

▶ **Smartphone or tablet Internet sharing:** Smartphones and tablets are generally available with built-in SIM cards and cellular data connectivity of their own, and some can share that connection over Wi-Fi with other devices and PCs, much like a wireless router. This process is sometimes called Internet tethering, because sharing a smartphone's Internet connection in particular can lead to a quick loss of battery life. So it's advisable to connect, or tether, the phone to your PC via a USB cable to keep it charged. Windows 8 interacts with these networks as it does with any Wi-Fi type wireless network.

FIGURE 13-8: A portable wireless router can connect multiple PCs and devices to a cellular data network.

▶ **USB dongle:** Many wireless carriers also provide small USB devices that plug into a PC (or Windows-based device with a USB port), providing cellular connectivity directly to that PC. These devices typically come with their own software stack, so that they work with all modern versions of Windows, and if you use such a device, it's likely that you'll need to install this software before you can get online. In such cases, usage will vary, since the provided utilities will vary from device to device. A typical cellular data dongle is shown in Figure 13-9.

FIGURE 13-9: You can add cellular data connectivity to any PC using an external USB dongle.

If you've purchased a modern Windows 8 PC or device, especially a portable computer such as a laptop, Ultrabook, tablet, or hybrid PC, chances are good that it came with at least a SIM module, which would allow you to later add a SIM card and associated data plan from your wireless carrier of choice and use that connectivity to access the Internet on the go.

The placement and accessibility of this SIM port will vary from machine to machine. They're generally well-hidden, hard to access, and only need to be fiddled with once (if at all): when you install the SIM card the first time.

Availability and cost of cellular data will also vary by wireless carrier, so you'll want to consider your needs—that is, whether you'll typically use the connectivity from the same basic location (home, work, the local coffee shop) or while traveling. That's because cellular data coverage varies from place to place, and while certain carriers offer great coverage in one area, they may offer terrible coverage elsewhere, if at all.

You'll also need to consider your data needs, planning, and shopping accordingly. Some wireless carriers offer pay-as-you-go plans, while others require you to sign up for 2 years and pay a standard monthly fee for a set amount of data (with additional payments made for overages). We happen to use AT&T Wireless in the United States at the time of this writing, and this company offers the following pay-as-you-go data plans for Windows-based PCs and tablets with a built-in LTE-based SIM card.

Prepaid plans with an auto-renew option and anytime termination:

250 MB monthly pass $15

3 GB monthly pass $30

5 GB monthly pass $50

These plans expire when you have used all the data in your plan or your time expires, whichever occurs first. Any "leftover" never carries forward to the next time period, sorry. But AT&T also happens to offer international data add-ons for world travelers, another option to consider. However, this is just an example; you'll want to shop around.

Determining how much data you need can be difficult. Fortunately, with a pay-as-you-go plan, you can adjust over time until you settle on the plan that makes the most sense for you.

Setting Up a Cellular Data Connection

To set up a cellular data connection in Windows 8, you use the same Networks pane that is used for wired and wireless (Wi-Fi) connections. This is accessed from Settings (Win-key + I), Network, or by clicking the Network icon in the Notification Area in the desktop environment. Either way, you'll see a Mobile broadband area in the Networks pane, as shown in Figure 13-10, with an entry representing your cellular data connection.

When you select the cellular data connection, the Networks display expands to show additional options. As you can see in Figure 13-11, these include View my account, Connect automatically, and Roam automatically.

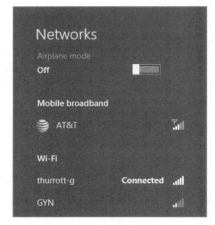

FIGURE 13-10: Cellular data connections receive their own special area in the Networks pane.

We'll look at these options in a moment. For now, the goal is to get this connection set up. So click Connect to continue.

After a bit of configuration, you'll be connected to the wireless carrier's custom Metro-style experience where you can create a (or connect to an existing) account, determine which data plan you would like to use, and so on. This experience will vary by wireless carrier, but in Figure 13-12, you can see an AT&T account portal for a pay-as-you-go data plan.

Meanwhile, back in the Networks pane, the cellular data connection will note that it's connected. You will need to disconnect from that network to configure the two other options noted previously. These include the following:

▶ **Connect automatically:** If selected, your cellular data connection will attempt to connect anytime you are otherwise not connected to the Internet via a wired or Wi-Fi connection. Most users with 2 GB of more of monthly data allowance are probably safe with this option enabled, though you'll want to monitor it and ensure that it's configured as a metered connection; both of these options are discussed in the next section.

▶ **Roam automatically:** If selected, your cellular data connection will attempt to connect anytime you are otherwise not connected to the Internet, even if you're outside of your own wireless carrier's network. This is *not* recommended unless your carrier explicitly allows this and doesn't charge extra for the privilege; such connections often come with additional charges. Check with your wireless carrier to be sure.

FIGURE 13-12: AT&T Wireless has adopted the Metro design style for its own Windows 8 connectivity experience.

Further Configuring a Cellular Data Connection

As with a wireless (Wi-Fi) connection, you can right-click (or tap on and hold) a cellular data connection to view additional options. These include the following:

▶ **Show/Hide estimated data usage:** This option is actually a toggle. When it's enabled, you'll see a data usage estimate whenever you select the connection.

▶ **Set as metered/non-metered connection:** This option is enabled by default for cellular data connections, meaning that Windows 8 correctly treats such networks as metered. A metered connection is one that is limited to a certain amount of bandwidth for a certain period of time, typically a month. Most wireless carriers offer tiers of service, with monthly allotments of 250 MB, 2 GB, 5 GB, and so on. So most users will want to ensure that their device isn't sopping up the available bandwidth each month. And this is where Windows 8 provides some interesting functionality.

When you're connected to the Internet with just a metered connection, Windows 8 changes its behavior to be less data hungry. For example, Windows Update will not automatically download updates in the background, even if you have Auto Updates enabled (as you should). There's no exception to this: If Microsoft feels that a security update is particularly important, it will enable the downloading of that fix regardless of the connection type.

And just in case it's not clear why this ability to configure a connection as metered is important, consider this example: In the writing of this book, your authors of course spent a lot of time testing things—a process that involves reinstalling Windows 8 again and again and reconfiguring the OS from scratch to ensure that the behaviors we see and describe aren't colored by other user or application configurations. While doing that for this chapter, the process of updating the OS and the bundled Metro-style apps (through Windows Store) consumed an entire 250 MB monthly cellular allotment in about half an hour. The ability to configure a metered connection isn't just useful, it's necessary.

▶ **Forget/Remember this network:** Cellular data networks are configured to be remembered by default. If you'd like to forget the network for some reason, you can do so.

▶ **View connection properties:** Choosing this option displays an old-school desktop-type configuration window, as it does for wireless networks.

▶ We're not sure why this isn't enabled by default for a cellular data connection, since it is such useful information. Our advice is to enable it and, especially on connections with a limited data allowance, keep an eye on usage.

However, there is one useful option in this window when used with a cellular data connection: You can enable a PIN for the PC or device's SIM card to help protect against theft.

Comparing this list to that of a wireless network, you may have noticed that the Turn sharing on or off option is unavailable. This makes sense since a cellular data connection, by definition, cannot connect you to your local network. It is instead used to connect to the Internet directly and thus will always be public.

Using Airplane Mode

Like a smartphone, Windows 8 actually supports a useful Airplane Mode toggle that instantly disables all of the wireless (Wi-Fi and cellular data) connections in your PC or device without requiring you to fumble with multiple interfaces, as you did in previous Windows versions.

You access Airplane Mode from two different locations. The easiest is the Networks pane (Winkey + I, Network). As you can see in Figure 13-13, it's the toggle right at the top of the pane. So if you're on an airplane, literally, or wish to otherwise disengage the various antennas in the device to preserve battery life, this is your go-to toggle.

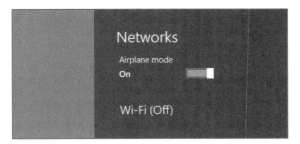

FIGURE 13-13: Airplane mode is available from Networks.

You can also access Airplane Mode from PC Settings under the Wireless entry. As shown in Figure 13-14, this interface lets you toggle Airplane Mode as you would from the Networks pane, but you can also individually toggle the availability of specific wireless (Wi-Fi plus cellular data) connections.

This is dramatically simpler than with previous Windows versions. Before, you had to find the Network Connections explorer and then manually disable each device individually.

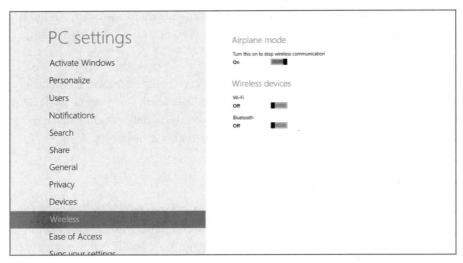

FIGURE 13-14: From PC Settings, you can enable Airplane Mode or configure individual wireless connections.

SHARING FILES, MEDIA, AND PRINTERS AT HOME WITH HOMEGROUP

Prior to Windows 7, most home users with two or more PCs would employ a simple strategy to easily share files over their home networks: They would simply configure each PC with at least one user account with the same username and password. This way, they wouldn't need to enter a username and password combination each time they accessed a shared folder on the other PC.

This type of workgroup networking scheme worked well enough but it also required users to understand how to actually share folders, too—a process that was fairly arcane even after the addition of a Simple Sharing functionality in Windows XP Home Edition. So with Windows 7, Microsoft finally moved to formalize a simpler method for sharing resources on a home network, which included not only files, but also printers and digital media (for streaming purposes via Windows Media Player and Media Center). Dubbed HomeGroup, it was one of the nice, consumer-oriented innovations in Windows 7, though we suspect it was underutilized in that release.

HomeGroup sharing didn't replace the old-school workgroup-style sharing technique, and that's still true in Windows 8. This means you're free to share as you'd like. But in Windows 8, HomeGroup sharing is more desirable than ever, thanks to the addition of Microsoft account sign-ins, as you'll soon discover. But first, let's review what HomeGroup sharing is all about.

> **NOTE** Microsoft's use of the word *HomeGroup* may seem inconsistent because the word appears variously as *HomeGroup*, *Homegroup*, and *homegroup* through-out the Windows user interface. However, Microsoft tells us this is all by design. The word *HomeGroup* is a trademarked term and refers to the sharing feature itself. A *homegroup*, meanwhile, is the generic "thing" that is created by the feature. And if you see it spelled as *Homegroup* (with a capital *H* but a small *g*, that's just because it's a title or other place in the UI where an initial capitalization is required. Seriously, they told us this. And yes, they really believe it.

HomeGroup sharing works much as it does in Windows 7, though as part of a wider effort to streamline, well, virtually everything in Windows 8, it's no longer an option during Windows Setup. So you'll need to create—or join—a homegroup after you're done installing Windows 8.

HomeGroup allows you to easily share three items that, prior to Windows 7, required three different interfaces. They are as follows:

▶ **Libraries:** Previously, you could create individual folder shares to share documents and other files, but now you can share these through your various libraries—Documents, Music, Pictures, and Videos—and individually determine which ones are shared. This is more powerful than sharing individual folders for many reasons, but one obvious reason is that since libraries by definition aggregate multiple physical locations in the filesystem, what you're really sharing are discrete groups of files (or documents) rather than individual folders.

▶ **Printers and devices:** When you configure a printer or other attached device for one PC, it can be made automatically available to all the other home PCs that join the homegroup.

▶ **Media devices:** You can provide access to your media collection for purposes of media streaming to compatible devices such as an Xbox 360 or other Windows 8 PCs using software such as Windows Media Player. As with library-based sharing, this makes far more sense than being forced to remotely browse folders of content on your PC from a device. Instead, you can simply connect to a media library and browse the actual content.

In addition to not being part of the Windows 8 Setup process, the interface you use to configure a homegroup is now a Metro-style experience that can be found in PC Settings. To access this interface, navigate to Settings (Winkey + I) and select More

PC settings at the bottom of the Settings pane. This will load the full-screen PC Settings interface. When you select HomeGroup from the list of options on the left, you'll see a screen like that in Figure 13-15.

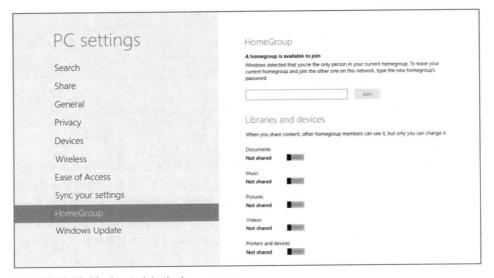

FIGURE 13-15: It's time to join the homegroup.

Enter the homegroup password and click Join. Once the PC is connected to the homegroup, you'll be able to choose which items to share, including individual libraries—Documents, Music, Pictures, and Videos—as well as printers and devices, and media devices.

When you're done, you can exit PC Settings.

You can access the shared resources of other PCs on your homegroup using new Metro-style apps that support this feature. Your homegroup is also available via the standard Metro-style file picker, which can of course be integrated into any app. As you can see in Figure 13-16, the file picker displays each of the machines in your homegroup, letting you dive into the shared libraries on each and find what you're looking for.

Homegroups are also available from the Windows desktop, of course. When you open an Explorer window, you'll see a Homegroup node in the navigation pane, and you can easily browse through the shared items on your home network-connected PCs. This works as it did in Windows 7, as you might expect, where files and other resources exposed through the homegroup are available to any desktop-type application, too. For example, applications can open and save files to homegroup locations.

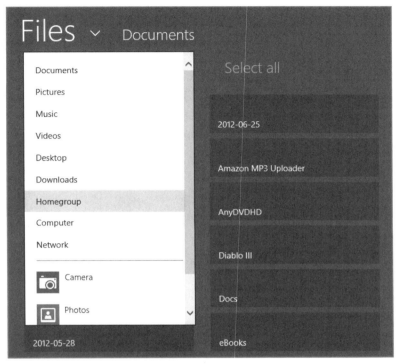

FIGURE 13-16: Your homegroup is accessible by any Metro-style app, including via the standard file picker.

Put simply, HomeGroup works much as it did in Windows 7, aside from the new Metro-style configuration interface. But there is one more wrinkle.

As you know, Windows 8 provides a new sign-in model where you use a Microsoft account (previously called a Windows Live ID) instead of a traditional local account to sign in to the PC. This new sign-in type provides many advantages related to PC-to-PC sync settings and more, and as a result we recommend eschewing old-fashioned local accounts in favor of this new sign-in type. But using a Microsoft account also comes with a few challenges. And key among them is home network interoperability. If you need to access shared resources on other PCs on your home network, whether they're using Windows 8, Windows 7, or whatever Windows version, you could experience some difficulty.

That is, if you use the standard Network explorer to access shares on your other PCs, you're going to be seeing the dialog in Figure 13-17 all too often. And that's because you're now signing in with a Microsoft account. If the other PC isn't also signed in with the same account, you won't be automatically authenticated to access that shared resource.

FIGURE 13-17: Not-so-seamless network connectivity

You could of course enter a correct username and password combination, and chances are you know what these entries are since it's your home network. And Windows 8 even fixes a long-standing bug in Windows networking so that when you select the option "Remember my credentials," it actually—get this—remembers your credentials.

So that works. But you could also simply choose to use HomeGroup sharing instead of the Network explorer. (That is, you will access shared resources via the homegroup and not through the Network interface.) This method requires that all of your home machines are running Windows 7, Windows 8 (or, interestingly, Windows Home Server 2011). So if you are using an older Windows version (Vista, XP) on your home network, this method won't work.

Long story short, you should use your homegroup for all home network-based sharing activities when possible: It's simpler, more powerful, and it's automatic. But if you are still using older Windows PCs on your network, Network explorer will make their shared resources available to you as well ... as long you know the credentials.

SUMMARY

Windows 8 offers all of the power and flexibility of the networking and connectivity services offered in its predecessor, but improves on matters enormously with new Metro-style interfaces that work across the OS, and features new capabilities that make this version of Windows the best yet from a connectivity standpoint.

Key among these new capabilities is the native support for cellular data connections, which achieves first-class status in Windows 8 alongside wired and wireless (Wi-Fi) networking types. If anything, cellular data support is superior to those older types of networking, thanks to intelligent integration with your wireless carrier's metered and costly data plans. It's even more powerful than the cellular support in most smartphones.

Windows 8 also expands on the HomeGroup sharing functionality from Windows 7, by adding a new Metro-style interface. And HomeGroup-style sharing is more important than ever because of the prevalence of Microsoft account sign-ins, which makes old-school sharing schemes a bit more difficult. But if you do need to access the network resources of a PC running an older Windows PC, too, the hidden Windows Credentials feature will make that happen.

CHAPTER 14

Windows 8 for Business

IN THIS CHAPTER

- ► Joining a domain with Windows 8
- ► Enabling EFS to protect files and folders
- ► Using BitLocker and BitLocker To Go to protect entire disks
- ► Using Client Hyper-V to install virtual environments
- ► Managing your virtual resources with Hyper-V Manager
- ► Accessing virtual machines with Hyper-V Virtual Machine Connection
- ► Integrating virtual hard disks with the Windows shell
- ► Using Remote Desktop, Remote Desktop Connection, and Remote Desktop Host
- ► Understanding which features are unique to Windows 8 Enterprise
- ► Understanding how consumer-oriented Windows RT tablets can be used in corporate settings securely

Let there be no doubt: Windows 8 is quite definitely a consumer-focused release of Windows, the first since perhaps Windows Me to cater almost exclusively to that part of the market. This is understandable, given the rapid rise of competing consumer technologies from companies like Apple and the rapid adoption of those technologies, even in businesses. This trend, called the consumerization of IT, has revolutionized many aspects of technology used in business, including areas that were once sacrosanct. And it's led to a loosening of the reigns, so to speak, as the workforce has evolved to engage in computing activities away from the office.

Microsoft has embraced this trend with its client and server products and cloud services, and while Windows 8 may seem a bit light on the business technology side, this needs to be viewed in perspective. First, as a superset of Windows 7, Windows 8 does include all of the business-oriented features and functionality that graced that product, often in upgraded or enhanced form. That means that it shares the same basic deployment tools, manageability, and other back-end technologies, as well as its general feature set.

But Windows 8 also includes some new business-oriented technologies of its own. And while consumers are having fun with the Metro-style experiences that dominate this product, what you're about to discover is this version of Windows also offers a compelling upgrade case for businesses, too.

> **CROSSREF** Windows 8 isn't just about Metro. There are numerous updates to the desktop environment, which we discuss in Chapter 4, plus a new desktop version of Internet Explorer, amazing new file and system recovery tools (Chapter 11) and network and connectivity capabilities (Chapter 13). Metro is fun, and beautiful to look at. But Windows 8 is a productivity champion, too. It's in the product's DNA.

> **NOTE** Most of the features described in this chapter require Windows 8 Pro, the business- and enthusiast-focused version of Microsoft's latest operating system. Some require Windows 8 Enterprise, which is only available via Microsoft's volume licensing program, Software Assurance. Those features that also work with the base version of Windows 8 will be noted as such.

DOMAIN JOIN AND GROUP POLICY

When you think about it, traditional home-based Windows PCs are unmanaged in the sense that there's no central oversight available, either by the head of a household or a central server. This type of computing, which has been formally described as workgroup computing makes a certain amount of sense at home, where each PC is an island of functionality onto itself. In the workplace, however, especially at mid-sized businesses and enterprises where there can be hundreds or thousands of PCs, the go-your-own route doesn't actually make any sense. Corporations need a central way to manage users, PCs, devices, and other entities, and ways to secure and update their computing products. They need what's called a managed solution.

The most popular managed solution for businesses is called Active Directory, or AD. It requires a centralized Windows Server infrastructure and uses Group Policy to establish rules for its computing services. While AD and Group Policy haven't made a lot of headway with smaller businesses—though that could change with the adoption of these services in cloud-based solutions like Windows Azure, Office 365, and Windows Intune—it's the standard at larger businesses. And chances are, if you're provided with a PC at work, you'll be required to sign in to your AD domain, not just to the PC using a local account or Microsoft account. Domain joined computers are controlled via policy, so they can be very restrictive, especially for such things as application installation and certain system customizations. But they're also typically better locked down from a security standpoint and, when configured properly, allow you to access your company's secure network resources, even while working remotely.

Domain join works in Windows 8 as it did in previous Windows versions. If your Windows 8 PC hasn't been pre-configured with your user account, you can sign in to the domain in two ways: from the lock screen or through the Advanced System Properties control panel.

To sign in to your domain from the lock screen, select Other user. Then, in the screen shown in Figure 14-1, you must provide your domain, username, and password credentials.

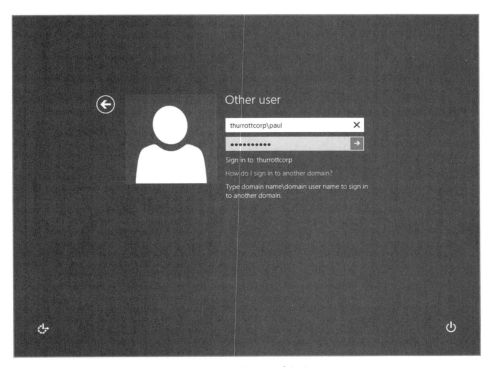

FIGURE 14-1: Signing in to a domain from the Windows 8 lock screen

This sign-in must take a specific form, like *domain\username* or *username@ domain*, in the username field. (Your employer will provide the domain name.) Assuming the domain name is *mydomain.com* and the username is *paul*, the username would then be *mydomain\paul* or *paul@mydomain.com*.

Alternatively, you can connect to your domain first from a local (or Microsoft) account using the Advanced System Properties control panel. You might use this method if you wanted to access your work account from your own home PC, for example, though again your workplace would likely provide you with additional tools (such as a VPN) or information for making the connection.

First, of course, you must find Advanced System Properties. The easiest way is to use Start Search from the Start screen, type *advanced system*, and then choose Settings from the Search bar. In the search results list, select View advanced system settings. You'll see a window like the one in Figure 14-2. (If not, navigate to the Computer Name tab.)

FIGURE 14-2: Advanced System Properties

To sign in to your domain, click Change. In the Computer Name/Domain Changes window, enable Domain and type your fully qualified domain name (*yourdomain. com*) in the Domain field. (Again, this will be supplied by work.) Then, in the dialog that appears, type your username only (for example, *paul*, and not *mydomain\paul*) and password. You'll be prompted to log off and then sign in with the new domain account. Here, again, you'll need to use either the *domain\username* or *username@ domain.com* syntax for the username (for example, *mydomain\paul*).

When you sign in with a domain, Windows 8 works largely as it does otherwise, aside from whatever policy-based limitations your corporation has applied. Two obvious areas of difference include the new Metro-style Mail app, which is discussed in Chapter 8: When you run this app, you may be required to accept the workplace's more stringent Exchange ActiveSync (EAS)-based policy, as you can see in Figure 14-3. This requirement exists outside of whatever domain-based policies you may have in place as well.

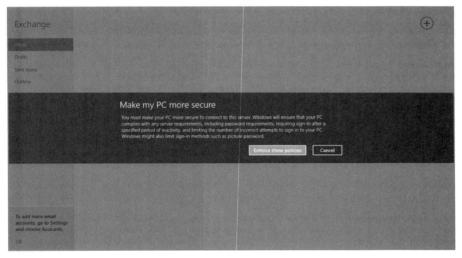

FIGURE 14-3: EAS clients like Mail app will be required to conform to your workplace's policies before they can be used with a work-based account.

Likewise, the User Account control panels work differently with a domain. We discuss these differences in Chapter 12.

BETTER TOGETHER

As is the case with each new version of Windows, Windows 8 comes with a number of new group policies that help administrators control new features that are specific to Windows 8. Some of these policies are Windows 8-specific, so they don't require a certain version of Windows Server. This means they can be used with older versions of Windows Server, like Windows Server 2008 R2. Others are related to technologies that also require Windows Server 2012, the Server version of Windows 8. These products can work in tandem to deliver certain technologies in truly modern workplaces. Suffice to say, that's pretty rare.

Domain users are probably familiar with the myriad of ways in which their corporate overlords can control their computing experience. And in each new version of Windows, Microsoft adds to these capabilities, which are exposed through a technology called Group Policy, part of Active Directory. To give you a taste of what to expect, Table 14-1 highlights some of the over 150 new Windows 8-specific policies that have been added to Group Policy.

TABLE 14-1: Top New Windows 8 Group Policies

POLICY NAME	DESCRIPTION
Allow all trusted apps to install	Manage the installation of app packages that do not originate from the Windows Store. When enabled, you can install any trusted app.
Do not display the lock screen	Controls whether the lock screen appears for users. If enabled, users will see their user tile after locking their PC.
Turn on PIN sign-in	Controls whether a domain user can sign in using a numeric PIN. If disabled or not configured, a domain user can't set up and use a PIN.
Turn off picture password sign-in	Controls whether a domain user can sign in using a picture password. If disabled or not configured, a domain user can't set up and use a picture password.
Turn off switching between recent apps	If enabled, users will not be allowed to switch between recent apps and the App Switching option in PC Settings will be disabled.
Windows To Go Default Startup Options	Controls whether the PC will boot to Windows To Go if a USB device containing a Windows To Go workspace is connected, and controls whether users can make changes using the Windows To Go Startup Options control panel item.
Turn off File History	Allows you to turn off File History. If enabled, File History cannot be activated to create regular, automatic backups. Otherwise, File History can be activated.
Turn off access to the Store	Specifies whether to use the Store service for finding an app or application to open a file with an unhandled file type or protocol association.
Turn off the Store application	Denies or allows access to the Windows Store app. If enabled, access to the Windows Store application is denied.

POLICY NAME	DESCRIPTION
Turn off app notifications on the lock screen	Allows you to prevent app notifications from appearing on the lock screen.
Do not sync	This turns off and disables the "sync your settings" switch on the "sync your settings" page in PC Settings. If enabled, "sync your settings" will be turned off, and none of the "sync your setting" groups will be available. Note: Additional related policies let you control syncing of app settings, passwords, personalization, other Windows settings, browser settings, desktop personalization, and more.
Prevent users from uninstalling applications from Start	If enabled, users cannot uninstall apps from Start.
Allow Secure Boot for integrity validation	Configures whether Secure Boot will be allowed as the platform integrity provider for BitLocker operating system drives. Secure Boot ensures that the PC's pre-boot environment only loads digitally signed firmware.
Configure Windows SmartScreen	Manages the behavior of Windows SmartScreen.
Start Windows Explorer with ribbon minimized	This policy setting allows you to specify whether the ribbon appears minimized or in full when new File Explorer windows are opened.
Set Cost	Configures the cost of Wireless LAN connections on the local machine. If enabled, a drop-down list box presenting possible cost values will be active. Selecting one of the following values from the list will set the cost of these connections. (There are related policies, Set 3G Cost and Set 4G Cost, for cellular data connections.)
Turn off tile notifications	If enabled, apps and system features will not be able to update their tiles and tile badges in the Start screen.
Turn off toast notifications	If enabled, apps will not be able to raise toast notifications. (This policy does not affect taskbar notification balloons.)
Turn off toast notifications on the lock screen	If enabled, apps will not be able to raise toast notifications on the lock screen.

DISK ENCRYPTION

Windows 8 supports a number of disk encryption technologies, which prevents thieves from accessing sensitive data should your computer be physically stolen: If the thief removes your hard drive and attaches it to a different computer, any encrypted files cannot be read even if the thief figures out a way to access the hard drive's filesystem. There are two major technologies at play here: the older Encrypting File System, or EFS, and BitLocker, a more modern and easily managed system.

EFS

▶ When files are copied or moved out of an encrypted folder, the encryption is retained unless you move them to a location where encryption is not supported, such as to another machine on your home network.

EFS, while still available in Windows 8, has been somewhat deprecated. It was created as a way to encrypt individual files or, more commonly, a folder. With the latter approach, encryption works for both new files as well as those that were present when the folder was encrypted. That is, as you add new files to the encrypted folder, those files are automatically encrypted.

To encrypt a folder with EFS, right-click it and choose Properties from the menu that appears. Then, in the Properties window that appears, click the Advanced button. In the Advanced Attributes window shown in Figure 14-4, select the option titled Encrypt contents to secure data.

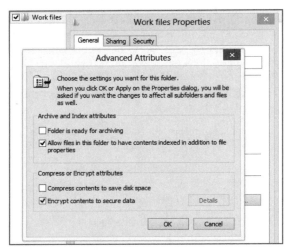

FIGURE 14-4: Encrypting an individual file or folder is easy and generally quite fast.

When you click OK (or Apply), you'll be asked to make the change to the folder only (which includes all of its contained files) or to the folder and any of its subfolders and their contents. Windows will encrypt the appropriate items and immediately suggest that you back up your encryption certificate and key, which is required for recovery should you try to access the folder contents later via a different PC or future reinstall of Windows. Microsoft recommends backing these items up to removable media. But we'd go a step further and make copies in multiple places, including cloud storage like SkyDrive.

Encrypted folders are easily identified later: When you open an encrypted folder, you'll see that all of the enclosed files have a green (rather than black) filename. This is a visual indicator that they're encrypted.

BitLocker and BitLocker To Go

EFS is good for what it is, but it has a few limitations. First, it's ponderous to encrypt an entire hard disk with this technology since it only works with individual folders and files; a set-it-and-forget-it whole-disk encryption makes more sense. And second, EFS only provides software-based encryption services. A technology that integrates with on-PC security chipsets would be far more difficult, impossible really, to crack. And finally, EFS encryption sticks with files as they travel around. It would be nice if the encryption was automatically removed if a file was copied or moved from an EFS-protected folder.

Enter BitLocker and its baby brother, BitLocker To Go. They're both managed from the same control panel, but use slightly different technologies under the hood. From a usability perspective, BitLocker is used with fixed disks—those disks mounted inside your computer—while BitLocker To Go serves the needs of external, removable disks.

Like EFS, BitLocker enables you to encrypt data on your hard drive to protect it in the event of physical theft. But BitLocker offers a few unique twists:

- ► BitLocker is full-disk encryption, not per-file or folder encryption. If you enable BitLocker on a disk, it encrypts the entire hard disk, and all future files that are added to that drive are silently encrypted as well.

- ► BitLocker can also provide full-disk encryption services to both system and non-system partitions, so in addition to encrypting the entire hard disk on which Windows 8 is installed, you can encrypt any other partitions, too.

- ► BitLocker protects vital Windows system files during boot-up: If BitLocker discovers a security risk, such as a change to any startup files (which might indicate that the hard drive was stolen and placed in a different machine), it will lock the system until you enter your BitLocker recovery key or password (discussed shortly).

▶ BitLocker works in conjunction with Trusted Platform Module (TPM) security hardware in some PCs to provide a more secure solution than is possible with a software-only encryption routine. No hacker will defeat a BitLocker-protected hard disk.

▶ Files copied or moved from a BitLocker-protected disk are automatically decrypted as part of the copy or move procedure.

There isn't a heck of a lot to configure for BitLocker. It's either on or it's not, and you either have TPM hardware or you don't: If your system does have TPM hardware, BitLocker will use it.

To unlock a BitLocker-protected disk, you must use a recovery key. This key can take different forms, including a password or smartcard PIN. BitLocker-protected disks can be configured to auto-unlock when you sign in to Windows, which is the recommended approach for day-to-day use.

BitLocker is generally a seamless experience, with one exception: Some software installs are blocked when BitLocker is enabled on your disk. For this reason, you can temporarily suspend BitLocker, install the software, and then re-enable BitLocker.

> **WARNING** If you lose your recovery key—forget the password or smartcard PIN, for example—it's game over. There is literally no other recovery option available. Microsoft Support can't help you.

▶ *You can't use any old password: It must meet certain minimum length and complexity requirements, which could be set by corporate policy.*

Not scared off?

To enable BitLocker, launch the BitLocker Drive Encryption control panel (as always, Start Search is your friend). Shown in Figure 14-5, BitLocker is straightforward.

To enable BitLocker (or BitLocker To Go), simply click the Turn on BitLocker option next to the appropriate disk. The BitLocker Drive Encryption wizard will step you through the process of encrypting the disk and creating a recovery key, which can be a standard password or smartcard with PIN.

▶ *We recommend you do all three. (Be sure to keep the printed copy secure, in a safe perhaps.)*

The wizard will also ask whether you'd like to back up the recovery key, which is certainly desirable. You can save to SkyDrive, to a file, or print the recovery key.

Once this is complete, the wizard will present two options, new to Windows 8, for encrypting the disk: It can encrypt the entire disk, including the empty space, which is slower, or just encrypt the used disk space, which is faster and perfectly acceptable for unused disks.

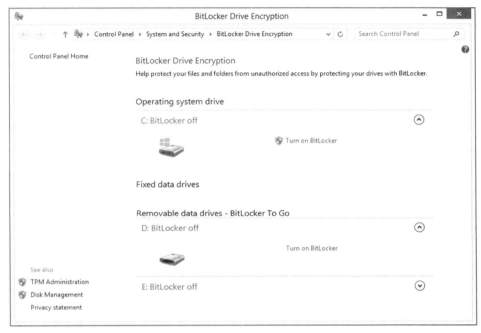

FIGURE 14-5: BitLocker and BitLocker To Go utilize the same configuration interface.

Encrypting an entire fixed disk can be a very time-consuming process. In fact, you may want to do this overnight, though the process doesn't impact your ability to use the disk.

When the encryption is complete, you'll see that the disk appears different in both Explorer, as shown in Figure 14-6, and in the BitLocker Drive Encryption control panel.

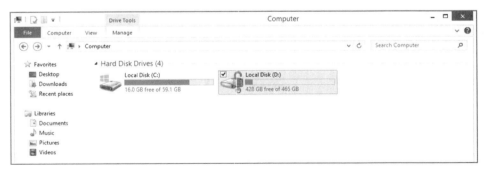

FIGURE 14-6: BitLocker-protected disks are visually differentiated and now provide other options.

They also have some new options in the control panel. These include the following:

▶ **Back up recovery key:** While the BitLocker Drive Encryption wizard won't complete without ensuring that you back up your recovery key in some fashion, you can back it up again at any time.

▶ **Add or Change password:** If you're using a password, you can change the password at any time. Or, if you're using a smartcard PIN, you can add a password as a second way to enter the recovery key.

▶ **Remove password:** You can remove the password if you've separately configured a smartcard PIN.

▶ **Add or Change smartcard:** If you're using a smartcard PIN, you can change the PIN at any time. Or, if you're using a password, you can add a smartcard PIN as a second way to enter the recovery key.

▶ **Turn on (or off) auto-unlock:** By default, BitLocker-protected disks will prompt you for a password (or PIN) each time you sign in to Windows or, in the case of an external, removable disk, when you plug the drive into the PC. The password entry interface can be seen in Figure 14-7. You can use the Automatically unlock on this PC option, found under More options, to disable this tiresome requirement.

▶ **Turn off BitLocker:** If you'd like to remove BitLocker encryption from a disk, this option will reverse the process.

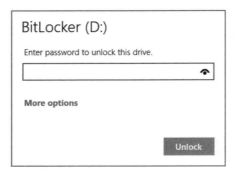

FIGURE 14-7: By default, BitLocker-protected disks require you to enter a password or PIN each time they're first accessed.

VIRTUALIZATION

In Windows 7, Microsoft provided a virtualization solution called Windows Virtual PC that allowed users to run virtualized instances of Windows XP, Vista, and 7, and even individual applications within those environments, side by side with native Windows 7 applications. And it did so without forcing users to manage the complexity of dealing with two desktops, one virtualized and one native.

Windows Virtual PC offered decent functionality but middling performance because it was based on an older form of virtualization technology purchased long ago from Connectix Corporation. So in Windows 8, Microsoft has dramatically expanded the virtualization capabilities of its desktop OS. And let's just say that performance is no longer going to be an issue.

Thanks to the integration of its previously server-only hypervisor technology, Hyper-V, Windows 8 offers the same core virtualization features as does Windows Server 2012, albeit aimed at a few core scenarios. And it doesn't stop there: Windows 8 also includes some interesting and useful virtualization integration features that really put this version over the top.

▶ Users of Windows 7 Professional, Enterprise, and Ultimate could also download a free feature called XP Mode, which was essentially a copy of Windows XP that could only be used inside of Windows Virtual PC.

Client Hyper-V

Client Hyper-V, as Microsoft calls the Windows 8 version of Hyper-V, has been added to the OS for two primary reasons. One is for software developers who need to test applications and web apps on a variety of operating system and browser combinations. The other reason is for IT pros who are managing virtualized environments using Microsoft's enterprise virtualization tools—Hyper-V on Windows Server 2012, but also Application Virtualization (App-V) and Microsoft Enterprise Desktop Virtualization (MED-V)—and want to work with virtual machines (VMs) and their Virtual Hard Disks (VHDs) locally on a PC before deploying them elsewhere in their workplace.

These reasons bear little resemblance to the stated mission of Windows Virtual PC/ XP Mode, which existed for a completely different reason: to provide users with a fairly seamless way to access Windows XP-based applications that, for one reason or another, simply wouldn't run natively on Windows 7. And while that may be confusing for some, if you need the XP Mode functionality from Virtual PC, you're still welcome to use it in Windows 8 Pro. Client Hyper-V is a completely different animal.

Generally speaking, it's more capable and powerful than Virtual PC. It offers much better performance and you can run multiple virtual machines simultaneously. It runs both 32-bit and 64-bit operating systems, and not just 32-bit like Virtual PC. And it comes with an amazing management interface, just like the version from Windows Server. (In fact, they're identical.) This means that your experience using Client Hyper-V in Windows 8 will be directly applicable to Windows Server 2012 as well.

HYPER-V REQUIREMENTS

Of course, with this power comes some responsibility. And Client Hyper-V comes with some important system requirements that can't be circumvented. These include the following:

- ▶ **64-bit PCs only:** Client Hyper-V only runs on 64-bit PCs that are running the 64-bit version of Windows 8 Pro (or Enterprise).

- ▶ **Chipset requirements:** Hyper-V requires modern Intel and AMD microprocessors that include Second Level Address Translation (SLAT). This is a feature of all current generation microprocessors (for example, Intel "Sandy Bridge" and newer) at the time of this writing.

- ▶ **RAM:** Your PC must be configured with at least 4 GB of RAM. But with virtualization, more is *always* better, and if you wish to run multiple virtualized OSes, you're going to need a lot of RAM.

INSTALLING HYPER-V

Assuming you meet these requirements, you're free to install and use Hyper-V. Because this is a feature of Windows, you install Hyper-V in the Windows Features control panel. This can be hard to find, but the easiest way is Start Search: Type *windows features,* then select Settings, and then choose the option titled Turn Windows features on or off. The Windows Features window is shown in Figure 14-8.

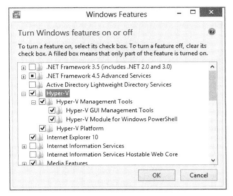

FIGURE 14-8: You can add Hyper-V to your PC using Windows Features.

Expand the Hyper-V entry in the list of Windows features, and you'll see two entries: Hyper-V Managements Tools and Hyper-V Platform. Any Windows 8 PC can install the management tools, so that option should always be available. But if Hyper-V Platform is grayed out, it can mean only one of two things: Either you don't meet the system requirements or the CPU's virtualization features are disabled in the PC firmware or BIOS.

If it's the latter case, you'll need to examine the firmware and enable the correct features. How you do so, of course, will vary from PC to PC, so there's no way to provide general instructions here. Consult your PC's documentation for the details.

Once you've selected all of the Hyper-V features (and do select them all if you'll be using Hyper-V on that PC), click OK to install Hyper-V. The PC will need to be restarted. Once it does so, you can use the various Hyper-V tools to create and work with virtual machines. There are two primary interfaces: Hyper-V Manager and Hyper-V Virtual Machine Connection (VMC).

USING HYPER-V MANAGER

Hyper-V Manager is the Hyper-V management console and the exact same utility that is provided with Windows Server 2012 and the Remote Server Administration Tools

(RSAT) for Windows Server 2012. As you can see in Figure 14-9, Hyper-V Manager is a modern and full-featured tool, and all you need to create, manage, and run virtual environments on your PC.

FIGURE 14-9: Hyper-V Manager

Hyper-V Manager is such a feature rich application that describing all of its features would require a book in its own right. But here are the top things you can do with this utility:

- ▶ **Connect to other PCs or servers:** While you can of course work solely on your PC, you can also connect to other Hyper-V installs on other PCs or servers in your environment. In fact, you can connect to multiple Hyper-Vs, which is useful for copying virtual machines from machine to machine, within Hyper-V Manager, using drag and drop.

- ▶ **Create a virtual machine:** The primary function of Client Hyper-V, of course, concerns the creation and configuration of virtual machines, or VMs. To create a new virtual machine, click New and then Virtual Machine in the Actions pane and then step through the wizard to complete the action. Each virtual machine can be configured with a name, (dynamic) RAM allotment, a network, one or more virtual hard disks (VHDs), and an attached installation media (which can be a physical disc, an ISO, or other source).

- **Create and manage a virtual hard disk:** Separate from your virtualized environments, you can create and then edit virtual disks that can be used by any of these environments (or accessed as physical disks from the host OS—your PC—using a new VHD shell integration feature we'll describe shortly). To create a new VHD, click New and then Virtual Hard Disk in the Actions pane and then step through the wizard. Note that Client Hyper-V now supports the newer VHDX format, which provides support for virtual disks up to 64 TB. But VHDX is not supported in OSes earlier than Windows 8 and Windows Server 2012. Also, VHDs can (and should be) configured to be dynamically sized. That way, a 2 TB virtual disk—which appears as a single file to the host system—won't take up much too much disk space unless you later fill it up with content. To edit a virtual disk, select Edit Disk from the Actions pane.

Don't have Hyper-V Manager? You can also create VHDs from Disk Management. From that application, choose Action, Create VHD.

- **Create and manage virtual switches and SANs:** Useful in both testing and production environments, you can create and manage both virtual switches—external, internal, or private networks—and virtual SANs, which emulate a corporate storage area network.

- **Manage virtual machines:** Once you've created a virtual machine, you can access its settings and configure far more features than were available in the New Virtual Machine wizard. Among other features you can configure are the device boot order, the memory (RAM), the number of virtual processor cores, the attached hard disks (which can be virtual or physical), and much, much more. As you can see in Figure 14-10, virtual machines come with a dizzying array of settings.

- **Install and run an operating system in virtual machines:** At some point, you are of course going to need to install an operating system in that virtual machine, configure it to your liking, and then possibly install applications within it. You do so as you do when installing Windows or other OSes on a physical PC, except in this case it's running virtually and is accessible in a window as shown in Figure 14-11.

- **Import and export virtual machines:** If you've created a virtual machine in another instance of Hyper-V, you can use the Import functionality to import it to whatever machine you're connected to (the host PC or a remote PC). Likewise, you can export virtual machines so they can be used elsewhere. You may do this, for example, when you've completed configuring a VM and would like to deploy it to a product server.

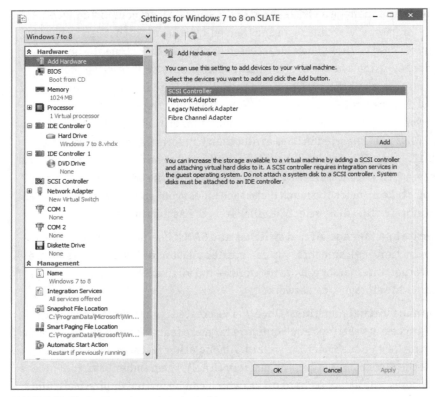

FIGURE 14-10: Settings for a virtual machine

USING HYPER-V VIRTUAL MACHINE CONNECTION

Hyper-V is a one-stop shop for creating and managing virtual machines and other virtual resources, but sometimes all you need to do is connect to a virtual machine, which can be found on your own PC or in a Hyper-V install on a different PC or server in your environment. When you want to just work with a single virtual machine that's already created and configured, you can use Hyper-V Virtual Machine Connection (VMC) instead of Hyper-V Manager.

As you can see in Figure 14-12, VMC looks an awful lot like the desktop version of the Remote Desktop Connection utility from Windows 7 (which can be found in Windows 8 as well).

To connect to a virtual machine, you'll need to select the server first. This can be a bit tiresome; if you don't see the server name in the top drop-down list (named

Server), choose the option called Browse for more, then click Advanced and then Find Now to search the local network for Hyper-V servers.

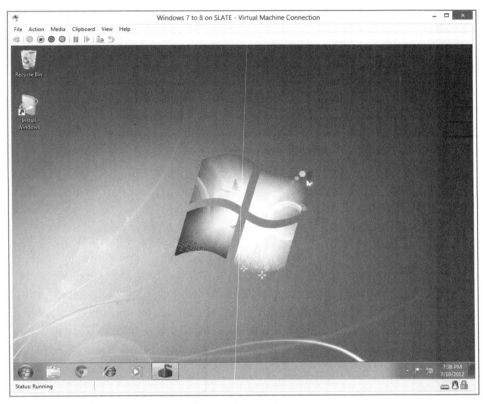

FIGURE 14-11: Virtual machines are often run in a window so you can access the host machine simultaneously.

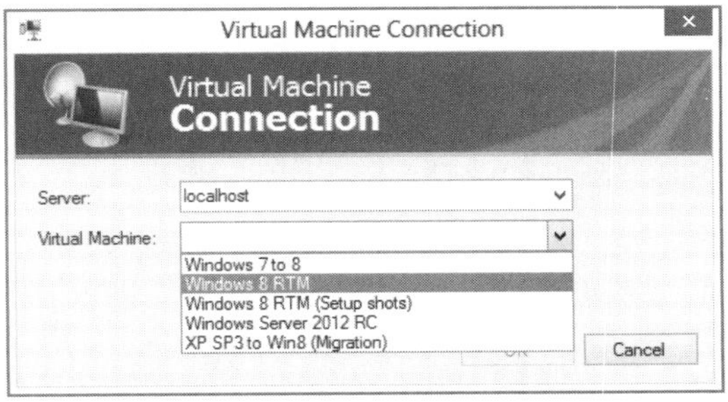

FIGURE 14-12: Virtual Machine Connection

Then, select the virtual machine you wish to use from the Virtual Machine drop-down list and click OK to connect. When you do, VMC will resemble the Virtual Machine Connection window shown back in Figure 14-11. This gives you the opportunity to interactively access the virtual OS and its virtual apps and resources in a window on your host PC.

> **NOTE** If it's configured correctly, you can also connect to a virtual machine using Remote Desktop Connection (RDC). By *configured correctly*, we mean that it's attached to the same network and includes remote desktop host function-ality (see later in the chapter) that is enabled. You'll also need the VM's host name or IP address and the proper sign-in credentials.

VHD Shell Integration

Windows 8 now offers direct shell integration with VHD files, letting you seam-lessly "mount" them as if they were physical disks and then browse through them using File Explorer. To do so, all you need to do is locate the VHD file in question in the filesystem—remember, you can create them with Hyper-V manager—and then double-click it in File Explorer. (Or, right-click and choose Mount.)

When you do, the VHD is mounted and made accessible as the next available drive letter, much as is the case when you insert a USB drive or memory stick. This can be seen in Figure 14-13.

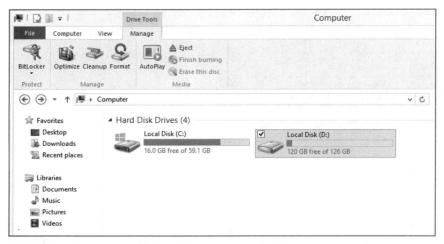

FIGURE 14-13: Mounting a VHD as if it were a physical disk

OK, fine. But why do this? Working in virtual environments can sometimes be a lot slower than doing so with physical PCs and disks. By bridging the gap—accessing a virtual disk from your host, physical PC—you can perform actions like bulk file copies more quickly than if you do so from within a virtual OS. When you're done, simply right-click the disk in Explorer and choose Eject to unmount it.

CROSSREF We describe Windows 8's VHD shell integration further in Chapter 4.

Remote Desktop and Remote Desktop Host

All versions of Windows 8, including Windows RT, include the desktop-based Remote Desktop Connection software and have access to the free Metro-style Remote Desktop app from Windows Store, allowing you connect to remote computers using Microsoft's RDC technology and access them through a window, much as you access virtual machines in a window using Hyper-V Manager or Hyper-V Virtual Machine Connection.

As a Metro-style app, Remote Desktop offers a full-screen experience and lets you configure multiple remote connections, though you can only access one at a time. The Remote Desktop interface can be seen in Figure 14-14.

Remote Desktop Connection is a bit more useful. It runs on the desktop, but you can run multiple instances of this application at a time and thus connect to multiple remote computers as well. Remote Desktop Connection can be seen in Figure 14-15.

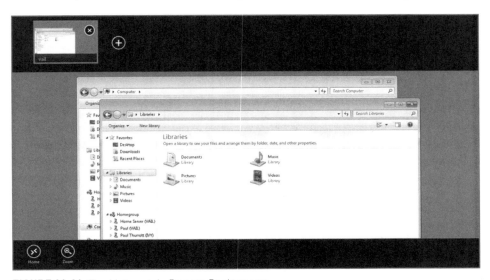

FIGURE 14-14: The Metro-style Remote Desktop app

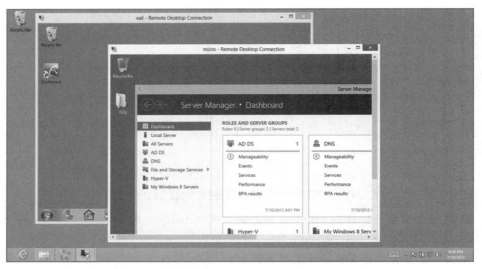

FIGURE 14-15: Connect to multiple remote machines simultaneously with RDC.

With Windows 8 Pro, you can also host remote connections, a feature that is generally available only on server operating systems like Windows Server 2012. That way, you or another user (with the proper credentials) could use Remote Desktop or Remote Desktop Connection to access your PC across the home network or, with a VPN solution (or Windows Server's DirectAccess feature), across the Internet. This feature is called Remote Desktop Host.

To enable RDH, you need to access the System Properties window. But the easiest way to find this interface is to use Start Search: Type **remote**, select the Settings filter in the Search pane, and then choose the option called Allow remote access to your computer. The System Properties window, with the Remote tab preselected, will appear as shown in Figure 14-16.

By default, remote desktop connections are not allowed for security reasons. To enable this type of connection, choose one of the following options instead:

▶ **Allow connections from computers running any version of Remote Desktop (less secure):** While it's possible you may want to choose this option, only do so if you'll be connecting to your PC from a very old PC running Windows XP or Vista, a non-Windows PC running some other OS, or a mobile device like an iPad.

▶ **Allow connections only from computers running Remote Desktop with Network Level Authentication (more secure):** If you will be connecting to your PC from a PC running Windows 7 or Windows 8 (or Windows Server 2008 R2 or 2012), this is the way to go. These OSes support Network Level Authentication (NLA), and this will provide you with a more secure connection in which you're authenticated against the remote PC *before* the connection is fully established.

TIP There's an additional layer of complexity that occurs if you wish to access a home computer that is sitting behind a router of some kind from outside your home, perhaps from work. To do this, you will need additional software, such as a Virtual Private Network (VPN), or you will need to configure your router to allow such a connection. Since the latter is complex and router-specific, we recommend the former. LogMeIn Hamachi (`logmein.com`) is a great option for this, and it's free for noncommercial use.

FIGURE 14-16: You configure RDH from this, ahem, remote location.

Optionally, you can further lock down the RDH by specifying which users can access the PC. That is, when you use Remote Desktop or RDC to connect to your PC, you will be prompted to supply a username and password. By default, the currently signed-in user is automatically OK'd at the time you enable RDH. But if you want to configure other user accounts (or user groups) for this access, click Select Users. Then, in the Remote Desktop Users window shown in Figure 14-17, add the users and/or groups you want via the Add button.

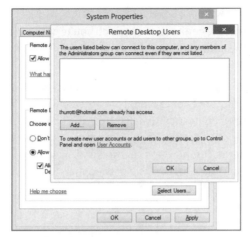

FIGURE 14-17: Adding additional users to
RDH with Remote Desktop Users

Note that these users must be already configured for use on the PC, as they will
sign in to their custom environment when they access the PC remotely.

To test that Remote Desktop Host is working properly, use the Remote Desktop
client on another PC on your network to try and connect to your PC.

FEATURES EXCLUSIVE TO WINDOWS 8 ENTERPRISE

In addition to the Windows Pro-based business features that were discussed in this
chapter, Microsoft is also providing a unique set of features for users of the Windows 8
Enterprise edition. This high-end Windows 8 product edition is available only to corporate customers that subscribe to Microsoft's Software Assurance volume licensing program. So while it doesn't make sense to spend too much time describing each feature,
we can at least provide a rundown of what most of us are missing.

Unique features in Windows 8 Enterprise include the following:

▶ **Windows To Go:** This feature lets you deploy a new, fully manageable Windows 8
environment on a bootable external USB flash drive, enabling the "Bring
Your Own PC" (BYOPC) usage scenario. Employees can use Windows To Go on
any company PC as well as from their home PC, securely accessing corporate
resources on an encrypted device that would be useless in the hands of others.
Windows To Go is a feature we hope to see ported to other Windows editions in
the future, and it would be a huge boon to lab environments of all kinds, including those used by educational institutions.

▶ **DirectAccess:** This is a more modern take on VPN functionality, letting remote users seamlessly access corporate network resources without dealing with the hassles common to VPN solutions. DirectAccess is based on the proven HTTPS (secure HTTP) tunneling technology Microsoft first used with Exchange Server. There's no VPN configuring, connecting, and reconnecting. In fact, there's no VPN at all. Instead, DirectAccess-enabled PCs are simply always connected, securely, to the corporate network. As long as you have an Internet connection, you're in. And for the end user, there's nothing to see or configure. You're simply connected. And on the administrative side, IT pros and admins can configure which corporate resources are available to which users, and they can direct Internet-based network traffic as they see fit.

▶ **BranchCache:** Aimed at distributed corporations, BranchCache lets servers and users' PCs in branch offices cache files, websites, and other content that is sent from a central office over the WAN, so that it is not repeatedly down-loaded at great cost by different users in the same location. With more and more corporate mergers and acquisitions, and larger companies maintaining separate physical offices in different locales, this is a real need.

▶ **AppLocker:** Introduced with Windows 7 as a replacement for Software Restriction Policies (SRP), AppLocker is more flexible and malleable but offers the same basic functionality: It uses Group Policy-based rules to determine which applications users can and cannot access. But it goes deeper than SRP by introducing the concept of publisher rules, where admins can specify which application versions are allowed or disallowed. For example, suppose there's a known vulnerability in an out-of-date ver-sion of Adobe Reader, the popular PDF viewer utility. With AppLocker, you could specify that users are allowed to install and use Adobe Reader 10.01 (or whatever) or newer, only. Problem solved: Users retain the ability to view PDFs and you, the administrator, don't need to worry that they're doing so with obsolete and potentially dangerous versions of the software.

▶ **VDI enhancements:** With updates to RemoteFX and Windows Server 2012, users can access virtualized instances of Windows 8 Enterprise from the data center and receive rich desktop experiences via thin clients, including, interestingly, Windows RT-based tablets. (See the following section for more information about Windows RT in the enterprise.)

▶ **Windows 8 (Metro-style) app deployment:** Domain-joined PCs and tablets running Windows 8 Enterprise will automatically be enabled to "side-load" internal, Windows 8 Metro-style apps, bypassing the Windows Store.

WINDOWS RT AND BUSINESS: A TABLET FOR ALL SEASONS

While ARM-based Windows RT tablets and devices are aimed squarely at the consumer market, Microsoft also knows that these devices will be hugely popular at work, because they're deployed by the employer or because users will simply choose to use them to get work done. There's just one problem: Windows RT, like the basic version of Windows 8, doesn't support domain join, so you can't integrate your Windows sign-in with your employer's Active Directory environment. Fortunately, Windows RT has two things going for it that will somewhat mitigate this issue.

First, Windows RT, like all versions of Windows 8, fully supports the Exchange ActiveSync (EAS) management protocol, the same technology that businesses use to manage devices all of kinds, including Windows Phones, Apple iPhones and iPads, Android handsets and tablets, and many other devices. EAS provides a ton of management functionality, including:

> **Push-based corporate e-mail, calendaring, tasks, and contacts:** And these all integrate with the appropriate Metro-style apps on Windows RT, including Mail, Calendar, and People.

> **Password:** Your workplace can specify a minimum password length, that a password is required to use the device, that an alphanumeric password is required, and password reset intervals. After a failed number of sign-in attempts, the device can be remote wiped or disabled. And many, many more password policies are available.

> **Timeout:** Your workplace can specify that if the device is left unused for a set period of time, it will be locked automatically.

> **Device encryption:** Your employer can require that any disks attached to the device be encrypted. This can include the primary storage device (the internal hard disk or SSD) as well as external storage. Windows RT provides this support with device encryption.

> **Hardware device disabling:** Your workplace can specify that certain devices in the Windows RT tablet be disabled, including the camera, Bluetooth, IrDA, and more.

> **Software disabling:** Your employer can specify that certain types of software be disabled, including consumer e-mail, POP3/IMAP e-mail, web browser, and more.

Second, Microsoft is providing a special Windows RT management client that will allow users to connect to a self-service portal on their employer's servers and browse and install Metro-style line of business (LOB) apps that would otherwise require a domain connection, as well as perform other duties. Key among these is the ability of the employer to specify compliance around certain EAS-type policies such as device encryption, the enabling of Auto Updates, and the configuration of antivirus and anti-spyware solutions.

While these capabilities don't quite amount to domain join, they do remove most of the pain with using a Windows RT-based device for work in a managed environment. It remains to be seen how many companies will be forward leaning enough to implement this in the years ahead, however.

SUMMARY

There's no doubt that Windows 8 is a huge upgrade for consumers, a revolutionary new version of Windows that will allow Microsoft's most successful product line to enter new markets for touch-based portable devices. But Windows 8 isn't just about fun and games. Like previous Windows versions, it comes well-stocked with an abundance of business-oriented features, including updated versions of many preexisting features like domain join and Group Policy support, EFS, BitLocker and BitLocker To Go, and more.

Windows 8 includes new business features, too. It picks up the powerful Hyper-V virtualization platform from Windows Server 2012, providing users with an astonishing new tool for managing virtual environments and resources. And Hyper-V is further bolstered by new VHD shell integration and a new Virtual Machine Connection client. Remote desktop users will find both Metro-style and desktop clients as well as a secure version of Remote Desktop Host that will allow you to access your own desktop PC remotely.

Those corporations that opt for Windows 8 Enterprise will see several other additional features. And even consumer-oriented Windows RT tablets can make their way into businesses thanks to Exchange ActiveSync compatibility and a unique management client.

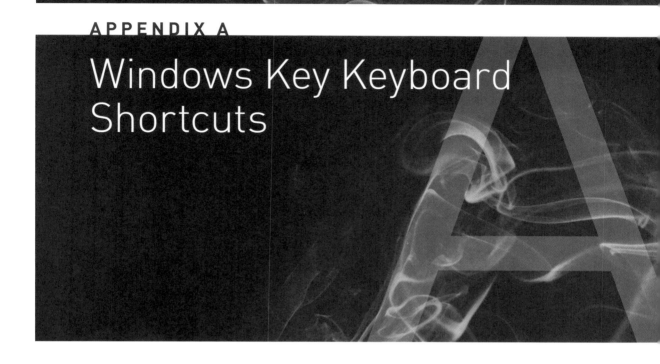

Windows Key Keyboard Shortcuts

TABLE A-1: Windows Key Keyboard Shortcuts

WINKEY +	COMMAND
C	Charms
D	Show desktop
E	New File Explorer window (desktop)
F	Search for files
H	Share charm
I	Settings charm
J	Switch focus between snapped and main apps
K	Devices charm
L	Lock computer

continues

TABLE A-1: *(continued)*

WINKEY +	COMMAND
M	Minimize all desktop windows
O	Lock the screen orientation (on devices that support rotation)
P	Second screen (projection)
Q	Search charm
R	Run window (desktop)
T	Set focus to taskbar (desktop), tap repeatedly to select pinned applications
U	Ease of Access Center (desktop)
V	Cycle through notifications
W	Search for settings (and control panels)
X	Open power user menu (desktop)
Z	Open app bar
1-9	Open the app at the given position in the taskbar (desktop)
=	Magnifier (zoom in) (Magnifier must be running first)
-	Magnifier (zoom out) (Magnifier must be running first)
, (comma)	Peek at desktop
. (period)	Snap a Metro app to the right (Use Shift to snap to left)
Enter	Narrator
Spacebar	Switch input language and keyboard layout
Tab	Switcher (tap repeatedly to switch between running Metro-style apps)
Esc	Exit Magnifier (Magnifier must be running first)
Print Screen	Takes a screenshot and saves it to the Screenshots folder in Pictures
Home	Minimize non-active windows (desktop)
Page Up	Move Start screen to monitor on the left
Page Down	Move Start screen to monitor on the right
Break	System control panel

WINKEY +	COMMAND	
Left arrow	Snap window to the left (desktop)	
Right arrow	Snap window to the right (desktop)	
Up arrow	Maximize window (desktop)	
Down arrow	Minimize window (desktop)	
F1	Windows Help and Support	

Note that some Windows key shortcuts can be used in tandem with the Shift key to cycle objects in the opposite direction.

Index

Index

SYMBOLS

3G cellular networks, 448–449
  definition, 449
4G/LTE cellular networks, 448–449
  definition, 449
32-bit version, 45
64-bit version, 45

A

accessibility, 68. *See also* Ease of Access button
accounts
  Guest account, 428–429
  PC Settings
    adding users, 423
    Microsoft account connect/disconnect, 420
    password change, 420–421
    picture passwords, 421–422
    PINs, 422–423
    switching to local or Microsoft, 420
  People app and
    configuration, 253
    Exchange, 252
    Facebook, 252
    Google, 252
    LinkedIn, 252
    Microsoft/Hotmail, 252
    Twitter, 252
  types, changing, 424–425
  UAC (User Account Control), 426–427
  user account, 42–43, 414–415
    Active Directory, 414–415
    domain accounts, 415, 417–419
    local accounts, 415–419

    Microsoft accounts, 416, 418–419, 437
    picture, 159–160
    settings, 160–161
  Windows 8 product editions, 7
  Windows Store, 212–214
  Xbox LIVE, 360–362
Accounts pane (Mail app), 262–267
Action Center
  drive status, 438
  File History, 438
  HomeGroup, 438
  maintenance, 438
  Microsoft account, 437
  Windows activation, 437
  Windows SmartScreen, 435–437
AD (Active Directory), 414–415, 464–465
  Group Policy and, 464–465, 468–469
adaptive screen brightness, 22
address space layout randomization (ASLR), 439
administrator, Run as administrator option, 83
Advanced System Properties control panel, 466
advertising in Windows Store, 187
Aero, 104–105
  Peek, 108–109
Airplane Mode, 455–456
all-in-one computers, 15–16
Alt+Tab. *See* Windows Flip
animation, Start screen, 71
antivirus, Windows Defender, 431–433
app groups, sign in with Microsoft account, 418–419
App settings, 165
Apple iTunes, 32
AppLocker, 10

apps, 65. *See also* Windows Store
  Back experience, 89
    moving from, 113
  background, photos as, 315
  Bing, 208
  communications, 208
  connected apps, 249
  core Microsoft apps, 207–208
  desktop, file associations, 136–138
  entertainment, 208
    Camera app, 321–322
    Microsoft account and, 307
    Photos app, 210–321
    VLC Media Player, 347
    Windows Movie Maker, 347–348
    Xbox Companion app, 371–375
    Xbox Games app, 364–370
    Xbox Music app, 327–337
    Xbox Video app, 339–347
  in-app purchases, games, 354
  installation and, 35, 51
  Internet Explorer 10 Metro, 234
  launching, 74–75
  Microsoft account, 248–249
    Bing apps, 293–300
    Calendar, 272–281
    Mail, 262–272
    Messaging, 281–286
    People, 250–261
    SkyDrive, 287–291
    Windows Reader, 292–293
  pinning to taskbar, 130–131
  Search and, 142–143
  sharing between, 86–87
  Snap, 91–93, 113
  Start Search, 82
  switching, 139–140
    swiping, 88–89
    Switcher, 89–90
  tiles, photos as, 315
  uninstalling, 211–212
  web searches, 201–203

ARM processor, 3
  chipsets, 12
  Intel comparison, 11–14
ASLR (address space layout randomization), 439
associating files, 136–138
AutoPlay, 98, 319–320
avatar (Xbox LIVE), 360

B

Back experience, 89
  apps, moving from, 113
Back stack, 110–111
background
  desktop, multiple monitors, 172–174
  lock screen, 148
  photos as, 315
backups
  cloud and, 409–411
  File History, items backed up, 395
  installation and, 35
Bing apps, 208
  Bing, 298–299
  Bing Finance, News, Sports, and Weather, 299–300
  Bing Maps, 294–298
    appearance, 295
    Directions, 296–298
    location searches, 296
  My location, 295
BIOS (basic input/output system), 433
BitLocker, 8, 471–475
BitLocker To Go, 8, 471–475
Boot Camp Assistant, 58–59
Boot from VHD, 9
bootable media, 47–48
bootable Windows Setup disc or USB key, 46–47
booting
  to desktop, 180–181
  Secure Boot, 434
  to WinRE, 401
    boot interruption and, 402
    boot menu and, 402
    system recovery drive and, 402
    Windows Setup media and, 402

boot-time security, 433–435

BranchCache, 10

brightness of screen, 80
  sensors, 22

browser. *See also* Internet Explorer 10
  preferences, 165

business features, 463–464
  BitLocker, 471–475
  BitLocker To Go, 471–475
  disk encryption, EFS (Encrypting File System),
    470–471
  domain joined computers, 464–465
    EAS (Exchange ActiveSync), 467
  Group Policy, 468–469
  Remote Desktop, 483–486
  VHD, 482–483
  virtualization, 475
    Client Hyper-V, 476–482
  Windows 8 Enterprise, 486–487
    app deployment, 487
    AppLocker, 487
    BranchCache, 487
    DirectAccess, 487
    VDI enhancements, 487
  Windows 8 product edition, 8
  Windows RT

C

Calendar app, 272–273
  account management, 275
  configuration, 277
  Day button, 274
  EAS (Exchange ActiveSync), 273
  events
    Calendar, 276
    How long, 276
    Message, 276
    new, 276–277
    Show more, 276
    Start, 276
    Title, 276
    When, 276
    Where, 276

live tile, 280–281
  Lock Screen, 279–280
  Month button, 274
  navigating, 274
  reminders, 277
  Snap and, 277–278
  Week button, 274

Camera app, 307, 321–322

cameras, Photos app and, 318–321

cellular data networks, 448–450
  automatic connection, 453
  automatic roam, 453
  connection properties, 454–455
  connection setup, 452–453
  data usage estimate, 454
  Forget/Remember this network, 454
  metered/non-metered connections, 454
  portable wireless router, 450
  smartphones, 450
  tablets, 450
  USB dongle, 451

Charms bar, 77–81
  accessing, 120
  Devices, 78
  opening, 118–119
  Search, 78
  Settings, 79–81
  Share, 78, 86–87
  Start, 78
  Start experience and, 107–108

chrome
  Internet Explorer 10, Metro, 220
  Start screen, 71

clean install, 28, 35

Client Hyper-V, 9
  Hyper-V Manager, 477–480
  installation, 477
  requirements, 476
  VMC (Virtual Machine Connection), 480–482

cloud, 176, 305–306
  backups, 409–411
  connected apps, 249
  SkyDrive, 143–144, 177–178, 287

color, Windows Explorer, 166–167

communications, apps, 208

compass, 22

compatibility, 31–33

computer shopping tips, 14–20

configuration, dual boot, 52–57

connected apps, 249

Connected Standby, 7, 21

connections
  cellular data networks, 452–453
  networks
    Wi-Fi, 445–446
    wired, 443–444

contacts
  Messaging app, 282
  People app, 250
    Contact information, 255
    details, 255
    editing, 255–256
    favorites, 254, 256–257
    interacting with, 254–255
    new, 256
    photos, 255
    searches, 258–259
    What's new, 255, 259–261
  pinning to Start screen, 257–258
  tiles, 257–258

Control Panel, 121
  accounts, types, 424–425
  EAS (Exchange ActiveSync), policy reset, 429–430
  Family Safety, 427–428
  File History, 395
  Guest account, 428–429
  PC Settings, 423–431
  Storage Spaces, 383
  UAC (User Account Control), 426–427
  User Accounts, account type change, 425

copying
  files, 127–129
  in Mail messages, 269

Credential Manager, 439

customizing
  desktop, 164
  Metro

lock screen, 148–151
  PC Settings, 146–148
  Start screen, 151–159
  password, 165

PC Settings
  devices, 161–162
  East of Access, 162
  notifications, 161
  synchronization, 162
  Windows Update, 162

user accounts
  picture, 159–160
  settings, 160–161

D

data usage
  cellular data networks, 454
  Wi-Fi networks, 447

Delete Browsing History (IE 10 Metro), 237

desktop
  accessing, 75–76
  applications, file associations, 136–138
  background, multiple monitors, 172–174
  booting to, 180–181
  Explorer, color, 166–167
  Metro and, 104
    features, 109–123
  personalization, 164
  pinning items to Start screen, 154
  remote desktop, 9
  Settings, 120–121
  snapping, 116
  transitioning to Metro, wallpaper and, 178–180
  Windows 7, 104
  Windows 8 product editions, 6
  Windows Photo Viewer, 322–323

desktop PCs, 15
  Storage Spaces and, 390

Device Manager, 29, 50

device selection tips, 10–24

devices, 96–97. *See also* peripherals
  monitors, secondary, 100
  PC Settings, 161–162
  Photos app and, 318–321

printers, 97–98

sharing, 457

storage, portable, 98–99

Storage Spaces and, 382–383

  new, 390–391

Windows Store, 187

Devices charm (Charms bar), 78

Devices charm, printers, 97–98

digital media, Windows 8 product editions, 7

DirectAccess, 10

directions, 22

Directions (Bing Maps), 296–298

disk encryption, EFS (Encrypting File System), 470–471

disk images, 133

Disk Management Utility, 52–53

  external storage devices, 382–383

documents, SkyDrive

  editing, 289

  opening, 289

domain accounts, 415

  connecting to Microsoft, 417–418

  sign in, 465–466

domain joined computers, 464–465

  EAS (Exchange ActiveSync), 467

domains, 9

downloads

  apps, Windows Store, 203–205

  email messages, 266

  Internet Explorer 10 Metro, 228–229

  SkyDrive and, 289–290

drag and drop, Mail app, 264

Drive Extender, 380

drive status, 438

drivers, 46

  Device Manager, 50

  installation, 48–51

dual boot, 52–57

E

EAS (Exchange ActiveSync), 273

  domain joined computers, 467

  policy reset, 429–430

Ease of Access, 68, 162, 165

edge UIs, 76

  Internet Explorer 10, Metro, 220

  Start experience and, 106–107

EFS (encrypting file system), 9

  disk encryption, 470–471

email. *See* Mail app

emoticons in email messages, 270

encryption

  BitLocker, 471–475

  BitLocker To Go, 471–475

  EFS (Encrypting File System), 470–471

entertainment apps, 208

  Camera app, 321–322

  Microsoft account and, 307

  Movie Maker, 347–348

  Photos app

    connected PCs, 309

    deleting photos, 316

    devices and, 318–321

    digital cameras and, 318–321

    Facebook, 308–315

    Flickr, 308–315

    memory cards and, 318–321

    photo viewing, 315–317

    Pictures library, 308, 313–315

    printing photos, 317–318

    searches, 317–318

    sharing photos, 317–318

    SkyDrive, 312–315

    slideshows, 315–317

  VLC Media Player, 347

  Windows Movie Maker, 347–348

  Xbox Companion app, 371–375

  Xbox Games app, 364–365

    Friends group, 367

    Game Activity group, 368–370

    Gamertag, 365–367

    Spotlight group, 368

    Windows Games Store group, 370

    Xbox Games Marketplace, 370–371

  Xbox Music app

    accessing collection, 327–334

    Albums view, 329

Arranged by option, 328
Artists view, 329
Back option, 328
Most Popular option, 327
My Music option, 326–327
Now Playing experience, 330–332
Now Playing option, 327
Play option, 329
playing music, 327–334
Spotlight option, 327
View menu option, 328
Xbox 360 play, 332–333
Xbox Companion app, 332
Xbox Music Store, 334–337
Xbox Video app, 339
  Movie Store, 344–347
  navigating videos, 340–342
  playing video, 342–344
  Television Store, 344–347
EULA (End User License Agreement), 34
Excel, 302
Exchange, People app, 252
exFAT, 378
Explorer, 65
  HomeGroup, 458–459
Express Settings installation, 38–39
external storage, 131–132

F

Facebook
  Messaging app and, 281
  People app, 252, 259–260
  Photos app, 308
    configuration, 310–311
    navigating, 313–315
Family Safety, 427–428
FAT. *See* exFAT
Favorites
  Internet Explorer 10 Metro, 226
  People app, 254
    adding new, 256–257
file associations, 136–138
File Explorer, 123–126

File History and, 398
  File tab, 125
  Home tab, 126
  Share tab, 126
  View tab, 126
File History, 378, 394–395
  Action Center, 438
  advanced settings, 397
  configuration, 395–397
  drive change, 396
  duplicate files, 399
  enabling, 395–397
  File Exploder, 398
  file recovery, 397–400
  folders, excluding, 396–397
  items backed up, 395
  Options icon, 399
  Recover button, 399
  replacing files, 399
  Restore personal files, 397–398
  Storage Spaces and, 400
file management
  copying, 127–129
  File Explorer, 123–126
  moving, 127–129
  renaming files, 129–130
File menu, 125
File tab (File Explorer), 125
files
  downloading, Internet Explorer 10 Metro, 228–229
  installation and, 35
  recovering, File History, 397–400
  ReFS (Resilient File System), 379
  sharing, SkyDrive, 291
  Windows 8 product editions, 7
filters
  Start Search, 84–85
  Task Manager, 142
flash drive, Windows 8 install, 61
Flickr, Photos app, 308
  configuration, 310–311
  navigating, 313–315
Flip ahead, 239

folders
  File History, excluding, 396–397
  mail, pinning to Start screen, 264
  SkyDrive, 287–289
formatting, pool (Storage Spaces), 384
Friends group (Xbox Games), 367
full-screen notifications, 94, 122

G

Gadgets, 72–73
Game Activity group (Xbox Games app), 368–370
Gamer Picture (Xbox LIVE), 360
Gamer Zone (Xbox LIVE), 360
Gamertag
  Xbox Games app, 365–367
  Xbox LIVE, 360
gaming, 349
  in-app purchases, 354
  installation, 356
  Metro and, 350–354
  Window Store, 355
  Windows Store, searches, 357–358
  Xbox Games app, 364–365
  Xbox LIVE, 350
    account, 360–362
    achievement points, 362–363
    arcade games, 362–363
glance and go interface, 68
Google, People app, 252
Group Policy, 468–469
  Active Directory and, 464–465
groups, 9
  tiles (Start screen), 154–158
Guest account, 428–429

H

hard disks, Storage Spaces, 382
hardware
  compatibility issues, 33
  Connected Standby, 21
  multi-touch support, 20–21
  sensors, 21–22
  Tap to Send, 22–23
  UEFI firmware, 23
  USB 3.0, 23
  Windows 8 product editions, 4, 5
Help, 121
Help protect and update your PC option, 39–40
Home tab (File Explorer), 126
HomeGroup, 438
  Explorer, 458–459
  sharing, 442, 456–457
    devices, 457
    libraries, 457
    media devices, 457
    printers, 457
hot corners, 76
Hotmail, People app, 252
hybrid installation, 35
hybrid PCs, shopping tips, 19–20
hyperlnks, Internet Explorer 10 Metro, 224

I

image formats. *See* disk images
images
  Internet Explorer 10 Metro, 224
  user account, 159–160
in-app purchases in Windows Store, 187
  games, 354
in-place upgrade, 28
InPrivate browsing, Internet Explorer 10 Metro, 227
installation
  applications, 35, 51
    pinning to Start screen, 138–139
  apps, Windows Store, 203–205
  backups, 35
  bootable media, 47–48
  Check online for solutions to problems, 40
  clean install, 28, 35
  compatibility, 31–33
  downloading, 31
  drivers, 46, 48–51
  EULA (End User License Agreement), 34
  Express Settings, 38–39
  files and, 35
  flash drive, 61
  games, 356
  Help protect and update your PC, 39–40

hybrid, 35
Macintosh, 57–58
  Boot Camp Assistant, 58–59
  keyboards, 59
  OS X, 60–61
migration, 35
OOBE (out-of-box experience), 37
partitions, 33
Password, 40
product key, 45
purchasing Windows 8, 30–31
Send Microsoft info to help make Windows and apps
    better, 40
Setup, 26–27
Sharing and Connect to Devices, 39
sign in to PC, 42
virtual machine, 61
web-based Setup, 28–30
Windows Easy Transfer, 27
Windows settings, 35
Intel *versus* ARM, 11–14
interfaces
  chrome, 71
  Edge UIs, 76–77
  glance and go, 68
  hot corners, 76
  keyboard shortcuts, 76
  SkyDrive, 287–289
Internet Explorer 10, 215
  default browser, 243–245
Internet Explorer 10 desktop, 217, 239–240
  configuration
    add-ons, 242
    browsing history delete, 241–242
    tab options, 242
    versions, 242
  versus IE 10 Metro, 242–243
Internet Explorer 10 Metro, 216, 218–219
  apps, 234
  Back button, 224–225
  chrome, 220
  configuration
    Deleting Browsing History, 237
    encoding, 239
    Flip ahead, 239

Permissions, 237–238
    zoom, 238
  downloading files, 228–229
  edge UI, 220
  Favorites, 225–226
  Forward button, 224–225
  Home, 224
  hyperlinks, 224
  versus IE 10 desktop, 242–243
  images, 224
  InPrivate browsing, 227
  live tile, 219
  navigation bar
    Address bar, 222
    Back button, 221
    Forward button, 223
    Page Tools, 222–223
    Pin to Start button, 222
    Refresh/Stop button, 222
    Site icon, 222
  pinned websites, 234–237
  printing, 233–234
  searches, address bar, 222
  sharing web pages, 231–232
  tab switcher, 223
    active tabs, 223
    new tab, 223
    Tab menu, 223
  tabs, 227
  text, 224
  web navigation, 224–237
  web searches, 229–231
  websites, specific, 225
  zooming, 227–228
ISO format, 133
  Windows Explorer, 133–134

J-K
kernel, Windows, 439
keyboard
  Back stack, 111
  icon, 81
  Macintosh, 59
  shortcuts, 76

Start experience and, 111
Switcher, 112
Winkey shortcuts, 491–493

L

language preferences, 165
laptops, selection tips, 16
launching apps, 74–75
  Windows Store, 189
libraries, 175, 309
  sharing, 457
  SkyDrive, 176–177
  Storage Spaces and, 381
Library
LinkedIn, People app, 252
live tiles, 73
  Calendar app, 280–281
  Internet Explorer 10 Metro, 219
  on/off, 158–159
local accounts, 415–416
  switching to Microsoft, 417
    PC Settings, 420
Local Group Policy Editor, lock screen, 150
location, 22
Lock Screen, Calendar app, 279–280
lock screen, 66, 67–68
  background picture, 148
  bypassing, 68
  disabling, 150
  notifications, 149–150
  status updates, 149–150
log in/log out, 66

M

Macintosh install, 57–58
  Boot Camp Assistant, 58–59
  keyboards, 59
  OS X, 60–61
Mail, tiles, 73
Mail app
  accounts
    adding, 265
    settings, 265–267

Accounts pane, 262–267
configuration, 271
Delete, 263
downloading new mail, 266
drag and drop, 264
Mark as read/Mark as unread button, 264
messages
  attachments, 269
  bold text, 270
  colored text, 270
  copying in, 269
  drafts, 269
  emoticons, 270
  fonts, 270
  forwarding, 268
  italic text, 270
  lists, 270
  pasting in, 269
  receiving, 268
  responding to, 268
  selecting multiple, 267–268
  sending, 268
  smileys, 270
  underlined text, 270
  writing new, 268
Messages pane, 263
Move button, 264
New, 263
notifications, 266
Pin to Start button, 264
Reading pane, 263
Respond option, 263
searches, 270–271
Snap and, 272
Sync button, 263
maps, Bing Maps, 294–298
Me view (People app), 251
Media Center, 9
media devices, sharing, 457
memory, security and, 440
memory cards, Photos app, 318–321
menus, File, 125
Messages pane (Mail app), 263

Messaging app, 281–286
  account management, 283
  contacts, 282
  Delete command, 283
  Facebook, 281
  Invite command, 283
  MMS messages, 281
  notifications, 284–286
  People chooser, 284
  SMS messages, 281
  Snap and, 286
  Status command, 283
  Threads pane, 282–284
  Windows Live Messenger, 281
metered connections
  cellular data networks, 454
  Wi-Fi, 448
Metro, 5–6, 37, 64–65
  Back stack, 110–111
  design, 72
  desktop and, 104
  games, 350–354
  Internet Explorer 10, 216
    chrome, 220
    edge UI, 220
    live tile, 219
    navigation bar, 221–223
    tab switcher, 223
  lock screen, customizing, 148–151
  multiple displays, 176
  name origins, 72
  PC Settings, customizing, 146–148
  Push Button Reset, 405
  Start experience, 111
  Switcher, 112–114
  transitioning to, wallpaper and, 178–180
  UAC (User Account Control), 427
  Windows 8 Enterprise, 10
Metro-style user experience, 70
  Netbooks, 168
Microsoft account, 416
  Action Center, 437
  apps, 248–249
  Bing apps

Bing, 298–299
  Bing Finance, News, Sports, and Weather, 299–300
  Bing Maps, 294–298
Calendar app, 272–273
  account management, 275
  configuration, 277
  Day button, 274
  EAS (Exchange ActiveSync), 273
  events, 275–276
  live tile, 280–281
  Lock Screen, 279–280
  Month button, 274
  navigating, 274
  reminders, 277
  Snap and, 277–278
  Week button, 274
connecting to from domain account, 417
entertainment apps and, 307
Mail app
  account settings, 265–267
  Accounts pane, 262–267
  attachments to messages, 269
  bold text, 270
  colored text, 270
  configuration, 271
  copying/pasting in messages, 269
  Delete, 263
  draft messages, 269
  emoticons, 270
  fonts, 270
  forwarding messages, 268
  italic text, 270
  lists, 270
  Mark as read/Mark as unread button, 264
  Messages pane, 263
  Move button, 264
  New, 263
  Pin to Start button, 264
  Reading pane, 263
  Respond option, 263
  responding to messages, 268
  searches, 270–271
  selecting multiple messages, 267–268
  sending/receiving messages, 268

smileys, 270

Snap and, 272

Sync button, 263

underlined text, 270

writing messages, 268–270

Messaging app, 281–282

account management, 283

Delete command, 283

Invite command, 283

notifications, 284–286

People chooser, 284

Snap and, 286

Status command, 283

Threads pane, 282–284

Office, 300–302

password, 42–43

People app, 250

account configuration, 253

contacts, 255–261

Exchange, 252

Facebook, 252, 259–260

Google, 252

LinkedIn, 252

Me view, 251

Microsoft/Hotmail, 252

Notifications view, 251

persona, 261

snapping, 251

Social view, 251

Twitter, 252, 260

What's new view, 251

sign in, 249

to app groups, 418–419

SkyDrive app, 287

downloading files, 289–290

editing documents, 289

file sharing, 291

interface, 287–289

opening documents, 289

uploading files, 290–291

switching to from local account, 417

PC Settings, 420

Windows Reader, 292–293

Microsoft Excel, 302

Microsoft Office, 300–302

Microsoft OneNote, 302

Microsoft PowerPoint, 302

Microsoft Security Essentials, 32

Setup and, 36

Microsoft Word, 302

migration, 28, 35

Windows Easy Transfer, 27

mirroring, Storage Spaces, 387–389

MMS messaging, Messaging app and, 281

Modern apps, xix, 65. *See also* apps

Modern UI, xix, 65. *See also* Metro, Metro-style user experience

monitors

multiple

advanced configuration, 171–172

basic configuration, 169–170

desktop background, 172–174

Metro, 176

Span option, 173–174

taskbar, 174–175

orientation, 171

resolution, 172

Second Screen, 170–171

secondary, 100

visual positioning, 171–172

motion, 22

Start screen, 71

motto (Xbox LIVE), 360

mouse

Back stack, 110

Snap and, 116

Start experience and, 106–107, 111

Switcher, 112

Movies Maker, 347–348

Movies Store, 344–347

moving files, 127–129

MSE (Microsoft Security Essentials), 431–432

multiple monitors. *See* monitors, multiple.

multi-touch support, 20–21

music, 306

Windows Media Center, 338–339

Windows Media Player, 325, 338–339

Xbox Music app, 325–327

accessing collection, 327–334

Albums view, 329

Arranged by option, 328
Artists view, 329
Back option, 328
Most Popular option, 327
My Music option, 326–327
Now Playing experience, 330–332
Now Playing option, 327
Play option, 329
playing music, 327–334
Spotlight option, 327
View menu option, 328
Xbox 360 play, 332–333
Xbox Companion app, 332
Xbox Music Store, 334–337
Zune, 325
My location (Bing Maps), 295
My Network Places. *See* Network explorer

N

navigation bar, Internet Explorer 10, Metro, 221–223
Netbooks
Metro-style apps, 168
selection tips, 16–17
network, File History, 395
Network and Sharing Center, 442
Network explorer, 442
Network icon, 79, 444
network locations, 443
networking
connections, 442
HomeGroup, 456–457
sharing, 442
Network and Sharing Center, 442
Network explorer, 442
network locations, 443
networks
cellular data networks, 448–450
automatic connection, 453
automatic roam, 453
connection setup, 452–453
portable wireless routers, 450
smartphone sharing, 450
tablet sharing, 450
USB dongle, 451

Wi-Fi
connecting, 445–446
connection properties, 448
data usage, 447
Forget/Remember this network, 448
metered connections, 448
password, 447
wired, 443–445
Networks pane, 444
New messages (Mail app), 263
news, Bing Finance, News, Sports, and Weather, 299–300
NFS (Near Field Communication) chipset, 22–23
Notification Area, Network icon, 444
notifications, 72–73, 93–96, 161
Calendar, 277
full-screen, 94, 122
lock screen, 149–150
Mail messages, 266
Messaging app, 284–286
Start notification tip, 91
toasts, 94, 122
Windows SmartScreen, 436
Notifications icon, 80
Notifications view (People app), 251
NTFS, 378–379

O

OEM versions, 2
Office, 300–302
OneNote, 302
online persona, People app and, 261
OOBE (out-of-box experience), 27
installation and, 37
Settings, 38–39
Open file location option, 83
Open new window option, 83
OS X, 60–61

P

Parental Controls, 427–428
Parity resiliency type (Storage Spaces), 381
partitions, 33

passwords
  changing, 420–421
  Microsoft account, 42–43
  personalization, 165
  picture passwords, 421–422
  sign in, 68–69
  Wi-Fi networks, 447
pasting in Mail messages, 269
PC Info, 121
PC Settings, 146–148
  accounts
    adding users, 423
    Microsoft account connect/disconnect, 420
    password change, 420–421
    picture passwords, 421–422
    PINs, 422–423
    switching to local or Microsoft, 420
  Control Panel, 423–431
  devices, 161–162
  East of Access, 162
  notifications, 161
  Sync your settings, 163–165
  synchronization, 162
  Windows Update, 162
PDF documents, Windows Reader, 292–293
Peek, 108–109
People app, 250
  account configuration, 253
  contacts, 255
    details, 255
    editing, 255–256
    favorites, 254, 256–257
    interacting with, 254–255
    new, 256
    photos, 255
    searches, 258–259
    What's new, 255, 259–261
  Exchange, 252
  Facebook, 252, 259–260
  Google, 252
  LinkedIn, 252
  Me view, 251
  Microsoft/Hotmail, 252

  Notifications view, 251
  persona, 261
  snapping, 251
  Social view, 251
  Twitter, 252, 260
  What's new view, 251
People hub (Windows Phone), 250
peripherals, 96–97
  monitors, secondary, 100
  printers, 97–98
  storage, portable, 98–99
permissions, Internet Explorer 10 Metro, 237–238
persona online, People app and, 261
Personalization control panel, 121
Personalize option, 164
Photos Gallery, 323–324
photos, 306
  as App background, 315
  as App tile, 315
  Camera app, 321–322
  contacts, 255
  as Lock screen, 315
  People app, 255
  Photo Gallery, 323–324
  viewing, Photos app, 315–317
  Windows Photo Gallery, 323–324
  Windows Photo Viewer, 322–323
Photos app, 307
  connected PCs, 309
  deleting photos, 316, 317–318
  devices and, 318–321
  digital cameras and, 318–321
  Facebook, 308
    configuration, 310–311
    navigating, 313–315
  Flickr, 308
    configuration, 310–311
    navigating, 313–315
  memory cards and, 318–321
  photos
    as App background, 315
    as App tile, 315
    as Lock screen, 315

Pictures library, 308
  navigating, 313–315
  printing photos, 317–318
  searches, 317–318
  sharing photos, 317–318
  SkyDrive, 308, 312–313
  navigating, 313–315
  slideshows, 315–317
  viewing photos, 315–317
picture passwords, 421–422
pictures, user accounts, 159–160
pinned websites, Internet Explorer 10 Metro,
  234–237
pinning
  mail folders to Start screen, 264
  to Start screen
    contacts, 257–258
    new installs, 138–139
  to taskbar, 130–131
PINs, 422–423
Pin/Unpin
  from Start, 82
  from taskbar, 83
podcasts, 337
pool (Storage Spaces), 380
  configuration, 386–687
  creating, 383–386
  disks, adding, 385
  drives, adding, 386–387
  formatting, 384
  renaming, 386–387
portable wireless routers, 450
portable workstations, selection tips, 16
Power icon, 80
power user features, Windows 8 product edition, 8
PowerPoint, 302
preferences
  browser, 165
  language, 165
  Windows Store, 212–214
Previous Versions, 378, 379, 394
printers, 97–98
  sharing, 457

printing
  Internet Explorer 10 Metro, 233–234
  photos, 317–318
processors, Windows 8 product editions, 5
product key, 45
Program Manager, 66
Push Button Reset, 7, 44, 378, 404–407
  Metro, 405
  Refresh Your PC, 404, 407
  Reset Your PC, 404, 406–407

Q-R

rating apps, 209–210
Reading pane (Mail app), 263
recovery, 378
  File History, 397–400
  Storage Spaces, 393–394
  system recovery disc, 401
  WinRE
    Automatic Repair, 403
    command prompt, 404
    startup settings, 404
    System Image Recovery, 403
    System Restore, 403
Recovery Media Creator, 401
Refresh Your PC, 403
  Metro, 407
refresh/reset PC, 403
ReFS (Resilient File System), 379
  Storage Spaces and, 381
reliability features, 7
reminders in Calendar, 277
Remote Desktop, 483–486
remote desktop, 9
Remote Fetch, 143–144
renaming files, 129–130
Reset Your PC, 403, 404
  Metro, 406–407
resiliency types (Storage Spaces), 381
reviewing apps, 209–210
right side Snap, 117
routers, wireless, portable, 450
Run as administrator option, 83

S

screen
  brightness, 22, 80
  Lock Screen, Calendar app, 279–280
  lock screen, 66, 67–68
    background, 148
    bypassing, 68
  resolution, 170–171
  rotation, 22
  Second Screen, 170–171
  Start screen, 44, 69–70
searches. *See also* Start Search
  applications, 142–143
  Charms bar, 78
  email messages, 270–271
  Internet Explorer, address bar, 222
  Internet Explorer 10 Metro, 229–231
  People app, 258–259
  Photos app, 317–318
  Start Menu Search, 142–143
  Windows Store, 200–201
  Xbox Music Store, 336–337
Second Screen, 170–171
secondary monitors, 100
Secure Boot, 434
security
  ASLR (address space layout randomization), 439
  boot-time, 433–435
  Credential Manager, 439
  memory, 440
  MSE (Microsoft Security Essentials), 431–432
  passwords, picture passwords, 422
  Secure Boot, 434
  UEFI (Unified Extensible Firmware Interface), 433–434
  Windows 8 product editions, 7
  Windows Defender, 431–433
  Windows kernel, 439
  Windows SmartScreen
    configuration, 435–436
    notification, 436
sensors, 21
  adaptive screen brightness, 22
  compass, 22
  directions, 22
  location, 22
  motion, 22
  screen rotation, automatic, 22
  tilt, 22
Set Network Location wizard, 443
Settings, 38–39
  Charms bar, 79–81
  desktop, 120–121
settings, installation and, 35
Setup, 26–27
  bootable Windows setup disc, 46
  bootable Windows USB key, 47
  Microsoft Security Essentials, 36
  Push Button Reset, 44
  Upgrade Advisor, 27, 29
  web-based, 28–30
  Windows Easy Transfer, 29
Setup files
  DVD, 34
  USB memory device, 34
Share, Charms bar, 78
Share tab (File Explorer), 126
sharing
  between apps, 86–87
  files, SkyDrive, 291
  HomeGroup, 442, 456–457
    devices, 457
    libraries, 457
    media devices, 457
    printers, 457
  Network and Sharing Center, 442
  photos, 317–318
  smartphones, 450
  tablets, 450
  web pages, Internet Explorer 10 Metro, 231–232
Sharing and Connect to Devices option, 39
shopping tips, computers, 14–20
shortcuts
  keyboard, 76
  Winkey, 491–493
side-by-side mode, 114–118
sign in, 68–69, 413–414
  domains, 465–466

SIM (subscriber identity module) cards, 450

sizing, tiles (Start screen), 158

SkyDrive, 143–144, 177–178, 287

  documents

    editing, 289

    opening, 289

  files

    sharing, 291

    uploading, 290–291

  interface, 287–289

  Photos app, 308, 312–313

    navigating, 313–315

SkyDrive app, files, downloading, 289–290

SlapDash Podcasts, 337

slate style devices, shopping tips, 17–19

sleep, 65

slideshows, Photos app, 315–317

smartphone sharing, 450

SmartScreen

  configuration, 435–436

  notification, 436

smileys in email messages, 270

SMS, Messaging app and, 281

Snap, 91–93, 113–118

  Calendar app, 277–278

  close snapped app, 118

  desktop, 116

  Mail app, 272

  Messaging app and, 286

  mouse use, 116

  People app, 251

  right side, 117

  swapping apps, 118

  touch mode, 116

social networks

  Facebook, People app, 252, 259–260

  People app, 261

  Twitter, People app, 252, 260

Social view (People app), 251

Software Assurance licensing program, 4

space (Storage Spaces), 381

  creating, 389–390

Span option, 173–174

sports, Bing Finance, News, Sports, and Weather, 299–300

Spotlight group (Xbox Games app), 368

SSD (solid state storage), 378

Start, Charms bar, 78

Start button, 106

Start experience, 106–108

  Charms bar, 107–108

  Metro, 111

  mouse and, 106–107

  Switcher, 107–108

Start Menu Search, 142–143

Start notification tip, 91

Start screen, 44, 69–70, 106

  animation, 71

  chrome, 71

  customizing, 74

  design, 72

  interface chrome, 71

  live tiles, 73

  Metro-style user experience, 70

  motion, 71

  pinning items to

    contacts, 257–258

    desktop items, 154

    mail folders, 264

    new installs, 138–139

  Search, 82

  Start tip, 107

  theme, 151–152

  tiles

    adding, 153–154

    arranging, 154–158

    grouping, 154–158

    live tile on/off, 158–159

    removing, 152–153

    sizing, 158

  typography, 70

  white space, 70

  Windows desktop and, 72

Start Search, 81–82

  Apps, 82

  filtering, 84–85

Open file location, 83
Open new window, 83
Pin/Unpin from Start, 82
Pin/Unpin from taskbar, 83
Run as administrator, 83
Uninstall, 83
Start tip, 107
Start8, 181
status updates, lock screen, 149–150
storage
    external, 131–132
    portable, 98–99
    Windows 8 product editions, 7
Storage Spaces, 378–382
    configuration, 387
    Control Panel, 383
    Create a Storage Pool, 392
    creating spaces, 389–390
    data redundancy, 380
    deleting drives, 387
    desktop computers, 390
    devices, new, 390–391
    disks, removing, 390
    File History and, 400
    pool, 380
        adding, 385
        configuration, 386–687
        creating, 383–386
        drives, 386
        renaming, 386–387
    recovery, 393–394
    ReFS-based disks, 381
    resiliency types, 381
        pool creation and, 385
    size maximum, 389
    space, 381
    storage devices, 382–383
    Take offline link, 384
    thin provisioning, 380
    three-disk configuration, 392–393
    two-way mirroring, 387–389
swiping, switching apps, 88–89

Switcher, 89–90
    activating, 112
    Back stack and, 113
    Snap and, 92–93, 113
    Start experience and, 107–108
    switching between apps, 139
    versus Windows Flip, 114
switching apps, 139–140
    swiping, 88–89
    Switcher, 89–90
switching windows, 139–140
Sync settings on this PC, 164
Sync your settings (PC Settings), 163–165
synchronization, 162, 165
system recovery disc, 401
system requirements, 25–26

T

tab switcher, Internet Explorer 10 Metro
    active tabs, 223
    new tab, 223
    Tab menu, 223
tablets
    sharing, 450
    shopping tips, 17–19
    Windows 8 product editions, 4
    Windows RT, 488–489
tabs, Internet Explorer 10 Metro, 227
tap and hold, 224
Tap to Send, 22–23
Task Manager, 140–142
Task Scheduler, 180–181
taskbar
    multiple monitors, 174–175
    pinning applications, 130–131
    Pin/Unpin from taskbar option, 83
Television Store, 344–347
text
    Internet Explorer 10 Metro, 224
    Windows Explorer, 167–168
themes, Start screen, 151–152
thin provisioning, 380

Threads pane (Messaging app), 282–284

Three-way mirror resiliency type (Storage Spaces), 381, 392–393

tiles (Start Screen), 22
  adding, 153–154
  arranging, 154–158
  contacts, 257–258
  grouping, 154–158
  live tile on/off, 158–159
  live tiles, 73
  photos as, 315
  removing, 152–153
  sizing, 158

toasts, 94, 122

touch
  Back stack, 111
  Snap, 116
  Start experience and, 111
  Switcher, 112
  tap and hold, 224

trial versions in Windows Store, 187

Twitter, People app, 252, 260

Two-way mirror resiliency type (Storage Spaces), 381, 387–389

typography of Start screen, 70

U

UAC (User Account Control), 426–427

UEFI (Unified Extensible Firmware Interface), 23, 433–434

UIs (user interfaces), Edge UIs, 76

Uninstall option, 83

uninstalling apps, 211–212

updates, apps, 205–206

Upgrade Advisor, 27, 29

Upgrade version, 45

upgrades
  in-place upgrade, 28
  Windows 7 Pro, 8
  Windows 7 Ultimate, 8
  Windows 8 product editions, 5
  Windows Easy Transfer, 27, 29

uploading, SkyDrive and, 290–291

USB, bootable USB key, 47

USB 3.0, 23

USB dongle, 451

USB/DVD Download Tool (Windows 7), 34

user account, 42–43, 414–415
  Active Directory, 414–415
  domain accounts, 415
    connecting to Microsoft, 417–418
  Guest account, 428–429
  local accounts, 415–416
    switching to Microsoft, 417
  Microsoft accounts, 416
    sign in to app groups, 418–419
  picture, 159–160
  settings, 160–161

User Accounts control panel, 430
  changing account type, 425

user experiences, 76
  Auto Play, 98–99
  Charms bar, 77–81

user interface. *See* interfaces

users, adding, 423

V

VDI (virtual desktop infrastructure), 10
  Windows 8 Enterprise Edition, 487

VHD format, 133
  shell integration, 482–483
  Windows Explorer, 134–135

video, 306
  Movie Maker, 347–348
  VLC Media Player, 347
  Windows Movie Maker, 347–348
  Xbox Video app, 339
    Movies store, 344–347
    navigating video, 340–342
    playing video, 342–344
    Television store, 344–347

View tab (File Explorer), 126

virtual machine installs, 61

virtualization, 475
  Client Hyper-V
    Hyper-V Manager, 477–480
    installation, 477

requirements, 476

    VMC (Virtual Machine Connection), 480–482

VLC Media player, 347

Volume icon, 79

W

wallpaper, transitioning to Metro and, 178–180

weather, Bing Finance, News, Sports, and Weather, 299–300

web, browsing. *See also* Internet Explorer 10

web pages, sharing, Internet Explorer 10 Metro, 231–232

web searches, apps, 201–203

web-based Setup, 28–30

websites, pinned, Internet Explorer Metro, 234–237

What's new view (People app), 251, 255, 259–261

whitespace of Start screen, 70

Wi-Fi networks

    Airplane Mode, 455–456

    connecting, 445–446

    connection properties, 448

    data usage, 447

    Forget/Remember this network, 448

    metered connections, 448

    password, 447

WIM (Windows Imaging), 30

windows, switching, 139–140

Windows 7

    Aero, 104–105

    desktop, 104

    upgrades, 8

    USB/DVD Download Tool, 34

    versions, 3

Windows 8, 3

    compatibility, 31–32

    OEM versions, 2

    product editions, 2–3, 45

        account features, 7

        business features, 8

        desktop, 6

        digital media, 7

        file and storage features, 7

        hardware choices, 4–5

        power user features, 8

        processors, 5

        reliability features, 7

        security features, 7

        upgrades, 5

        Windows 8 Enterprise, 4

        versus Windows 8 Pro, 8–9

        Windows 8 Pro edition, 3

        Windows 8 Starter, 4

        Windows RT edition, 3

    purchasing from website, 30–31

    Start screen, 44

    versus Windows 8 Pro edition, 8–9

Windows 8 Enterprise

    app deployment, 484

    AppLocker, 10, 487

    BranchCache, 10, 487

    business features, 486–487

    DirectAccess, 10, 487

    Metro-style apps, 10

    VDI, 10

    VDI enhancements, 487

    Windows To Go, 9

Windows 8 apps, xix, 65. *See also* apps

Windows 8 Pro edition, 3

    Windows 8 comparison, 8–9

Windows 8 UI, xix, 65. *See also* Metro, Metro-style user experience

Windows Backup, 407–408

Windows Defender, 431–433

Windows Easy Transfer, 27, 29

Windows Explorer, 65

    color, 166–167

    File History and, 398

    ISO format, 133–134

    text size, 167–168

    VHD files, 134–135

Windows Flip, 87

    versus Switcher, 114

    switching between apps, 139

Windows Flip 3D, switching between apps, 139

Windows Gadgets, 72–73

Windows Games Store group (Xbox Games app), 370

Windows kernel, 439

Windows key, 106

Windows Live ID, 413. *See* Microsoft account
Windows Live Messenger, Messaging app and, 281
Windows Marketplace, 184
Windows Media Center, 338–339. *See* Media Center
  Windows RT, 325
Windows Media Player, 325, 338–339
  Windows RT, 325
Windows Movie Maker, 347–348
Windows Phone, 249
  People hub, 250
Windows Photo Gallery, 323–324
Windows Photo Viewer, 322–323
Windows Reader app, 292–293
Windows Recovery Environment. *See* WinRE
Windows RT apps, xix, 65. *See also* apps
Windows RT edition, 3, 4, 488–489
  Office and, 301
  Windows Media Center, 325
  Windows Media Player, 325
Windows Runtime, 67
Windows Setup, WinRE and, 400
Windows shell, 65–66
Windows SmartScreen
  configuration, 435–436
  notification, 436
Windows Store, 183–186
  accounts, 212–214
  apps
    core Microsoft apps, 207–208
    downloading, 203–205
    installing, 203–205
    updating, 205–206
    viewing downloaded, 207
  browsing
    by app, 198–199
    by category, 194–196
    by list, 196–197
  categories, 192–194
    browsing by, 194–196
  games, searches, 357–358
  Games group, 355
  home screen, 190–192
  launching, 189
  preferences, 212–214

rating and reviewing apps, 209–210
rules, 186–188
Search, 200–201
searches, games, 357–358
uninstalling apps, 211–212
web searches, 201–203
Your apps interface, 207
Windows To Go, 9, 486
Windows Update, 162
Windows Virtual PC, 475
Winkey keyboard shortcuts, 491–493
WinRE, 400
  Automatic Repair, 403
  booting to, 401
    boot interruption and, 402
    boot menu and, 402
    system recovery drive and, 402
    Windows Setup media and, 402
  command prompt, 404
  Push Button Reset, 403–407
    Refresh Your PC, 403, 407
    Reset Your PC, 403
  startup settings, 404
  System Image Recovery, 403
  System Restore, 403
WinRT, 67
WinRT apps, xix, 65. *See also* apps
wired networks, 443–445
wireless networks. *See* Wi-Fi networks
  routers, portable, 450
Word, 302
workgroup accounts. *See* user account

X

Xbox, 306
Xbox Companion app, 332, 371–375
Xbox Games app, 364–365
  Friends group, 367
  Game Activity group, 368–370
  Gamertag, 365–367
  Spotlight group, 368
  Windows Games Store group, 370
  Xbox Games Marketplace, 370–371
Xbox Games Marketplace, 370–371

Xbox LIVE, 350, 359
  account, 360–362
  achievement points, 362–363
  arcade games, 362–363
  friends list, 361
  Gamercard, 361
  Gamerscore, 361
  messages, 361
  profile, 361
  rep, 361
Xbox Marketplace, 184
Xbox Music app, 307, 325–327
  accessing collection, 327–328
  Albums view, 329
  Arranged by option, 328
  Artists view, 329
  Back option, 328
  Most Popular option, 327
  My Music option, 326–327
  Now Playing experience, 330–332
  Now Playing option, 327
  Play option, 329

  Spotlight option, 327
  View menu option, 328
  Xbox 360 play, 332–333
  Xbox Companion app, 332
  Xbox Music Store, 334
    buying songs, 334–335
    searches, 336–337
    Xbox Music Pass, 335–336
Xbox Music Pass, 335–336
Xbox Music Store, 334
  buying songs, 334–335
  searches, 336–337
  Xbox Music Pass, 335–336
Xbox Video app, 307, 339
  Movie Store, 344–347
  navigating videos, 340–342
  playing video, 342–344
  Television Store, 344–347

Y-Z

zooming, Internet Explorer 10 Metro, 227–228, 238
Zune, 325